The Heart of Encouragement

THE HEART OF ENCOURAGEMENT

176 Reflections to Build You Up and Empower You to Build Up Others

Stavros N. Akrotirianakis

Foreword by Tim Tassopoulos

XULON ELITE

Xulon Press Elite
2301 Lucien Way #415
Maitland, FL 32751
407.339.4217
www.xulonpress.com

© 2022 by Stavros N. Akrotirianakis

All rights reserved solely by the author. The author guarantees all contents are original and do not infringe upon the legal rights of any other person or work. No part of this book may be reproduced in any form without the permission of the author.

Due to the changing nature of the Internet, if there are any web addresses, links, or URLs included in this manuscript, these may have been altered and may no longer be accessible. The views and opinions shared in this book belong solely to the author and do not necessarily reflect those of the publisher. The publisher therefore disclaims responsibility for the views or opinions expressed within the work.

Unless stated otherwise, all scripture references come from the Revised Standard Version translation of the Bible, copyright 1946, 1962 and 1971 the Division of Christian Education of the National Council of the Churches of Christ in the United States of America. Used by permission. All rights reserved.

Paperback ISBN-13: 978-1-6628-6025-6
Ebook ISBN-13: 978-1-6628-6026-3

And there appeared to Him an angel from heaven, strengthening Him.

Luke 22:43

Therefore, encourage one another and build one another up, just as you are doing. But we beseech you, brethren, to respect those who labor among you and are over you in the Lord and admonish you, and to esteem them very highly in love because of their work. Be at peace among yourselves. And we exhort you, brethren, admonish the idlers, encourage the fainthearted, help the weak, be patient with them all. See that none of you repays evil for evil, but always seek to do good to one another and to all. Rejoice always, pray constantly, give thanks in all circumstances; for this is the will of God in Christ Jesus for you. Do not quench the Spirit, do not despise prophesying, but test everything; hold fast to what is good, abstain from every form of evil. May the God of peace Himself sanctify you wholly; and may your spirit and soul and body be kept sound and blameless at the coming of our Lord Jesus Christ. He who calls you is faithful, and He will do it. Brethren, pray for us. Greet all the brethren with a holy kiss. I adjure you by the Lord that this letter be read to all the brethren. The grace of our Lord Jesus Christ be with you.

1 Thessalonians 5:11–28

Table of Contents

Acknowledgments... xv

Foreword: Encourage One Another xvii

Why This Book? xix

Introduction
Encouragement Defined 1
Encouragement Was Very Important to St. Paul 3
Encouragement—A Call to Action 5

Part One: Encourage One Another
The Need for Encouragement... 8
Something Everyone Can Do 10
Encouragement Is a Choice... 12
What Encouragement Looks Like and Sounds Like..................... 14
Low-Cost, High Benefit 16
Getting over the Wall 19
Why Social Media Is Discouraging 22

Part Two: Esteem Others Highly
The Golden Rule... 26
Our Neighbor Is Whomever Is Closest at This Moment 28
The Basic Building Block to Any Relationship Is Respect 30
Respecting Others by Not Pressuring Them to Change 32
It's Okay to Be a "Smith" and Not a "Jones"................................. 35
Encouragement to be the Person God Created You to Be............. 38
Leaders Need Encouragement Too 40
Do THIS above Everything Else 43

Part Three: Be At Peace
Encouraging Peace 48
Affirming and Encouraging Peace in Your Home 50
How to Build an Encouraging Environment in Your Home........ 53
F.A.M.I.L.Y. 55

    Mary versus Martha 57
    It's Okay to Eat off a Paper Plate Sometimes 60
    The "Theology" of Fred Flintstone 63
    Finding Peace in Authentic Relationships 65
    Peace in the Midst of Conflict 67

PART FOUR: HELP AND BE PATIENT
    The Encouragement Languages 70
    Solving the Maze of Inconsistent Voices 73
    We Are All Pretty, but We Have to Work at Being Attractive 77
    Using Encouragement Even When Someone Disappoints You 80
    Speak Carefully to Those Closest to You 83
    Don't Be a Victim, Be a Survivor 85
    I Believe in You, and I Believe in Me 88
    It's Okay to Admit Weakness 90
    Love Is Patient and Kind—So Are Encouragers 93
    Two Sides of a Tapestry 96

PART FIVE: SEEK TO DO GOOD
    Kill Pain with Kindness 100
    Be a Light in the World, Lead with Kindness 103
    One Scenario Where Encouragement Is Bad 105
    Criticism Is Encouraging When It Is Constructive 108
    Praise versus Encouragement 110
    God Is an Optimist—We Should Be as Well 113
    Charlie Brown and Lucy 116
    Paderewski and the Piano 118
    Time Does Not Heal Most Wounds 120
    The Art of Forgiveness 122
    Be Part of the Solution, Not Part of the Problem 125

PART SIX: REJOICE ALWAYS
    Be Someone Who Builds Joy 128
    A Matter of Perspective 130
    Breaking the Cycle—I Will Not Do That Today 133
    Get a Win Today! 135
    Don't Look Past Today 137
    Make Each Moment Count 140
    A Lot of It Won't Matter Next Week 143
    You Can Rewrite the Narrative 145

Have a Great Day! Really, It's Okay 147
Is That Even Possible? Yes, It Is 150

Part Seven: Pray Constantly
Encouragement to Pray 154
Little Bits Add Up to a Lot 157
Are You a Good Quarterback? 159
Alone with God 161
How to Pray: 5-5-5-1 163

Part Eight: Give Thanks
Give Thanks IN All Circumstances, Not FOR All Circumstances 168
Our First Words Should Be Words of Thanks 171
The Power of a "Thank You" 173
Gratitude Spawns Generosity 176
Generosity of Time 179
Generosity with Money 181
Would Anyone Describe You with This Word? 183
We're Supposed to Be Satisfied with How Much? 185
God Wants Us to Succeed 187
The Highest Goal Is Holiness 190
Keep Your Eyes on the Prize 192
Remember Those Who Have Helped You 194

Part Nine: Let the Spirit Lead
The Holy Spirit—Let the Spirit Lead 198
Be a Follower, Not a Fan 200
God's Glory Will Change You 203
I Sin Most on Wednesdays 206
You Don't Do Stupid Things When You Feel Full 209

Part Ten: Hold Fast
My Struggle Is too Ugly, so I Suffer in Silence 214
Coming Out of the Dark: It Can't Happen Here. No, It Can and It Does. 216
Mental Illness 219
Managing the Things That Cannot Be Changed 222
Empathy–Getting in the Sufferings of Others 225
Vulnerability 227
Creating Environments Where It Is Safe to Be Vulnerable 230
My Secret Heart 233

    Test Questions 236
    Hold Fast to Your Boundaries—Drinking and Drugs 238
    Hold Fast to Your Boundaries—Honesty 241
    Hold Fast to Your Boundaries—Truth. 243
    Hold Fast to Your Boundaries—The Tongue 246
    Hold Fast to Your Boundaries—Time 248
    Hold Fast to Your Boundaries—What Is Purity? 251
    Hold Fast to Your Boundaries—Our Bodies Are Temples 254
    Hold Fast to Your Boundaries—Sexual Purity 257
    Hold Fast to Your Boundaries—The Faith 262
    Make a Mantra and Use It 265
    We Have to Know Him, Not Just about Him. 268
    There Is No Need for Self-Pressure. 271
    Hold Fast to Your Boundaries—Be (the Good Parts of) You 275

Part Eleven: Abstain From Evil
    Stick with the Good, Stay Away from the Bad 278
    What Do You Fill Your Empty Spaces With?. 280
    We've Forgotten How to Argue 282
    Relationships: Competitive, Cooperative, or Indifferent. 285
    Consequences of Positive, Negative, and No Input 288
    Be the Salt of the Earth. 290
    An Important Conversion for Parents. 293
    Getting Rid of Guilt and Shame 296
    Then What?. 299
    The Signs Have to Match 303

Part Twelve: Keep Sound
    God and the Church Are Encouragers 306
    Having Rules Makes You Free. 309
    A Buddy to Keep You Accountable 311
    Be a Light in the World. 313
    Preparing the Soil of Your Heart. 315
    Go for Excellence, Not Mediocrity 318
    Course Corrections Are Important. 320

Part Thirteen: God Is Faithful
    God Knows Your Storms 324
    Walking on Water Is Possible with Encouragement and Faith. 326
    When God Feels Absent. 328

Yes, But What about My Crosses?.. 333
The Lord Is My Shepherd... 335
God Rewards Effort.. 337
The Parable of the Talents—The Best I Can with What I Have on a Given Day 339
The Parable of the Talents—Don't Be Discouraged If You Only Have One Talent 342
The Parable of the Talents—Be Careful What You Wish For 346
The Parable of the Talents—I Want to Die Exhausted 348
Filling the Gap between the Life We Want and the Life We Have—The Rick Ankiel Story 351
God Is Faithful, Even When We Are Not... 354

Part Fourteen: Pray For Us

We Do Not Exist in Isolation... 358
Intercessory Prayer.. 361
I'm Going to God for You.. 363
Praying with Someone... 366
There Is No Shame in Asking for Help 369
I Need Help to Get to Christ—I Can't Get There Alone 372
You Can Ask for Encouragement... 376
You Are Worthy... 378

Part Fifteen: Greet One Another

Are Our Churches Places of Encouragement or Discouragement? 382
Encouragement to Serve 385
Fellowship with Others.. 388
One Body with Many Members.. 390
No One Should Ever Feel Alone 392
BE the Church!... 395
Consumers versus Producers, Cruise Ships versus Battleships....................... 397
The Church Should Be a Safe Environment....................................... 400

Part Sixteen: Read With All

The Importance of Scripture... 404
Encouragement from the Bible... 407
Getting the Full Experience—Worship 410
The Divine Fellowship—Holy Communion 412
Confession as Encouragement 414
The Sacraments... 416

Part Seventeen: The Grace of our Lord

What Is Grace?... 420

    Let Him Lead 422
    God Is Rooting for Us 425
    Easy to Entreat, Easy to Forgive 428
    Authenticity Starts with Christ 430
    If I Could Be like Christ 433

CONCLUSION
    The Riddle 436
    Who Is the Loudest Voice in Your Life? 439
    The Paralytic—Who Are Your Go-To People? Are You a Go-To Person? ... 442
    We Are Called to be Barnabas 444
    A Summary of Four Existential Questions 447
    For Whom Do We Exist? 450
    It's Not Goodness but Godliness We Are Aiming For 453
    Positive In-Positive Out, Negative In-Negative Out, Nothing In-Negative Out 455
    I Wish the Best for You 457
    The Encouragement Walk Experiment—The Gift Is You 460
    Swimming against the Current 463
    Practical Ways We Can All Make a Difference 465
    Who Is Going to Take the First Step? 468
    We Can All Solve This Problem 470
    Are You All In? 472
    Proclaim Encouragement from the Rooftops 474
    Go Do It 476
    About the Author 479
    Endnotes 481
    Bibliography-Suggested Reading 487

Acknowledgments

In February 2015, a parishioner approached me with an idea about creating a prayer team—a group of parishioners who would commit to daily praying for the church and me during the upcoming Lenten period. I have always enjoyed writing and decided that for the period of Lent in 2015, I would write a daily reflection and send it to whoever joined the Prayer Team. I had hoped that thirty people would join, and the intention was to do this for forty days. Over 150 people joined the Prayer Team, and as Lent came to an end, they asked me if I would continue the daily reflections, so I did.

Now, nearly eight years into writing daily reflections, I write on various topics related to prayer, the Orthodox faith, and the Christian life. This is the seventh book that has come out of the daily reflections of the prayer team. The first is *Let All Creation Rejoice: Reflections for Advent, the Nativity and Epiphany*. The second is *The Road Back to Christ: Reflections on Lent, Holy Week and the Resurrection*. The third is *Blessed Is the Kingdom, Now and Forever: Reflections on the Divine Liturgy*. The fourth is *The Heart of Encouragement: Reflections on the Sunday and Feastday Scripture Readings of the Orthodox Church*. The fifth is *Engaged: Called to Be Disciples, Reflections on What It Means to Be a Christian*. The sixth is *Commissioned to Be Apostles: Love, Worship, Community, Learning, Service*.

I wish to thank those who have helped and encouraged me in this project:

To His Eminence Metropolitan Alexios of Atlanta, the Greek Orthodox bishop of the Metropolis of Atlanta, for his prayers and blessings.

To Tim Tassopoulos, who graciously accepted my invitation to write the foreword for this book. Tim is not only an accomplished businessman, but he is also a devout husband, father, friend, servant, encourager, and most of all, a man of deep faith.

To the anonymous donor who provided the funds what made this publication possible.

To the many parishioners of St. John the Baptist Greek Orthodox Church in Tampa, Florida, for their support of the Prayer Team and encouragement to move forward with this project. Many of the experiences related in this book have come from my work with them.

To all the members of the Prayer Team, for reading my reflections, for your prayers, and for your encouragement.

To the Orthodox Christian Network (OCN) for posting my writings.

To Father John Bociu, who designed the cover for this book.

To Catherine Mitseas and Rose Wilson, who offered helpful suggestions for the back cover.

To His Eminence Metropolitan Methodios of Boston, Christine Selochan, Alkis Crassas, Dr. Pete Copsis, Elizabeth (Poulos) and Stone Hendrickson, St. Luke's Cabin of Week Two of St. Stephen's Camp 2021, the California High School Class of 1990, Fr. Dean Gigicos, Fr. Steve Dalber, Fr. Aris Metrakos, Dr. Timothy Evans, Connie Simopoulos, Lygia Karagiozis, Fr. John Bociu, Fr. Larry Richards, Fr. James T. Adams, Artemis Xenick, Mia Lenardos, Kristina Hixson, and the clergy, staff, and campers of St. Stephen's Greek Orthodox Summer Camp, who provided inspiration for many of the reflections contained in this book.

To my mom and dad (of blessed memory) for their encouragement and help and for encouraging me from a young age to develop my writing skills.

To my son, Nicholas, who already enjoys writing, for his unconditional love and the beautiful stories he tells.

To my wife, Lisa, for her support of my ministry, the many sacrifices she makes for our family, and her encouragement to write.

Finally, and most especially, to the Lord, for the great blessing to serve as a Greek Orthodox priest and for His grace to stand before the holy altar and celebrate the Divine Liturgy; for giving me a talent to write and a desire to share that gift through this project. I am thankful for the continued inspiration He provides and this blessing He has given me to share my thoughts on the commission we each have to be His apostles.

> *For I long to see you, that I may impart to you some spiritual gift to strengthen you, that is, that we may be mutually encouraged by each other's faith, both yours and mine.*
> Romans 1:11–12

Foreword: Encourage One Another

Encouragement is a difference maker, a force multiplier, a gift to be shared, and a habit and practice that is often too rare in our often fast-paced, hectic culture. I'm grateful to Father Stavros Akrotirianakis, or "Father Stav" as he is known in our family, for capturing the essence of encouragement in this very readable and applicable book.

Encouragement can be productively applied in all settings, whether it is at work, at home, on a sports field or court, in a classroom, in the community, or in a church. I'm so fortunate to have experienced the power of encouragement throughout my forty-five-year professional career, starting as an hourly restaurant team member at a Chick-fil-A restaurant in Atlanta during high school and throughout my time as a corporate staff member as well. I was the recipient of encouragement from my first day on the job cleaning tables and serving guests.

The young owner-operator of my Chick-fil-A restaurant, Gary Gettis, didn't have decades of business experience, but he did have the gift of encouragement, and he shared if frequently and authentically. When I finished my shift on my first day, Gary told me "thank you" in a personal and caring way. Then he said "thanks" again on my second day. And I soon noticed that he told my fellow team members "thank you" after each of their shifts as well. The appreciation was important, but it was the intentionality and consistency of Gary's encouragement that made all the difference. Encouragement is a difference maker.

I also experienced genuine encouragement when Gary introduced me to the founder of Chick-fil-A, Truett Cathy. Truett was a master encourager. His willingness to spend dedicated, focused time with young people was consistent and often life-changing. Truett prayed with me, counseled me, and supported me from my years as a college intern at the Chick-fil-A Corporate Office until his passing thirty-five years later. But Truett didn't just encourage me. He was a multiplier of encouragement in every environment, whether it was the workplace, in school, or the community. Truett asked all of us at Chick-fil-A over and over again, "How do you know if someone needs encouragement?" And he would quickly answer his own question, "If they are breathing." Yes, everyone needs encouragement. And part of Truett's legacy at Chick-fil-A has been the intent of those of us who worked closely with him to build a culture of encouragement that lifts up our team members, owner-operators, corporate staff, suppliers, customers, and communities in which we do business. Encouragement is a force multiplier.

But, as Father Stav reminds us in this engaging and insightful book, encouragement is also a choice. It is a personal choice that we can make each and every day. It is a choice that is expressed in our words and actions. It is embodied in our focus and attention to others, and it is strengthened in our prayers and petitions for God's blessings on our families, friends, colleagues, and neighbors. My encouragement to each and every one of you—just as I am encouraging myself—is to acknowledge the gift that encouragement can be if we accept it gracefully and share it wholeheartedly. I'm encouraged by this book and the principles and practices in it, and I hope and pray that you will be too. I hope you will enjoy, apply, and share Father Stav's "lessons learned" from *The Heart of Encouragement*. Let's encourage one another and make a difference in our families, schools, teams, churches, businesses, and communities. And by doing so, we'll be making a difference in our own lives as well.

Tim Tassopoulos
President and COO, Chick-fil-A, Inc.

Why This Book?

Very few people have this right. If you ask most people, and they answer honestly, most would say that they are lacking in confidence. A lack of confidence leads to low self-esteem, which leads to low productivity, which leads to anxiety, which then leads to a lack of confidence, and a vicious cycle occurs. This is not just a teenage thing. If it was, we could call it simply one stage of life. And yes, perhaps this is exacerbated in the teenage years. However, many people never break this cycle. They lack confidence throughout life.

On the flip side, some people are supremely confident. They might even have narcissistic tendencies and lack humility. They are confrontational, and many people feel uncomfortable around them. Some of these may also lack confidence deep down. They just go overboard in hiding it.

There is an overall problem with honesty in our society. In many pockets, it's not safe to be honest or vulnerable. So we create stories about ourselves based on lies—we don't tell people we are stressed out, lack confidence, or need help because we think we can't. Because it might cost us a job or a reputation. Or because we might be subjects of gossip. So, we play this game where we are less than honest.

This book is about encouragement, building up others, and creating safe spaces where it's okay to be honest and vulnerable. The older I get and the more life I experience, the more I think it is necessary to encourage and reassure others and create safe spaces. These three things—encouragement, reassurance, and safety—will create environments of honesty, confidence, and productivity. When I say productivity, I'm not talking about work ethic only. Many people can't be productive at anything because they are anxious, sad, and discouraged. By encouraging others, we can help one another be the best version of ourselves, and rather than feeling isolated with our thoughts and our worries, we can get out and enjoy life with a little more confidence.

This book contains 176 reflections. Each contains a verse of Scripture, a reflection, and a prayer. Each is written with the hope that it will encourage you and build you up in one area of life and will, in turn, give you some concrete ideas of how to encourage and build up others. Most reflections also include an "Encouragement Challenge," something to do on a given day that will infuse encouragement into our world.

Its nineteen sections are based on 1 Thessalonians 5:11–28, a mere eighteen verses of Scripture that provide an amazing amount of encouragement and a solid framework of how to become a good encourager.

You don't have to read the whole book or read it in order. Look over the table of contents and find areas of your life where you need some encouragement and read those. If something in particular strikes you or reminds you of someone, feel free to share that reflection with them as you wish. There is so much tearing down in the world today. I hope this book will serve as a way to build you up and help you build up others as well.

No one wants to lack confidence. No one likes feeling anxious. Narcissism is not the answer. Living at either extreme will not allow us to be the best version of ourselves. The answer is somewhere in the middle. Encouragement, I believe, is an important component in getting us to the middle, where we can be the best version of ourselves and help others to do the same.

I have served as a Greek Orthodox priest for nearly a quarter of a century, and I have been an Orthodox Christian my entire life. This book is written for a "general Christian" audience. However, there are occasional references that are specific to the Orthodox Christian church.

Further, one of the greatest joys in my life has been to serve as the director of a Greek Orthodox summer camp, which I have done for twenty years. I've learned many lessons on encouragement from summer camp as well as from my ministry, and many of those lessons and stories will appear throughout this book.

+Fr. Stavros N. Akrotirianakis

INTRODUCTION

Encouragement Defined

Therefore, encourage one another and build one another up, just as you are doing.
1 Thessalonians 5:11

Over the past several years, encouragement is a topic that I have become more and more convicted about for a few simple reasons:

~Encouragement is something we all need.
~Encouragement is something we can all give.
~Encouragement is something we don't get enough of.
~Giving encouragement is something that involves low-cost but high benefit.

Encouragement is a topic I write about and frequently speak on. It seems like common sense when I'm writing or speaking about it; nothing earth-shattering, scientific, or profound. Yet, when people feel encouraged, it becomes a game-changer for their lives. When they encourage others, they see how much it changes other people for the better. I hope that in these writings, you will find encouragement as well as inspiration to encourage others and make encouragement an important part of your daily life.

Let us begin by defining the word encouragement. In 1 Thessalonians 5:11, the verse that this study will be based around, the Greek word that is translated as encourage is *parakalite*, which comes from the Greek verb *parakaleo* and can be translated as "exhort," "comfort," or "encourage."[1] Different translations of the Bible translate it differently. In the New King James Version (NKJV), the translation is "comfort," while in the Revised Standard Version, the word is "encourage." Related to the word *parakaleo* are the words *Paraclete*, one of the names given to the Holy Spirit and is often translated as "Comforter," and the word *Paraklesis*, which is an Orthodox Christian service of comfort and supplication.

The modern English word for encourage comes from an early fifteenth-century French word *encoragier*, which means "to make strong, hearten." *En* means to "put in" or "make," and *corage* means "courage" or "heart." So to encourage means to make one strong in heart or to put in courage in the heart of another. Encouraging others is something we can all do. To feel encouraged means to feel strong in one's own heart. Receiving encouragement is something we all need.

In Matthew 24, Jesus warned His followers about the signs of the end of the world. One of the signs, in Matthew 24:12, is "And because wickedness is multiplied, most men's love will grow cold." There is no doubt that wickedness is multiplying in the world today. Almost every day, we read about a mass shooting or other act of senseless violence. It happens so often that we are no longer shocked. We are practically numb to it. The prevalent emotion among many is anger: angry drivers, angry music lyrics, angry workers, angry arguments, anger and politics, and anger and social unrest. Because of anger and wickedness, as Jesus predicted, hearts are growing cold. Whether the world is about to end or not, none of us knows. We do know that love is growing cold with the increase of anger and wickedness.

Could encouragement be the antidote? I'm not sure if would be right to characterize encouragement as the key to solving all of our societal problems, but it certainly is a step in the right direction. So, I invite you to join in on a journey to better understand something beautiful, powerful, needed, and most important, accessible to any person alive today—encouragement.

The title of this book is *The Heart of Encouragement*. I chose this title for two reasons. First, we will get to "the heart of the matter" and define and discuss the meaning of the word encouragement. Second, I hope this discussion on encouragement will change hearts and make us more committed encouragers, and as individual hearts change, the result is that hearts in our respective little corners of the world change to be hearts that are positive, encouraging, and help build others up.

Perhaps the best definition of encouragement is one I read recently in an article from a pastor named Sean DeMars, entitled "Don't Flatter, Encourage!" He wrote that "encouragement is pointing out the grace of God in the lives of others."[2] Encouragement is not only something essential in everyone's life, but it is also an essential part of the Christian life. I suppose one can give encouragement and not be a Christian, but it would be hard to be a Christian and not be an encourager.

Lord, thank You for the gift of this day. Help me to better understand the meaning of encouragement so that I can be a better encourager to others and so that I can feel encouraged as well. Amen.

I pray that our hearts will be changed by this book on *The Heart of Encouragement*!

Encouragement Was Very Important to St. Paul

May the God of steadfastness and encouragement grant you to live in such harmony with one another, in accord with Christ Jesus, that together you may with one voice glorify the God and Father of our Lord Jesus Christ.
Romans 15:5–6

You could say that encouragement was very important to St. Paul, as he used the word over thirty times in his epistles. The Epistles of St. Paul were letters to the early churches in the years immediately following the resurrection. These new Christians and their respective new communities needed a lot of guidance and teaching. Occasionally, they needed some admonishing. As with any new endeavor, there were growing pains. However, St. Paul was not only careful but purposeful in giving them not only information to digest and correction when they were making missteps, but he was also careful and purposeful to give them encouragement as well. After all, if all we received from some new endeavor was teaching, information, and admonishing, we wouldn't stick with anything.

Think back to your school years and how you learned your multiplication tables, for example. There was repetition, repetition, repetition. There was correction when you got something wrong. There might have been admonishing when you didn't stick to the task, weren't focused in getting homework done, or when you didn't do as well as you could have on a test. But without some encouragement along the way, you would have given up on math. Someone recognized when you did well and told you so. Maybe it was a teacher, parent, or peer. Something positive kept you interested in learning. It wasn't just self-driven.

St. Paul knew that the fledgling churches were learning, just the way children learn. His epistles are still valued to this day because we are still fledgling in our understanding and practice of Christianity, and we need to learn just as the early church did. We will make mistakes, just like the early Christians did. In fact, we will make the same mistakes that the early Christians did. That's why the epistles of St. Paul are so timeless.

The encouragement found in St. Paul's Epistles are as critical for us today as they were for the early Christians of the first century. We need to hear these words as much today as they did back then. We need to hear encouragement inside and outside of our church communities.

The Scriptures give us instruction on what we believe and how to apply what we believe. We believe in God and apply that belief through love and service. An important part of love and service is encouragement. Thus, what we read in Scriptures and what we will study in this book on the heart of encouragement are not just things to know but things to apply in our lives.

The verses from Romans 15:5–6 encourage us to live in harmony with one another, to be with one voice as we glorify God. They call us to unity. Imagine if we invoked this blessing over everyone we meet today and if we encouraged everyone to live in harmony and unity. What would happen? Well, the cynical part of me says we'd probably get laughed at. Can you imagine saying this to your neighbors, co-workers, or friends? In politically correct circles, someone would probably get mad that God's name was said out loud. However, let's say you said it once and then you actually lived it out, if you gave encouragement and looked for opportunities for harmony and unity, imagine what could happen in your life.

Let's take St. Paul's number of encouragements, conservatively thirty, and took ONE-TENTH of that, three, and made it a goal to encourage three people a day. Imagine if everyone reading this message encouraged three people a day. That would be a lot of encouragement.

St. Paul was very real and very bold. He wasn't afraid to call people out. He wasn't all fun and fluff. However, St. Paul, for all of his boldness, had a great sense of love and compassion. He knew that encouragement needed to temper admonishment. He understood that one couldn't be changed only by tearing them down but by building them up. Thus, as we seek to imitate what we read in Scripture and apply it to our daily lives, as St. Paul made encouragement an important part of his writings to the churches of his day, and that we still make important to the churches today, we need to encourage one another. We may have to call people out, admonish, correct, and guide. However, in all of that, we can't forget to encourage.

Lord, help me to balance my tone today. Give me the grace to offer even in admonishing someone in a way that is constructive and not destructive. Give me the eyes to see three people who could use some encouragement today. Give me the heart and words to offer them what they need. Amen.

Encouragement Challenge: Intentionally encourage THREE people today!

Encouragement—A Call to Action

Then His mother and His brothers came to Him, but they could not reach Him for the crowd. And He was told "Your mother and your brothers are standing outside, desiring to see you." But He said to them, "My mother and my brothers are those who hear the word of God and do it."
Luke 8:19–21

Learning without application is a pointless exercise. Learning the multiplication tables is valuable when it is applied to a real-life situation. For instance, knowing that 4×5 equals 20 is of little value by itself. The value to knowing this is when one wants to buy four hamburgers that cost five dollars each and knowing that one needs twenty dollars for this to happen.

Knowing many Bible verses or religious things is just trivia if these things are not applied to life. Winning the "Bible trivia contest" does not get one into the kingdom of heaven.

This book will be based around 1 Thessalonians 5:11–28. I like to call this section of the Bible, "The Encouragement Chapter." In these eighteen verses of Scripture, we find twenty-two verbs, each one a call to some action. This book is about encouragement, why it's important, and how we can all become better at it. This chapter, which we will study in detail, will give us more than twenty specific things we can do. There are many parts of Scripture that seem difficult to interpret. Some of St. Paul's letters seem to require supplemental material to understand them. First Thessalonians 5:11–28 is actually pretty straightforward. Though we will go into a good deal of depth on each verse, St. Paul, in these verses, is essentially telling us, "If you want to be a good encourager, do this."

Christ came into the world to change the world. His message wasn't just a call to learn but a call to action. That's why we can study even a small piece of Scripture in great detail because each passage of Scripture contains a call to some kind of action. He didn't tell us to absorb as many of His words as possible but to use His words to love and serve each other while giving glory to God.

The few verses quoted above this reflection remind us that Christ identifies "His people" as the ones who not only hear the Word of God but who do it. When told "Your people (Your mother and brothers) are here," His response was that His people (His mother and brothers) "are those who hear the word of God and do it" (Luke 8:21). God's "people" are not the ones who just show up in church on Sundays and sit and absorb information. They are the ones who leave from the service and go out and apply what they have learned.

Of course, some will make the argument that they are good people who do good things and don't need to come to church to worship and learn. Worship is a necessary component to every Christian life. Worship is where we gather as a community to offer prayers to God as a whole group. Worship is the context in which we commune as well. In the context of worship, in Scripture and in sermon, we learn. But the experience of worship is supposed to extend beyond Sunday morning. It is supposed to lead us to a life of action. On Sunday mornings (and on other days we worship), we come to recharge, reconnect, recommit, and learn more deeply. Outside of worship, we are to serve, putting into action the things we've learned.

In this in-depth study of 1 Thessalonians 5:11–28, we are sure to learn a lot. However, the goal is to apply what we've learned, not merely learn for the sake of learning. That's why each reflection will end with some call to action, something we can do on a given day to be an encourager. By the time you reach the end of this book, we will have discussed dozens of small and practical ways to encourage others as well as feel encouraged ourselves.

> *Shine in our hearts, O Master Who loves mankind, the pure light of Your divine knowledge, and open the eyes of our mind that we may comprehend the proclamations of Your Gospels. Instill in us also reverence for Your blessed commandments so that, having trampled down all carnal desires, we may lead a spiritual life both thinking and doing all those things that are pleasing to You. For You, Christ our God, are the illumination of our souls and bodies, and to You we offer up glory, together with Your Father, Who is without beginning, and Your all-holy, good, and life-creating Spirit, now and forever and to the ages of ages. Amen. (From the Divine Liturgy of St. John Chrysostom, Translation of the Greek Orthodox Archdiocese of America, 2015, p. 19-20)[3]*

Let's open our minds and hearts and allow St. Paul, through this beautiful chapter of 1 Thessalonians 5:11–28, to help us be more encouraged in our lives and able to better encourage others. Let us prepare to both learn and apply what we've learned.

Part One
ENCOURAGE ONE ANOTHER

Therefore, encourage one another and build one another up, just as you are doing.

1 Thessalonians 5:11

The Need for Encouragement

Therefore encourage one another and build on another up, just as you are doing.
1 Thessalonians 5:11

Having surveyed a number of people of all ages, from teens at summer camp to our Sunday school teachers to parishioners of all ages, there is an almost unanimous agreement that the number of voices we hear in our daily lives are voices of discouragement rather than encouragement. People are much more likely to feel torn down than built up. Because we are all treated this way, we also tend to treat others in this way.

Because most of our sensory input (what we see, hear, read, and say) is discouraging, we need to tip the scales and put some more encouragement into our lives to bring things into a balance we all need, even if we don't realize it. Many times we want to give up because the discouraging voices outweigh the encouraging ones.

Encouragement builds confidence. Lack of encouragement erodes confidence and leads to doubt and despair. Confidence is important because it helps us to be more productive and see things with more joy and optimism. We aren't as productive in anything—marriage, parenting, career, exercise, health, spirituality, etc.—when we receive messages of discouragement. We become more productive and thrive more in all of our roles when we are encouraged.

There is a secondary problem to not enough encouragement, and that is people lack safe spaces in which to talk about their thoughts. Oftentimes, in the sacrament of confession, I have found a person will quickly confess their sins and then ask, "Can we just talk? I have no place to put certain thoughts and feelings." Thus, many of us lack not only encouragement, but we also lack a safe space in which to put our thoughts, work through our challenges, and share our doubts and fears.

Not only are most of us at a deficit when it comes to encouragement versus discouragement, but many of us also lack someone even to talk to honestly about our struggles and successes. Many feel discouraged. Few feel encouraged. Not enough are intentionally encouraging others. Not enough are listening, and many are not feeling that they are heard.

The other struggle we all have, because we are human beings living in a fallen world, is that we each contribute to the problem of discouragement. Whether we gossip, speak negatively, or have indifference, at times, we all contribute to the problem.

The goal of this book on the *Heart of Encouragement* is to bring encouragement to the forefront of our minds. Because we all crave encouragement and have few places to go get it, an infusion of encouragement into our daily consciousness and incorporated into our daily lives will hopefully lead you to a greater sense of joy and optimism in your life, relationships and faith. In line with encouraging, we can help create safe spaces where honest conversation can happen. We can work to build authentic relationships based on love and respect, where gossip, negativity, and indifference are intentionally and purposely cast aside.

This reflection begins a study on 1 Thessalonians 5:11, the central verse in this chapter on encouragement. This verse gives us two specific things we are to do for each other—encourage and build up one another. The two concepts go hand in hand. Encouraging builds up. Discouraging tears down. We must consciously seek to do the one while purposefully avoiding the other because encouragement is not only a doing of the positive but an avoiding of the negative. When it comes to encouraging and building up, we are either doing both, or we are doing neither. We can't do one and not the other. So, start the process today by looking for opportunities to encourage and build up.

Lord, I begin today by offering thanks to You for the gift of a new day. I know that today will have challenges. I know that I may not even know what these challenges are. Help me to trust that You will walk with me in all of them. I know that there will be opportunities for joy today. Help me to seize on those moments. And I know that there will be an opportunity to encourage someone today. Open the eyes of my soul to see those opportunities and the eyes of my heart to be an encourager. Bless me and everyone I will meet today. Amen.

Encouragement Challenge: Have a great day! Be encouraging today! Start off with good and positive intentions for your day today!

Something Everyone Can Do

So if there is any encouragement in Christ, any incentive of love, any participation in the Spirit, any affection and sympathy, complete my joy by being of the same mind, having the same love, being in full accord and of one mind.
Philippians 2:1–2

One of the best things about encouraging others is that it is something we can all do. Everyone has the ability to be an encourager. For some, it is natural. For others, it is learned. Even if encouragement doesn't come naturally to you, it is something you can easily learn. You don't need a college degree. You don't need to invest any money or own a home, be famous, well-read, or articulate. To be an encourager requires heart, patience, and interest.

Encouraging is something that comes more naturally to some people than others. Some lack experience, and some are just not in the habit yet. Encouragement is something we can all do, and for those who are already doing it, it is something we can all do even better. It takes a conscious choice and consistency.

One Sunday in church, I encouraged everyone to send at least one "encouraging" text message to a different person every day this week. I told them not to expect to get a text back. I asked them not to do it for any other reason than a one-way expression of encouragement they are giving as a gift to someone. Many people reported that they had received positive responses. Those who were texted felt good, and those who had sent the text felt good. It was a win-win for everyone.

One week, I did an experiment. I sent ten moms in my parish a text that read, "You are a great mom!" and sent ten dads in my parish a text that read, "You are a great dad!" I even had copied and pasted the same message so I sent twenty text messages in literally two minutes. I received nearly twenty positive responses. Giving a message of encouragement is actually one of the easiest things a person can do.

Here is another great thing about encouragement—you don't have to be old to send a message to a young person. You can't be too young to send an encouraging message to an older person. Anyone can send encouragement to pretty much anyone. It's really that easy.

They say that to acquire a new habit takes thirty days. I encourage you to send out an encouraging text to someone every day this week. It will take you a minute or less. And after this week, see if you can make this a habit for the next month.

Of course, we know that text messaging isn't the only way to encourage. It's convenient, though. We will discuss many other ways to encourage others as well as what to say and what to do as we go along.

We know that the greatest commandments are to love God and love our neighbor. And one of the easiest ways to love your neighbor is to encourage your neighbor because encouragement brings joy and builds confidence. Discouragement steals joy and erodes confidence. It distracts and causes doubt as well.

Remember, encouragement is something we can all do. All it takes is a loving heart, interest, and consistency.

Lord, thank You for the gift of today. As I go through the day today, help me to see the good in people. Help me to seize on what is good in others rather than focusing only on flaws. Help me to have the discipline to be an encourager and to make encouraging others a daily habit, starting today. Amen.

Encouragement Challenge: Send an encouraging text message to at least one person today!

Encouragement Is a Choice

For I long to see you, that I may impart to you some spiritual gift to strengthen you, that is, that we may be mutually encouraged by each other's faith, both yours and mine.
Romans 1:11–12

One of God's greatest gifts to us is the gift of freedom. Freedom means that we have choices. We are free to engage in certain behaviors and avoid others. We are certainly not robots. One of the challenges to life, then, is how to exercise freedom in such a way that our choices are good ones.

Interacting with other people is something we do virtually every day. I would venture to say that every day, there is an opportunity to offer both encouragement and discouragement. No one can force you to do one or the other. What you do in these moments is purely your choice.

There is great power in encouragement. Likewise, there is a great power in discouragement. One builds morale and confidence. The other erodes both. In forming our own identities, do we want to see ourselves as confidence builders or confidence breakers? When we go and stand in front of the Lord and answer for our lives, do we want to present a life record that is one of encouragement or discouragement? As you can see, not only does the choice to encourage or discourage bring a daily consequence to those around us, but it also brings an eternal consequence to us as well.

Let's move back to the practical. Not everything that happens on a given day will be positive. Someone will annoy us. What then will be our response? Will we "rip into them"? Can we correct and still maintain our love and their dignity? Can we be constructive in our guidance rather than destructive? Can we correct misbehavior in a way that actually encourages the desired behavior to happen next time?

In whatever negative situation happens today, as you decide on how you will react, think of this: "What can I say that will encourage a better outcome next time?" Think of encouraging thoughts and offer encouraging words even in moments of discouragement. This not only has potential benefit for your relationships, but it also has potential benefit for your own soul.

Encouragement is intentional and purposeful. Encouragement doesn't happen by accident, nor does it happen by itself. Encouragement is a choice we are each given the opportunity to make probably several times a day. Encouragement is something we have to be intentional about. We have to be deliberate in offering it. Encouragement serves a purpose, which is to build people up rather than tear them down. Thus, the choice to be an encourager needs to be intentional and purposeful if it is to be genuine and effective.

One final thought, and that is on the word indifference. Many times we are quick to correct bad behavior but are slow to encourage good behavior. Sometimes we only correct the bad and are indifferent to the good. In youth ministry, people have pointed out that we are so quick to try to save the "bad kids" that we forget to spend time with the "good" ones. So make sure that when something good happens, when someone makes a positive gesture to you, you encourage and praise that as well. We need to encourage good behavior in people who are acting badly, but we also need to encourage good behavior in people who are doing things that are good.

How about encouragement for people who are just "there," people whose names we don't necessarily know, but if they weren't in our lives, we'd have some significant things missing? Like the bank teller, the cashier at the store, the mail carrier, or the sanitation engineer. Merely telling someone to have a great day and doing it with a smile or telling someone that they do good work is encouraging. We can all do a better job of being intentional and purposeful encouragers for people we know, and most especially for people we don't know well.

Lord, give me patience in my discouraging moments today. Help me to be constructive and not destructive toward those who disappoint me. Create in me a greater desire to encourage the things that I see are good. Open my eyes so that I don't miss these opportunities, and open my heart to offer encouragement to people who help me, whose names I don't even know, like the cashier at the store or the teller at the bank (or fill in the blank with people you'll interact with today who you don't know well but can't make it without). Remember these people who serve me and help me to remember to encourage them as well. Amen.

Encouragement Challenge: Choose to encourage today!

WHAT ENCOURAGEMENT LOOKS LIKE AND SOUNDS LIKE

Everyone helps his neighbor, and says to his brother, "Take courage!" The craftsman encourages the goldsmith, and he who smooths with the hammer him who strikes the anvil, saying of the soldering "It is good"; and they fasten it with nails so that it cannot be moved.
Isaiah 41:6–7

There are very few people who don't respond to well positive reinforcement. There is virtually no one who doesn't like to hear "You've done well." On the other hand, most people do not respond well to negative reinforcement. No one likes to hear "You did a bad job."

Some people handle negative reinforcement better than others. For instance, when a coach tells a player, "If you don't play well today, you won't be in the lineup tomorrow," some people respond positively to pressure like that. Most people, however, do not. When the coach says, "I believe in you, you are playing tomorrow even if it's a bad game today," then the player can relax. And most athletes play better when they are relaxed.

For some, negative reinforcement is a turn-off—they tend to write off the negative reinforcers. However, there is virtually no one who turns off positive reinforcement. It is something we all like and something that we all need.

It's amazing how powerful of a tool one's mouth is. The mouth can be used to build people up or tear them down. Speaking personally, I know that I thrive on affirmation. I don't need a lot of it, nor do I need it constantly. I do, however, need it regularly.

Affirmation can come effectively in three ways. First, affirm a person. "You are doing a great job." "You are a talented secretary." "I wish all doctors were as friendly as you." It is important to say these things to those who work for us because encouragement and affirmation inspire people to work even harder at what they do.

Secondly, affirm a relationship. "You mean a lot to me." "I'm really glad that you are in my life." It is important that we say these things to those we care about because encouragement and affirmation inspire relationships to strengthen.

Third, encourage even when the behavior is not what you wanted. Instead of saying, "You are wrong," it's more effective to say, "I know you can do better. I still believe in you."

Many people forget affirmation in relationships. Saying "I love you" is certainly an affirmation, but affirming should go beyond that. Many times in marriage, more than "I love you," a spouse wants to hear "you are a great provider," "you are a great mom/dad," or "I love coming home to you every night." In long-term friendships, many people forget to say things like "I really treasure our friendship." If that is a true statement in one of your friendships, why not say it?

Finally, we all do things wrong, and we all make mistakes. When we affirm someone, even when they have made an error, we can correct without shattering someone's confidence or tearing apart a relationship. Affirming someone's value while correcting them or even telling them you are disappointed is one of the most mature things a person can do.

Encouragement includes affirming those around us on a regular basis with thoughts that are positive and, in the case of a mistake, reassuring.

Lord, I begin this prayer by affirming Your importance in my life. Thank You for creating the world I live in. Thank You for giving me the talents I have. Lord, direct my words so that they can be words of affirmation and encouragement. Even when I'm disappointed with someone or something, help me learn to speak in ways that are still constructive and encouraging. Help bring out the best in me. Help me to bring out the best in others. Amen.

Encouragement Challenge: Affirm someone today!

Low-Cost, High Benefit

But where shall wisdom be found? And where is the place of understanding? Man does not know the way to it, and it is not found deep in the land of the living. The deep says "It is not in me," and the sea says, "It is not with me." It cannot be gotten for gold, and silver cannot be weighed as its price. It cannot be valued in the gold of Ophir, in the precious onyx or sapphire. Gold and glass cannot equal it, nor can it be exchanged for jewels or fine gold. No mention shall be made of coral or of crystal; the price of wisdom is above pearls. The topaz of Ethiopia cannot compare with it, nor can it be valued in pure gold.
Job 28:12–19

Just about everything in life that is worthwhile comes at a cost. We have to spend time and money to get some benefit. Sometimes that time is significant, like years of education to land a good job or a sizeable mortgage to have a nice home. There are obvious benefits to having a good job and a good home. There are costs to having a job but definite benefits in the form of compensation, which allows us to go on trips, acquire material goods, and many other things.

There is even a high cost to being a Christian because to be a good Christian, one must "deny himself and take up his cross and follow" (Mark 8:34). This means that at many forks in the road, we will have decide to do what God calls us to do and what we might want to do. This is the lifelong struggle of the committed Christian. Of course, there is an eternal benefit for one who is a follower of Christ, which is eternal life, and there are plenty of benefits in everyday life as well.

Encouragement is one of the few things in life that comes with a low cost and high benefit. As we will discuss, it doesn't cost much time to encourage someone. It doesn't cost any money. A smile or a compliment or an encouraging word takes mere seconds.

There is benefit to both encourager and the one receiving encouragement. To the one receiving encouragement, their confidence receives a boost, which, in turn, makes them more joyful and hopeful. The one giving the encouragement also benefits, to see someone else feel good and know that you are the cause of their good feelings. I must say, I love seeing people who feel good, especially the ones where I play a direct role in encouraging. There is virtually no cost and just high benefit that comes from encouraging someone.

Let's talk about the cost of feeling discouraged because discouragement comes with little to no benefit and high cost. A "benefit" from being discouraged might be more motivation. However, most people just get down when they are discouraged. They feel anything but motivated and empowered. Discouragement leads to doubt, and doubt stifles confidence, causes depression, fuels frustration, and reduces efficiency. I know that when I feel discouraged, it is harder to get out of bed, stay focused on tasks, and feel confident in what I'm doing. Encouragement puts a "spring in my step," motivates me to jump out of bed rather than slink out of it, gets me to work in a good mood instead of a bad one, helps me be more patient, and makes the day more productive and efficient overall.

The bottom line is, it costs very little to encourage. It brings a benefit to both the one being encouraged and the one who encourages them. There is a high cost when one does not receive encouragement, i.e. when one feels discouraged. Can we afford *not* to build environments of encouragement? Can we afford to have people more frustrated, less focused, more inefficient, and less confident than they already are? *No.*

It takes money to overcome financial deficits. It takes time to overcome deficits of knowledge. But it requires only desire to overcome the encouragement deficits in our world. I can't fix my own deficit of encouragement, but others most certainly can. Encouragement is really a work of the heart, not of the mind. That's why this book is called *The Heart of Encouragement* because it is not intelligence, fame, or fortune that makes one a good encourager. Those with the biggest hearts become the biggest encouragers. If there is anything tangible we can all work on is our own hearts. Focus on a tender heart, and you are a few steps closer to being a good encourager.

The Scripture quote from the book of Job talks about the value of wisdom and how you can't put a price on it. Encouragement is the same thing. What good is all the fortune and material possessions in the world when one feels discouraged?

Encouragement is one of the few things in life that has low cost and high benefit. It's also a vital need, something we can't put a price on. Since there is such a large need for encouragement, and it is so easy for us to encourage others, there really isn't much excuse for why there isn't more encouragement going on in our world today. We've all got a role to play in being encouragers. Let's get to work.

Lord, help me to honor You this day by bringing something that is so desperately needed, encouragement, to as many people as possible. Give me the eyes to see those who need the most encouragement, give me the words to encourage them, and give me the heart that rejoices in encouraging others and grows in the desire to do so. Amen.

Encouragement Challenge: Because there is no cost and high benefit to sending a message of encouragement, send at least three today!

Getting over the Wall

Yea, Thou does light my lamp; the Lord my God lightens my darkness. Yea, by Thee I can crush a troop; and by my God I can leap over a wall. This God—His way is perfect; the promise of the Lord proves true; He is a shield for all those who take refuge in Him.
Psalm 18:28–30

One of the great joys in my ministry has been my involvement in summer camp. I will periodically make references to camp in this book. One of the things we promote at camp is encouragement, and this is especially prevalent on the ropes course, a collection of obstacles that cabins complete as a group. These experiences have a direct correlation to the Christian life and to life in general.

One of the obstacles on the ropes course is a twelve-foot-high wall. Each cabin must get their entire cabin over the wall by working as a team. The first person who gets over the wall may have assistance from his/her cabin mates on the ground. They can hoist the person up, but they must pull themselves over the wall. On the back side of the wall is a deck where a couple of people can stand. Once two people are over the wall and standing on the deck, they may help to lift cabin mates from above while others lift from below. The last person who goes over the wall has to go over with no help from below but can jump and be pulled up from above.

The wall teaches participants several things:

1. Some people are afraid of heights and the wall teaches them about overcoming fear;
2. Trust is an important lesson on just about every element, and there is certainly a trust element in allowing people to lift you and pull you over the wall;
3. There is a teamwork element to this activity. The cabin has to work together as a unit to make sure the ones lifting and the one being lifted are moving in sync; and
4. There is an element of planning involved as the cabin must decide who will go over first and who will go over last because these will go with minimal assistance.

The wall illustrates something else that is very important. If there are two people on top of the wall lifting someone, and one person runs and grabs the ankles of the person being lifted up, do you think that the two lifters can overcome the guy who is pulling the climber down? The answer is no, and that is because of gravity. One person is climbing up, two people are lifting, and then one person jumps on the ankles of the climber, and now it's the weight of two plus gravity against the strength of the two up top. The climber loses every time.

How many people do you think it would take to lift the climber from up on top to counterbalance the one tearing the climber down? The answer is probably FIVE. This supports the 5:1 ratio we will later discuss on the amount of encouragement to discouragement one needs to receive to be in any kind of balance.

However, before we go to that, something that we will address much later, the easy lesson of the wall is that it is much easier to pull someone down than to pull them up. It is much easier to tear someone down than to build them up. The questions we ask the campers are these:

- Are there more people in your life who are pulling you up or tearing you down? And who are these people?
- Are you someone who pulls people up or who tears them down?

The wall describes every human life. Every human life has walls to get over. Every human being requires help getting over the walls. That help might be something significant like being lifted by someone else, and that lift could be as simple as an encouraging word or as significant as doing the bulk of the work for someone for them to conquer something. In any case, we all have walls, and we all need help getting over them.

When we build people up, we are like the people on the top of the wall doing the lifting. We are the ones helping someone get over their "walls," whatever those might be. When we are the ones who jump on the person climbing and tear them down, we not only cause someone to fail and be discouraged, but we also hurt and discourage the ones above who are helping. We actually can cause collateral damage to a lot of people.

In our lives, we require many more people who will build us up rather than tear us down. Thus, we need to be cognizant of the people we associate with—are they people who bring us up? Or people who bring us down? The bringing down is not only in the form of discouragement; it might also be in the form of temptation. For instance, the person trying to be a good student may be "torn down" from his or her studies by friends who are always distracting. We all have walls to get over in life. Do we have people around to help us?

We will also be in a position to lift up someone else in life. Are we people who bring others up? Or as we people who tear others down? We need to ask ourselves in our daily decisions of what we say and do, is what we are doing going to build up someone and help them get over a wall, or will it tear them down from the wall and discourage and sabotage them? Simply put, when making a decision that involves someone else, what we say or do, we need to ask ourselves, "Is this going to build them up or tear them down? And then we need to act accordingly.

Everyone has "walls" to get over in life. Everyone needs people to lift them up. No one needs people to tear them down. Everyone will have an opportunity to lift up or tear down. We will each be presented with that choice and often. Which will you be?

The last part of 1 Thessalonians 5:11 reminds us that part of encouraging is building up others. The exercise of the wall illustrates why and how building up others is needed.

Lord, there are many walls in my life (name some of them). Please put people around me who will help lift me over them. Please give me the trust to place my hands in theirs, and most especially to place my hands in Your hands. Lord, there are people around me who are struggling with their own walls (name some of them). Help me to be a good friend and give me the wisdom to know how to lift them and the opportunity to lift them up. Keep me away from the temptation to tear down others. Help me to be someone who lifts others. Amen.

Encouragement Challenge: Surround yourself with people who will lift you up. Make sure that you are someone who lifts up others. "Lift" someone up today!

Why Social Media Is Discouraging

But the Lord said to Samuel, "Do not look on his appearance or on the height of his stature, because I have rejected him; for the Lord sees not as man sees; man looks on the outward appearance, but the Lord looks on the heart."
1 Samuel 16:7

Rarely it seems that we read bad news on social media. Occasionally, someone will write "I'm missing my dad" if he has passed away recently. But we are not likely to read "I didn't make the football team," "Didn't get into the college of my choice," "Was just chewed out by my boss," or "Status: fired."

I recently heard someone call Facebook "Fakebook" because there is not much stuff that's authentic on there. It's generally true that we tend to put only the pretty, dressed-up, happy versions of ourselves on social media.

There are at least two reasons why we do this. The first is pride. We don't want people to see the less-than-best us. We post photos of our achievements, not our failures. We don't regularly see things on social media like someone posing with a photo of the police officer who just gave them a ticket, there are no selfies at divorce proceedings, and no one posts "feeling annoyed that my kid failed math."

Second, there is genuine fear about what people would think if they saw the real us. Would they be judgmental? Would they be sympathetic? Would they run away from someone who "has issues?" Would they avoid us for fear that failure is contagious?

There is a vicious cycle where everyone says everything is okay. And we are, for whatever reason, afraid to break the cycle.

There is a problem with "fake," and it is that we can fool many people, but deep down, we can't fool ourselves, and we can't fool the Lord. He knows our struggles. We know our struggles. Without some authenticity, we will keep struggling. The only way to win the struggle or even manage it is with some degree of honesty.

There are at least two bad things that result from the dishonesty of social media. The first is anger. We have the misguided notion that everyone's life is perfect except ours. If "everyone" appears perfect (even though we know on some level they are not), posing with perfect clothes, on trips to exotic places, and putting only their best faces forward, it's upsetting to wonder, "Why aren't those things happening for me?" For instance, when someone posts, "Celebrating twenty years together with the love of my life," the person who is in a struggling marriage feels angry and sad about their own situation, wondering why the couple on social media looks perfect together. Of course they do! (And maybe they really do have a great marriage.) They are never going to post "Celebrating twenty years together with the love of my life even though we've been to the brink of divorce several times and he cheated on me ten years ago, and after years of therapy, I forgave him."

That brings us to the second by-product, which is isolation. Because we think everyone is doing well, and we know we are not, we feel isolated. How can I tell the perfect people about my imperfections? I'll stand out like a sore thumb. I'll be a pariah. They'll laugh at me.

What happens when people are isolated and angry? They eventually implode or explode. Implosion includes things like alcohol and drug abuse to take the edge off of a sad reality that can't be shared or fixed. Unchecked, implosion can lead to destructive behavior that, in some cases, leads to suicide.

Explosion includes acting out, which can include something small like gossiping about others as a cover for someone's own inadequacy or can include something more destructive, like bullying. In extreme circumstances, explosions include violent outbursts, and with access to a gun, the acts of mass violence are becoming all too common.*

I believe more and more that social media causes more problems than it solves. It divides people more than it unites them. I use social media to share good news and encouraging messages. I post pictures of positive events in my life and in my parish. And yes, I don't generally air failures on social media. However, I do not let social media affect me by constantly comparing myself with others or counting how many people "like" or "comment" on the things that I post. In fact, as time goes on, I'm using social media less and less because I want to be an authentic and truthful person, I want to associate with authentic and truthful people, and I'm realizing that social media does not help either of these pursuits.

The purpose of this book on the *Heart of Encouragement* is to inspire us to encourage others and build them up. A good place to start is by being creating environments where it is safe to be honest. We need to change "fakebook" to honesty and move from Facebook to face-to-face conversation.

The heart is the center of the human body. Without the heart beating, there is no thinking or doing. A body can work without hands. A person is still alive even when their brain is damaged. But without a heartbeat, there is no life. At the heart of encouragement is honesty and authenticity. Without these, there can't be genuine relationships. If encouragement is part of the solution, then eliminating the problem of being fake must also be part of the solution.

Lord, help me always to know that You are real. Help me to build an authentic relationship with You. May I be inspired to bring to You my good things and my failings. Please help me to encourage authenticity in my relationships with others. Please bring others to me who will encourage me to be authentic. Bring people into my life with whom I can be authentic. Give me the courage to be honest, take away my temptation to be fake, and surround me with people with whom it will be safe to be honest. Amen.

This first section of our study has been about 1 Thessalonians 5:11, which reminds us that we are to both encourage one another and build up one another. For encouragement and building up to occur, there needs to be honesty and authenticity.

Part Two

ESTEEM OTHERS HIGHLY

But we beseech you, brethren, to respect those who labor among you, and are over you in the Lord, and admonish you, and to esteem them very highly in love because of their work.

1 Thessalonians 5:12–13

The Golden Rule

And as you wish that men would do to you, do so to them.
Luke 6:31

One of the first Bible verses I memorized as a child was the Golden Rule. Truth be told, I memorized the Golden Rule and later put it together that this was actually a verse from the Bible. In fact, the translation I remember was "Do unto others as you would have them do unto you."

As we move into the second section of this study, we will examine 1 Thessalonians 5:12–13a (the first half of verse 13). This verse includes encouragement to "respect those who labor among you" (your equals), those who "are over you" (your bosses), and those who "admonish you" (even those who treat you rudely). We are to hold all in high esteem, even those we don't get along with.

The Golden Rule provides a good barometer for how we are supposed to interact with one another. We are to put ourselves in their shoes. For instance, if we find ourselves in a position of authority, that is, we are the boss, we should see our workers as if we were one of them. We should ask ourselves, how would I want to be treated if I was in their shoes? We should lead with kindness, patience, and love, not with shrewdness and fear.

This idea of putting ourselves in the shoes of someone else is not something that comes natural to many of us. This is something we all need to work on. As an example, if we have no sense of empathy and compassion, it will be difficult to offer that to someone else. This is an important reason why we must teach our children empathy and compassion along with reading and math. If they don't learn it as a child, they may have a harder time learning it as an adult.

We also tend to judge one another by our own yardstick. If we are dishonest, we are likely to think others around us are dishonest. Thus, in learning how to hold others in high esteem, we have to learn to hold ourselves in high esteem. To see value in others, we need to see value in ourselves.

We can't give away to others what we don't have ourselves to give. If we are harsh on ourselves, we are more likely to be judgmental about others. If we have a good sense of belonging, we can give others a sense of belonging. If we have a sense of self-worth, not in an arrogant way, but in a quiet and confident way, then we can help give worth to others.

We have to build a sense of self-esteem so that we can esteem others. We have to build up and encourage others so that they have a sense of self-esteem because esteem ultimately happens in a cycle. If I have no self-worth, I can't give you self-worth, which contributes to lowering your self-worth, which perpetuates on mine. Encouragement and esteem work in a cycle. When we build the esteem of others, others feel encouraged, and they have the confidence to lift others.

One modern interpretation of the Golden Rule is that we tend to do unto others what has been done to us. If we feel blessed, we are likely to impart blessings to others. If we feel cursed, we are likely to curse others. Because so many people feel angry, they inflict their anger on others. Think about the last time you felt cranky or grouchy; you probably inflicted that on others. After all, when we are cranky, it is hard to put on a happy face for others. (An even worse modern interpretation of the Golden Rule is "Do unto others BEFORE they do unto you," as if to say, "everyone is out to get me, so let me get one over on everyone else before they get one over on me.")

Encouragement helps break a cycle of low self-worth and helps create the cycle of good self-worth in others. Encouragement and self-esteem are very closely tied together. When we help others in the esteem category, we actually get a benefit ourselves.

Going back to the Golden Rule, if you want to be encouraged by others, be an encourager yourself.

Lord, thank You for the gift of my life, talents, skills, successes and even my failures because even in failure, I can grow. Help me to have confidence in myself. Help me to remember that everything I have that is good is a blessing from You. Help me to impart confidence in others by esteeming others and encouraging others. In the moments when I lack confidence, bring others to me who will encourage me. Amen.

Encouragement Challenge: Encourage someone today because it will benefit both them as well as you!

Our Neighbor Is Whomever Is Closest at This Moment

Which of these three, do you think, proved neighbor to the man who fell among the robbers?" He said, "The one who showed mercy on him." And Jesus said to him, "Go and do likewise."
Luke 10:36–37

Most of us are familiar with the parable of the Good Samaritan. As we remember, a lawyer asked Jesus what the two greatest commandments were, to which He replied that we are to love God and love our neighbor as ourselves. The man asked Jesus to quantify who our neighbor is. And Jesus told the parable of a Jewish man who was beaten by robbers and left by the side of the road to die. A priest and a Levite, two Jewish men, who should have been the FIRST ones to run to the man's aid, passed him by without stopping to help. The man who finally stopped was a Samaritan, the sworn enemy of the Jewish robbery victim. The Samaritan spent time (a day and a night) and money (two denarii, or two days' wages) to make sure the man was cared for.

Then Jesus asked the lawyer which man acted like the neighbor to the man who had been beaten and robbed. The man answered, "The one who showed mercy on him" (Luke 10:37). And Jesus told him to go and do the same. The meaning of this parable is that our neighbor is everyone, even our enemy. The Samaritan showed mercy, kindness, and sacrifice for an enemy.

Let's look at this with an even more practical definition of neighbor. Most people, when they hear the word neighbor, think of the person who lives next door to them. By extension, our neighbor is the person who is "residing" closest to us at this moment. At work, our neighbor might be the person whose desk is ten feet away from ours. If we are teachers, our neighbors are the students in a particular class at a particular moment in time. For the doctor, the neighbor is the patient he or she is seeing at a particular moment, for the waiter or waitress, the neighbor is the customer, and for the customer in the restaurant, the neighbor is the person you are eating with as well as the waiter or waitress. Our neighbor can be the driver next to us on the road, the teller at the bank, the clerk at the grocery store, or the fan in the seat next to us at the ballgame. Our neighbor might be someone we know well or someone we don't know at all. Our neighbor might be someone we see every day or someone we will see once and never see again. Our neighbor is everyone, but at any particular moment in time, our neighbor is the person who is physically closest to us.

Encouragement should not just be limited to those we know or those we know well. We aren't only supposed to build up our friends, and we shouldn't only hold people in high esteem who are authority figures. Encouragement, building others up, and holding others in high esteem are things we should be giving our neighbor, whoever is next to us at a given moment. If we love our "neighbors" as we love ourselves, then we are constantly putting ourselves in their shoes.

Do we like when people notice us? When they thank us? When they encourage us? Of course, we all like these things. To love our neighbor as ourselves means to do for the neighbor as we hope to have done for ourselves. Loving our neighbor includes encouraging, building up, and holding in high esteem.

How often do we thank the waiter for excellent service or the teller at the bank? How often do we fail to? How often do we hold a door open for someone or even just simply smile? We are so preoccupied on our phones and with ourselves that we often forget to hold our neighbor in any kind of regard. Sadly, our society in some corners has become so unsafe that many times we think twice about even acknowledging our neighbor for fear they will do us harm.

St. Paul reinforces Christ's command to love our neighbor when he tells us to esteem highly in love those who are among us, whether they are working with us, working for us, or working over us. Since everyone needs encouragement, we should look for opportunities to encourage all of our neighbors, which may mean something as simple as a smile, holding the door open, or even saying, "Good morning." Thanking someone who has served us in a restaurant or bank is something we should all do. I make a point of thanking all people who wear the uniform of the United States military or police officers. They need encouragement as well. In a world where people are feeling increasingly isolated, lonely, and frustrated, a little encouragement is like a drink from a desert oasis, a refreshing change.

Lord, I know that You gave us a commandment to love our neighbors as we love ourselves. Help me to see everyone person who comes into my path today as a neighbor and help me to love each neighbor and to offer encouragement to as many neighbors as possible. Bring someone into my life today who needs encouragement, whether I know this or not, and allow me to be an instrument of encouragement so that they walk away from our encounter feeling more positive about their day. Amen.

Encouragement Challenge: Look for opportunities to encourage your neighbors today, the people who are occupying the spaces closest to you today!

The Basic Building Block to Any Relationship Is Respect

There is no fear in love, but perfect love casts out all fear. For fear has to do with punishment, and he who fears is not perfected in love.
1 John 4:18

In this verse on esteeming others highly, 1 Thessalonians 5:12–13, we encounter the word respect. This is significant because the basic building block to any human relationships, well before we get to love, is respect. In fact, the order of building blocks for a relationship is this: respect, then finding things you have in common, spending time, building a rapport, earning trust, and eventually love.

The Scripture verse from 1 John 4:18 reminds us that fear and love cannot co-exist. Because encouragement is an expression of love, one cannot be fearful and feel encouraged at the same time. Being stressed out and encouraged is possible, but fear tends to shut down our other positive feelings, so it is difficult if not impossible to feel encouraged and afraid at the same time.

From the standpoint of the encourager, one cannot encourage and put fear into someone at the same time. For instance, a boss cannot threaten to fire an employee and say something encouraging in the same sentence, such as, "You are doing a decent job but if you don't improve, I'm going to have to fire you." "You are doing a decent job" on its own may sound encouraging, but placing it beside a threat of termination will not sound encouraging.

Thus, in establishing encouragement in relationships and in environments, one basic step is making sure people are safe and feel safe. (I qualify this using both "are" and "feel" because one is truth and the other is perception, and many times, perception is more important than truth because perception is what people believe. One could have a safe environment, but if it is perceived as not safe, that's what people will believe.) And what we're talking about here isn't a place where it is safe to be vulnerable; we'll get to that much later. We're just talking about a place where one feels safe.

There are many instances in life where we're not thinking about whether it's safe to be vulnerable; we're thinking about whether it's safe to even open our mouths. We're not talking about deep conversation; we're afraid to say even one word. I'm sure we've all had the experience of being nervous making a phone call or seeing someone's name on our caller ID because we are afraid of someone. We all know someone that when they walk into the room, our blood pressure goes up, and we try to avoid contact. I hope that I will never be classified as one of those people—someone who makes people nervous, someone people want to avoid, or someone whose name strikes fear if it pops up on caller ID.

The basic building block of any relationship is respect. That means that a person feels safe around you, and you feel safe around them. You feel physically safe and don't worry that some physical harm will come to you. The back alleys of the inner cities are not places of encouragement because one doesn't feel safe walking them. When walking in a bad part of town, the only thought I have is to let me safely pass through here.

One has to also feel emotionally safe to feel encouraged. Encouragement can't mix with insincerity or sarcasm any more than it can mix with a threat. If the person who makes me the most nervous suddenly offers encouragement, I most likely won't hear the encouragement because I'll be so nervous based on past experience that I won't hear it or believe it is sincere.

Creating environments and relationships based on safety is a necessary precursor to encouragement. Again, referencing my experience at summer camp, the number one rule is safety first. What good is a great program, or even a great lesson, if it is not done in a safe environment?

There have been a few Sundays during my ministry in Tampa, Florida, where we canceled Sunday services because a hurricane was coming through Tampa, and it wasn't safe to go out on the streets and come to church. No one would be thinking about praying in peace in the midst of a storm threatening to damage cars and people who ventured out in it.

Lord, protect me today in all that I do. Protect me from anyone who wishes to harm me. Protect me from myself and thoughts I have that might harm other people. Help me to create environments where safety abounds. Give me wisdom to see the safe way through the day and all the challenges this day will bring. Allow me to serve others in a way that keeps them safe. Amen.

Encouragement Challenge: Safety is a necessary precursor to encouragement. So esteem people first and foremost by making sure they are (and feel) safe.

Respecting Others by Not Pressuring Them to Change

For this very reason make every effort to supplement your faith with virtue, and virtue with knowledge, and knowledge with self-control, and self-control with steadfastness, and steadfastness with godliness, and godliness with brotherly affection, and brotherly affection with love.
2 Peter 1:5–7

One of the most prevalent challenges in life is peer pressure. Just about everyone is a victim at some point in life. And if we are all honest, just about everyone is or has been a perpetrator of it at some point in life.

What is peer pressure? Simply put, it is pressuring someone to change a belief or behavior to comply with the idea of a peer.

Peer pressure comes in two forms. One is direct pressure from one peer to another. An example from high school and college is when a peer pressures a peer to drink or drink too much. Let's say that a high school student decides he or she is not going to drink (after all, it is against the law), but his or her peers (friends) pressure him or her to go to a party and once there to partake in drinking. In college, even once one has reached the legal drinking age, there is pressure to drink excessively. In adult life, peer pressure might come in the form of someone being pressured into volunteering for something they don't have time or ability to do. It could be pressuring someone to spill dirt on a co-worker. Peer-to-peer pressure comes in many forms.

The other form of peer pressure is more of a societal one, not necessarily peer to peer. There is pressure on young people to get into a college, then to get into the right college, then to get the right job, for the right pay, so one can buy the right things. We will discuss this kind of pressure in the next reflection.

For now, let us stick with the peer-to-peer pressure. If we are supposed to esteem one another highly, what does it say for us when we try to pressure people to be what they don't want to be and do certain kinds of behaviors that they don't want to do? Those who esteem one another highly do not pressure people to change in ways that run contrary to their beliefs. Rather, they encourage people to be the best versions of themselves, celebrating their triumphs and values while gently encouraging offering suggestions for improvements on shortcomings.

Most people do not like peer pressure. It's like we all hate it. So, if we all hate it, why do we all perpetuate it? If it's something we all can't stand, then why don't we collectively stand against it? The solution to this problem lies within each of us. Collectively, we have the power to solve it. Individually, we have the power to lessen it.

There is a critical difference between encouragement and pressure. Pressure to do something is not encouragement—it's actually closer to bullying. Encouraging someone to run faster or practice harder is encouragement, not peer pressure. Pressuring someone to continue running when they are obviously exhausted and teetering on dehydration is pressure, not encouragement. Challenging someone also walks a fine line between encouragement and pressure. Challenging someone to try something they've never done many times falls in the encouragement category. Challenging someone to do something that is risky and unsafe goes into the pressure/bullying category. Part of understanding the heart of encouragement is knowing the difference between what is a challenge and what is pressure.

To esteem others highly means to encourage, even challenge, without pressuring. Again, the goal is for each of us to be the best versions of ourselves, to be who God created us to be. We should encourage and challenge one another to this end. And we should accept encouragement and challenge from others to this end.

We spoke in the last reflection about creating spaces where we feel safe and where others feel safe. Peer pressure not only creates spaces that are unsafe, but peer pressure ultimately is disrespectful and costs relationships the opportunity to attain trust and love.

The above Scripture verses remind us that faith is supplemented through virtue, which starts a chain of positive things like knowledge, self-control, steadfastness, godliness, brotherly affection, and ultimately love. Peer pressure is nowhere to be found on this list because it doesn't lead to any of these things. In esteeming others, encouragement and challenge is good. Peer pressure, generally, is not.

I want to make one exception to peer pressure being a good thing, and that is when friends "pressure" friends to do good. For instance, pressuring someone to avoid a tempting situation or to go to a study group can be a good thing. However, pressure generally has a negative connotation. In trying to get someone to do something good, encouragement is probably the better word, as it reflects something that is a positive (encouragement) rather than a negative (pressure).

Lord, help me to be someone who can encourage without pressure. Surround me with people who will challenge and encourage me. Help me to avoid succumbing to peer pressure. Help me to stay true to who I am, to be the best version of who You created me to be. Help me to bring out the best in other people. Amen.

Encouragement Challenge: Esteem others through encouragement and challenge but avoid peer pressure, either pressuring others or succumbing to pressure put on you by peers.

It's Okay to Be a "Smith" and Not a "Jones"

If your sons keep My covenant and My testimonies which I shall teach them, their sons also forever shall sit upon your throne.
Psalm 132:12

In the last reflection, we talked about pressure that comes from individual peers. This reflection will discuss peer pressure from a societal point of view and how this pressure has caused us to become inauthentic on our relationships. This runs counter to esteeming others highly because when we esteem others highly, we are encouraging them to be the best versions of themselves rather than an inauthentic version of whatever the "society of the day" is pressuring them to be.

Many of us have seen the epic movie *Titanic*[4] with Leonardo DiCaprio and Kate Winslet. As much as that movie covered the historical event of the sinking of Titanic, the movie was so lengthy because it did a study into the character of the many different kinds of people on the ship. The story takes place in 1912 and is about the maiden voyage of a ship thought to be "unsinkable," which would make the crossing of the Atlantic Ocean more quickly and more luxuriously than any ship before. The people who booked passage on the ship were mostly of the upper class of society. The movie was very good at showing the dichotomy between the first-class passengers and those consigned to "steerage." It was the upper-class people who insisted on getting in the lifeboats first and didn't want to return to rescue any of the "other people."

There was a certain way that people were expected to dress, walk, talk, and hold their tea cup. They were willing to sacrifice comfort for image. And conversation remained on the surface; no one would dare show weakness for fear of being put out of the upper class. Mothers passed these "traditions" to daughters, and fathers passed them to sons. Having watched the movie many times, I find this "society" with all of its unwritten rules to be not only inauthentic but actually oppressive.

Fast-forward a hundred years, and we see that not much has changed. We don't care about tea and crumpets any more, but there is pressure to own a certain brand of handbag, you wouldn't be "caught dead" in a certain brand of shoes, and most women cannot stand the thought of being seen without makeup. There is a saying, "Keeping up with the Joneses." This saying probably came from the fact that one of the most popular last names in America is "Jones," and so this saying means that we need to keep up with everyone else.

And the fact is we don't. Who says we need to? Everyone?

When I was a pre-teen, I didn't so much care about my appearance or what anyone else thought. I was a geeky kid who wore a sweatshirt covered with patches from the space program. I wore my socks up to my knees, and I wore braces. And I was happy.

When I got to high school, I felt "pressure" to look different. I felt compelled to have shorter socks and longer hair and even had cosmetic surgery on my nose (my droopy cleft nose) at age sixteen because people made fun of it. As I look back at that time in my life, that pressure was horrible. In fact, without a doubt, high school was the hardest and worst four years of my life.

As I have gotten older, I have felt less pressure to be a certain way. Maybe that's because I've matured, and probably it's because I hang around people who don't pressure one another to look a certain way. Now that I have a teen, I know it's just a matter of time before his image starts becoming important to him, and I'll be reliving high school pressures again through him.

The point of this message is that it's okay to be a "Smith" and not a "Jones." It's okay to not have a fancy handbag or wear designer shoes. A car is a means by which we get from one place to another—it shouldn't be a status symbol. And a home doesn't need to be as clean as a museum. It's a home because people "live" in it—it's okay to have Legos on the floor or have the bedspread crooked. That's what an authentic home looks like. And we don't have to be "prim and proper" all the time because that's not what an authentic person looks like.

Dr. Martin Luther King Jr. said in his famous "I Have a Dream" speech that he dreamt that "little children will one day live in a nation where they will not be judged by the color of their skin, but by the content of their character."[5] To me, it's not the color of skin, value of clothes, or which neighborhood one lives in that garners respect. It's the authenticity of character that draws me to people.

As we strive to esteem others highly, let's encourage others to be authentic rather than inauthentic by encouraging them to be the best versions of themselves rather than the inauthentic people society is pressuring us to become.

Lord, thank You for who I am. (List things about yourself that you are proud of and thank God for them). Help me to see the good in others. Help others to see the good in me. Help me to have strength of character and see the beauty in the character of others. Amen.

It's okay to be a "Smith." You don't have to keep up with the Joneses!

Encouragement to be the Person God Created You to Be

Then God said, "Let us make man in Our image, after Our likeness; and let them have dominion over the fish of the sea, and over the birds of the air, and over the cattle, and over all the earth, and over every creeping thing that creeps upon the earth." So God created man in His own image, in the image of God He created him; male and female He created them.
Genesis 1:26–27

I recently heard a podcast where the speaker talked about becoming the "best version of yourself."[6] It was by Matthew Kelly, a notable Roman Catholic writer/speaker. His intention was not to say that we should become anything we feel like becoming, but rather to become the best version of who God created us to be. This is an important distinction because in today's society, it seems that we are continually told that the "best version of ourselves" is really anything we want to be. So, if society tells us that the best version of ourselves is rich, we start obsessing about money. A "society" of friends in college may tell us that the best version of ourselves is to live life to the fullest and encourage us to be drunk and fun-loving. A "society" of our peer group may tell us the best version of ourselves is to have children who are successful athletes and students who can get into the best college. And then the children of this "society" will have it ingrained in them that you can't be the best version of anything without the right college, the right sport, the right car, the right handbag, and so on.

It seems that society's message to us is that the best version of ourselves is either a) whatever society is telling us is right "this year" or b) whatever an individual thinks is right, right now. The message we receive speaks nothing of God and His desire for us to be the best version of who He created us to be, which would include using our talents and caring for others.

God calls us to use our talents to serve others and honor Him. In this way, we are all the same. Our individual talents and how we use them to serve others and honor Him varies from person to person. There is no "best talent" or "best way to serve." Rather, we are to do our best with what He has given us. When we do the best with what we have been given by God to serve others and honor Him, then we are the best versions of who He created us to be, the best versions of ourselves according to His measuring stick.

Our present challenge is that our society tells us to be anything we want to be and do anything we want to do, even if it is at odds with what God tells us, as if the greatest authority now is ourselves rather than God. Our individual challenge then becomes how to be the best version of who God created us to be in a society where it's all about ourselves. It's hard to stick close to what God wants when it seems that everyone is trying to direct us away from that.

Encouraging others to be the best version of who God created each of us to be is part of esteeming others highly. Many people think respect is accepting people just as they are. Respect, however, is really encouraging people to be the best version of who God created them to be. As an example, take a teenager who doesn't like studying and spends all his time playing video games. Society might send a message that this teenager is academically challenged and that it's okay to play video games all the time if one is so inclined. To affirm, that message is actually disrespectful to this student. The right message is to be more focused and more diligent about studying. If one is so obsessed with video games, perhaps he should get the proper education so he can design games in the future. Real respect, really esteeming others highly is not to placate them for whoever they want to be but to encourage them to be the best they can be.

The above verses of Scripture remind us that we are ALL created in God's image, regardless of our talents and differences. We all are created in the same image, in the image of God. So when we honor one another, when we esteem one another highly, we are honoring God through the image of another. And when we are the best versions of who He created us to be, we are honoring His image in us.

Lord, thank You for the gifts and talents that are unique to me (list them). Thank You for the opportunities that present themselves to me because of my talents (list them). Provide opportunities for me to serve others, and in so doing, honor You this day. Open my eyes to see these opportunities. Give me the strength and wisdom to be the best version of who You created me to be. Help me inspire others to be their best versions of who You created them to be. Amen.

Encouragement Challenge: Encourage one another to be the best version of who God created us to be!

Leaders Need Encouragement Too

Obey your leaders and submit to them; for they are keeping watch over your souls, as men who will have to give account. Let them do this joyfully, and not sadly, for that would be of no advantage to you.
Hebrews 13:17

There are a lot of people who react negatively to this verse of Scripture. Those who don't like their priest, the president of the United States, their boss, or whoever is in authority that they don't like often voice and objection to the word submit. I know from personal study and spiritual discussion that as a priest, I have to give an accounting for the souls I watch over, the people of the flock I have been entrusted. However, this responsibility and accountability doesn't apply only to priests but also extends to everyone in a leadership position. At some points in life, we will all be in the position to lead. The followers will put their trust in us. And thus, we will all have to account to someone—our boss, our spouse, God—for how we take care of what has been entrusted to us. Because leadership can be such a daunting thing, it is important to remember in esteeming others highly, those who are "over you" (1 Thess. 5:12–13) need just as much encouragement from the followers as the followers need encouragement from their leaders.

A few years ago, I needed to have some sinus surgery to correct my breathing. As any patient does who is hospitalized, they "submit" to medical experts to whom they cede control. I submitted my body to them to be put to sleep, be cut, altered and repaired, and recover. For someone who is a "control freak," this is never an easy task. For someone who has had a lifelong fear of needles (and has had too many surgeries to count), this is still very stressful for me. During my hospitalization, I was tended to by a nurse named Christine.

As I said above, I have had a lifelong phobia of needles, specifically IV needles. Thankfully, my doctor ordered a sedative so I could be somewhat calm for the IV start. I was met upon my arrival by a nurse named Christine. She took my blood pressure and said, "Well, this is a tick above normal, but that's normal; most people in here are nervous." When I didn't respond, she said, "You look as white as a ghost." When I still didn't respond, she said, "Let's try this, why don't you put your own clothes back on (I had already put a hospital gown on and was laying in the bed, dreading what was coming, and was so nervous that I couldn't talk), hop off the bed, and let's just talk." So I did. We sat in chairs like two friends, and I told her about my IV fear. She was so calming that I almost let her start it without the prescribed sedative that was very late in arriving. That's how calming and trustworthy this stranger was quickly becoming, using only encouragement and empathy.

At another hospital a few years earlier, I had been talked down to by a nurse who said, "Are we going to have to give you gas like a little kid?" and "I'm not trying to belittle you," which is exactly what she was doing. Somehow in that experience, the nurse not only didn't help my nerves but she actually made me feel even worse than I already did.

Back to Nurse Christine. As I was about to drift off into unconsciousness, Christine said to me, "You won't mind if I say a little prayer for you as you slip out?" and I said, "Of course not." The last sound I heard was her quiet voice talking to God about me. When I woke up, Nurse Christine was right there, calming, reassuring, and encouraging. That day, I happened to be the follower, I submitted to the leader, Nurse Christine, and she rewarded my trust with comfort and encouragement.

I'm not a nurse, but I imagine nursing is a stressful job. My situation wasn't an emergency. If it was, I'd be smart enough, I hope, not to be debating or discussing the fine points of how to start an IV. But in the situation I was in, there was time, this wasn't an emergency, and one nurse's kindness made all the difference in keeping me calm and confident.

The story doesn't end there. When I got better, I went back to the hospital to thank Christine in person and give her a small gift as a token of my appreciation for what she had done. I went a step further. I stopped by the administration wing of the hospital, collected the names of all the important people who run the hospital, and wrote each of them a letter telling them how much Christine had done for me, how much I appreciated it, and what a great nurse they have on their staff. And, in turn, they recognized her with a special ceremony that I got to be part of.

Christine later told me that she had worked for the hospital for many years and rarely got any kind of positive feedback from her patients, which is sad. She is a great nurse!

A year later, I needed to have a colonoscopy done, and it was at the same hospital. I arranged for Christine to be my nurse and even let her start the IV without a sedative, a major accomplishment for me. And a few years later, again, I needed a colonoscopy and again was fortunate enough to have Christine as my nurse, and she was patient, understanding, reassuring, and accommodating. I know that I will never conquer my fear of IV needles, but they are part of life as we get older, and as long as it's not an emergency, I'm grateful for a nurse who takes the time to help me, not as just a patient but as a person.

Something great came out of something stressful because of encouragement. Christine encouraged me the first time I was a patient, but because of my gratitude, that was a big dose of encouragement for her. And I got the encouraging behavior to repeat on my second and third hospital visit.

The lessons here are two:

1. When you are the leader, encourage the followers because their souls and, in this case, my life, was in her hands.

2. When you are a follower, and the leader does something right, recognize that. Encourage your leaders. Why? Because leaders need feedback and specifically positive feedback. People are much quicker to criticize a leader than to thank a leader. And second, when you praise a leader, you are more likely to motivate that leader to repeat the behavior you liked.

We all play the role of the patient and the nurse in this story many times in our lives. When we are the nurse, will we take the role of Christine? Will we be the encourager? Or the discourager? And when we are the patient, will we take time to thank and encourage? Or feel entitled or ungrateful and forget to thank and encourage?

Lord, thank You for the opportunities I have to be a leader (list areas in your life where you are a leader, like in your house, with your kids, etc.) Help me to be an encouraging leader. Help me also to be a good follower (list areas in your life where you are a follower). Help me to be a loyal follower. Help me to always remember to encourage both the leaders and followers in my life and to esteem others highly, whoever they may be. Amen.

Encouragement Challenge: Encourage someone who is a "leader" in your life today!

**Dedicated to Christine Selochan, who has made a difference for me now on three occasions when I have been in the hospital.

Do THIS above Everything Else

Jesus said to His Disciples: "A new commandment I give to you, that you love one another; even as I have loved you, that you also love one another. By this all men will know that you are My Disciples, if you have love for one another."
John 14:34–35

The Bible is filled with "commandments." Most know the Ten Commandments. The Ten Commandments are actually ten out of 613 commandments that are found in the Old Testament books of Exodus, Leviticus, Numbers, and Deuteronomy. The 613 commandments became so cumbersome that no one could follow all of them. People had a hard time even memorizing them.

Jesus summarized all the commandments into two—love God and love your neighbor. And He summarized them even further into one word: love. To serve God is to manifest love. Sin is the absence of love.

I remember during my seminary studies, one day I felt overwhelmed by the sheer amount of stuff we needed to know. And I called my spiritual father (In the Orthodox tradition, a spiritual father serves as a mentor and guide and is the priest one utilizes especially for the sacrament of confession) in a panic and said, "What is it that I absolutely have to know to be a priest?" His answer was simple. He said I needed to know how to love people. He said, "If you don't love people, you will never be an effective priest." That doesn't mean that I didn't learn a lot of things but that the primary job of the priest is to manifest the love of God to people—through worship, prayer, preaching, teaching, and counseling.

St. Paul, in his treatise on love in 1 Corinthians 13, tells us:

If I speak in the tongues of man and of angels, but have not love, I am a noisy gong or clanging cymbal. And if I have prophetic powers and understand all mysteries and all knowledge, and if I have all faith, so as to remove mountains, but have not love, I am nothing. If I give away all I have, and if I deliver my body to be burned, but have not love, I gain nothing (1 Cor. 13:1–3).

So, if you ever feel overwhelmed by all of the stuff you think you have to master to be a Christian, remember that one thing is more important than everything else, and that is love. That doesn't mean to not pray, read the Bible, or follow the commandments. If you focus on love, it will lead you to these things.

We are all overwhelmed with the business of the world. We forget to tell others we love them. We forget to offer gestures of love and unexpected kindnesses to people. Love is something that is given to someone else. While there may be self-respect or self-confidence, one cannot love himself because, by definition, love is taken from one person and given to another. To take and give back to oneself is not love. Use today and offer as many expressions of love as possible—whether it is courtesy to other drivers on the road or a kind word to the clerk in the store. Show love today.

We are wrapping up our discussion of 1 Thessalonians 5:12–13 on the subject of esteeming others highly. We have discussed this over the course of several reflections. And just like my seminary experience, looking at the Bible, word by word, can be intimidating. It is important to study the words of the Bible in-depth, just like it was important to study the various aspects of theology in-depth when I was at the seminary. However, the study of Scripture doesn't amount to much if there is no application of it to our lives. The takeaway from any section of the Bible should be a greater desire to love God and love others. Every section of Scripture reinforces this idea. So in esteeming others highly, let love lead the way.

As for our Scripture verses today, there are many ways to advertise something. Banners, websites, t-shirts, commercials, and ads are ways companies market their products. Jesus told His followers that it's not fancy slogans and billboards that will bring people to Him. People will know we are followers of Christ because of love. Christ led with love, which is why He died for us. We follow Him because of this. Others will come to Him because of love. In esteeming others, whoever you esteem today, let love lead.

As a practical matter, tell those who are close to you that you love them. It is important that we demonstrate love. It is important that we say it. It is also important that we hear it. Saying "I love you" to others is very encouraging and empowering for them. Hearing others say it to you has the same effect on you.

Love God. Love other people. Love. This is what matters most in esteeming others highly.

Lord, thank You for your example of what it means to love others. You showed that by loving us so much, You died for us. Help me to offer love freely and joyfully to others. Surround me with people who encourage love. Remember those who I love most in my life (name your family and close friends). Allow our love to grow. Allow our love to honor You. Allow me to honor You with expressions of love today and every day. Amen.

Encouragement Challenge: Show love today!

Part Three

BE AT PEACE

Be at peace among yourselves.

1 Thessalonians 5:13

Encouraging Peace

Jesus said, "Peace I leave with you; My peace I give to you; not as the world give do I give to you.
John 14:27

Peace means the absence of conflict. However, to have peace does not mean there will never be conflict. To have peace means that there is a desire to work through conflict when it arises.

To have peace is to be still. However, to have peace doesn't mean that we don't work or have stress. To be at peace is a heart that is still—meaning that it is filled with God and God's love so that the work and stresses of life don't knock it off kilter.

To have peace is to desire unity with others. It doesn't mean complete agreement with others but a desire to work together.

There are many places in the Bible where peace is mentioned:

In Matthew 5:9, during the Sermon on the Mount, in a section of Scripture called The Beatitudes, Jesus says, "Blessed are the peacemakers, for they shall be called sons of God."

The message of the angels at the nativity was "Glory to God in the highest, and on earth peace among men with whom He is pleased!" (Luke 2:14). This verse is often mistranslated as "Glory to God in the highest and on earth peace, goodwill towards men." This implies that peace is a gift to everyone. However, this is not what the verse says. Peace isn't something we get merely by living. Peace is a gift that is given to people of goodwill, people with whom the Lord is pleased, people who make an effort to encourage peace, people who make an effort to live peacefully.

In Psalm 133:1, we read, "Behold how good and pleasant it is when brothers dwell in unity!"

Peace is one of the nine Fruit of the Spirit listed in Galatians 5:22–23, Christian values that we seek to cultivate.

The decision to cultivate peace comes from within oneself. One can be in a war-torn area and still find peace, just as one can live in a safe society and not have peace. Peace is a gift from God. However, it is a gift we must choose to cultivate—it is not cultivated for us.

Peace is a desire to work through conflict, have a calm heart, and work for unity. Encouragement and peace work hand in hand. When someone encourages me, it lessens conflict, calms my heart, and brings me closer to my encourager. When someone discourages me, it creates conflict, burdens my heart, and builds walls between me and [7]the discourager. The choice to be an encourager helps one to become a peacemaker and a promoter of peace.

One of my favorite songs at Christmas is "Let There Be Peace on Earth," which is what I'll use as the prayer for this reflection. This song highlights that the decision to have peace on earth begins with the individual. Peace in the world begins with peace with yourself. Encouragement has a large impact on the peace of the individual. And if individual peace is the first step toward peace in the world, we see how important encouragement is in relation to peace. I encourage you to listen to the song below today and let its words become a mantra for you.

> *Let there be peace on earth, and let it begin with me.*
> *Let there be peace on earth, the peace that was meant to be.*
> *With God as our Father, brothers all are we.*
> *Let me walk with my brother, in perfect harmony.*
>
> *Let peace begin with me, let this me the moment now.*
> *With every step I take, let this be my solemn vow.*
> *To take each moment and live each moment in peace eternally.*
> *Let there be peace on earth and let it begin with me.*

(Written by Jill Jackson Miller and Sy Miller, 1955)[7]

Encouragement Challenge: Let peace begin with you today. Do your part for peace by encouraging someone today!

Affirming and Encouraging Peace in Your Home

And thus you shall salute him: "Peace be to you, and peace be to your house, and peace be to all that you have."
1 Samuel 25:6

We know that the overwhelming majority of messages we receive outside of our homes are discouraging, which is why the overwhelming majority of messages we receive inside of our homes need to be encouraging. This helps to tip the balance or at least balance out the discouragement we hear every day. Many people, however, forget to say words of affirmation and encouragement inside their homes. It's not that they are discouraging. They perhaps assume that those in the house know how they feel. That is, my kids know I love them; why do I need to say it? The fact is, you need to say it! They need to hear it! This goes for things we say to our spouses, our children, what children say to their parents, and what close friends say to one another. Words of encouragement need to be said and be said often because they affirm others, and affirmation builds confidence.

So, what do words of encouragement sound like? I recently saw an article entitled "66 Positive Things to Say to Your Child."[8] I would argue that these are things that can be said to your spouse as well, most of them. And some of them can be said to close friends as well. Let me share a few of them that are taken from this article:

> I'm grateful for you.
> You make me proud.
> I love being your parent (or wife/husband).
> You don't have to be perfect to be great.
> I know you did your best.
> You were right.
> We can try your way.
> You make me happy.
> I trust you.
> Seeing you happy makes me happy.

I appreciate you.
That's a very fair point.
You are beautiful inside and out.
I love you.
I could never stop loving you.
You make my heart full.

Here are some other things we should say often:

Thank you.
I'm very lucky.
Life is better with you in it.
You are beautiful.
You mean the world to me.
You make my heart overflow with happiness.

I can just about guarantee that there isn't anyone who doesn't like hearing words of affirmation. Some people need it more than others. It is a fact that most men need to hear affirmation more than women. But that doesn't mean women don't like to hear these words. Who doesn't want to feel needed, appreciated, and loved?

In a world that seems to constantly send messages to us that we are not okay, not good enough, or that we are sorely lacking if we don't have the latest "in thing," words of affirmation are needed more than ever. And they don't cost anything to give.

Saying something is great. Writing it down is a great thing too. We send so many text messages. How about a quick text to your spouse in the middle of the day that says, "I'm thinking about you"? How about a little love note in your child's lunch box that says, "I love being your mommy/daddy"" A Post-it Note in the car or on the counter can work, a love letter, or a kind comment on the way out the door. Make it a point to affirm and encourage as much as possible.

At prayer time, have each family member say something that affirms everyone else in the family.

Be sure to have the last comment before you leave each morning be a positive, affirming, and encouraging one. "Have a great day" is much better than "See you later."

Finally, a note to married couples. If you want to know one of the best ways to safeguard your marriage, make a promise to your spouse to pray together each day and use these words in prayer: "Thank You Lord, for our marriage." If you make a commitment to pray this together every day, even on days you are mad, you will not stay mad for long.

Lord, thank You for the many special people in my life (list some of them). Help me to affirm and encourage each of them in some way today and every day. Help me to see the good in them and quickly move past the bad so that I can be a source of positive reinforcement to them. Surround me also with people who will encourage and affirm me. And when I receive encouragement, help me to receive it with humility and gratitude. Amen.

Encouragement Challenge: There are many possibilities for encouragement and affirmation. Make it a point for the next week to send one affirming message via text or note every day to your children and your spouse. Make sure you stop and deliberately say something affirming every day to your children and your spouse.

How to Build an Encouraging Environment in Your Home

Be glad in the Lord, and rejoice, O righteous, and shout for joy, all you upright in heart!
Psalm 32:11

"My family is so discouraging."
"My parents are always on my case."
"I can't seem to do anything right by my (parents, spouse, kids)."
"My spouse is always nagging me."
"My kids never listen."

Any of this ring true for you?

I hear these laments all the time. At times in my life, they've been my lament as well. If we're honest, we've all had these thoughts at some time or other, and probably a lot of us are feeling these laments right now.

While we can't always control what someone else does, we can certainly control how we react to what other people do. If you are relating to the above laments, the first thing to do is take a real honest look at yourself and ask, "Is anything they are lamenting about true?" For instance, if you are a teenager, and your parents are always nagging you about your homework because you don't get it done in a timely manner, well if you want the nagging to stop, just be more responsible and independent about getting it done. If your spouse is always complaining that you leave your clothes strewn around the room instead of putting them in the clothes basket, start putting them away, and that nagging will stop. Our efforts go a long way to the kind of interactions and feedback we get.

Despite our good intentions and even good actions, there is some amount of unnecessary "getting on our case" that happens to all of us from all corners. There really are some people (be they parents or spouses or our children) that, no matter what, they will not be satisfied. What do we do about that?

I wonder what would happen if we were more intentional about gratitude and encouragement. For the teenager whose parents are on their case all the time, what would happen if you were more intentional with gratitude and encouragement? What if you said thank you more often for a meal or the ride they are always giving? What if you said, "Thank you for being my parent" more often?

For the spouse who is discouraged, what if you thanked your spouse more often, even for the mundane things that you take for granted? What if you were more intentional about complimenting and encouraging them for things they do well instead of always looking for the things that annoy you?

For the worker who struggles either with another co-worker or a boss, what if you were more intentional with compliments and encouragement for the things that are going right?

People are actually caught off guard in a good way when people pay them a compliment. Most of the time when people call me, they want something. Most of the time when I call people, they think I want something. It is a pleasant surprise when someone out of the blue just calls to say, "thank you," or "I appreciate you." It is positive and motivating.

Imagine what could happen if we went out of our way to thank and appreciate the people closest to us, our families. Many times we take our families for granted, perhaps we feel like they have to like us because we are family, or we don't have to impress them or be careful with them because they are stuck with us. If there isn't a culture of positivity in your family, you can start one by being positive, affirming, and encouraging. Be patient, as it may take the rest of the family a while to catch on. It's hard to see how affirming and encouraging could be negative.

The simple answer to how to build an encouraging environment in your home is to just start encouraging. Make a decision to encourage and affirm, even if you don't get anything in return. If you only do it once or do it inconsistently, someone may question your motives and question your sincerity, that is, they are only doing this to get something or get out of something. When you do it consistently over a period of time, it will be harder to question your motives or sincerity. Most important, believe in what you are doing. Once you become convinced that encouragement and affirmation are important things, it will be much easier to give them and give them consistently.

Lord, thank You for the gift of my family (name your family members). Help me to love and appreciate them more. Help me to express my love and appreciation of them through encouragement. Help us to love one another closer and more deeply. Amen.

Encouragement Challenge: Encourage people in your immediate family today!

F.A.M.I.L.Y.

You are witnesses, and God also, how holy and righteous and blameless was our behavior to you believers; for you know how, like a father with his children, we exhorted each one of you and encouraged you and charged you to lead a life worthy of God, who calls you into His own kingdom and glory.
1 Thessalonians 2:10–12

Family is both a gift and a challenge. Through family, we get the close, intimate, and permanent relationships that we all crave and need. We also get some permanent and sometimes deep-seeded challenges and conflicts.

Father Larry Richards, a Roman Catholic priest, speaker, and writer, has made an acronym of the word FAMILY that I would like to share with you today.[9]

F is for faith and forgiveness. The number-one thing that parents are called to do is to get their children to heaven. This is done by the way you live and the example you set. You must lead your children to Christ. Pray as a family, read the Bible as a family, and attend church as a family. Both mothers and fathers must be involved in the building of the faith.

We must have **forgiveness** in the family. The people you love the most can hurt you the most. To keep the relationships moving forward is to offer and accept forgiveness. The Lord's Prayer demands it of us to forgive. What better place to start than in your own family.

A is for affirmation. In our families, we must build each other up. Offer a kind word of encouragement each day to your family members. No one has ever gotten hurt from too much praise, but every minute, a kid dies inside from the lack of it. **In a family, we must know that we are loved as I am, not as I should be.**

M is for making memories. This happens when we spend time with each other. Have dinner at least once a week at the table. Do not watch TV during dinner. Limit technology at the table. Ask questions, even silly ones, to get your kids talking. Laughter in the family and at the table creates memories your family will always remember. This is the ultimate "insurance policy" for making memories in the family.

I is for intimacy. This is not only a physical description but one of the soul. **"In to me see"**—this is going beyond the external and seeing what is inside. We must ask of our family members, **"How are you?"** and minister to their needs. Respect, trust, and vulnerability are all precursors to intimacy. Intimacy is based on unconditional love and is the ultimate goal of every close family relationship.

L is for love. Love is not a feeling; it is a commitment! It is an action that you would give your life for your family members. You must show that you love them and tell them that you love them. Our family members need to hear this **EVERY SINGLE DAY.** In John 15:9, Jesus said to His disciples, "As the father loved Me, I also have loved you." We might strive to express Christlike love for our family members.

Y is for it's all about you, meaning it's all about the needs of our family members. Our posture with our family members needs to be: How can I put your needs in front of my own? How can I serve you? We must put God first, family second, and ourselves third.

Father Larry not only spoke on this acronym but challenged listeners to do a homework assignment, which is to write a letter to your family members, telling them that you love them and why. Kids should write a letter to each parent. Parents should write a letter to each child. And spouses should write a letter to each other. For additional motivation, he suggested that we should imagine that we will not be alive tomorrow, so we should write the letter today. Though he says that at least 50 percent of people reading this won't do it, he says that those who do won't have any regrets.

He concluded his presentation by encouraging people to tell the people you love that you love them **every day**. Live every day, so that everyone—especially your family—will know that you love them because you've told them. You have to show them AND tell them.

Lord, thank You for my family. Thank You for (my spouse, children, parents, cousins, fill in the names of all of your family here). Help me to forge strong relationships with each of them. Help us to express love freely and joyfully. Help us through difficult times. Help us to love each other more and more each day. Help us to express that in both words and actions. Build our faith, help us express affirmation, inspire us to make memories, help us to express intimacy, deepen our love, and help us serve one another. Amen.

Encouragement Challenge: Write a letter to your family members today.

**With grateful appreciation to Fr. Larry Richards, pastor of St. Joseph Church/Bread of Life community in Erie, PA, and the founder and president of The Reason for our Hope Foundation.

Mary versus Martha

Now as they went on their way, Jesus entered a village; and a woman named Martha received Him into her house. And she had a sister called Mary, who sat at the Lord's feet and listened to His teaching. But Martha was distracted with much serving; and she went to Him and said, "Lord, do you not care that my sister has left me to serve alone? Tell her then to help me." But the Lord answered her, "Martha, Martha, you are anxious and troubled about many things; one thing is needful. Mary has chosen the good portion, which shall not be taken away from her."
Luke 10:38–42

Many of us are familiar with the story of Mary and Martha. They were good friends of Jesus, together with their brother Lazarus, who Jesus would later raise from the dead. There are many interpretations of this gospel story. The most obvious is the tension of time management. Many people are quick to rush to Martha's defense because work is a necessary part of life. Who has time to sit with Jesus all day when there is work to be done? Many criticize Jesus for His telling Mary that she is right in focusing on the one needful thing. After all, aren't work, raising children, family responsibilities, and even household chores "needful" things? Here is another way to look at the story:

Martha had a tangible output for her efforts. She was running around, cooking dinner, setting the table, showing hospitality, and being a good host. There was a tangible outcome for her efforts. Mary, on the other hand, was listening to the words of the Lord. She was not accomplishing anything tangible. Let's say that after an hour, Martha had put out a meal that her guests could see and taste. Mary, on the other hand, perhaps had a softer heart, a cleaner spirit, and was wiser in the ways of the Lord. All of these are good things, but they are not tangible.

When we become obsessed with the tangible, we forget the *"needful thing"* that Christ mentioned, the genuine relationship with Him. And when the tangible doesn't work out—and let's be honest, there are many times it doesn't work out—because we've burned the dinner, been in a car accident, or despite our efforts to be successful parents, our child behaves poorly at school or fails a test, then we break down because we have failed at both the tangible things and the intangible ones as well. This leaves us feeling fragile and struggling with identity because there is a palpable tension between being the *Mary* that Christ calls us to be and the *Martha* that the world calls us to be.

There is no question that we play both the role of Mary and Martha. I've even heard people use the phrase, "trying to be Mary in a Martha world." There is no escaping that the Martha elements are always present. There is always a child who needs us, a job that demands our time, a person we are trying to impress, or a project we've put off.

However, what do you think pleases Christ? The stressed-out running around of Martha or the inner peace of Mary? No matter what, there will be Martha elements in our lives. Being "Martha" is part of our identity, whether we are a mother or a father or a worker. We tend to tie our sense of self to what makes us successful instead of tying our identity to Christ. This makes us feel fragile and broken down when whatever we identify ourselves with goes badly. We tend to feel things like, "My house is a mess, therefore I am a mess" or "My kids are difficult, so I am a bad parent and therefore bad." And again, what is more important, gathering the finest furniture you can find and taking it, even if it means you stole it? Or it is better to live within your means, content with the purchasing of your own equipment, and paying for it via honest means? The world may reward the things that Martha can purchase, but it is the way Mary chooses to live her life that pleases God.

We tend to forget that the "needful thing" is an authentic relationship with Christ. From this relationship, all other things in life slot the right way. When we are solid "Mary's" in terms of making our relationship with Christ the number-one priority, then we keep the "Martha" stresses in check and in the proper balance. Remember what Christ told Martha—it's not the running around that is needful. Maybe it is expected by the world or some standard we've created for ourselves and our peer group. Christ told Mary that one thing was needful, and that was a relationship with Him.

So, in the midst of living in a Martha world, don't forget that it is more important to have the needful thing of Mary. And just so we can recount the story correctly, Martha actually more than redeemed herself. In John 11, it was Martha who said in the presence of Jewish leadership hostile to Jesus, "Yes, Lord, I believe that You are the Christ, the Son of God, He who is coming into the world" (John 11:27). This is a high "confession" of Christ as the Son of God. Indeed, *Martha* had the "needful thing" as well.

In this section about "being at peace," we will find the greatest peace in Christ. No matter how busy life gets, when we make time for the "needful thing," Christ, we will also find His peace, which, as St. Paul writes in Philippians 4:7, is "the peace of God, which passes all understanding." This peace, which is peace in the midst of conflict, provides encouragement to us in the midst of our life stresses. And it comes through cultivating a relationship with Christ daily.

Lord, thank You for Your many blessings. Thank You for walking with me in my challenges. Please help me to know what the "needful thing" is. Show me the path to righteousness and give me the courage to walk it. In times of material setback, help me to focus on the spiritual victory. Help quiet the voices that seek to drag me into materialism and consumerism, and fill my heart with love for You, that I may not only be "successful" in my career and my home but that I may be successful in my heart, that it may always know You. Amen.

Encouragement Challenge: Focus on being a "Mary" this week instead of a "Martha."

It's Okay to Eat off a Paper Plate Sometimes

Now may our Lord Jesus Christ Himself, and God our father, who loved us and gave us eternal comfort and good hope through grace, comfort your hearts and establish them in every good work and word.
2 Thessalonians 2:16–17

One of the hardest things to figure out in life is the proper balance between work and family. In the ideal life, there would be a perfect balance of work, family, leisure, prayer, and rest. The truth of the matter is that I've never met anyone who has found the perfect balance. It is a struggle for EVERYONE. So, let me offer some encouragement for seeking a sense of balance.

The next two reflections will be about work/family balance. The last reflection referenced the story of Mary and Martha and when Jesus visited them in their home. Mary listened to the Lord's teaching. Martha was running around, trying to get dinner on the table. Martha complained to Jesus on why her sister Mary was not helping. Jesus said to Martha, "You are anxious and troubled about many things; Mary has chosen the good portion which shall not be taken away from her" (Luke 10:41–42).

As we discussed, many people interpret this passage as Jesus demeaning work, that we should all sit around and pray all day. Others criticize this passage and dismiss the words of Jesus. After all, who can afford to sit all day and not work? Neither is correct. Jesus was pointing out the need for balance. He was saying that the most needful thing in our life is to work on our salvation. And if we are running around, anxious and troubled, we will neglect this most important thing. He didn't dispute that working hard at a job isn't a necessary part of life, only that we should be anxious and troubled about work.

I heard a sermon once on this story, which I will ever forget because the story of Mary and Martha was examined in a completely different way. We know that Jesus was friends with Mary and Martha. He went to their home to relax. Perhaps Martha was running around, feeling pressure to put out the nicest food on the finest dinnerware, when Jesus would have been happy ordering out for pizza (obviously, they did not have pizza back then, but you get the point). Jesus perhaps was saying, "I came over here to relax; don't stress. The needful thing is your company, not the food."

It is okay to order out for pizza occasionally or eat off paper plates. It's okay to sit around the table and talk after dinner and not do the dishes right away. I would never suggest not cleaning the house, but it is okay to have a house that looks like it is lived in, not one that looks like an immaculate cathedral. I'm reminded of a country song by Toby Keith (" My List", by Toby Keith):

> *Wouldn't change the course of fate,*
> *If cutting the grass just had to wait,*
> *Cause I got more important things,*
> *Like pushing my kid on a backyard swing.*
> *I won't break my back for a million bucks I can't take to my grave,*
> *So why put off for tomorrow what I could get done today?*
> *Like go for a walk, say a little prayer, take a deep breath of mountain air,*
> *Put on my glove and play some catch, it's time that I make time for that,*
> *Wade the shore, cast a line, look up an old lost friend of mine,*
> *Sit on the porch and give my girl a kiss,*
> *Start living that's the next thing on my list.*[10]

Work is important and necessary. It is necessary because a vocation is what puts food on the table and roof over our heads. It is important because work is how we use our talents to help others and fulfill God's plan for us. However, God does not intend for us to work all the time. He intends for us to relax and recharge. He has blessed us with families for us to enjoy.

So, work hard, for sure. But make sure that you keep some sense of balance in your life. We can't have the perfect job, perfect family, perfect house, perfect food, and so on. So, don't put stress where it isn't needed, and don't pressure yourself to be the perfect worker, parent, housekeeper, and cook. Do your best. And when it comes to housekeeping and cooking, ordering out for pizza or eating off paper plates is not the worst thing you can do. In fact, some days it's the needful thing.

Tune in to the next reflection for a way to get more out of your workday.

Lord, thank You for the many wonderful things that fill my life (list them—family, job, home, hobbies, etc.). Help me to find the right balance between all of these responsibilities and joys. Help me to always see You as the most needful thing in my life and to center the rest of my life around You.

Help me to find the proper balance between work, family, leisure, spirituality, and rest. Give me patience with family and friends who are also engaged in this struggle. Give patience to them as they support me in my struggle to find balance. Amen.

Encouragement Challenge: In the next week, make a night where you order out or eat off paper plates, and in the time you save, do something fun with your family.

The "Theology" of Fred Flintstone

Remember the Sabbath day, to keep it holy. Six days you shall labor, and do all your work; but the seventh day is a Sabbath to the Lord your God; in it you shall not do any work, you, or your son, or your daughter, your manservant, or your maidservant, or your cattle, or the sojourner who is within your gates; for in six days the Lord made heaven and earth, the sea, and all that is in them, and rested the seventh day; therefore the Lord blessed the Sabbath day and hallowed it.
Exodus 20:8–11

Many of us remember the Fred Flintstone cartoons. Fred worked in a rock quarry. He sat on the back of a dinosaur, chipping away at rocks all day. And at quitting time, a bird would squawk, Fred would drop his tools, slide down the back of the dinosaur, yell "yab-ba-dabba-doo," and run home to his family.

This image from a silly cartoon provides us a powerful metaphor for the work-family balance. Fred worked hard all day. And at quitting time, he quit and went home. There are two lessons we learn from Fred Flintstone—work hard during the work day, and then go home when the work day is over.

The concept of "quitting time" is vanishing. Why? Because when it is time to work, many of us are distracted. We all know people who "quit" (in the sense that they are mentally checked out) well before the workday ends. Texting, social media, and the internet contribute to our sense of distraction during the workday. If a person spends six minutes an hour surfing the web for non-work-related things, like reading the sports scores on ESPN.com, or texts with friends or updates their status on their social media accounts, that is 10 percent of work time being lost. If a person earns $50,000 a year, he or she is stealing the equivalent of $5,000 a year from the boss. So, work is not getting done at work, and that cheats your employer and customers. But it also cheats you.

When quitting time comes, people have to take work home because they didn't get it done at work. Or they have to stay overtime to get done what didn't get done during the day.

I recognize that the forty-hour work week is gone for many of us, including me. I have a job that I could work at twenty-four hours a day and still not get it all done. My solution? Appoint a quitting time, work hard until quitting time, and at quitting time, quit and go home. I look at Fred Flintstone for inspiration.

If your quitting time is 5:00 p.m., then work hard until 5:00 p.m. Don't get distracted. Don't quit at 4:00 p.m. or start texting and get on social media at 3:00 p.m. And if your quitting time is 5:00 p.m., and you've worked hard all day, then quit and go home and don't feel guilty about going home and relaxing.

Be present in whatever you are doing. Try not to think about home while at work. Try not to think about work while at home.

One of the Ten Commandments is quoted above: "Remember the Sabbath day to keep it holy." Of all of the commandments, this is the longest, four verses. In it, God gives more details than any of the other commandments. God's intention for us is to live in balance.

His idea that we need rest is not a suggestion. It is a commandment!

We are to dedicate time each week to worship. That is not a suggestion. It is a commandment!

And we are to dedicate time to resting. That is not a suggestion. It is a commandment!

As you seek to live a balanced life, build in time to rest. Find a hobby. Build in time to worship. Make Sunday mornings sacred to the Lord. And when it is time to work, work without distraction so that you can rest without distraction or guilt.

Work/family/leisure/spirituality/rest—the struggle to find balance between all of these things will be a lifelong struggle. The first key to finding balance is to be present and undistracted when doing each.

Lord, help me to focus today. At work, help me to be present and not distracted. Help me to be efficient in the tasks I need to finish. When it is time to quit, help me to leave work without guilt over what didn't get done. Give me a time to enjoy my family. Help me to find balance in all aspects of my life. Help me to put You first in all things. Amen.

Encouragement Challenge: Work hard at work. Quit at quitting time. Be present.

Finding Peace in Authentic Relationships

I hope in the Lord Jesus to send Timothy to you soon, so that I may be cheered by news of you. I have no one like him, who will be genuinely anxious for your welfare. They all look after their own interests, not those of Jesus Christ.
Philippians 2:19–21

It seems that the idea of an authentic relationship is becoming more and more rare in today's world. We seem to live in a very superficial society; just check out the tabloid magazines at the supermarket check-out line. And this affects us having authentic relationships with Christ and with one another.

This reflection is about what it means to have an authentic relationship. Being at peace is dependent, at least in some part, to the relationships we establish with others and most especially with Christ. Relationships that are inauthentic contribute to chaos and internal conflict. Relationships that are authentic contribute to being at peace with oneself and others.

The word "authentic" means "genuine," "original," and "true."[11] The first example of authentic that comes to mind is uniform jerseys of sports teams. I'm a big sports fan, as you all know by now. I recently bought an "authentic" jersey of the Tampa Bay Lightning. Authentic means it is the exact replica jersey of what is worn by the hockey players. I also have a T-shirt that says "Tampa Bay Lightning" on the front and have the number and name of a player on the back. This is a Tampa Bay Lightning product, but it is not an authentic jersey. It is nice, even comfortable to wear, but it is not authentic.

The word relationship means how we exist in comparison with someone else. A close relationship means that we share many things with someone. An honest relationship means that we are not afraid to tell the truth to someone. A superficial relationship means that there might be a surface level or appearance of closeness, but beneath the surface or outward appearance, there is no closeness or honesty.

Now, having an authentic jersey doesn't make me more or less of a fan; it's honestly not that important. Having an authentic relationship, on the other hand, is very important. Authenticity is vital to an honest and deep relationship. And that goes for a relationship with

Christ or with another person. In an authentic relationship, there are things like respect, communication, a genuine desire, trust, love, and vulnerability.

In Genesis 2, we see the picture painted of Adam and Eve walking with the Lord in the cool mist of the garden of Eden. This relationship was authentic. Adam and Eve loved each other, they loved the Lord, and there was no envy, jealousy, pretense, or anything else that was negative. It was an authentic and pure relationship. Then Adam and Eve went away from the Lord, they committed a sin, and they severed themselves from the authentic relationship with the Lord. Where they had been naked and unashamed, they were now ashamed and covered themselves. Where they had been open and honest, they now lied and were deceitful.

Christ showed us the way to an authentic relationship—love, sacrifice, vulnerability. This is how He made His relationship with us. This is how He showed us to make our relationships with Him and with one another. Somewhere deep down in each of us, and I truly believe this, is a desire for an authentic relationship with Christ and one another. The problem is that there are layers of sin, doubt, anger, and so on that cover over this place of authenticity. There is a fear of removing the layers and what we'd find beneath them. Yet, if we all made the collective decision to remove the things that cover up authenticity, we'd again capture the paradise enjoyed by Adam and Eve with each other and the Lord. So, this is one of life's challenges, to build authentic relationships.

Authentic relationships help us to be at peace. We don't have enough authenticity—in close relationships like marriage and with children, relationships with close friends, and relationships with co-workers that we are with every day. I encourage you to examine your relationships with others and the Lord and reflect on whether they are authentic or inauthentic, the barriers that keep relationships from being authentic, and how to bring more authenticity to them.

Lord, thank You for the gifts You have so richly poured out upon me. Thank You for the people I know (list names of your family and friends). Help us to work together toward more authentic relationships, with one another, and most especially with You. Open my mind and my heart to desire more genuineness and honesty in my relationships. Give me courage as I look within myself. And give me courage to explore with my family and friends on how to deepen bonds of love and friendship. Amen.

Encouragement Challenge: Reflect on the word authentic and whether that is a word that you'd apply toward your relationships with Christ and others. Why is that, or isn't that a good word to describe your relationships?

Peace in the Midst of Conflict

Have no anxiety about anything, but in everything by prayer and supplication with thanksgiving let your requests be made known to God. And the peace of God, which passes all understanding, will keep your hearts and minds in Christ Jesus.
Philippians 4:6–7

It is easy to dismiss 1 Thessalonians 5:13, as "pie in the sky," that is, how can we hope to be at any kind of peace in this stressful world? Even these verses from Philippians 4 may cause us to shake our heads. I mean, how can we not have any anxiety about anything?

For those who know Christ, there is a peace of God, which, as St. Paul writes, "passes all understanding." This is the kind of peace we can experience in the midst of conflict. Most often, people think of peace as the absence of conflict. God's peace is a peace that comes in the midst of conflict.

It's kind of ironic that even in times of peace, we may struggle with inner conflict. There may be peace all around us, and yet we will not feel peace, or we will feel insecure or struggle with our confidence.

The peace of God is what allows us to feel calm and secure even in the midst of chaos all around us. The peace of God is what allows us to stay above the fray, so to speak, to keep our focus and feel confident and secure even in the midst of a storm.

In Tampa, Florida, where I currently live, we get a lot of rain in the summer. We get afternoon thundershowers that dump large amounts of rain quickly. The wind sometimes picks up during these thunderstorms and blows trees and scatters leaves. The rain is so hard that I could get soaked walking from my car to the office, a space of not even ten feet. When I'm driving the car with the radio on, in air conditioned comfort, with the windows up, and sealing out both the water and its sound, I feel at peace. The car is like a little cocoon. It's keeps me safe and dry in the midst of the squall.

The peace of God is a lot like this scene. It protects us and makes us feel warm and secure in the midst of conflict. The peace of God is like the cocoon that protects us in the middle of the storms and stresses of life.

When I have to leave the office and it's raining, I run to the car as fast as I can. I can't wait to shut the door and enjoy its protection. And in the midst of life's storms, ideally, I run to God as fast as I can so that I can feel protected by Him. I write ideally because, honestly, in my weakness, I don't always do that or do it fast enough. I try to go against the storm on my own, and for anyone who's experienced a thunderstorm in Florida, when the rain falls sideways and quickly soaks everyone and everything, we know not to linger on our own or even try it with an umbrella but rather get to shelter and covering quickly.

When St. Paul writes to us to "be at peace," he wasn't naïve enough to suggest that there will never be conflict in our lives, that every day will be sunny and have no storms. Rather he is encouraging us to seek out the peace of God, so that in the midst of life's storms, we can truly be a peace.

Finally, he writes that this peace of God, which passes all understanding, will keep our hearts and minds in Christ Jesus. If we seek after God in prayer and in the way we conduct our lives, it will be easier to keep our hearts and minds on Christ, stay hopeful during setbacks, stay upbeat when we are down, and stay faithful even as the rest of world seems to go away from God. The ultimate stress in any life is when it comes to an end. Those who have the peace of God see the end of life as the greatest triumph. So, focus on the peace of God, which comes through prayer, repentance, obedience, and effort, so that setbacks are kept in perspective and the end of life can be viewed through a lens of anticipation rather than trepidation.

Lord, thank You for this day, regardless of what the day will bring. Today is another day to glorify You, live for You, and serve You by serving others. Bring peace into whatever stresses I will encounter today. Help me to stay focused on You even when I'm tempted to get angry or frustrated. Pour over me Your peace, which passes all understanding. Give me peace with the things I do not understand. Bring peace into the situations I will have a hard time understanding and knowing what to do with today. Help me to be a person of peace, and may I radiate Your peace in the way I conduct myself today. Amen.

Be at peace! Share God's peace with others!

Part Four
HELP AND BE PATIENT

And we exhort you, brethren, admonish the idlers, encourage the fainthearted, help the weak, be patient with all.

1 Thessalonians 5:14

The Encouragement Languages

When the day of Pentecost had come, they were all together in one place. And suddenly a sound came from heaven like the rush of a mighty wind, and it filled all the house where they were sitting. And there appeared to them tongues as of fire, distributed and resting on each one of them. And they were all filled with the Holy Spirit and began to speak in other tongues, as the Spirit gave them utterance. Now there were dwelling in Jerusalem Jews, devout men from every nation under heaven. And at this sound the multitude came together, and they were bewildered, because each one heard them speaking in his own language. And they were amazed and wondered, saying, "Are not all these who are speaking Galileans? And how is it that we hear, each of us in his own native language?"
Acts 2:1–8

We constantly here about how diverse the world is. There isn't a one-size-fits-all in just about anything in life, including encouragement. Diverse people and diverse situations require diverse forms of encouragement.

One of the best books I have ever read is called *The Five Love Languages* by Dr. Gary Chapman.[12] This is a great book for marriages and relationships in general and also good for self-awareness. Dr. Chapman's thesis is that there are five love languages—words of affirmation, quality time, giving gifts, acts of service and physical touch—and each person has one of them as their primary love language. The person to whom we are married may or may not have the same language, and the book details the nuances of each language so that if two spouses "speak different love languages," they can learn the things that best serve the needs and language of the other. If you are married, I highly recommend this book.

Using this idea of different languages of love, there are also different languages for encouragement. Some people respond well to verbal affirmation. Some people actually need and thrive on it. In some way, we all need verbal affirmation, though some more than others. So, we encourage through affirmation.

We encourage through spending time with others. When we are sad, sometimes we don't need words of comfort. It is enough for someone to just "be present" with us, even if few words are said. In learning how to be an encourager, sometimes we don't need to use words. Being a good listener or just being patient while being present is encouraging.

Everyone enjoys getting gifts. The gift of encouragement is one that doesn't cost any money; we don't have to shop for it, we don't have to wrap it, and we don't have to wait for a birthday or Christmas to give it. Encouragement is a gift that anyone can give to anyone at any time. Writing an encouraging letter to someone is a great gift because an encouraging comment is said and may be forgotten, but an encouraging letter is something one can read over and over again.

To encourage is not only to say things but to do things. So acts of service are also a form of encouragement. When someone does something for us, we feel uplifted. And the doing doesn't have to involve a lot of money. Someone who holds a door open, helps carry groceries, or who passes on an edifying article via email, these are all examples of acts of service that are encouraging.

And physical touch is encouraging. Athletes of all ages high-five and fist bump. Hugs and pats on the back are good too. Looking someone in the eye when you are talking to them shows sincerity. A smile is encouraging. And sitting close to someone who is having a hard time shows concern. Obviously, there is a time and an appropriateness for this language that we have to keep in mind.

The Scripture passage for this reflection from Acts is the account of Pentecost. This was the day that the Holy Spirit descended onto the apostles and empowered them to speak in all the languages of the world. People were amazed to hear the gospel in their own language. They were also comforted. The words of the gospel were no longer a foreign tongue but one that was familiar.

For many people, encouragement is just as foreign as a foreign language. They don't get enough encouragement, or they don't get it in a language that they can understand or appreciate because maybe a person who needs affirmation has plenty of people present who never say anything. Or the person who needs people present gets text messages of encouragement but doesn't have someone to sit and patiently listen. Each of us needs encouragement, and each of us will prefer a different way to receive it. Therefore, it is important for each of us to learn various "languages" of encouragement so that those around us can hear and benefit from encouragement in "their own language."

Lord, show me today how I can encourage others. Help me to speak different languages of encouragement to people—my family, my friends, and complete strangers. Help me be a voice of positivity and compassion. Give me opportunities to encourage others. Bring people who need encouragement into my path today. May my encouragement help someone today, and may it always glorify You. Amen.

Just as some people are young and some are old and some are strong in personality and in faith and others aren't, the diversity in personalities, talents, and life stories merits a need for diversity in encouragement.

Solving the Maze of Inconsistent Voices

Now the whole earth had one language and few words. And as men migrated from the east, they found a plan in the land of Shinar and settled there. And they said to one another, "Come, let us make bricks, and burn them thoroughly." And they had brick for stone, and bitumen for mortar. Then they said, "Come let us build ourselves a city, and a tower with its top in the heavens, and let us make a name for ourselves lest we be scattered abroad upon the faith of the whole earth." And the Lord came down to see the city and the tower, which the sons of man had built. And the Lord said, "Behold, they are one people, and they have all one language; and this is only the beginning of what they will do; and nothing that they propose to do will now be impossible for them. Come, let us go down, and there confuse their language, that they may not understand one another's speech." So the Lord scattered them abroad from there over the face of all the earth, and they left off building the city. Therefore, its name was called Babel, because there the Lord confused the language of all the earth; and from there the Lord scattered them abroad over the face of the earth.
Genesis 11:1–9

One of our team-building activities at summer camp is called "the maze of encouragement." This activity consists of one thousand feet of rope strung around dozens of trees, creating a very complex web of ropes that are about four feet off the ground. (Think of a movie where there are laser beams all across the floor, but instead, these are ropes.) A bandana is tied to one of the ropes somewhere in the maze. All of the campers of a particular cabin stand around the outside of the maze. A couple of campers who have not done this activity stay a distance away from the maze so as to not see it or hear the instructions. They are brought in one at a time, blindfolded, and told that they are to find a bandana that has been tied onto one of the ropes.

The cabin mates who are around the outside of the maze have been told that when the person makes a step in the right direction, they are all to clap. When they make a step in the wrong direction, they are all to remain silent. The activity begins. The blindfolded participant will eventually catch on that the clapping means they've gone in the right direction, and silence will mean they've taken a misstep. This person will have to use the audio cues to figure out his or her way around trees and under ropes and eventually to find the bandana.

Here is how this activity relates to real life. The clapping in this activity represents encouraging voices in our lives. The bandana tied on the rope represents various goals we set in life. The goal might be an educational goal, like going to college. It might be an athletic goal, like making the basketball team. Or it might be a spiritual goal, like getting closer to Christ. The person being blindfolded represents our inability to get to our goals without help and encouragement from others. Tell the blindfolded person to find the bandana with no help, and they are not very likely to succeed. In fact, the most likely outcome would be that they quit or end up getting hurt.

This activity is successfully done when two things happen. First, when the blindfolded participant listens to the audio cues and takes them, that is, doesn't just keep going when the clapping has stopped. Second, the people clapping must be consistent. They need to start and stop clapping at the same time. They need to immediately clap when the participant makes a good decision, and they need to immediately stop when they don't.

Here is where this activity, at least the way we do it at camp, is NOT like real life. Sure, it is true that we need encouragement to help us reach our goals. However, we hear many voices in our lives, some encouraging and some discouraging. Which voices win? The loudest ones? If this activity were to mirror real life, it would be much more difficult. If half of the group clapped for the right direction and half clapped for the wrong direction, it would be virtually impossible to find the bandana. That's a lot like real life, especially for teenagers. For example, they hear voices telling them, "Drinking and drugs are bad," and they hear voices telling them, "Drinking and drugs are cool." Which voices do they listen to? Adults hear conflicting voices as well. For example, the Bible and the church tell us to live simply. Advertisements tell us we need expensive clothes. Which voices do we listen to?

What if we did the activity this way? Let's say fifteen campers are standing around the maze, and we tell fourteen of them to clap when the participant does wrong and one to clap when they do right. Will the participant figure out that the one lone voice is actually the right one? Or will they think that fourteen couldn't possibly be wrong?

What if we told ten to clap all the time, whether the participant moved right or wrong? And we told five to snap their fingers when the participant did something right? The clapping of ten would certainly drown out the snapping of five.

This is how real life works. The voices we hear are inconsistent. And this inconsistency causes confusion, just like the confusion at the tower of Babel that we read about in the above Scripture verses. We are often both encouraged and discouraged to do the same thing. It's hard to know what is right when this happens. Sometimes we hear many voices of discouragement and only a single voice of encouragement. These are the times when it's hard to make the right choice or feel confident when it's just one voice of encouragement against many voices of discouragement. And sometimes, we hear loud clapping and faint snapping, and we wonder, which is the right voice to follow? It's really hard to figure that our when you can't see where you are going!

We've discussed before that the proper ratio of encouraging to discouraging voices in our lives should be five encouraging voice to every one discouraging voice. If we had fifteen people clapping for encouragement and three people snapping for discouragement, the sound of the clappers would overwhelm the sound of the snappers. And sadly, that often mirrors real life for many of us.

I ask the campers whether they hear more encouraging voices or discouraging ones, and the answer, for anyone in high school or above, is that they hear more discouraging voices than encouraging ones. These discouraging voices include their friends, the media, and sometimes even their parents.

Each of us takes on both roles in this exercise, probably daily. As the blindfolded person trying to find Christ, success, or whatever we are trying to find, do we have enough voices of encouragement around us, do we listen to them, are we confused as to whether we are hearing encouragement or discouragement, are we moving confidently, or are we about to quit? We all walk uncertain paths at times, which, hopefully are filled with more encouragement than discouragement, more clarity than confusion.

When we are the people who are "clapping" for others, are we encouraging them to do right, encouraging them to do wrong, or are we a voice of inconsistency and even confusion? This is a challenge for each of us, to be voices of encouragement and clarity for others. Will we be one of the five voices of encouragement or one of the voices of discouragement that will take five people to overcome? It's a choice we make daily. Many people around us are stuck in the "maze" of life, and encouragement can make a real difference in helping them get to their goals.

Lord, be with me in the challenges I face today. Many days, my life resembles a maze, and it is hard to know exactly the right thing to do. Give me the patience to listen to the voices of encouragement around me. Bring people around me that will encourage me. Give me the discernment to hear their voices. Give me the discernment to know which voices not to listen to. Help me to be a consistent voice of encouragement for people. Put someone in my path today who I can encourage. Amen.

Encouragement Challenge: If we are to help others, we need to be encouragers. Take a few minutes today and write a message of encouragement (can be a text, email, or real letter) to someone today! If you want a challenge, make a short text of encouragement to someone part of every day!

We Are All Pretty, but We Have to Work at Being Attractive

Jesus said, "The eye is the lamp of the body. So, if your eye is sound, your whole body will be full of light; but if your eye is not sound, your whole body will be full of darkness."
Matthew 6:22–23

Many people have insecurities about the way they look. It's not just girls and teenagers. Plenty of adults and males struggle with body image. I'm going bald, and I accept that, but I am also a middle-aged male, and many of my male peers are going through the same thing. How we see ourselves can affect our self-esteem and self-confidence. If you think about it, most women's products are marketed on the premise that women are not pretty. Their marketing essentially says, "You will only be pretty if you wear our makeup, our lipstick, our eyeliner, or this sweater." And basically, "You are not pretty if you don't."

People are so desperate to be "pretty" that they will buy just about anything. And yet, many still don't feel pretty. However, beauty is not what our bodies look like, the clothes we put on them, the way we style our hair, or what kind of handbag we might carry. The beauty in the human being is found in the eyes. Jesus tells us in Matthew 6 that if the eye is sound, the rest of the body is sound. Thus, if the eyes are pretty, the rest of the body is pretty.

Most people do not have pretty eyes because their eyes are beset with sadness, loneliness, tiredness, and discouragement. People are not encouraged to be honest, truthful, decent, and noble. They are taught that winning is the only thing, even if it involves the downfall of our neighbor. We are taught that there is a threshold of beauty or success that is almost unattainable, but that doesn't stop people from trying to attain the unattainable. And along the way, they cross lines of honesty and integrity in the attempt to achieve "beauty." In their attempt to be outwardly pretty, they become inwardly ugly, and this is manifested in eyes that become filled with darkness and lose their joy.

When people are honest, strive for integrity, decency, and nobility, their eyes become pretty, and they become attractive as people. People are actually attracted to decency, honesty, honor, and nobility. People are attracted to sincerity rather than superficiality.

Because so many voices we hear each day are coming from advertisements making being pretty more important than being attractive, we go after material things to be pretty, and we forget the things that make us attractive. If the prettiest part of any body is the eye (and again, Christ said that, not me), then we don't make our eyes pretty with makeup. (Let's think about this word for a minute—makeup—the idea that I can use a product to make me something that I'm not. By using makeup, we are not sincere or honest; we are "made up.") Instead of using makeup to make our eyes pretty, let's use honesty and sincerity to make our eyes attractive. If the eyes are attractive because they are honest and sincere, the rest of us will be attractive as well. When we have to use makeup (and I don't mean this literally but metaphorically; when we have to "make up" stuff about ourselves to feel pretty or worthwhile), we actually make our eyes darker and less pretty because when we use too much makeup (too many lies or exaggerations), we are less truthful and less attractive.

We did an icebreaker at camp that involved catching fish and living out the Great Commission, Christ's command to make disciples of all nations. The exercise involved campers making a fishing pole out of a dowel, yarn, and a clothespin. The "bait" was a gummy worm. They had to catch fish by getting people to eat the gummy worm without using their hands. One of the lessons of this game was that to "catch fish," the "bait" needs to be attractive. If we had put a piece of liver on the end of the "fishing pole," no one would have wanted to participate. But because it was a gummy worm, something that looks and tastes good, people wanted to participate, and the game became very attractive.

If we want to attract people to us, whether it is to be Christians, or even more simply, just to be friends, the idea of "bait" works the same way it does when catching fish. If we are superficial, we will attract people who are superficial because superficial people find superficiality attractive. If we want to attract honest people of integrity to be our friends, we have to be honest and have integrity. We certainly don't need to make ourselves up with dishonesty. We need to work on the beauty of our eyes more than other things we think need to be pretty.

It is important, by the way, that we tell people they are pretty. I tell many people, especially ones who struggle with self-esteem and self-image, that they are pretty. That is important.

It is even more important to tell people they are attractive. I tell even more people that they are attractive because when they are struggling for honesty and integrity, when they are loyal and trustworthy, these things are very attractive. And it's important to remind people of that.

We can spend lots of money to try and look pretty. No amount of money makes a person attractive. Being attractive is something that comes from within, a desire to have sound eyes, eyes that are filled with honesty, integrity, trust, love, patience, and hope.

By the way, we are all pretty because we are all made in God's image and likeness. God doesn't make ugly. We are all pretty, but we have to work at being attractive.

Lord, thank You for creating us after Your image and likeness. Thank You for the gift of Scripture and for assuring us that it is only our eyes that need to be sound for us to be beautiful. Thank You for the gift of my own body, that it allows me to do all the things I do, starting off with breathing. Help me to be a person of honesty, nobility, and decency so that my eyes can be sound and the rest of me can be sound. Help me to see beauty in the eyes of others. Amen.

Encouragement Challenge: Work on being attractive today! Tell someone else they are pretty today! Encourage others to be attractive based on their eyes, not their makeup!

USING ENCOURAGEMENT EVEN WHEN SOMEONE DISAPPOINTS YOU

Let the word of Christ dwell in you richly, teach and admonish one another in all wisdom, and sing psalms and hymns and spiritual songs with thankfulness in your hearts to God.
Colossians 3:16

I Thessalonians 5:11–28 is a section of Scripture where the overwhelming sentiment is one of encouragement and positivity. Overall, this study is intended to be one of encouragement and positivity. However, it would be naïve to think that everything will be positive at all times with everyone. People will inevitably disappoint us. First Thessalonians 5:14 even uses the word admonish, which means to correct someone who has done wrong, call them out, even scold.[13] Is it possible to admonish someone and be encouraging at the same time? Under certain circumstances, I believe it is.

There are certain relationships in life that will run their course. For instance, if you are an employer and have an employee who is not performing, you might need to let that person go. That is truth. Not all relationships last forever. In this case, you can terminate someone constructively or destructively. Constructively would be to say it didn't work out, it will hopefully work out somewhere else, point out what could have been done differently, and offer best wishes for success in the future. Destructively would be to terminate someone using demeaning language, say they did nothing good, and publicly ruin their reputation so that it is difficult for them to find another job. None of that is really necessary. If an employer/employee relationship doesn't work out, so be it. However, cut ties without being destructive.

A friendship can run its course. I've read that some friendships last for a reason, a season, or a lifetime. And I believe that, eventually, all friendships will end up in one of these three categories. I have lived in several cities in my life. When I was in college, I made good friends, people I enjoyed spending time with, people I confided in, people I trusted, people who I helped, and people who helped me. When college ended, so did many of those friendships because I moved to another city, to graduate school, where I made a new set of friends. Most of the college friendships ended after college—those were friendships for a season. I've made many friends through working at summer camp. That is the only reason I met certain people.

Without camp, I wouldn't have met them. These are friendships of reason, people I enjoy working with each year, people I work well with each year, but people who I don't see by and large outside of summer camp.

Some relationships are supposed to last a lifetime. Specifically, the ones with our families. We are supposed to love our parents for as long as we have them. We are supposed to love our spouses and children for the rest of our lives. We can't change our parents or trade in our children, and the intention of marriage is to be with the same person for the rest of life. These aren't relationships of reason or season. And because they are supposed to be for a lifetime, we have to be more careful with how we negotiate them. We can't be overbearing when someone has done wrong and needs to be admonished. Neither can we be a pushover. If we keep encouragement in mind as we admonish, we are more likely to be constructive and positive rather than destructive and negative and get the results we hope for.

Admonishing, when done out of love and not with meanness is a form of encouragement. Telling your spouse you want them to correct a few things to strengthen a relationship that you are committed to for life does not have to be a bad thing. Telling your child you love them as you correct something they are doing wrong can be encouraging as well. Challenging someone to do better, give their best effort, or be the best version of themselves is a form of encouragement. Helping someone figure something out can be encouraging. Acknowledging a failure while working toward a solution can be encouraging.

Telling someone they have disappointed you but affirming that you value the relationship is encouraging. It's encouraging because it is honest. It doesn't avoid the conflict or "kick the can down the road." It tackles the problem head-on. However, while admonishing, it also affirms commitment. It says, "Even though I'm disappointed or frustrated, I'm not going anywhere. I'm in this with you for the long haul." This is encouraging. Admonishment followed up by encouragement provides a safe environment where it's okay to fail, and it's okay to be truthful. And let's be honest, we all frequently fail to some extent, every time we disappoint someone.

Admonishment when mixed with encouragement fosters patience. And patience tells someone, "You are important to me, and even though it is taking you more time to do something, understand something, or even correct something, I'll be patient. You are worth it."

We can't avoid all pains. We can't avoid people inflicting pain on us. And because of our fallen nature, there is no way we will get through life without inflicting pain and disappointment on others. Admonishing seems to naturally follow disappointment. However, admonishing when coupled with encouragement, in the relationships that really matter, bring people together rather than drive them apart and helps get the desired results. It is certainly an "art" to learn to encourage while scolding. It requires an understanding of the importance of building up, even when tearing down. It requires a commitment to a 5:1 ratio of encouragement to discouragement so that when it is necessary to admonish (which does tear people down), there is intentional encouragement (which builds people back up).

Lord, thank You for the people in my life that I'm closest to (mention names of family and closest friends). Help me to remember in these relationships that I treasure the most how to combine admonishing and encouragement. Help me to admonish with kindness and sensitivity while also being firm and honest. Help me to see the good in others even when they frustrate me. Give me the wisdom to work through moments of disappointment in my relationships. Amen.

Encouragement Challenge: Learn to encourage even while admonishing!

Speak Carefully to Those Closest to You

Honor your father and your mother, that your days may be long
in the land which the Lord your God gives you.
Exodus 20:12

Most of us know the Ten Commandments, one of which is that we are to honor our father and mother. By extension, those of us who are married are supposed to honor our spouses, and those of us who have children are supposed to honor our children.

In the last reflection, we discussed the idea that admonishing others is a part of life. When someone does something wrong, they need to be corrected. When each of us does something wrong, there is a good chance we will be corrected or called out on it. This is what admonishing is. However, admonishing can happen in a positive way or a destructive way. And we discussed how it is actually possible to be encouraging even while admonishing. It primarily depends on the spirit in which admonishing is given, which, hopefully, is a spirit of love.

I once read an article that basically said that we are more likely to treat family disrespectfully, even more so than how we treat our friends. Perhaps that is because we think of family as people who are stuck with us, while friends choose to have relationships with us. We tend to choose our words more carefully with friends or even strangers than we do for our own family sometimes.

Because we are around family more than we are around anyone else, we probably admonish family more than others in our lives. Because our families are "always around," we also tend to take our families for granted, which is why we admonish family more carelessly.

This reflection is an encouragement to speak carefully to those who are closest to us so that we don't take our families—our parents, our spouses, and our children—for granted. Reflect on these questions for a moment: Are you more likely to "blast" your spouse or your children than to blast your friends, relative strangers like the mailman, the teller at the bank, or the clerk at the store? For most of us, sadly, the answer is yes.

Here is the challenge for us this week. When you want to raise your voice to admonish your spouse, parents, children, ask yourself, "Would I talk to a friend like this?" or "would I talk to the mailman/garbage collector/bank teller, and so on like this?"

There is a phrase that says, "you only hurt the ones you love." Ideally, we shouldn't be hurting anyone. And if we are careful with friends and even strangers, we should be careful about what we are saying, especially to the ones we love the most.

Finally, when we are around someone all the time, we tend to think we don't need to encourage them. We might even think that repeatedly saying the same thing, like, "I'm proud of you," or "Thanks for being my spouse" might get redundant. We might make the mistake of thinking, "Well, they KNOW I'm proud of them." Well, when we don't hear encouragement, we might wonder what someone thinks of us. When we don't hear "I'm proud of you" from our parents, we might wonder if they are proud of us. When we don't hear "I love you" from those closest to us, we might actually wonder, "Do they really love me?"

I've often wondered why the commandment to honor your father and mother (and by extension your family) is the only commandment that connects obedience to longevity. Here are two answers I've come up with (I'm sure there are more): First, it is our parents who were the first to tell us to look both ways before crossing the street. If we didn't listen to our parents when they gave this advice as well as other advice (don't play with fire, don't put things in your mouth, etc.), there is a good chance we wouldn't be alive today. Secondly, because we are with our families more than with others, there is the potential for greater stress. After all, we are more likely to have stress with people we see every day than with those we rarely see. We know that stress brings on illness and wears our defenses down. Ultimately, stress contributes to sickness and death. If we keep our stress down, we are more likely to live longer. Encouraging one another and being careful in our families will lower stress and lead to longer life. So, when we honor our parents, our spouses, and our children, it is more likely that our days will be long.

Lord, thank You for the gift of my family. Thank You for (mention the names of your family members and closest friends). Help me to treat everyone with kindness, especially those who are closest to me. Help me to always have a spirit of gratitude for my family and to speak with everyone in a respectful way that reflects my love for them. Help me to be a better (child, spouse, parent). Bless my (parents, marriage, children) today and always. May these relationships reflect and honor You always. Amen.

Encouragement Challenge: Don't forget to encourage those who are closest to you. And when it is necessary to admonish someone in your family, choose your words as carefully as you would choose them if you were talking to a friend.

Don't Be a Victim, Be a Survivor

In that day the branch of the Lord shall be beautiful and glorious, and the fruit of the land shall be the pride and glory of the survivors of Israel.
Isaiah 4:2

To thrive means to do well. To survive means to get through. It is certainly more preferable to thrive than to survive. After all, who wants to have just enough money to get by, a marriage that is barely holding on, or a child who is barely passing their classes? In most areas of life, thriving is preferable to surviving. However, many times we have to focus on just surviving before we can thrive.

When I was nineteen years old, I was not in a good place at all. An injury to my elbow meant that I would never play competitive sports again. The injury had happened over time, but when I woke up one day with paralysis in my right arm, the prognosis for never playing sports again was decided in mere minutes. There was a serious surgery, a lengthy recovery and rehabilitation, and the loss of something I enjoyed that helped boost a fragile self-esteem, and all these things came crashing down on me at the same time. Now that I'm in middle age, with the life experience I now have with setbacks and comebacks, I would probably handle that situation differently if it happened now. It's not like I had been diagnosed with a terminal illness, but back then, as a nineteen-year-old, it was as if I had.

My thought patterns were not good. People close to me were reassuring that I could still have a great life, and to be honest, I wasn't great at sports anyway; it's not like I was going to make a career in athletics, but I didn't see it that way at that moment. In one of my lower moments, I made an appointment to see my priest. I figured it couldn't hurt. I went to see him one afternoon, told him about my situation, that I was profoundly sad, that I didn't see what good would come out of my situation, I wondered where God was, and I wondered loudly, "Why me?!"

Despite the fact that I went to church every Sunday and was still serving in the altar faithfully at age nineteen (and was having thoughts about the priesthood), I couldn't really tell him that my relationship with Christ was very strong. It was very surface. Other than a children's Bible my parents used to read to us when we were kids, I had never really read the Bible. Daily prayer was not part of my life. I had gone to confession once when I was nine, so that didn't really count. And an attitude of "I am a victim here" really prohibited a joyful relationship with the Lord.

The priest offered some advice and encouragement. He suggested I go for confession, which I said I'd have to think about. He suggested how I could start reading the Bible. He gave me some prayers to offer each day, and he gave me a book entitled *When Bad Things Happen to Good People* and told me to read it. I must confess that I left his office a little frustrated. I had gone in expecting empathy and validation and instead got homework. I even told myself that this priest's advice would not work. However, I decided to take his advice, do the things he asked me to do, then go back in thirty days as he asked, and tell him that his advice didn't work.

When I opened the book he had given me, inside the front cover, he had written a few words that have stuck with me to this day: Stop being a victim and start being a survivor. God does not want victims. He wants survivors.

I read the book, and it had a profound impact on me. I started praying and reading the Bible. I went back to his office thirty days later and had my first confession. And I can safely say now that encounter at age nineteen changed my life. It certainly changed my attitude. I began to think of myself more as a survivor than as a victim. And I began to think more about how to survive things than become a victim to them. I stopped being afraid of setbacks—that doesn't mean I like them—I just honed a survival instinct rather than one of being a victim when it comes to setbacks.

The encounter with this priest really helped propel me to the priesthood. Up to that point in my life, the priesthood was about services and vestments. In this moment, he showed me that the priesthood is about people and that a priest could have an impact on someone's life by just being there and offering encouragement. When I thought about the priesthood, it was no longer just about what it would be like to celebrate the Liturgy but what it would be like to do for others what he had done for me.

Now, nearly thirty years later, I thank God for that low moment in my life because it prepared me to work with people in their low moments, and I approach people in their low moments with the same advice (and sometimes the same book) that my priest gave me back in 1991: Don't be a victim, be a survivor. When it's not possible to thrive, focus on survival. Of course, once one is comfortably at the survival stage, then it is time to focus on thriving.

When 1 Thessalonians 5:14 tells us to "encourage the fainthearted," one way to do that is to encourage them to be survivors and not victims. There are some challenges in life that cannot be overcome—that could be a financial situation, a health diagnosis, a learning disability, or many other things. So to tell someone to overcome something that cannot be overcome is not helpful. However, to encourage someone to be a survivor, to somehow survive the things that cannot be overcome rather than putting up the victim flag is helpful, genuine, and actually possible. There are some things in life that won't allow us to thrive—a diagnosis with a terminal illness is the first one that comes to mind. But we can spiritually survive anything that comes our way. And that is the goal, survival during life's bleak moments when we put our faith and trust in God rather than being a victim of our circumstances.

Lord, thank You for the many blessings in my life (name a few of them). Please be with me in my challenges as well (name a few of them). Help me to thrive in my circumstances. And when that is not possible, give me the wisdom and strength to just survive. Help me not to see myself as a victim but as a survivor of setbacks. Help me to encourage others to do the same. Bring someone into my path today who could use some encouragement. And bring someone into my path today who will encourage me. Amen.

Encouragement Challenge: I encourage you to be a survivor, not a victim, of whatever adverse circumstance you face today. And I encourage you to encourage others to do the same.

**In memory of Fr. James T. Adams, a priest whose advice back in 1991 changed my outlook and my life. I am forever grateful!

I Believe in You, and I Believe in Me

Have I not commanded you? Be strong and of good courage; be not frightened, neither be dismayed; for the Lord your God is with you wherever you go.
Joshua 1:9

Encouragement seeks to eliminate negative talk, not only our negative talk about others but negative talk to and about our own selves.

First, let's talk about eliminating negative talk to and about others. If a person hears over and over again, "You are a loser," that person will eventually start feeling like they are a loser. If ninety-nine people tell someone they are a loser, and one person tells them they are a winner, the positive voice will not be heard through the sea of negative voices. On the other hand, if a person hears from ninety-nine people that they are a winner, and one person tells them they are a loser, the voice of negativity will most likely be lost in the sea of positive voices.

It is important when we have to be critical or even negative that what we offer is constructive and objective and that correction is given positively. One phrase that none of us hears often enough is "I believe in you." It seems that we more often hear some version of "I'm disappointed in you." Just as with the example above, when a person consistently hears, "I'm disappointed in you," they may begin to believe that they are an overall disappointment. Just as when a person consistently hears "I believe in you," they will believe that people have confidence in them, and they will have confidence in themselves. On the occasion when we must correct someone and even voice disappointment, it is important to make sure there is still some confidence mixed even amidst the disappointment. The best way to do this is simply to combine the two phrases: "I may be disappointed in you, but I still believe in you."

Many of us played sports at some point in our lives. And many of us have experienced coaches of varying temperaments. Many of us are familiar with the coach who says, "If you don't play well today, you'll be on the bench tomorrow." And hopefully some of us are familiar with the coach who says, "Win or lose today, you're still starting tomorrow." Which kind of coach do you prefer? I'm sure the answers vary. Some people do very well under intense pressure. Others wilt. I have always played better for the second kind of coach, the kind of coach who expresses confidence and optimism in me, who says, "If it doesn't go well today, there is still a tomorrow for you."

Whether it's coming from a coach, boss, friend, or parishioner, when someone expresses confidence in me, I tend to be more confident. When someone expresses a lack of confidence in me or makes a threat that if some level of performance is not achieved, I will receive something negative, I tend to be less confident. For me, anyway, positive reinforcement works much better than negative reinforcement. I'd rather work for reward than to avoid punishment, and I would venture to say that many of us prefer it this way as well.

Now, let's discuss negative self-talk. Again, using a sports analogy, let's say that I'm throwing a ball back and forth with someone from a distance of fifty feet. And let's say that while throwing the ball, I start thinking negatively: *What if I throw the ball too hard, it will go over the other person's head. What if I throw the ball too soft and it doesn't get to them? What if I throw the ball badly several times in a row? Will they still want to play catch with me?* Inevitably, the negative self-talk will result in a negative outcome. If I'm too worried about throwing the ball over someone's head, my worry will become a self-fulfilling prophecy. That's exactly what will happen; it will go over their head. If instead of negative self-talk, I engage in positive self-talk, there will still be times when I get a negative outcome, but more times than not, the outcome will be positive.

One phrase I've adopted in my life is "If you play to win, sometimes you'll win and sometime you'll lose, but if you play not to lose, you just about always lose."

This positive self-talk helps whether we are talking about tossing the ball around, giving a presentation, writing, or just about anything else we do. Going into something with a positive outlook makes it much more likely you'll get a positive result. Giving a positive outlook to someone else through encouragement makes them much more likely to have positive results in what they are doing.

Lord, thank You for my gifts and talents. Help me to use them for Your glory and in service to my neighbor. Help me to see the good in those around me and to encourage others. Help others to see the good in me and encourage me. And help me to see the good in me and have confidence in the abilities that You have given me. Help me to use them as best as I can. Give me confidence today in myself, and give me the opportunity to inspire confidence in someone else today as well. Amen.

Encouragement Challenge: In addition to encouragement from others, we need encouragement from ourselves. Play to win today and encourage others to play to win as well! Believe in yourself. Believe in others. Most importantly, believe in God!

It's Okay to Admit Weakness

> *To keep me from being too elated by the abundance of revelations, a thorn was given me in the flesh, a messenger of Satan, to harass me, to keep me from being too elated. Three times I besought the Lord about this, that it should leave me; but He said to me, "My grace is sufficient for you, for My power is made perfect in weakness." I will all the more gladly boast of my weaknesses, that the power of Christ may rest upon me. For the sake of Christ, then, I am content with weaknesses, insults, hardships, persecutions, and calamities; for when I am weak, then I am strong.*
> 2 Corinthians 12:7–10

One of my favorite spiritual stories is about a monk at a monastery who asked his abbot if he could go into the city near the monastery to see if he could find a demon. His abbot gave him leave, so the monk went out into the big city and searched everyone, trying to find a demon. Finally, he found one demon asleep under a tree. The monk returned to the monastery, and as he was about to pass through the monastery gates, he saw many demons coming in and out of the windows of the monastery. When he saw his abbot, he questioned why, in the big city, there was only one demon to be found, and he was sleeping, but here at this small monastery, where there were a few monks trying to grow in their faith and pray, the demons were all around. The abbot explained that out in the big city, people are so busy, there is no work for the demons to do. The people are so distracted that they don't need the help of the demons to lose focus. However, the demons will seek to attack the monks who are trying to grow in their faith.

If we believe in the presence of God in the world, then we must believe in the presence of the devil in the world who tries to discourage us from following after God. Even the most positive and encouraging people will feel discouraged at times. No one will feel encouraged all the time. And in some ways, the devil will go after the encouragers in the world as well as those who are encouraged to discourage and distract them.

In the above Scripture verses, St. Paul writes about a thorn in his side, given to him to keep him from feeling too elated or encouraged. This thorn sought to weaken his faith and his resolve to spread the faith. God assured St. Paul that God's power can be found even in times of weakness, and by extension, we can feel God's strength even when we are discouraged. St.

Paul then wrote that he could find contentment even in weakness because he knew even when he was weak, he could become strong again in Christ.

Similarly, we will all go through times where we feel discouraged. And that's okay. In fact, it is to be expected. In these times, it is important to remember that encouragement need not be far away. It can be as close as a friend offering encouragement to us or us offering encouragement to someone else, even when we don't feel encouraged ourselves. When no friends are around, encouragement can come through prayer, reading Scripture, through the satisfaction of getting something done, or even just surviving a tough day.

It's okay to admit when we feel weak, ask for encouragement, and ask for a little bit of time to feel down. Sometimes, well-meaning people are so quick to lift us up that they don't allow us to mourn and be sad when mourning and sadness might be very appropriate emotions to have. This is why discernment is so important in the life of the encourager. We have to allow ourselves time to grieve and feel weak. It's part of our makeup as human beings to have moments of weakness and sadness. It's also important to allow others to lift us up so that we don't stay in this state for too long.

As encouragers, we should look to lift people up and build them up. But we should also be patient and recognize that when someone has suffered a loss or is having a time of weakness, they may need empathy more than encouragement. That's why as we study this verse of 1 Thessalonians 5:14, we have to remember that sometimes to "help the weak" means to encourage, and sometimes it just means to be present and empathetic, not to have all the answers or push someone beyond where they are capable of going on a given day. After all, it's hard to feel uplifted if you've just been laid off, gotten a bad medical diagnosis, or someone has just passed away. When you are going through a hard time, it's okay to admit weakness and ask for empathy and patience instead of encouragement. And when someone else is going through a hard time, it is important to be sensitive to their situation, and sometimes that involves being present and silent. Discernment helps us to know what to do in moments of weakness—our own and that of those around us.

Lord, thank You for the many people I know and the friends that I have. Help me to be a good friend to all. Help me to be a discerning friend. Give me words of encouragement to offer to others and the discernment to know when to use them. Help me to always remember to be sensitive and empathetic to friends who are going through moments when they don't feel strong. Help me to be able to articulate my needs in moments of weakness and send me the right people who will be present when I need comfort and who will offer encouragement when I need to be lifted up. Help me to see You at all times, even in moments of weakness. And help me to come back strong from setbacks that

I suffer. Please help those who have suffered setbacks to get back on the path to wholeness and feel encouraged once again. Amen.

Encouragement Challenge: It's okay to admit weakness. And it is critical to be sensitive to the weaknesses of others.

Love Is Patient and Kind—So Are Encouragers

If I speak in the tongues of men and of angels, but have not love, I am a noisy gong or a clanging cymbal. And If I have prophetic powers, and understand all mysteries and all knowledge, and if I have all faith, so as to remove mountains, but have not love, I am nothing. If I give away all I have, and if I deliver my body to be burned, but have not love, I gain nothing. Love is patient and kind.
1 Corinthians 13:1–4

Love is probably the most important word we have.

God created us out of love.

Love was the motivation for sending Christ into the world (John 3:16).

The greatest commandments given by Christ are to love God and love our neighbor.

The Bible has been described as God's love letter to His children.

Sin can be defined as failure to love.

Christ told us that love would be the thing that identified us as His disciples (John 13:35).

St. Paul, in his "treatise" on love in 1 Corinthians 13, writes that "If I have prophetic powers, and understand all mysteries and all knowledge, and if I have all faith, so as to remove mountains, but have not love, I am nothing."

What is love? How do we love? Books upon books have been written seeking to answer these questions. St. Paul first defined love as being patient and kind, so that is a great place to start. Nowhere is love defined as easy or fun. Many people associate love with a feeling. However, if love is only based on feelings, then every relationship would eventually fall apart because when negative feelings enter a relationship, love would disappear.

Rather than a feeling, love is a choice we make. We can still love our spouses and our children, even when we are mad at them because love isn't based on how we feel but on a deep-seeded commitment, a choice to love.

It is safe to say that all gestures we make fall under one of three classifications—there are gestures of love, negativity (hate is too strong of a word, but a word that is the opposite of love), and indifference. Encouragement falls under the first gesture—encouragement is a gesture of love. If encouragement, therefore, is tied to love, then the top two characteristics of love—patience and kindness—can be attached to encouragement and encouragers. If we want to be good encouragers, it is necessary to learn how to love, and it is necessary to learn patience and kindness.

Being an encourager, just like love, is not always easy, and it is not always fun. There will be times when we will encourage and get no feedback. There may even be times when we encourage and get negative feedback. There are people who are not ready or able to receive encouragement on a particular day. Perhaps because they've suffered a setback. There are also people who are eager and ready and need some encouragement. Of course, it is great to encourage these because we will get positive feedback right away.

Encouragement, like love, can't be based on a feeling or even the prospect of feedback. Encouragement, like love, is a choice. We can choose to encourage others regardless of how we are feeling, how they are feeling, and even whether they will react favorably or unfavorably to our encouragement. And because there are so many variables when it comes to encouragement, just as with love, the encourager must be patient. That perhaps is the most important quality of the encourager—to be patient, and give encouragement, not necessarily expecting anything in return.

Encouragers are kind since encouragement is an act of kindness. Kind gestures are not to be given in expectation of any reward. Any expectation of return constitutes an "exchange" rather than a gift. Kindness is a gift we offer to others. Kindness is also a choice. When someone is unkind to us, we can still choose to be kind in return. We can be kind even when we've been wronged, even when we disagree. We can go up to an "enemy" and still make a gesture of kindness.

As we will shortly reach the conclusion of our discussion on 1 Thessalonians 5:14, we are reminded that as we "admonish the idlers, encourage the fainthearted, (and) help the weak," we must be patient with all. Encouragement, like love, begins with patience and kindness.

Lord, thank You for loving me. Thank You for being patient in overlooking and forgiving my sins. Thank You for the many gestures of kindness You bring into my life (list some of them). Help me to be a more loving person. Help me to be patient with others. Open my eyes and my heart to opportunities to be kind today. Send people into my path who need some encouragement, and give me the wisdom to lift them up today. Amen.

Encouragement Challenge: Encouragement is a choice. Choose to encourage today. Choose to be patient. Look for opportunities to be kind, and choose those as well.

Two Sides of a Tapestry

Who has believed what we have heard? And to whom has the arm of the Lord been revealed? For he grew up before him like a young plant, and like a root out of dry ground; he had no form or comeliness that we should look at him, and no beauty that we should desire him. He was despised and rejected by men; a man of sorrows, and acquainted with grief; and as one from whom men hide their faces he was despised, and we esteemed him not. Surely he has born our griefs and carried our sorrows; yet we esteemed him stricken, smitten by God, and afflicted. But he was wounded for our transgressions, he was bruised for our iniquities; upon him was the chastisement that made us whole, and with his stripes we are healed.
Isaiah 53:1–5

Do you know who this Scripture passage from Isaiah describes? The person who is being described as despised, rejected, sorrowful, and afflicted? The Prophecy of Isaiah, chapter 53, foretells of the passion of Jesus Christ. For us to be healed, which is the resurrection, it took a man bearing our griefs and sorrows. Jesus Christ, whom we now esteem as our Lord and Savior, was once bruised, battered, and killed.

Had anyone of us come up on Golgotha two thousand years ago, we almost certainly would not have felt encouraged and uplifted. Without knowing the rest of the story, I'm not sure I would have felt uplifted. Here was a man dying on a cross—the most painful and humiliating way to die, reserved for the worst of the worst of the criminals. Yet, we now know that this scene of pain and suffering paved the way for the greatest triumph in the history of humanity, the resurrection, which paves the way to salvation for each of us.

A tapestry is a fabric woven by hand that has a picture or design on it. The front side of the tapestry that we see will be a beautiful picture or design, made of threads woven by hand or with a loom. The back side of the tapestry will be all the loose ends of the thread or yarn. While the front side will look beautiful and finished, the back side generally looks unkempt and not in order. If we only saw the back of a tapestry, we would not be impressed. Most likely, we'd be very disappointed. However, when we look only at the front of a beautiful tapestry, we don't understand the complexities of what lies on the other side.

Had people witnessed the crucifixion, they might have compared it to the back side of a tapestry—lacking beauty, completeness, structure, and order. The resurrection is the front of our analogous tapestry—it weaves together beauty and glory and hope. When we look at the resurrection, it may be easy to forget what was on the other side, what was behind the resurrection. Just like if we look at only the crucifixion, the resurrection lacks meaning, and we just see a jumbled and painful mess.

In many ways, we are like tapestries. We each have the outward appearance, the place where we might appear beautiful, accomplished, and confident. The back side of our tapestry looks entirely different. It looks disorganized and chaotic. If we look at only the front side, we don't see the whole picture. If we look only at the back side, we don't see the whole picture either. This is true whether we look at others and even when we look at ourselves.

There is no person who is completely organized and beautiful like the front of the tapestry. Everyone has some "loose threads" behind their public persona. Likewise, there is no person who has no outward beauty, who is just a mess of disorganization. At least there is no one who has no potential of outward beauty. Just as we all have some chaos and loose ends in our lives, we also have beauty.

As we wrap up our discussion of helping and being patient, we need to be patient with others, and we need to be patient with ourselves. God created each of us to be a beautiful tapestry, made in His image and likeness, and able to project His beauty and glory. Because of our fallen world, there is not one of us who doesn't have challenges below the surface. This is why things like being part of a community are so important and why encouragement is so vital. We need others to encourage us and let us know that they see the front of our tapestry, even when we are focused on the back of it. And we ourselves need to understand both sides of our tapestry, there can always be a beautiful side, and there will always be a side that needs some work.

Lord, thank You for the joys in my life, the outward manifestations of happiness and hope (list some). Lord, You know the secret hurts of my life (list some of them). Give me the patience to manage the parts of me that are chaotic and disorganized. Help me to see the good in myself and the good in others. Help me to encourage others to improve their shortcomings that can be managed and to accept the ones that cannot. Bring others around me who can do the same for me. Amen.

Encouragement Challenge: There are two sides to every person. Be encouraged to share the front side and to see the beauty of the front sides of the tapestries of others. Be encouraged to be patient with the back side, our own and those of others.

Part Five

SEEK TO DO GOOD

See that none of you repays evil for evil, but always seek to do good to one another and to all.

1 Thessalonians 5:15

Kill Pain with Kindness

He who pursues righteousness and kindness will find life and honor.
Proverbs 21:21

Pain is a part of life. Some pain is necessary, even good. For instance, it's not all that pleasant at the dentist when they are scratching the plaque off of your teeth. I can't exactly say I look forward to that. However, after I'm done, the pain is worth it to have clean teeth.

Inflicting pain on others is also necessary at times. If you tell your child to turn the TV off and do his or her homework, you are causing pain to your child, who gets upset. But ultimately, that pain is for the child's own good because if he or she doesn't do well in school, they won't do well in life.

Most pain, however, is bad. It is no fun to be home sick. I would gladly give up being sick to go back to work. However, sickness is unavoidable. At many points in life, we get sick, and that's just part of living in a fallen world. So that pain is "justifiable." We can rationalize that we will all have the pain of sickness.

The pain of losing a loved one really stings. The hardest thing to intellectually wrap our heads around is when someone dies. It's the finality of it that is so hard to comprehend. We can lose a job and go get another one. We can lose money and then go get more. We can get really sick and still have hope for recovery. Our children will leave and go to college, but it's not like we won't ever see them again. When someone passes away, the finality of no tomorrow is very hard to comprehend. This pain is awful. However, even this pain is normal and expected, and we will all go through it.

There is another kind of pain that is avoidable. It's not a good pain either. It is not a purposeful pain. It is the pain we inflict on one another for no reason. No, this is not the pain a parent causes a child when he tells his son he's had too many French fries this week and tonight he's eating asparagus. This is not even the pain of a relationship breaking up because it is not working. It is the pain that is senseless. It's the pain of a bully who mercilessly picks on someone. That is not necessary, productive, or positive in any way. It is the pain of someone who pokes and needles someone for no reason. It is the pain of someone who puts people down constantly. It is the pain of someone who speaks loud enough to trample on anyone who raises a voice in opposition. It is the pain of someone who goes and speaks against someone and ruins their reputation for no reason. These kinds of pains are really unnecessary. And yet we experience them all the time. We all are on the receiving end of pains like this. And sadly, we are all on the inflicting end of pain like this.

I know that I cause pain to people, sometimes unintentionally and sadly, sometimes intentionally. This is an area in which I want to improve. Some people also cause me pain, unintentionally and sometimes intentionally. When it is unintentional, there needs to be forgiveness. When it is intentional, there needs to be patience on my part and repentance on the other person's.

Some people inflict pain, and they don't know it, or they don't think what they are doing causes pain to others. It's just "Johnny (or insert any other name) being Johnny." It's hard to know what to do with people in this category. Most people who do wrong deep down know that what they are doing is wrong, even when they pretend they aren't. Those who do wrong and can't conceive that what they are doing is wrong exhibit sociopathic tendencies. Left unchecked, people in this category inflict a lot of pain on a lot of people.

The key, I believe, to the problem of pain is kindness. If we resolve each day to be kind, speak kindly, and think kind thoughts, it will be much harder to turn around and inflict pain on others. Even if pain is involved, as it is when we correct a child, we can deliver the message with kindness. And when we find "Johnny being Johnny," we should encourage (even strongly encourage) Johnny to be kind by modeling kindness and applauding him when Johnny is kind. You'd be surprised how encouragement results in better behavior. It is better to "kill with kindness" or rather "build up with kindness" than to meet meanness with even more meanness.

We see acts of kindness and unkindness daily. We also see pain daily—some of which is necessary, and a lot of which is not. Most of the pain we inflict on other people is completely unnecessary. And I don't know what drives it, though most likely it is insecurity. Kindness and encouragement breed confidence, which tends to lessen insecurity.

So, be kind today. If you have to say something negative, say it as kindly as possible. Look for opportunities to encourage others. Lend an ear to someone who wants to talk. Many times, unkindness rears its head simply because someone is crying out for attention. There are many ways to express kindness. I'm sure there would be a lot less pain in the world if there were a little more kindness. Kindness can't stop all pain, and all pain isn't bad. However, there is a lot of pain that is unnecessary, and kindness can go a long way to stopping this kind of pain.

Lord, help me to be kind today. When I have to say something that is corrective, please help me to be kind as I do it. Bring people into my path today whom I can show kindness to. Help me to be an instrument of kindness is a world filled with so much pain. Amen.

Encouragement Challenge: Be intentionally kind today!

BE A LIGHT IN THE WORLD, LEAD WITH KINDNESS

*The people who sat in darkness have seen a great light, and for those
who sat in the region and shadow of death light has dawned.*
Matthew 4:16

There is a lot of anxiety in the world today. We don't need any more of it. In our fallen world, no one is perfect. There is no one who doesn't have a character flaw, no one who does not make mistakes. There is also no one who does not have destructive impulses. We all have them. If we say we don't have them, then we are lying to ourselves.

When we are anxious, either by our own circumstance or someone else who is causing us anxiety, many of us almost naturally run to our destructive impulse. We eat a bag of potato chips, have an ice cream sundae, suck down a twelve-pack, or go to the computer and look at something inappropriate. Under the wrong circumstances, we might even consider doing something permanent, and sadly, there are some who act on this and succeed.

Jesus told us to be lights in the world. It is the one quality we share with God. Light is the one thing that Jesus said that "I (he) amthe Light of the world,"(John 8:12, John 9:5) and "you (us) are the light of the world." (Matthew 5:14)

The light is not always bright in my world. People irritate me all the time, as I'm sure I irritate them. The challenge, and the Christian response, to our state of mutual irritation is to lead with kindness. It is never wrong to lead with kindness, mercy, and compassion. These are God-like qualities. God is full of kindness, mercy, and compassion toward us. Should we not offer these to one another? Anger, while it may seem to be a justified response, ultimately darkens our light. Anger is a part of life. There is no life where we will not experience anger. Even Jesus got angry from time to time. However, He did not stew in His anger. He expressed His frustrations and got right back to kindness, mercy, and compassion.

I'm reminded of the words of Psalm 4:4–5: *Be angry, but sin not; commune with your own hearts on your beds, and be silent. Offer right sacrifices and put your trust in the Lord.*

These are beautiful words that are indeed hard to live by. Yet, they light the path to our salvation. The Lord doesn't tell us not to be angry. Rather, He tells us to be angry but do so in a way that is not sinful. Be angry, but don't forget about kindness, mercy, and compassion.

Psalm 103:10–11 says: *He does not deal with us according to our sins, nor requite us according to our iniquities. For as the heavens are high above the earth, so great is His steadfast love toward those who fear Him.*

Multiple times each day, we will be faced with a choice to make—to contribute to the increase of anxiety in the world or the decrease of anxiety in the world. When we lead with mercy, compassion, and kindness through encouragement, we become part of the solution and help to lessen the problem. We each have the power to push people toward their destructive impulses or away from them. And only that, when we interact with someone who has done us neither harm nor good, someone who we don't know whether they are ready to succeed or self-destruct, a kind word might be the thing that rescues them from self-destruction or propels them further on their road to success. That's why it's never wrong to lead with kindness, mercy, and compassion, and making encouragement a deliberate and intentional part of our lives is of critical importance, especially in these days.

Lead with mercy, compassion, and kindness. Offer encouragement generously.

Lord, help me to be a light in the world today. Speak good things into my heart about mercy, compassion, and kindness. Help me to remember to lead with these things, even in the times when I am frustrated and angry, even with those who don't deserve these things from me. You are merciful, kind, and compassionate toward my shortcomings. Help me to extend this to others. Help me to see those who need encouragement today and to offer it generously. Amen.

Encouragement Challenge: Let your light shine through kindness today.

One Scenario Where Encouragement Is Bad

Be not envious of evil men, nor desire to be with them.
Proverbs 24:1

There actually is one kind of encouragement that is bad, and that is the encouragement to do bad things. Peers can encourage us to do things that are not good, and peer pressure might cause us to succumb to this kind of encouragement. Excessive drinking, especially in high school and college, is one example that comes to mind. Many people are pressured to drink, try smoking weed, abuse prescription drugs, or take performance-enhancing drugs to improve athletic performance. They are encouraged by their peers to engage in risky behavior. Sometimes it is difficult to tell the difference between peer pressure and encouragement. "Everyone's doing it," or "Let's go, and we'll have a great time" sounds encouraging. "You have to do this" sounds like peer pressure, but it can also be heard as encouragement. ("You have to read this book, it's so good," that's an encouraging way to use this phrase.)

We know that there is no fear in love (1 John 4:18). So if someone is pressuring someone else to do something, and that person being pressured feels that they need to do what is being encouraged or they stand to lose in some way, doing something out of fear in this instance would qualify as pressure rather than encouragement.

Encouragement is a positive thing and should be reserved for motivating people to do positive things. Let's say that a group of friends is meeting on a Saturday morning to go serve at a soup kitchen, and one friend is a little hesitant about going. The other friends encourage, saying, "C'mon, let's go; it is really important that we help those who are less fortunate than we are." That is an example of encouragement. On the other hand, let's say that two friends are shopping in the store, and one says to the other, "Hey, let's steal a pair of expensive shoes; the store won't miss two pairs." That is an example of peer pressure rather than encouragement.

I think that encouragement is something that is limited to pushing people to do the good. Pushing others to behave badly is not encouragement, at least as I understand it.

This brings a new word into the equation: discernment. It may take a good deal of discernment to understand where the line is between encouragement and peer pressure, when encouragement ceases to be encouragement and becomes something destructive rather than something that builds us up.

Prayer and counsel are invaluable tools in learning to be discerning. Prayer connects us with God. It opens up our hearts to listen to Him. It slows us down so that we can hear His voice speaking into our hearts. Prayer may be a prolonged event, for example five to fifteen minutes of intentional silence to be with God. Or it may be a short prayer before making a decision. Hopefully, it is both. Ideally, prayer is something that we set aside time for every day, time to be still and just be with God. There are many decisions that we make each day that are of no consequence—whether we eat chicken or a burger for lunch will generally not have long-lasting consequences. However, there are decisions we make each day that have longer term consequences. Stealing and getting caught is a decision that could follow someone for the rest of their lives. It could cost someone admission to college, a job, and more. So, praying before making decisions is important.

Almost as important is good counsel. Good counsel can come from a lot of sources. Parents can be a good source. So can teachers and clergy. A therapist or counselor is a good place to sort out ideas, to discern what is right and what might be wrong. And trusted friends are important. We are not talking about the friends who pressure you to do wrong, but the ones who encourage you to do right, the ones who always have your back, the ones with whom you always feel safe. I use this word "always" intentionally. Because most of us have friends that fall into two different categories—friends who are "always" good for us, and other friends who may be fun but may not always encourage us to make the right decisions.

In the area of encouragement, it's important to realize that not everything we are "encouraged" to do is a good idea. And we have to discern sometimes intentions that present themselves as noble, idealistic, or good to make sure that they really are. Proverbs 14:8 reads, "The wisdom of a prudent man is to discern his way, but the folly of fools is deceiving." Sometimes it is hard to discern between what is wise and what is foolish, especially when foolishness is presented in an attractive way. It is important to develop discernment to recognize the prudent person and listen to him or her and ignore those who deceive us into thinking that folly and foolishness are good things.

Lord, please help me to develop a good sense of discernment. Help me to see clearly that which is noble and right and true, even when what is in front of me seems attractive and inconsequential. Help me to make good decisions today, to slow down and think about the consequences of my actions. Surround me with people who will encourage me to do what is good and not pressure me to do things that are harmful. May I also be one who encourages the good and doesn't pressure others toward what is not good. Amen.

Encouragement Challenge: Make praying for discernment part of your daily prayers.

Criticism Is Encouraging When It Is Constructive

My soul will rejoice when your lips speak what is right.
Proverbs 23:16

No one likes criticism, and the reason is probably that most criticism is destructive rather than constructive. It focuses on what a person did wrong rather than what they did right. And the net effect is that criticism usually tears someone down rather than builds them up.

Many of us have had the experience of not making something we tried out for—maybe it was a sports team, a part in the school play, a choral group, or something else. If the coach/teacher only said, "Well, you didn't make it because you are just not good enough," that would be very discouraging because there is nothing to build on, and a comment like that doesn't really instill much hope for future success. A better way to deliver this kind of "bad news" would be if they said, "If you do this and this, you'd improve your chances." This is both constructive and hopeful.

We have to be critical at times with people and situations that might disappoint us. Yelling at your child who is about to touch a hot stove or cross a street without looking first is necessary because yelling carries a great sense of urgency, which is exactly what you want when your child is about to do something dangerous. However, when the danger has passed, making a secondary statement like "I love you so much, and I don't want to see you get hurt, that's why I yelled," adds something constructive and encouraging to a moment of anger that might make a child feel hurt or embarrassed.

When a co-worker does something wrong at work, it's not enough to only tell them what they did wrong. That can be demeaning and embarrassing even if it's warranted. And a string of criticisms will ruin a working relationship. A consistently critical boss is bad for company morale. A more effective strategy would be to tell a co-worker what to do differently next time, and also something affirming like "I'm glad we work together." Try to avoid comments that are belittling and demeaning.

Let's say that you are in a car, and the driver is going too fast. You pipe up and say, "Slow down. You are driving too fast." The driver answers, "No, I'm not." And then you respond,

"Yes, you are." "No, I'm not." "Yes, you are." As you can see, in very quick order, you will be getting nowhere. The driver will think you think he is a bad driver and, of course, is going to fight on this. Your criticism (warranted or not) is met with contempt rather than correction.

A better way to get someone to slow down if they are driving too fast is to say, "Would you mind slowing down, I'm a little nervous." The driver can't say, "No, you are not" because who can possibly argue with the feelings of someone else? In this case, the driver can slow down and not feel demeaned. The passenger will be successful in getting the car to slow down without putting friction between themselves and the driver; in fact, if anything, the passenger indicated the problem is more with the passenger being nervous than the out-of-control driver. Everyone wins—the passenger feels safer, and the driver doesn't have his or her ego destroyed.

We all do things wrong, just as we all have wrong things done to us. I'm not sure if there is anyone who likes harsh criticism. I think we all prefer to receive criticism that is constructive and couched in encouragement than in destruction. When pointing out things that someone has done wrong, it is important to point out the things they did right so that there is not only something to avoid (the wrong) but something to build on (that which is right).

Going back to the 5:1 ratio of encouragement to discouragement, when we must be critical, we must intentionally balance criticism with encouragement because people are more effective when they feel encouraged and hopeful rather than discouraged and torn down. Again, criticism is warranted in many situations. However, the way we criticize is important.

If we are supposed to do unto others as we would like to have done to us, criticize others in the way you'd want others to criticize you. No one likes to be stung or demeaned with criticism, so criticize without being destructive.

Lord, thank You for all of Your blessings. Please bless me with patience today. Help me to see the good in people. Help me in situations when I need to correct someone, to do so with kindness, patience, and in a constructive way. When I do wrong, help me to accept criticism with patience. Kindle the hearts of those around me so that they may also have patience with my shortcomings. Help me to learn from mistakes, and help me to bring encouragement even in situations when someone has done something wrong to me. Amen.

Encouragement Challenge: Criticism can be encouraged when it is constructive rather than destructive. Focus on being constructive when criticism is warranted. And couch criticism with encouragement.

Praise versus Encouragement

He who rebukes a man will afterward find more favor than he who flatters with his tongue.
Proverbs 28:23

There is a difference between praise and encouragement. The main difference is that encouragement can be given even when someone has done wrong. Praise can only be given when something has gone right. We need encouragement more than praise. It is actually possible that praise can be a negative. As the above Scripture verse from Proverbs tells us, the person who rebukes another will actually find more favor than one who flatters another. That is because flattery is often less than truthful, and people appreciate the truth in a rebuke more than a false instance of flattery.

Dr. Timothy Evans, who has studied and written extensively on encouragement, describes three levels of praise.[14] "Light praise" is typical flattery and politeness when we offer "what is expected," regardless of the truth. This occurs in social settings where we tell people they look nice even if they look bad, or we say that a meal was good even if it was terrible. Receiving this kind of praise is confusing because we don't know if someone is being truthful or only polite.

"Medium praise" is "when we use gold stars for good behavior." These are external motivators for good behavior. This kind of praise motivates based on some kind of recognition.

"Hurtful praise" is damaging. It makes use of superlatives like "You are the best," "You are great," or "You are better than everyone." While this makes someone temporarily feel good, these kinds of phrases are actually discouraging. Why? That doesn't seem to make sense. Don't people WANT to be told "You are the best"? Superlatives convey the message that we only count when we are perfect. Since none of us can be perfect all the time, and deep down we all know that, putting someone too high up on a pedestal will have a negative effect because they know it will be so hard to stay on top or get on top again that they will be discouraged from even trying. If one has to be the best to get praised, and it's impossible to do that every time, why even try?

Encouragement conveys faith in a person no matter how well or poorly things go. Legitimate praise can only be given when someone has done something right, though many people will praise even when something has gone wrong, and this is disingenuous at best and hurtful at worst.

Encouragement is focused on a person's effort or improvement. Praise focuses on outcome. We don't praise people for coming in last place. The people who finish first or who are "best" get praise. However, if a person is in a swimming race, for example, and comes in last place but shaves off time from their personal best, this is something worthy of encouragement.

Encouragement challenges us to develop our potential while praise threatens us to do what is expected. Using the swimming example again (our son has been swimming for years, so I'm familiar with this stuff), if he wins a race, but his technique is compromised, the praise for winning is actually pretty hollow because we know that in the long run, it is technique that will bring about improvement. So, if someone is going for praise all the time, their "technique" on a lot of things won't be good.

Another example that I was guilty of in college is learning for the test and not for the sake of learning. Many people, like me, could get top grades and hold the material in our heads only long enough to regurgitate it on a test. It would have been better had we been encouraged to learn rather than praised for scoring well.

Encouragement can be given at any time. Success isn't required for encouragement as it is for praise. Encouragement has more to do with effort than with success. Some of us are incapable of "success" under many circumstances. For instance, I'll never set a world record for running. I'm not really a runner. But I can run for exercise, and others can encourage the effort to get in shape. Encouragement is all about effort, and we are all capable of giving a good effort.

Encouragement frees us to be our unique selves. Praise obligates us to conform to standards set by another or to compete with others. To receive praise, we have to conform to some authority or what some authority says is praiseworthy. When someone compliments our car, that is praise. Society promotes the idea that a new expensive sports car is somehow better than an old beat-up car. So when a person buys a used beat-up car, they are not likely to receive praise from many people. However, when that person has worked hard and saved money to buy their first car, that is something to encourage. When we aren't feeling constant pressure to conform to what society says is good, it is freeing and encouraging in its own right.

Lord, we praise You because it is only You who is worthy of our praise. Help me to be genuine in opportunities to encourage others. Bring others in my path who will encourage me. Help me to be patient and see the "long game" in all I am doing, not to strive for that which is quick and temporary but that which is solid and lasting, be that in relationships, work, and especially faith. Amen.

Encouragement Challenge: Praise is like a temporary "high" that will never fully satisfy. Encouragement is more lasting!

God Is an Optimist—We Should Be as Well

He who diligently seeks good seeks favor, but evil come to him who searches for it.
Proverbs 11:27

When our son was young, one show that he watched was a cartoon about a young boy who was bald and kind of awkward. He had a mother and father and a baby sister, so thankfully, this cartoon presented what appeared to be a stable home life. However, when I watched this cartoon, the mother would consistently annoy me because she seemed to be the consummate pessimist. It seemed that she was always ten steps ahead on what could go wrong. If the little boy would say something like, "I'm going outside to play," she would respond with something like, "Well, I hope you don't get hurt or killed," "Don't fall off the swing set and die," or "I hope a car doesn't plow through our fence and kill you." Now I'm exaggerating a bit, but it's like she could never quite say, "Have a great time." She always managed to temper her son's joy with some kind of ominous warning.

We've all heard the terms "glass half-empty" and "glass half-full." These describe how people see a glass that contains 50 percent liquid and 50 percent space—some will see that glass as half-full and others as half-empty. Optimists are the ones who see the glass half-full while pessimists see it as half-empty. In the aforementioned cartoon, the mom was certainly a glass half-empty person.

Is God an optimist or pessimist? Does He see the glass as half-full or half-empty? I believe there is strong evidence that God is an optimist. In 1 Thessalonians 5:15, the verse that this unit is based on, we read that we are not to repay evil for evil. Rather, we are to seek to do good to one another. So, if a situation is evil, we are not supposed to meet evil with evil but instead to meet evil with good. In fact, St. Paul, in 1 Thessalonians 5:15, tells us that we are to "always seek to do good to one another and to all." "To all" means exactly that—we are supposed to do good to all, even those who are not good to us. Jesus is emphatic in Luke 6: 27–28 when He says, "But I say to you that hear, love your enemies, do go to those who hate you, bless those who curse you, pray for those who abuse you." In Matthew 18:21–22, we read that Peter asked Jesus, "'Lord, how often shall my brother sin against me, and I forgive him? As many as seven times?' Jesus said to him, 'I do not say to you seven times, but seventy times seven.'"

The Bible gives dozens upon dozens of examples of God's patience, mercy, and forgiveness. One would have to see some good in someone to have that degree of patience, mercy, and forgiveness.

Encouragement and optimism go hand in hand. That is because optimism sees the good in people and situations. Optimists see the good that can come out of a situation. Pessimists are always looking for the bad. That doesn't mean that optimists don't occasionally feel pessimistic or that they don't get upset, frustrated, or sad. Reality is somewhere between optimism and pessimism, and it's important that we are real.

However, optimism or pessimism are ways of looking at the world, a mindset that we develop over time. It's like the difference between the teacher who tells his or her students, "You are all starting off with an A, and it's yours to lose," versus the teacher who says, "You are all starting off with an F, and you have to earn your way out of it." Or saying, "I want you to succeed and will give you every opportunity" versus "You are going to fail, but I want you to prove me wrong."

We tend to find what we are looking for. If we are looking for good, we will probably find it. If we are looking for bad, we will probably find it. There are people who consistently look for the bad—a hair out of place, a small wrinkle or blemish, and they seize on the smallest thing gone wrong. They hear their children talk joyfully about going out to play with their friends, and rather than telling them to have a great time, they give a lecture about all the things that could go wrong. And then those children leave the house, many of them without confidence and their heads filled with doomsday scenarios. That doesn't mean that the optimist doesn't tell their children to be careful. That would be irresponsible. But rather than harp on what could go wrong, they think about what could go right as they encourage their children to have fun and make new friends.

If God is an optimist, and He must be, if He wants so badly to redeem a fallen world, then we as encouragers must be optimists as well. We are to see the good in things, people, and situations. Optimism is also tied to gratitude. When we are thankful, we are also optimistic; we see the good in what we have rather than frustration over what we do not have. God wants us to get to heaven. He wants us to be successful.

There is a beautiful line in an Orthodox prayer from the Sacrament of Holy Unction that reads, "You have not created man for destruction, but for the keeping of Your commandments, and for the inheriting of life incorruptible."[15] God did not create us to be destructive or negative. He did not create us to look at one another destructively or negatively. He created us so we might inherit eternal life. His message is one of encouragement. Our messages to one another should be encouraging as well.

God is an optimist. Encouragers are optimists as well. Work at learning to see the good in people. That doesn't mean there won't be bad or that we shouldn't correct the bad. It's developing a mindset to see the good in people and give people the benefit of the doubt rather than starting out with the doubt.

Lord, when You look at my life, please see the good in me. Forgive my shortcomings. Help me to learn from my mistakes. Help me to have a positive outlook on life and people. Help me to see the good in others and for others to see the good in me. Help me to be an optimist and encourager, to see the possibilities for joy and success in others and situations I will encounter today. Amen.

Encouragement Challenge: Choose to see the good in people and situations today, and when you see it, encourage it!

Charlie Brown and Lucy

And the word of the Lord came to Zechariah, saying, "Thus say the Lord of hosts, Render true judgments, show kindness and mercy each to his brother, do not oppress the widow, the fatherless, the sojourner, or the poor; and let none of you devise evil against his brother in your heart."
Zechariah 7:8–10

Most of us are familiar with Charlie Brown, the lead character of the long-running cartoon and comic strip, *Peanuts*. No matter how old I get, I always watch the Charlie Brown specials at Halloween (who can forget the "Great Pumpkin"), Thanksgiving (toast and popcorn for Thanksgiving dinner), and Christmas (thankfully they still read the Nativity story). Charlie Brown has a character we can all relate to. He has good days and bad ones, has times when he is optimistic and pessimistic, and has times when he feels confident and other times when he is nervous.

Linus, he of the ever-present blue security blanket, is Charlie Brown's best friend. Linus's sister, Lucy, is Charlie Brown's chief tormenter. She acts like his friend on many occasions, and the two talk often. Yet, Lucy acts like a bully toward Charlie Brown, making insensitive remarks about how much he is a failure and calling him names, especially "blockhead."

The most frustrating thing that Lucy does is "encourage" Charlie Brown to kick a football, which she eagerly holds for him. Every time Charlie Brown runs to kick the ball, she pulls it away at the last second, and he ends up on his back. This pattern continues often in the comic strips and cartoons. She "encourages" him to kick the ball, and promises that *this* time she will leave the ball in place and not pull it back; he believes that *this* will finally be the time he gets to kick the ball, he runs with optimism, and is inevitably disappointed when she pulls the ball back yet again. At some point, he knows that she won't let him kick the ball, and yet on some level, each time, he still tries, believing somewhere in his heart that this will be the time she helps him succeed.

I've often wondered why Charlie Brown doesn't just kick Lucy instead of the ball. She obviously will not let him kick it and will just continue to taunt and pick on him. Charlie Brown, however, is, if nothing else, very kind. While he might not be the "sharpest tack on the wall," he makes up for it with kindness. While he makes mistakes like everyone, we never see him unkind to someone. In fact, he goes out of his way to be kind to Linus, Schroeder, Franklin, and even embraces the perpetual mess that is Pig-Pen. Charlie Brown is not always an optimist, but he is a pretty good encourager.

One of the reasons why Charlie Brown has lasted so long and is appealing to people of all ages is because we see ourselves in the characters. We all have our quirks, like Linus. We all have our obsessions, like Schroeder and his piano. We all have days where we look messy, like Pig-Pen.

Most of us have Lucys in our lives, people who torment and who bully us. Most people have had a bad boss, bad teacher, or bad (former or current) friend. We all have people we want to believe in who consistently let us down. We all have had optimism in things we should just give up on, like kicking the football that "Lucy" is just never going to hold for us.

Sadly, each of us has Lucy tendencies, at least at some points. I hope no one thinks of me as a bad boss, priest, or friend, but I'm sure I have those titles with some people and honestly, with a few, it's probably deserved. We've all taken a turn pulling the ball back on someone, misleading someone, or pretending to encourage while secretly rooting for someone to fail.

Charlie Brown, as we discussed, was kind, if nothing else. If he ever had the urge to hurt Lucy or fight back, he never did. And while we may look at Charlie Brown as the perpetual victim, he is also the hero of the story. Why? Because he consistently tries to see the good in people. You never hear him use bad language. You never see him hit anyone. Charlie Brown may be a "blockhead" when it comes to certain things. However, we don't hear the Bible extol intelligence as a virtue, nor riches or popularity. Kindness, mercy, truth, and goodness, these are things that please God and also please others. These are the pillars on which genuine friendships are built. These are the virtues that make life truly meaningful. Because what good is it to have all the riches in the world if everyone thinks you are Lucy, a bully? We definitely need more Charlie Browns in the world.

Lord, thank You for simple gifts, like air to breathe, water, electricity, and life itself. Help me to be more appreciative of what I have. Help me to be an encourager to others. Help me to suppress thoughts of actions and words that can be harmful to others. Help me to see the good in others and encourage the good in others. Amen.

Which *Peanuts* character does your life most closely align with, Charlie Brown or Lucy?

Paderewski and the Piano

And calling to Him a child, He put him in the midst of them, and said, "Truly I say to you, unless you turn and become like children, you will never enter the kingdom of heaven. Whoever humbles himself like this child, he is the greatest in the kingdom of heaven."
Matthew 18:2–4

There is a beautiful story that can be found in many places on the internet about an incident in the life of the most famous concert pianist in Poland, Ignace Paderewski. While there is some dispute as to whether this is just a story or whether it actually happened, we know that Paderewski was a real person because he eventually became the prime minister of Poland. Here is the story:

> *A mother took her small child to a concert by Paderewski to expose him to the talent of the great pianist. She hoped as she did to encourage her son in his piano lessons, which he had just begun. They arrived early at the concert and were seated near the front. Standing alone on the stage was a marvelous Steinway grand piano. As they waited for the concert to begin, the mother entered into a conversation with the people beside her. Eventually, eight o'clock came, and the light began to dim. Everyone turned their attention to the stage and the grand piano. The mother looked up and was suddenly horrified. Her son was sitting at the piano and banging out with one little finger, "Twinkle, Twinkle, Little Star." "Oh no," she thought, "How am I going to get him down?"*
>
> *As she began to make her way to the platform, Ignace Paderewski himself appeared on stage. He went over and sat down beside the child. He whispered in the child's ear, "Don't quit; keep playing!" As the little boy continued to play, Paderewski reached down with his left hand and began to fill in the bass part. Then with his arm around the little boy, he added a running obbligato. Together, the old master and the young novice had the crowd mesmerized.*[16]

There are many times in life when we might feel like the little boy in this story. We wonder if we have any talent or think what we know is inconsequential or has no meaning. We wonder what we have to offer the world or what talent we have that God can possibly use. Just remember as you sit there on the piano bench, tapping out your little song, that God, the

Master of all, surrounds you with His love and whispers softly in your ear, "Don't quit, keep playing; together we can make a masterpiece."

There are many times in life when we might feel like the mom in this story. We wonder if our child has any talent or whether what our child has to offer the world will be of any consequence whatsoever. While we probably won't tell our child to "quit playing," we'll secretly think, *My child has no talent.*

Sometimes we actually play the role of the great Paderewski. We come upon the person (it could be a child or an adult) who is offering something as best as they can. That something might be very simple; it might even be the cause of snickering because of its simplicity. Will we join the crowd snickering? Or will we go beside this person, as Paderewski did with the child, and encourage them to keep playing and not quit? Can we take what talent they have and help make it a masterpiece?

Think about that boy for a minute. Imagine what joy he must have had to be on stage with a famous pianist in front of a crowd in rapt attention. What a humble gesture for the maestro to give the spotlight to someone else. In doing so, he not only gave that child a moment he'd never forget but probably increased both his love for music and confidence in himself. It is really a joy to give someone else the spotlight.

When we offer something to God, and especially when we offer it in a pure and innocent way, the way that this child did in the story, God takes what we do and can create a masterpiece with it. His masterpieces are not necessarily outwardly beautiful or materially expensive. His masterpieces, however, have the most lasting value and greatest inner beauty.

Lord, thank You for whatever talent I have and whatever good I am able to bring into the world. Help me to always see the good in others. Help me to find value in the gifts and talents of others. Give me the wisdom to see masterpieces in others, especially in times when the crowds see mediocrity. Give me the confidence to offer my talents, always reflecting Your glory in my offering of them. Amen.

Encouragement Challenge: Look for opportunities to encourage someone by giving them the spotlight!

Time Does Not Heal Most Wounds

Therefore, if any one is in Christ, he is a new creation; the old has passed away, behold the new has come. All this is from God, who through Christ reconciled us to Himself and gave us the ministry of reconciliation; that is, in Christ God was reconciling the world to Himself, not counting their trespasses against them, and entrusting to us the message of reconciliation.
2 Corinthians 5:17–19

I listened for a podcast by Rick Warren[17] (author of *The Purpose Driven Life*, Podcast of June 25, 2018) in which he described our struggle with conflict resolution. There are two things I took away from the program that I want to share in this reflection.

The first is the old adage, "Time heals all wounds." We've all heard it. Many of us believe it. Let's think about that for a moment. Time does not heal a broken leg, an open sore, or any other serious physical ailment. In fact, time is not on your side if you have an infection or serious disease. Waiting can make a wound much worse and have a much more serious impact on one's life. The best way to treat a serious physical wound is to quickly get medical treatment.

The same holds true for many of our conflicts in life. We sweep things under the rug and stonewall many conflicts, just thinking they will go away, and they don't. Often, they become worse. Think about unresolved conflicts you may have with a spouse, child, parent, or friend.

Why so much unresolved conflict? Well, the second thing I took away from this program was the fact that most of us have never had any training in conflict management. I had eight years of college and never once took a class in conflict management, never even heard of one. Yet, this is something that comes up in my life way more often than calculus or chemistry. It is something that most of us are not good at doing. And just as encouragement is an "art," so is effective conflict management.

The above Bible verse reminds us not to repay evil for evil. When wronged, it seems the inclination is to do exactly that, repay evil for evil. Sometimes when wronged, we do nothing, hoping it will just solve itself. That doesn't work either. When we are in conflict, the best thing to do is deal with the conflict, something that just about all of us do not enjoy and are not very good at.

In committed relationships, conflict resolution should be something we talk about with spouses, friends, and co-workers. We should talk about it before it happens, realizing that it will inevitably happen. As St. Paul writes in 1 Thessalonians 5:15, we are to *"always seek to do good to one another and to all."* Is goodwill possible all the time? Yes, it is possible to *offer* good will all the time. Is it possible that the person with whom we are in conflict will also *extend* goodwill all the time? No, there will inevitably be people who don't extend good will, who lack compassion. In our school years, there were bullies, and unfortunately, some adults are still bullies.

When conflict arises, pray for discernment to deal with it. Christ tells us in Matthew 18:15–17:

> *If your brother sins against you, go and tell him his fault, between you and him alone. If he listens to you, you have gained your brother. But if he does not listen, take one or two other along with you, that every word may be confirmed by the evidence of two or three witnesses. If he refuses to listen to them, tell it to the church; and if he refuses to listen even to the church, let him be to you as a Gentile and a tax collector.*

Christ advocated conflict resolution, not sweeping things under the rug, and He advocated for reconciliation whenever possible. Our intention should be to do the good, even if the outcome isn't always good. God commends the effort and intent.

Finally, healing what is wounded starts by looking at the good points of one another rather than the points of conflict.

In seeking to do good, it is critical that we work to resolve conflicts. Conflicts are discouraging. Resolving them is encouraging.

Lord, be with me in my conflicts. I pray for (names of people with whom you have conflicts), that you bless them today. Help us to heal the wounds that are between us. Help me to not repay evil for evil, but whenever possible, to reconcile. And when reconciliation is not possible, show me the way to personal peace. Surround me with people of peace and encouragement. Help me to be a peacemaker and a better encourager. Help me to see the good in others. Amen.

Encouragement Challenge: Talk to someone with whom you have a conflict, or talk to a close friend about how to deal with conflict when it happens.

THE ART OF FORGIVENESS

Then Peter came up and said to Him "Lord, how often shall my brother sin against me, and I forgive him? As many as seven times?" Jesus said to him, "I do not say to you seven times, but seventy times seven."
Matthew 18:21–22

Why did I entitle this reflection "The Art of Forgiveness"? To establish any thriving, long-term relationship requires forgiveness. And like a fine work of art, forgiveness is not painted with broad strokes but with delicate, intricate, and purposeful ones. There is no human relationship that can last without forgiveness. Spend any amount of time with someone, and there is bound to be a difference of opinion or outright transgression.

In seeking to do good, sometimes we will end up doing bad instead of good. No one can be good at all times except God. So, in seeking to do good, one good thing we must learn how to do is forgive others in the times when things are not good.

I suppose there are two kinds of forgiveness—forgiveness involving "people with whom we are close," like family members and close friends, and "people with whom we are not close." Let's start with the most important people in our lives, our families. A marriage will not last without forgiveness. If I have been married twenty years and I do one thing wrong a week, that would be one thousand wrongs. I'm sure there have been many more than that. If there are one thousand wrongs on a marital scorecard, there is no way to have a thriving marriage. The only way to survive is to forgive as we go. The Psalms say, *"If Thou, O Lord, shouldst mark iniquities, Lord, who could stand?"* (Ps. 130:3). This is very true in our lives. Without forgiveness, no one can stand.

Forgiveness with little children is a great model. We've all seen little kids lash out at each other and then five minutes later be playing together happily. Sadly, we the parents of those kids hold our grudges a lot longer. We forgive our own children easily. We chastise them, and fifteen minutes later, we are hugging them, another great model of forgiveness that we all see and practice.

So, why then does forgiveness become so complicated among adults? Because we don't work at it. As I said, forgiveness is an art form that needs to be developed and practiced throughout life. It takes a soft heart, generous spirit, and understanding of our own shortcomings. Our knowledge of our own shortcomings should make us seek forgiveness for our missteps, which should inspire us to offer forgiveness more freely to others.

Let's look quickly at the other kind of forgiveness. There are some relationships that are completely surface. We have a relationship with other drivers on the road, even though we don't know their names. Because we share the road together, there is a relationship. So, when the other driver cuts us off, we are not supposed to glare or swear at him; we should be forgiving. We all have our moments of poor driving. We should be forgiven when we make an error. We should offer forgiveness as well.

Not every relationship we have will go the distance. I have heard relationships as lasting for a reason, season, or lifetime. I have had many friendships that have died away during the years of my life. Some of those friendships have ended poorly. There are people that I no longer wish to be friends with. They've breached trust or wounded me in such a way that I no longer feel close to them. I'm sure people could say the same about me. I try to reflect on each of these "lost" relationships and understand that they were good for their "reason" or "season" and try to not harbor hostility toward former friends. This is an art in itself. It is very hard to master this.

We don't forgive well in modern times. When we do wrong, we say, "I'm sorry, but I had a reason." And the response is, "I forgive, but I'm going to sue," or "I forgive, but I'm going to keep track of this." Because we aren't sure we are going to be forgiven, we are afraid to own a wrong. Because we are not sure someone is actually owning a wrong, we are hesitant to forgive. We need to own our mistakes. We need to forgive the mistakes of others.

Forgiveness frees you. If I forgive someone who has wronged me, I am free. In relationships that go the long term, forgiveness is essential. In relationships that are permanently broken, forgiveness does not necessarily restore, but it provides freedom.

Finally, there is a difference between saying, "I'm sorry" and "Forgive me." The difference is that "I'm sorry" doesn't require action on the part of the person we say it to. Let's say that I say to someone, "I'm short on money." They can answer, shrug their shoulders, or ignore me. If I say, "May I have a dollar?" they are brought in, almost forced into the conversation. They have to answer either yes or no. If we say, "I'm sorry," someone can shrug their shoulder or ignore us. But if we say, "Can you please forgive me?" there is an answer that is required, either yes, forgiveness is possible, or no, it is not. And hopefully if the answer is no, some path to forgiveness can be offered.

It is certainly important that we learn how to forgive and that we also humble ourselves and ask for forgiveness. Saying, "I'm sorry" is easy. Saying, "Can you please forgive me?" is much more humbling and vulnerable. It is also much more effective and restorative when someone else says, "I forgive you."

If we expect the Lord to forgive us, we must learn the art of forgiving one another.

Lord, help me to forgive those who have wronged me. Give me the humility to ask for forgiveness when I've wronged someone else. Help free me from bad feelings I harbor toward others. Help forgiveness to be exchanged sincerely and often in my relationships with family and friends. Amen.

Encouragement Challenge: Forgive someone today. Ask forgiveness from someone today.

Be Part of the Solution, Not Part of the Problem

Bear one another's burdens, and so fulfill the law of Christ.
Galatians 6:2

We've all had the experience of sitting at a long traffic light, waiting to turn left. The special left-turn arrow turns green, and it seems like no one is moving. We know that the arrow won't be green for long; it never is. We wonder if we'll make it through the green arrow before it turns red and are stuck through another cycle of everyone else getting to move before the arrow turns green again. Our palms start to sweat. Our blood pressure starts to rise. Why is no one moving? Probably because the "stupid guy" (we say) in the front is looking at his phone. Cars start honking. Finally, the first car in the line moves, just as the light arrow turns yellow. And we're all stuck at the light for another three minutes, everyone except for the guy in the front who was probably on his phone and not paying attention.

Don't you just hate when this happens? I know I do. Time is the most precious commodity we have, and I don't like wasting time, particularly in traffic.

One day, I was sitting at a long light, at the front of the line, and, bored, I started reading emails. The left-turn arrow turned green, and I didn't notice. So I didn't move until people started honking their horns at me. Then I looked up, saw the light was green, and turned left. I'm positive that my delay in moving cost at least a few people getting the green light, cost them a few minutes of their lives, and probably raised their blood pressure, maybe led to them saying a few swear words, maybe had them late for work or picking up their children from school.

We've got a lot of anger in the world today: rude drivers, rude customers, cranky workers, and so on. The opposite of anger is joy and peace. So, we've got to ask ourselves, are we part of the problem? Are we anger-causing people? Or are we part of the solution? Are we injecting joy and peace into the world? Are we peacemakers or peace takers?

In the moment after I went through the green light and realized that, because of me, others wouldn't go through the light, I recognized, "in this moment, I am part of the problem, not part of the solution." We all have things that annoy us in life, like people being inattentive while driving. Ironically, I was doing the very thing that others do to annoy me. It was certainly a moment where I felt like a hypocrite, often complaining about how annoying inattentive drivers are, and in that moment, I'm sure others were complaining about me. And so I resolved to not look at the phone at red lights anymore so that I can be part of the solution and not part of the problem.

No one likes when people are rude to them. Thus, to be part of the solution, we shouldn't be rude to others. There is so much going on in the world, and we are so quick to point out the shortcomings of others. A well-known phrase comes to mind—when you are pointing your finger at someone else, there are three fingers pointing back at you. That's true. Point your index finger at someone, your thumb rests on top, and your other three fingers point back at you. So before we criticize others for causing problems, we need to ask ourselves how many problems we are causing. And we need to check ourselves from many different angles to make sure that what we are doing is part of the solution and not part of the problem. When we all work hard to be conscientious drivers, there won't be as many people missing green lights. When we all work hard to be courteous customers, there won't be as many rude ones. When we all work hard not to be cranky workers, our work environments will become more peaceful, and so on. When we all do our share to be part of the solution, we won't have as many problems.

There are people who are peacemakers—their presence brings peace to chaos. And there are people who are peace takers—their presence brings chaos where there was peace. Each day, we will be faced with opportunities to be both. And how we behave in each situation will either create problems or bring solutions.

Lord, thank You for today and the opportunities it will bring. As happens every day, I know that I will have opportunities to create both problems and solutions for others. Help me to put myself in the shoes of other people so that I can be a more attentive driver, more courteous customer, and friendlier worker. Help me to be a person who brings peace rather than takes it. Help me to be part of the solution and not part of the problem. Amen.

Encouragement Challenge: Be part of the solution, not part of the problem.

Part Six

REJOICE ALWAYS

Rejoice Always.

1 Thessalonians 5:16

Be Someone Who Builds Joy

*Let all bitterness and wrath and anger and clamor and slander be put
away from you, with all malice, and be kind to one another, tenderhearted,
forgiving one another, as God in Christ forgave you.*
Ephesians 4:31–32

Back when I went to college, we had a professor who routinely offered to let us out of class thirty minutes early unless someone had a question. And in this class, there was a student, who, every time he heard "unless someone has a question," his hand would immediately go up, as if it was a Pavlovian response. And he would chew up most of the thirty minutes where we might have gotten out early. Every class, there was a possibility to leave early. And every class, it seemed like he would steal that from us.

We call people like this "killjoy." They "kill" our "joy." I remember when said student wasn't in class, we would all be happy that he wasn't there. And when he came, which was most of the time, it frustrated us. He routinely, it seems, "killed our joy."

We all know people who fit this description. We all know people, who, when we call them, the palms of our hands start to sweat, and our hearts beat faster because they make us nervous. Some people are probably thinking of their bosses as they read this. Teachers have students like this. Sadly, some people feel like this about their parents, spouses, or children.

While I am sure that not everyone likes me, I hope that I'm not someone who makes people nervous. I certainly hope I'm not seen as a "kill joy." Reviewing what we've said so far about encouragement, being an encourager is serious business. It takes a serious commitment to be an encourager. It means putting aside any tendency we have that can make others nervous. It doesn't mean we have to be pushovers. It means that we strive for kindness even in moments of disagreement. We can be upset and still be an encourager.

What we need more of in this world are "build joys," people who build and encourage joy. We all know people who like to gossip and talk in negative terms about almost everything. Many times, we get frustrated with these people. We want to tell them, "Tell me something good." Sometimes, we all are negative, cynical, cranky, grouchy, or whatever you want to call it. Encouragers don't stay this way for long. Encouragers take joy with them wherever they go, and they seek to build joy among all people and in all (well, most) situations.

Going back to the words of St. Paul, we are to put away things like bitterness, wrath, anger, clamor, slander, and malice. These things breed discouragement. No one is encouraged when they are around people who cultivate these traits.

What people want and need in relationships is kindness and forgiveness. In short, we all crave encouragement. And we can all become encouragers.

One other piece of advice is to make sure you say something good. Don't be a bearer of only bad news. As one of my friends reminds me when I am too negative, "Tell me something good!" Make sure you get something "good" into every conversation today. Don't dominate conversations with negativity and try not to leave them on a negative note.

Lord, thank You for the gift of today. Thank You for the possibilities to glorify You. Thank You for the sun and its warmth. Thank You for the beauty of trees, sensation of the wind, and thank You for the moon and the stars as well. Help me to be a person who shows love, radiates joy, promotes encouragement, and focuses on the positive. Help me to be someone who builds joy. And strengthen my soul in the times when I am not joyful. May I project love and joy to all those I meet today. Amen.

Encouragement Challenge: Think about some concrete ways that you can encourage joy in your relationships today.

A Matter of Perspective

Blessed are you when men revile you and persecute you and utter all kinds of evil against you falsely on My account. Rejoice and be glad, for your reward is great in heaven.
Matthew 5:11–12

There is a book called *The Energy Bus* by Jon Gordon (Published by John Wiley & Sons, Inc., Hoboken, New Jersey 2007).[18] It is about how to create positive energy in your life. In the foreword to this book, written by Ken Blanchard, Mr. Blanchard mentions an exercise that he does at business seminars. He asks people to greet one another as if they are unimportant. There is a sense of dullness as people walk around, trying to ignore one another. Then he asks them to greet people as if they were long-lost friends. Suddenly there are laughter, enthusiasm, smiles, and hugs all around. The lesson here is that to run a successful organization, you need to have energy. Blanchard then writes: "'What did I do to change the energy in the room?' I ask. Then I answer: 'All I did was change your focus from a negative thought to a positive thought and the energy of the room increased tenfold.'"

This is an excellent exercise that I have tried both at summer camp with young adults and in my parish with our parish leadership. I asked them to greet one another with indifference and then to greet each other with enthusiasm. And it was amazing to see the dichotomy of doing this simple thing two ways.

So much of life works this way as well. Perspective is important, and so is attitude. One can choose to come to an event in either a positive or negative way. One can come to a positive event negatively, and then the positive event becomes negative. For instance, let's say you are offered free tickets to attend a sporting event with friends. That's a great thing, or it should be. At the very least, you are out with friends, and it is free. But let's say that your team doesn't play well, the food is not that great, and the line getting into the stadium is long, you can quickly change your perspective from a free night out with friends and make it a miserable experience.

On the other hand, if you choose to focus on the friends and the free night rather than the score, the food, or anything else, the night will be a great night. It's all a matter of perspective.

There are plenty of things we all do that we don't like doing. In every family, job, and life, there are numerous things we'd all rather not do. I hate (and that's the right word) sitting through programs where there are endless speeches. I've gone to way too many of them. We all know what the scene looks like. Big white plates with three pieces of overcooked meat on them, vegetables "au a word I can't pronounce," and some dessert that sounds disgusting with a price tag that I can't really afford. Then there are several speakers who think that if you don't talk for at least twenty minutes apiece, they aren't giving a good speech. I can't tell you how many times I've gone to an event like this and stopped at Taco Bell on the way home because I didn't get enough to eat at the hundred dollars-a-plate dinner.

I also can't tell you how many times I've been to events like this and made a new friend or met someone who played a prominent role in my ministry later on. I've met one of my doctors at an event like this. I've gotten ideas for sermons and reflections from conversations at some of these events. When I go to one of these events, I have to remind myself to be positive, to look for positive possibilities. If all I think of is negative things, I will have virtually no chance for any positive outcome.

Whether one feels encouraged and uplifted often depends on what they bring to the table. And whether one encourages or discourages others often depends on the same. Coming at a situation with indifference or worse will make for a "blah" experience, just like the experience of greeting people described in *The Energy Bus*. Coming at a situation with enthusiasm, even a situation we'd rather not be in, can turn something from being dreaded to actually being positive. Playing off the title of this book, does your life resemble an "energy bus" filled with energy, enthusiasm, and positivity? Or does your bus resemble an indifference bus, filled with negativity?

Something as simple as a smile versus a scowl changes energy and perspective. I was recently with two people both of whom I actually approached with a degree of intimidation. One of them smiled throughout our conversation and made me feel welcome and important. Though this is someone I didn't know well at all, I left with a positive impression and can't wait to interact with him again. The other scowled throughout the conversation and never made me feel comfortable; in fact, it's like he intentionally kept me off-balance. It was a relief when that conversation ended. It not only left me with a negative impression but a degree of trepidation when it comes to future conversations.

So much of how we deal with situations and people that come our way is dependent on our perspective, on how we approach them—do we come with energy or indifference? And so much of how we impact others is also based on perspective—do we approach with a smile or a scowl?

The above Bible verse is part of the Beatitudes, prescriptions for daily living as they have been called by many. We are reminded that when we are reviled and slandered, we should feel blessed; in fact, Christ tells us that we should "rejoice and be glad" (Matt. 5:12). If we make it a goal to rejoice and be glad in both good times and bad, to bring positive energy even to a negative situation, and wear a smile instead of a frown, it will make a difference, not only in our lives but in the lives of those around us.

Encouragers bring energy, positivity, and a smile. That doesn't mean that encouragers don't sometimes lack energy, positivity, or get sad. However, it means that they strive for energy and positivity, and they begin from this perspective.

Lord, thank You for the gift of a new day. Even if this day will be filled with challenges, thank You that I am alive to face them. Help me to see the good in situations and people today. Help me to have energy, even when I feel tired. Help me to be positive, even when I'm down. And help me to smile, even when I'm upset. Put people into my path today to need some positive energy, and give me the wisdom and patience to offer these things to them. Amen.

Encouragement Challenge: Bring energy, positivity, and a smile to whatever you do and whoever you meet today!

Breaking the Cycle—I Will Not Do That Today

Bear fruit that befits repentance.
Matthew 3:8

This reflection will focus on two words, repentance and habits. Repentance is a change of orientation so that one is pointed more toward God. Repentance is the antidote to sin. Sin is missing the mark and falling away from God. Repentance is when we correct our course so that we are pointed at God. Our life on earth involves a continual struggle to create habits that point us in the direction of God while avoiding habits that take us away from Him. Because we all have the inclination to sin, we have to also develop an inclination to repent.

In the battle of sin versus repentance, our daily habits will play a role in which wins. For example, a daily habit of prayer is important in fighting the battle against sin and toward repentance. Prayer, at the moment we are doing it, orients us toward God. We can't be sinning and praying at the same time. Sin happens at the moments when we are not praying. Theoretically, the more we pray, the less we sin. And the less we pray, the more open we are to sinning. Because in the *moment* of prayer, we are not capable of gossiping or harming our neighbor, and the majority of sins involve failing to love our neighbor.

All of us have bad habits. Habits are things we do on a regular basis, some even without thinking. Other habits are known to us—maybe we have a habit of drinking too much, gossiping or swearing, looking at pornography, judging, looking at others with envy, overeating, being too negative—the list is endless. And if we are honest, we all do at least a few things habitually wrong.

How does one break a bad habit? How does one stop a negative cycle? I've read that it takes thirty days to create a new habit. So, whether that means eating better or exercising or whatever we are trying to do better, if we do it for thirty days, it has a good chance of becoming a good habit.

To the person who is addicted to a bad habit, thirty days may seem like a very long time. At Alcoholics Anonymous, a support group that helps people stop drinking, the focus is on today. AA doesn't ask or expect an alcoholic to never drink again for the entirety of his or her life. That is too long of a period of time to wrap one's head around. So the focus is on not drinking today. This is why alcoholics go to meetings daily, to make a pledge to not drink today, and then they come back tomorrow to make the same pledge for a new day.

What does any of this have to do with encouragement? Our bad habits discourage us. They cause us to feel down about ourselves, our lives, our relationships, and our relationship with Christ. If you feel down and discouraged because of a bad habit you have, break the cycle of bad behavior by making a pledge to not do the behavior today. Much of what we will discuss in these reflections is to focus on today's challenges and not look at the big picture, which can be daunting.

As you begin each day, make a pledge to avoid a bad habit today. If you get through today, make the same pledge tomorrow. At the same time, make a pledge to work on a good habit today. If you make a step in the right direction, make the same pledge tomorrow. There is no waiting period when it comes to repentance. If you are not in the habit of praying, there isn't a period of probation or punishment until you can pray again; just pray today. If you have some bad habit, stop it today. (As a caveat, there are certain addictions that require professional help—a person with a drug or alcohol addiction will need professional help. Other kinds of addictions are a matter of willpower, such as controlling what we eat or what we say. The addictions that are overcome through willpower should be addressed through prayer. Prayer is a great tool in overcoming bad habits. So is being accountable to someone else).

If you aren't the best at praying or are addicted to some habitual sin, do not despair. Break the cycle of bad behavior and start a cycle of good behavior with a pledge to do the right thing today.

Lord, thank You for the gift of this day and the opportunities it will bring. Help me to avoid temptations (list at least one temptation you will strive to avoid today), and help me to bear fruit that befits repentance and shows love to You and others (list at least one good thing that you will commit to doing today). Give me the strength to avoid temptation and the heart that seeks to do good. Amen.

Encouragement Challenge: As you begin today, affirm something good that you will commit to doing today and make a commitment to avoid a temptation you struggle with today. Bear fruits that befits repentance by avoiding situations that cause you to sin.

Get a Win Today!

(Love) does not rejoice at wrong, but rejoices in the right.
1 Corinthians 13: 6

Sometimes even the best sports teams go on a losing streak. A major league baseball season lasts 162 games. It is not uncommon that even the best teams will have a losing streak of four or five games during the course of a season. Let's say that a team has lost five games in a row. What do you think their morale is like before their next game? Do you think that they think, *We are terrible?* Professional athletes will tell you that their mindset before every game is "Get a win today!"

Let's say that a team has lost many games in a row and they win on a particular day. What do you think the mood is like after the game? Do you think the team thinks, *Well, we still stink?* Professional athletes will tell you that their mindset after every win is, "We won today. Let's go win tomorrow."

In life, sometimes we go on "losing streaks." We go through a bad time at work, in marriage, with our children, even with our faith. We have crises and wonder if our marriage is doomed, our kids will not be successful adults, our jobs will work out, we'll feel overweight forever, or whatever myriad of things causes us to feel discouraged.

One of my best friends has a phrase, "Let's get some wins," which he uses to boost morale of his co-workers when he or they perceive there is a losing streak going on. And this is among the best pieces of advice and encouragement I have ever received. I think of this often. If today is the start of a new day, I haven't gotten in an argument, I haven't eaten poorly, I haven't failed to exercise, I haven't made a mistake at work, and so a "win" today is possible. Yesterday, whether I won or lost, is over. Tomorrow is tomorrow, and tomorrow isn't guaranteed. The challenge is to get a win today.

To the couple whose marriage is not what they want it to be, go on a few dates, have some good days, and get some wins.

To the person who hasn't exercised, go exercise today, and tomorrow, and the next day. Get some wins.

To the person who doesn't have a good work ethic, put in a good effort today, tomorrow, and get some wins.

To the person who doesn't pray or read the Bible, don't count all the days or years you haven't done these. Pray today. Read the Bible today. Get a spiritual win today! And then go for a repeat tomorrow and the next day.

If you've had a lot of wins but have had a few bad days, don't think of the bad days; get right back into winning form. And if you are on a good streak, get a win today and keep it going.

Today is all we have. The "games" of yesterday have already been played. You either won them or lost them. The "games" of tomorrow will not be played today. So play the "game" of today as best you can. And strive to get a win today.

And if you get a win today, celebrate it. Resist the urge to temper the win by already anticipating a future loss. Many people cannot celebrate a win because they are already contemplating the next loss. So, count the wins, and make the wins count; celebrate all of them. And when you've lost, don't despair. Get up tomorrow and go get a win. As the above Scripture verse reminds us, love (and God) rejoices in the right. So when we've done well, celebrate that! And when we've done wrong, correct it so we can celebrate a right, a win.

Lord, thank You for the gift of a new day. Thank You that each new day brings a new opportunity to succeed at something. Help me to focus on the needs and opportunities of today. Help me to focus today on prayer, reading Scripture, and following Your commandments. Help me to have a good work ethic today. Help me to be kind today. Help me to glorify You today. Amen.

Encouragement Challenge: Go get a win today!

**Dedicated to Alkis Crassas, who inspires me and so many others to "count the wins."

Don't Look Past Today

Give us this day our daily bread.
Matthew 6:11

Life is a balancing act, that's for sure. Ideally, we have a healthy balance of sleep, work, and recreation. We have a healthy balance of stress and relaxation, things that are challenging and things that are easy, and time with people and time alone. The truth of the matter is that very few, if any of us, live in balance. Most of us cheat when it comes to sleeping—we don't sleep enough. Most of us cheat when it comes to diet and exercise—we eat too much and don't exercise enough. Most of us are out of balance when it comes to encouragement versus discouragement. Remember the balanced ratio of 5:1, five encouraging things for every one discouraging thing is what keeps us in the encouragement balance. And remember when you are talking to others, how much encouragement versus discouragement you are giving.

I recently had a conversation with a friend of mine, and we were talking about issues with teens and adults today, and the subject of suicide came up. I don't know if it's just me, but it seems that this topic is coming up more and more today, not just with teens but with adults as well. We were discussing our thoughts on why these kinds of things happen. And he said something very profound that I want to share because it not only pertains to suicide but to many of our other life challenges. What he said is basically this:

> I walk my dog two miles a day, which adds up to sixty miles a month and 730 miles a year. That's a lot of miles. I can handle walking the dog two miles a day. If I try to do a month's worth of walking in a day, in other words, if I try to walk sixty miles in a day, I will probably die. My body can't handle walking that much. If I try to do a year's worth of walking in a day, I can't; it's actually impossible.

> This is how our stresses work. When we try to handle a month's worth of stress in one day, it's like trying to do sixty miles of walking in a day. Trying to handle that much stress at once will be debilitating. If we try to handle a year's worth of stress, or a lifetime's worth of stress, we simply cannot do it. And perhaps this is one of the reasons why people turn to measures that are harmful, be it suicide, excessive

drinking or eating, and so on because they are trying to deal with an amount of stress that we are simply not built to handle.

If we think too far ahead, anticipating stressful things that may not even happen, we will quickly sabotage our ability to properly function today. What future stresses cross your mind? Will my kid go to college? Will he get married? Will he have enough money to live on when I'm gone? Will I have enough money to retire on? Will my health be okay? Will I have to move? Will my job become obsolete? Will I get replaced by someone younger and less expensive? Will I suffer before I die—will I get cancer? Stroke? Dementia? Try to tackle all of these questions at one time, and two things are guaranteed—you will not be able to function well in what you are presently doing, and your stress level will go up, affecting your overall health.

This is why, like the example of walking the dog two miles a day, the Bible tells us to worry about the stresses of today and not to look too far ahead. Because we are all able to "walk the dog" two miles a day, but sixty miles will kill us, and 730 miles is impossible. Looking too far ahead on our stresses will make us sick, and looking at a lifetime of stresses and wondering how we will cope with them might make us despair even of life itself.

Therefore, we should focus on the things that are right in front of us, the challenges of today. It is no coincidence that the Lord's Prayer asks God to "Give us this DAY, our DAILY bread." It doesn't ask for our "yearly bread." This phrase refers to when God sent manna from heaven to feed the Israelites in the wilderness in Exodus 16. The people were wandering in the desert. They were discouraged. And God told them He would give them bread/manna, which they would find on the ground each morning, such as what was sufficient for the day. (On Fridays, there would be double the amount so they would have enough for the Sabbath, so they wouldn't have to gather it on the Sabbath and could rest.) He warned them not to store it up; otherwise, it would get worms and be inedible. They had to trust God that He would daily provide for them. And we have to do the same. When we pray the Lord's Prayer, in praying the phrase, "Give us this day our daily bread," we should ask God to give us the things we need to get through today, to be with us in the challenges of today, and help us not get too far ahead in worrying about the challenges that lie beyond today.

On a given day, our needs are actually few. Daily, I pray for five things—safety (since I'm in the car every day), wisdom (to make good decisions), efficiency (to be focused on tasks at hand and get them done as efficiently as possible), patience (a perpetual challenge and also the first quality of love), and to laugh (because I want to have at least one light-hearted moment each day). I have recently added a sixth thing to my prayers, asking God to give me an opportunity to serve someone. Thus, on a given day, I don't pray about our son going to college, retirement, or other things that are in the far future. Today is the first building block toward the future. If today goes well, it's one step closer to the future I hope to have. Plus, we can only handle so much stress, and the challenges of today will be stressful enough.

Our Father, who art in heaven, hallowed be Thy name. Thy Kingdom come, Thy will be done, on earth as it is in heaven. Give us this day our daily bread, and forgive us our trespasses as we forgive those who trespass against us. And lead us not into temptation, but deliver us from evil. For Thine is the Kingdom and the power and the glory, of the Father and of the Son and of the Holy Spirit, now and forever, and to the ages of ages. Amen.

Encouragement Challenge: Focus on the needs and challenges of today, and enjoy the opportunities that today brings as well! Don't try to "walk sixty miles" today. Just "walk two."

**Dedicated to Dr. Pete Copsis, a dear friend and valued encourager in my life.

MAKE EACH MOMENT COUNT

Therefore, do not be anxious about tomorrow, for tomorrow will be anxious for itself. Let the day's own trouble be sufficient for the day.
Matthew 6:34

In the last reflection, we discussed the importance of focusing on today. In this reflection, we focus on the importance of each moment of the day. For some, even the day is overwhelming, and it's important to focus on the moments throughout the day. Here's what I mean:

Despite that popularity of the term multitasking, it is really not possible to do more than one important task at a time. I can fold laundry while watching TV, as neither of those actions requires much brain power. I can talk on the phone while driving (if wearing an earpiece) or washing dishes. But if I'm doing something important, I can only do one thing at a time because at any given time, I have many things to do on my task list, and I have to focus on one task at a time to get any of the tasks done. But what happens when there is an event or appointment that is not on my task list? It is very easy to keep my mind on the list and away from the event if I'm not careful.

For instance, on many days, there is a church service in the morning. That commits me to two hours in the church. Doing those two hours, I cannot talk on the phone, sit at the computer, or meet with anyone. So, I have two choices during that two-hour period. I can either put all other thoughts of tasks out of my mind and focus on worship, or I can worry and brood over the tasks that I'm not getting done, and after two hours, I will not have worshiped or gotten any tasks done. I will have wasted two hours.

It's the same thing when I visit a hospital or meet with someone for counseling. I can either be *with them*, putting aside thoughts of other tasks, or I can be distracted with other thoughts, and this, again, wastes time; the tasks don't get done, and I'm not present with the person in front of me.

Regardless of what roles you have in your life, the scenario plays out in some way for all of us. Imagine your child needs help with their homework or asks you to play a game with them. You are preoccupied with writing Christmas cards and then paying bills. But you decide to be with your child. If you've made the decision to be with your child, then **BE WITH YOUR CHILD** because if you are trying to be with your child while thinking of something else, you won't get the something else done, and you won't be with your child either.

Many attempts at multitasking actually result in wasting time with no tasks being accomplished.

Being 100 percent present is something we really have to learn and strive for. With the phones and other media almost constantly available at our fingertips, there is a constant temptation to multitask or be distracted.

I'm still learning how to be present all the time and not get distracted. The moment that we are in is the only moment we have. Whatever happened an hour ago is over, and there is no guarantee there will be a next hour, really for any of us. Thus, we need to learn to make each moment count.

Imagine if we all made it a goal to make the person in front of us at any given moment the most important person in our lives. We've already discussed how our neighbor is the person closest to us at any given moment. So, imagine if when you are talking to someone, you view them as the most important person in your life because at that given moment, they are. When I meet with someone in my office, it's just the two of us. My wife is not present, our son is not present, and other parishioners are not present. My world, for that moment, has been reduced to one person. Ideally, that person should be treated as the most important person in the world because, for that moment, that person is my entire world.

The encouragement of this reflection is to focus on your day one moment at a time and treat each person you meet as if they were the most important person in the world because for the moments you are together, they actually are your whole world. Multitasking is okay when it comes to tasks that require little thought and no emotion. But when dealing with people and problems, it's really best and most respectful to deal with them one thing at a time. Finally, prayer is not a task you can combine with something else. We can't multitask when it comes to our quality time with the Lord. Time with God should be single-focused; it should just be about you and Him.

Of course, there is one critical way we can all multitask. We can give glory to God while doing any task. When it comes to glorifying God, we should be constantly multitasking.

Lord, thank You for the gift of today. Help me to make the most of this day by being focused and present with the people I will encounter today and in the tasks that I will attempt today. Help me to treat each person I encounter as if they were the most important person in the world during the time I spend with them. And help me to maintain a clear mind, so that I can focus on one task at a time and not become overwhelmed. Help me to glorify You in all the tasks and with all the people I will encounter today. Amen.

Encouragement Challenge: Be present in whatever you do today. And take today one moment at a time. Focus on one task at a time, and you'll find that you won't waste as much time.

A Lot of It Won't Matter Next Week

Consider the lilies of the field, how they grow; their neither toil nor spin; yet I tell you, even Solomon in all his glory was not arrayed like one of these. But if God so clothes the grass of the field, which today is alive and tomorrow is thrown into the oven, will He not much more clothe you, O men of little faith?
Matthew 6:28–30

I'm a planner. I like making plans. When I make plans, I have a hard time sometimes when those plans don't go just as I planned them.

One summer afternoon, I was mowing the lawn when dark clouds gathered overhead as they are prone to do on summer afternoons in Florida. So, I picked up the pace on my lawn mowing, anticipating that a thunderstorm would happen in the not too distant future. It started to rain lightly, but I was undeterred. I was determined to finish what I had started. Then it started to rain harder. And my resolve was even greater, even as my shoes became soaked. It began to thunder nearby, and then it began to thunder even more loudly. My ego took over. No way would I stop mowing; I must finish what I started. I can't stand the thought of looking at a half-mowed lawn for any amount of time. Then lightning struck very close to where I was working.

I started thinking as I frantically ran around the soaked yard, *Is finishing this job worth dying for? Will it really matter a week from now if I didn't finish this job?* I started thinking that if I got struck by lightning, that would have permanent catastrophic consequences for my family. I could die and leave my wife without a husband and my child without a father. I thought better of it, put the lawn mower away, and went into the house.

Two days later, I decided to mow the entire lawn again—yes, I'm obsessed with my lawn.

The lesson I learned that day is that we often get anxious about stuff that truly doesn't matter. It wouldn't change the course of my life if the lawn didn't get mowed during a rainstorm. However, if I got struck by lightning, my life would change. And as I thought about it, I wondered how many things in life that we stress out about won't matter next year, next month, next week, or even the next day. The truth is that a lot of things we stress and get angry about really don't matter. In the big span of life, it doesn't matter if the fries at McDonald's were cold or that I bought a pair of shoes I ended up not liking.

There are some things that truly do matter—a job promotion and our children getting into college. A lot of things really do not. So when you are deciding whether to stress out about something today, ask yourself, "Will this matter next year, next month, next week, or tomorrow?" If it will matter next year, then fight for it. If it won't matter tomorrow, don't stress out about it.

I remember my high school English teacher my senior year, Mr. P. Mr. P made our class do a timed write for ten minutes each day. If you didn't turn in anything, you got an "F." I remember at the beginning of the school year, students would complain that they couldn't think of anything to write. And occasionally throughout the year, even I couldn't think of things to write. Mr. P. said, "We have 185 days of school. Having writer's block on a few of them and getting an "F" won't be a big deal. Over the course of the semester, you have to be consistent. But on a particular day, if you can't get it done, don't stress." Yes, I had a few failing days but still got an "A" in the class, and Mr. P. is the one I credit with my ability to write quickly. He also taught me a valuable lesson about stress. Sometimes the failure of today matters tomorrow. But many times, it doesn't.

Whether you are failing at writing today or failing to get your lawn cut before the rain starts, ask yourself, will this matter next week or next month or tomorrow, and that will tell you whether it is worth stressing about today.

Lord, help me to discern the needs of today. Help me to manage the responsibilities that I must complete today. Help me to not stress about things I cannot control. Help me to be efficient in my tasks, to give my best effort in all things, and to make good decisions about which things I should stress about and which things I shouldn't. Walk with me in my decisions and in my work today. Amen.

Encouragement Challenge: Ask yourself when confronted with stress today—will this matter tomorrow? Or next week? Next month? Next year? And then act accordingly.

You Can Rewrite the Narrative

A man had two sons; and he went to the first and said, "Son, go and work in the vineyard today." And he answered, "I will not"; but afterward he repented and went. And he went to the second and said the same; and he answered, "I go, sir" but did not go. Which of the two did the will of his father?" They said, "The first." Jesus said to them, "Truly, I say to you, the tax collectors and the harlots go into the kingdom of God before you. For John came to you in the way of righteousness, and you did not believe him, but the tax collectors and harlots believed him; and even when you saw it, you did not afterward repent and believe.
Matthew 21:28–32

I read a book entitled *Addicted to the Monkey Mind: Changing the Programming that Sabotages Your Life* by J. F. Benoist. The thesis of this book is that we each have two competing voices in our head, a monkey mind, and an observing mind. The monkey mind are voices from our past, many put there by our parents, that guide the narrative of our lives at present. For instance, if our parents told us, "Be careful, you'll fail," then as an adult, people most likely will approach decisions expecting to fail. If a dad tells his son never to cry when the boy skins his knees, when he becomes a man, he may think it's never okay to cry, and he will not be emotionally balanced. The observing mind, on the other hand, is not handicapped by voices of the past and treats opportunities and challenges with a sense of possibility rather than resignation.

We are constantly writing the narrative of our lives and accumulating new voices of the monkey mind. For instance, a husband may lose the trust of his wife because he spends too many hours at the office. Then he does a better job of coming home earlier and spending more time with family. All seems well. Occasionally, he does have to work late. However, each time it happens, his wife starts to not trust him again because she is stuck in a narrative that he works too much and doesn't prioritize his family. No matter what he does, he can't seem to change her narrative.

The same thing can be said for the husband who feels neglected by his wife because she puts all her energy on the kids and never has energy left for him. She works hard to leave energy for him, but many times, something does come up. Even when they have a date night, he has a hard time relaxing because he thinks something inevitably will come up, she'll cancel the date, and go home early. She can't seem to change his narrative.

The above Scripture passage is about two sons who rewrote their story. One corrected a mistake while the other flaked on a commitment. A father addressed his two sons, asking each to go work in the vineyard. The first son refused but later repented and went to work in the vineyard. The second agreed to go but later did not go. The father, in his mind, had a narrative going about each son—he must have been disappointed in the first son and pleased with the second. Imagine if he was stuck in that narrative. He would have been disappointed despite the repentance of the first son.

This passage is encouragement to rewrite our narratives when they are wrong. When we've done wrong to someone, we should repent and do better. When we have been wronged by someone, we should allow them to repent.

It is not a stretch to say that I have sinned against and disappointed everyone I've ever known for any significant amount of time. It's inevitable that anyone we spend a significant amount of time with we will wrong at some point. So, who are the people we wrong the most? Our spouses, children, parents, close friends, and bosses. It is very easy to get stuck in a negative narrative with the people we are around the most.

We read in Psalm 130:3–4: "If Thou, O Lord, shouldst mark iniquities, Lord, who could stand? But there is forgiveness with Thee." Imagine if the Lord kept a narrative going on each of us based on our iniquities. As we read in the psalm, none of us would stand a chance before Him. If we hope for mercy from the Lord, we should extend mercy to one another. If we don't want the Lord to get stuck in a negative narrative about us, we should be willing to change the negative narrative we have on each other.

One of the greatest gifts we can give one another is to allow someone to rewrite their narrative through repentance and offer forgiveness and mercy. One of the most humbling and vulnerable things we can do is ask for forgiveness and ask to rewrite our narrative. Ideally, both parties work in sync for this to happen, one offering repentance while the other offers forgiveness. This is done with humility, trust, and patience.

Lord, please give me the humility to see when I have done wrong. Please give me the courage to repent. Please give me the grace to offer forgiveness to others. Help us to rewrite bad narratives and see others in Your light. Amen.

The negative narrative can be rewritten through forgiveness and repentance.

Have a Great Day! Really, It's Okay

This is the day which the Lord has made; let us rejoice and be glad in it.
Psalm 118:24

How are you?

What is the typical answer to this question? It's generally one of the following:

"I'm fine," which may or may not be the case. It's a polite answer.

Or, "I'm busy," which we use so often that "I'm busy" has become synonymous with "I'm alive." Another answer is, "I'm stressed."

When someone says, "I'm great, couldn't be better," we will almost automatically put that in the "I'm fine" category. And if someone really convinces us "I'm great, couldn't be better," we might send them a look of consternation in return because most of us aren't great or don't allow ourselves to feel great, and we become indignant about people who actually are.

There are people who actually feel great are afraid to let people know that since they think they will be looked down upon because the expected answer to "How are you?" is to say, "I'm busy" or "I'm stressed out," even if we are neither, and we feel pressured to conform by offering these answers. And there are some who don't allow themselves to have a good day. They wear their badge of tired, busy, or stressed out, with pride, like a badge of honor. It is sad to say, we might think people are weird when they say they are having a great day.

Does the question, "How are you doing?" get an honest answer? I'm sure the majority of the time the answer is the pat, "I'm doing fine." If someone says, "I'm struggling," they probably fear either being ignored (i.e., no one has time for someone who is struggling), judged (looked down on), or that someone will have something on them they can use against them later. And to answer, "I'm doing great" will be met again with consternation and even jealousy because most people aren't doing great.

Having a great day is something I hope happens to us often. The above verse from Psalm 118:24 says, "This is the day which the Lord has made; let us rejoice and be glad in it." It doesn't say, "let us struggle in it," "let us survive it," or "let us be exasperated in it." We are encouraged to rejoice and be glad in it. Many people struggle with this. Some even feel guilt, I'm guessing, that if they don't feel exasperated on a given day, they haven't made the most of the day as if the person who doesn't answer, "I'm busy," will be looked down upon.

If you are someone who never has a great day, you might consider talking to someone about that, like a priest or mental health professional because we should have great days. God wants us to have great days. Certainly not every day will be great, but some of them need to be. God wants everyone to have good days. So when people around us are feeling good and optimistic, we should celebrate with them, not throw a wet blanket over their feelings of joy.

A person can feel "blessed" even on a bad day because even on my worst day, on my most stressful days, I can feel blessed that I am alive, I am a Christian, I'm married and have a child, and I have a home and food. I have a lot of blessings, and I should recognize them, even on my stressful days, or even most especially on those days.

As for having a great day, I hope for every day to be a great day. Not all of them are great, but some of them sure are. It's hard to feel great around people who are down. So when we are down, we should at least find some joy for people who aren't feeling down. And we should wish others to have a great day; we should hope for that for them. We should hope for that for one another.

I have worked hard to drop three words from my vocabulary—busy, tired, and try. I'm always busy; most people are. So, I work hard to find different words instead of busy. As I said above, saying, "I'm busy" is almost like saying, "I'm alive" because just about everyone is busy. "Tired" is reserved for special occasions. That's because most people feel tired on a given day since all of us are stressed, and very few of us sleep enough. At the end of Holy Week or summer camp, I allow myself to say I'm tired. Finally, the word "try." In Star Wars, Yoda says, "Try out! Do or do not; there is no try." And he's right, we are either doing or not doing. There really is no try.

A "great day" is part of my vocabulary, perhaps not every day but on many days. I encourage you to wish for others to have a great day and for you to allow yourselves to have great days as well. No, they won't all be great, but many of them certainly can be. Part of being an encourager is being optimistic, for appreciating the good that comes our way, as well as appreciating the good that comes to others. The goal of every day should be a great day. And we should start off every day with optimism, that any day can be a good day. If we see every day as a gift from God, regardless of what kind of day it is, any day can really be a great day.

Lord, thank You for the gift of this day. Regardless of what happens to me today, I know that I am blessed to be alive on this day. Help me to see the possibilities for good things to happen this day. May I rejoice in the successes of others, and may they rejoice in mine. Help me to remember that this day is a gift from You. May I glorify You in this day, whatever it shall hold for me. Amen.

Have a great day! Really!

Is That Even Possible? Yes, It Is

Rejoice always.
1 Thessalonians 5:16

This verse from 1 Thessalonians is really challenging. It is not challenging to comprehend. We know the meaning of the word rejoice. It means "to celebrate." And always means "all the time." But what does that really mean in the context of our lives? Is this idea even possible?

The original Greek translation of this verse is *pantote hairete*. For those who don't know Greek, *pantote* means "atall times"[19] and *hairete* means "rejoice."[20] *Hairete* has an etymological connection with the word *hara*, which means "joy,"[21] and *haris*, which means "grace."[22] So, if the word rejoice is connected with both joy and grace, it is certainly possible at any moment in time to experience God's grace, even in moments when we are not having human joy.

Is it possible to rejoice at all times? In human terms, this is not possible. No one rejoices when they are sick, when they have failed, or when they are scared. There is no joy in losing a job, getting in a car accident, or finding out that your child is failing a class. Yet in all these moments, there can be *haris* or grace.

In 2 Corinthians 12:1–10, St. Paul writes to us about a struggle he was having. He writes that he had *"visions and revelations of the Lord"* (12:1). This abundance of revelations brought joy to St. Paul, just as positive things bring joy to our lives. However, this joy was tempered. St. Paul writes in 12:7 *"and to keep me from being too elated by the abundance of revelations, a thorn was given me in the flesh, a messenger of Satan, to harass me, to keep me from being too elated."* We can all relate to the *"thorn in the flesh."* How many times have we experienced life going well, only for us to be hamstrung by something or someone that keeps a situation from being what it could be. St. Paul even had the human reaction of complaining to the Lord about it: *"Three times I besought the Lord about this, that it should leave me"* (12:8).

The answer of the Lord to St. Paul is profound, and provides the answer to our challenge to *"rejoice always."* In 12:9–10, we read:

> *"But He said to me, "My grace is sufficient for you, for My power is made perfect in weakness." I will all the more gladly boast of my weaknesses, that the power of Christ may rest upon me. For the sake of Christ, then, I am content with weaknesses, insults, hardships, persecutions, and calamities; for when I am weak, then I am strong."*

We may not always be able to rejoice. We may not always feel joy. But God's grace is something that is accessible at all times. When we have the grace of God, when we feel God's grace through prayer and the sacraments, then we can feel joy even in the midst of sorrow. We can feel strong even when we are weak.

If *"every good and perfect gift is from above"* (James 1:17), and encouragement is a good thing, then grace can come upon us from the encouragement of others. If being a Christian is all about loving both God and our neighbor, then God's grace shines, not only through His love but through the loving gestures of our neighbors. Thus, encouragement helps us experience grace, which brings joy even in times of struggle. Think for a moment how your spirits are lifted by someone else's encouragement. Even their mere presence can be encouraging. For instance, when we are sick, and someone comes for a visit, their visit doesn't bring healing, but it brings encouragement, which leads to joy and is made possible by the mystical grace of God that often comes through other people.

So, can we rejoice always? The answer is, we can experience *haris* (grace) at all times, and *haris*, whether it comes directly from God or through someone else, leads us to *hara* (joy). Grace makes it possible to rejoice even in times of sadness. And encouragement from others is a key ingredient.

Lord, thank You for the gift of grace that is poured out upon us in so many ways. Thank You for putting people in my life who encourage and lift me up, especially when my spirits are down. Help me also to be someone who lifts up and encourages others. As You allow Your grace to come into me through the encouragement of others, allow Your grace to flow through me so that I may encourage others as well. Amen.

Encouragement Challenge: Lift someone's spirits today!

Part Seven
PRAY CONSTANTLY

Pray constantly.

1 Thessalonians 5:17

Encouragement to Pray

In these days, He went out to the mountain to pray; and all night He continued in prayer to God. And when it was day, He called His disciples, and chose from them twelve, whom He named apostles.
Luke 6:11–12

What is prayer? How do we pray? Why do we pray?

If we truly understand the answers to these questions, prayer will become more of a joy in our lives. Many people approach prayer the way that someone approaches a vending machine. They offer a prayer and expect an answer, the same way that when one approaches a vending machine, they put money in and get a product out, and not just any product but the one they specifically want. The problem with looking at prayer like a vending machine is twofold. First, we only go to the vending machine when we are hungry—most people don't go to the vending machine every day or multiple times a day. So, one problem with the vending machine approach to prayer is that in doing it this way, we only go to God in prayer when we need something.

Second, the vending machine spits out whatever candy or soda we punched the button for. If it put out something different, most certainly we wouldn't use it. The second problem with the vending machine approach to prayer is when God doesn't answer our prayer (or let's call it request or order because that's more accurate), we stop going to Him; we become discouraged from praying.

Prayer, simply put, is being with God. In the above Scripture verses, we see that Jesus was about to make an important decision. He had many disciples and was going to choose from them twelve who would be His apostles. Before making this important decision, Jesus went out to a mountain to pray, and He offered prayer continuously all night. Those who pray using the vending machine model are not likely to pray all night. They make their quick deposit and expect a quick answer. Jesus did not approach prayer like a vending machine. Instead, He approached prayer as sacred time with God the Father, and thus He went by Himself up to the mountain to pray, be with God, speak with Him, and listen to Him before making the important decision He was about to make.

What is prayer? Prayer is simply communicating with God, being with God.

Why do we pray? Prayer is an act of intimacy with God, where we speak, not to another human being but to the Divine God Himself. In prayer, we also hear from God. How is that? We don't necessarily hear an audible voice from God in answer to the things we say to Him. In establishing an intimacy of prayer, God stirs our hearts. In prayer, our hearts become open to "hearing" God's thoughts.

I can't tell you how many times I have been in a prayerful state, and God has put a thought on my heart or mind. For instance, many times I'm counseling someone, hearing them pour their heart out and crying about their problems and challenges. I often pray as I'm listening for God to give me a thought that provide guidance, direction, and encouragement to the person I am with. More times than I can count, a profound thought comes to my head, and I share it with them. Other times, a thought comes that surprises me, that seems to not relate at all to what is being discussed. And again, more times than I can count, I have shared what seems like an odd thought, and it ends up being just what the person needs to hear. I do not pray to God for material gain or even to do well at something. In my work, I pray only for God to guide my mind and my mouth so that I can be helpful in representing Him to others.

As for how we are to pray, let's first discuss how not to pray. Christ tells us not to make a spectacle of our prayers (Matt. 6:5–6) or heap up empty phrases (Matt. 6:7). While it is not necessary to pray out loud, especially when one is alone, I often choose to pray out loud, even when alone because it slows down my thoughts. I imagine if someone is standing next to me, and I speak slow enough that if someone were there, what I was praying would be easily understood. If we spoke at the speed we are thinking, no one would probably understand us. Slow prayer down. It's not the amount of words we offer and certainly not the speed at which we offer them that is important. It is that we offer them, that we offer them with honesty and sincerity, that we open ourselves up to God in a way that is intimate and vulnerable, and that we are patient in listening to the thoughts that God puts into our hearts when we are in a prayerful state.

While we ideally put aside specific time to pray each morning and night and also to pray at certain moments of the day, the most important thing about prayer is neither the amount of words of prayer nor even the amount of time we spend. Prayer is about a soft and sincere heart that longs for God, that longs to open itself to hear God's voice. Whether one prays from a book of prayers or from the heart, it is offering prayer that matters.

Lord, I know not what to ask of You. You alone know what my true needs are. You love me more than I know how to love. Help me to see my real needs which may be hidden from me. I dare not ask for either a cross or a consolation. I can only wait upon You; my heart is open to You. Visit and help me in Your steadfast love. Strike me and heal me; cast me down and raise me up. I worship in silence, Your holy will. I offer myself to You as a living sacrifice. I put all my trust in You. I have no other desire than to fulfill Your will. Teach me to pray. Pray Yourself in me. Amen.[23]

Encouragement Challenge: Pray today!

Little Bits Add Up to a Lot

Pray Constantly
1 Thessalonians 5:17

I work constantly. I write constantly.

Are these true statements? I guess that depends on how one defines constantly. In one sense, I do not do either of these constantly, as I spend time each day not working and not writing. When I'm sleeping, having dinner with my family, watching sports, or reading a magazine, I am not doing either. In another sense, though, I do engage in these things constantly in that I work throughout the day, and rarely a day goes by that I'm not writing.

One could look at the verse *"pray constantly"* in several ways. One can see this verse as unattainable and entirely dismiss it. After all, who, other than someone living in a monastery, can "pray constantly?" Most of us have jobs and families to tend to, houses to keep up, and most of us need down time where we do nothing more than relax. Unfortunately, this is the way that many people read this verse, and they just dismiss it, along with other verses of the Bible, almost entirely.

To pray constantly is to utter the words of prayer frequently throughout the day. Hopefully you begin the day with prayer. One does not need to pray for a long time to benefit from prayer, but spending a few minutes in prayer is important because it sets the tone of the day. There are other opportunities to pray during the day—before and after meals, before driving somewhere, and when you arrive at your destination, before you begin a task, before a meeting, before a conversation, and at the end of the day. These prayers can be short:

Lord, keep me safe in my journey to work. Amen.

Lord, bless me in the task I am about to begin, help me to be efficient, and glorify You in my work. Amen.

Lord be with me as I go into this meeting. Amen.

The Roman Catholics have a prayer called the Rosary, which is said repeatedly and is very short, so one can easily remember and repeat it. The Orthodox Christian church has a prayer called the Jesus Prayer. It is even shorter than the Rosary but works in much the same manner. It is a repetitive prayer that can be done over and over again, in time to your breath, at any time in any place. The prayer is: *Lord, Jesus Christ, Son of God, have mercy on me, a sinner.* This prayer is sometimes combined with a metanoia, or a prostration, which means that one bends at the waist and bows to touch the floor. While is it not necessary to do prostrations when praying, I realize that on a given day, I do at least a dozen "prostrations" without even trying—tying my shoes, picking up my bag, plugging and unplugging my phone, and when I drop things. And each time I do, I offer the Jesus Prayer. After years of doing this, I offer it almost unconsciously every time I bend at the waist for any reason.

Short prayers throughout the day add up to a good amount of daily prayer. Prayers throughout the day keep us checked in with God almost constantly. They remind us His love constantly. They remind us to glorify and serve Him constantly. They remind us to love Him and love our neighbor constantly. So, build a "habit" of prayer each morning and build in a habit of short prayers throughout the day.

Lord, Jesus Christ, Son of God, have mercy on me a sinner.

Lord, be with me today.

Lord, bless my interactions with people.

Give me wisdom in my decisions.

Help me be efficient with my time.

Allow me to glorify You in all the things I do today. Amen.

Encouragement Challenge: See how many short prayers you can offer today.

Are You a Good Quarterback?

Rejoice in your hope, be patient in tribulation, be constant in prayer.
Romans 12:12

In a football game, a team will typically run seventy offensive plays. Before each play, the offense will huddle, the quarterback will call a play, and the team will line up to run the play. There is a critical step that is made between the huddle and the running of the play, and that is that the quarterback will look over the defensive alignment of the other team and evaluate whether the play he called will work. If he doesn't like what he sees, he will "call an audible," a code of numbers, letters, and words that changes the play to something that will work better. This evaluation takes only seconds, yet without it, many plays will fail. No successful quarterback is so egotistical that he thinks every play he calls in the huddle will work. No successful quarterback doesn't do this evaluation before he runs a play. And when you watch a game, if you don't know the score, you won't be able to tell which quarterback is on the winning team or the losing team because they do the same evaluation regardless of the score.

In our lives, just like with the football team, we call about seventy plays a day; we make about seventy decisions each day. Unlike the football team, probably half of those decisions don't really matter. It doesn't really matter if you eat pizza or pasta for lunch. It doesn't really matter if you fold the laundry or put away the dishes first.

However, on a given day, there are probably thirty-five decisions (thirty-five plays) that really do matter, that will alter the course of the day and perhaps even the course of our lives. If you are running late, there is a decision to drive like normal or like a maniac. If you have to confront a co-worker, there is a decision to be calm, irrational, firm, or be non-confrontational. If you have to bring up a touchy subject with your spouse or your children, there is a question of how to do that. Which task to take on first at work? Is it worth getting upset with your child's teacher for a grade that seems unfair? And on and on.

Many of us make these decisions (call these plays) with our gut instinct. We don't necessarily take time to evaluate a decision and think through whether it is a good decision. That is why most of us make bad decisions at times.

Imagine if we did what the quarterback of the football team does if we took time to evaluate a decision or even a thought before we put it in play. This evaluation is prayer. Imagine offering a quick prayer before executing every important decision we make in a day. Like the quarterback on the football team, that quick pause might cause us to change our play. Now imagine never evaluating a decision. Not only will that result in many mistakes, but it will also make us egotistical, thinking that we never do wrong.

For most people, it is a challenge to pray. And one of the greatest challenges is finding the time to pray. Praying quickly before executing the thirty-five or so important decisions we make each day is a great way to pray often and will result in us making better decisions because we will have evaluated our decisions, not just from the standpoint of their successful outcome, but more importantly, we will evaluate whether our decisions are in line with what Christ teaches.

Prayer not only helps us experience intimacy with God, but it also helps us to keep ourselves in line with how God teaches us to live; it helps us to be holy and set apart, as He has called us to be. Imagine going into a difficult confrontation with a co-worker, and immediately before this confrontation, you pray, "Lord, help me to be kind." It will be near impossible to, in the next breath, confront the co-worker and be unkind because you have just asked God for help in being kind.

In these situations, while we can pray for God for the co-worker to be kind, that may or may not happen. Rather, we should pray to God to help us in how we behave since this is something we control.

A great way to improve our prayer life is to offer short prayers throughout the day, asking God to help guide our decisions. This will help us make better decisions, fewer mistakes, and keep our lives and decisions more Christ-centered and in line with Him.

Lord, each day I make many decisions. Give me the wisdom to make sound decisions, the patience to evaluate my decisions and the discipline to include You, through prayer, in all the important decisions I will make today. Amen.

Encouragement Challenge: Invite Christ into your decision-making process by making prayer part of your important decisions each day!

Alone with God

And after Jesus had dismissed the crowds, He went up on the mountain by Himself to pray. When evening came, He was there alone.
Matthew 14:23

Encouragement and discouragement are opposites. Both are present in our everyday lives, just like good and evil are opposites, and there is a presence of both in our lives. We know that everything that is good comes from God, as we read in James 1:17, "Every good and perfect gift is from Above." We know that encouragement is a good thing, and it takes a special person to be an encourager. We also know that the devil constantly tries to thwart the encourager, as he does with anyone that tried to do anything good.

It is critical then, for the encourager to maintain a good disposition of the heart. The heart needs to be continually conditioned so that it is always ready to encourage.

Part of what is needed to be a good encourager is to see yourself in a good light. Of course, it is important to be honest; we all have things we can improve upon. However, avoid things like negative self-talk and allowing negative thoughts to take root in your mind. These things thwart both our own sense of feeling encouraged and our ability to encourage others.

The best way to maintain readiness to encourage is to maintain a close relationship with God. Taking time alone each day to pray and meditate on Scriptures is essential. While faith is shared and celebrated and grown in the context of community, at the core of faith is a personal relationship with the Lord. And this is cultivated first and foremost through personal prayer and reading Scripture.

Christ set an example for us to pray, as we are told in Matthew 14:23 that He went up a mountain alone to pray with God. He wasn't constantly with the multitudes. He had a small group of friends, His disciples, and He wasn't even around them all the time. He took time out to pray, to spend time with God. If even the Son of God took time to pray, it is incumbent on each of us to do so as well.

Prayer need not be for long periods of time. The focus of prayer also does not need to be the amount of words that are said. "Lord, have mercy" is a prayer that can be repeated over and over again, the same with the Jesus Prayer, "Lord Jesus Christ, Son of God, have mercy on me, a sinner." Prayer and Scripture reading are about BEING in the presence of God. The focus isn't on talking or asking or getting. It's about being with God.

I can't tell you how many times I have found both answers to problems and comfort during stressful times in prayer and Scripture. The Bible contains so many passages, and you are certain to find passages that will speak directly to you. When you become familiar with the Bible, you will find "go-to" passages for the various life circumstances and challenges that come your way.

As for reading the Bible, read one chapter or only a few verses. Read a book of the Bible or read a random page. Read the Bible though. If you've never read the Bible, start with the Gospels and read through them several times so that you understand the life and teachings of Christ. And then move to the Epistles and then to the Old Testament.

Being an encourager doesn't require a lot of preparation. However, being a consistent encourager requires some routine maintenance of your soul. So, keep your soul fed with prayer and Scripture, and you will be better at many things in life, including encouraging others.

Another way to look at alone time with God is to compare it to recharging your phone or favorite electronic device. The phones don't just go and go and go. They need recharging. Most of us recharge the phones daily, and some of us even recharge in the middle of the day. Phones won't recharge if we don't plug them in. Like the phones, we work better when we are recharged. And we recharge our spirits when we plug in to Scripture and prayer and spend some time with our charger, God.

Lord, thank You that I am alive today to offer this prayer to You. Help me to understand that I have a need to recharge every day, and spending time with You is not a chore but a joy. Help me to better comprehend Scripture. Allow me to hear Your voice come through in prayer and Scripture so that I can receive not only spiritual renewal but needed guidance. Thank You for the gift of today. Amen.

Encouragement Challenge: Pray and read Scripture today! Spend time alone with God each day!

How to Pray: 5-5-5-1

As a hart longs for flowing streams, so longs my soul for Thee,
O God. My soul thirsts for God, for the living God.
Psalm 42:1–2

Many Christians do not know how to pray. Most know the Lord's Prayer, and for many, their knowledge of prayer ends with the Lord's Prayer. I can't remember in my childhood anyone teaching us how to construct a prayer. In fact, if anything, we were taught that prayer was like a vending machine. Insert prayer, wait for, and expect an answer. We never understood that prayer was simply being with God. And we never were taught the proper words to offer in prayer and that prayer is more than just giving requests to God.

Prayer should have a few elements. It should begin with a phrase that reflects God to Whom we are praying. We all know what the salutation a letter is. It could start, "Dear _____," "My dear friends," or "To my wonderful co-workers," and so on. It doesn't begin with "Hey," or with nothing. Likewise, our prayer should open with something addressing God. It could be as simple as "Lord," "Dear God," "Heavenly Father," or "Almighty Lord."

After we begin our prayer, we should have an element of thanksgiving. We should thank God for something, even something as simple as thanking Him for the day we are beginning. There are so many things to be thankful for—our families, friends, children, jobs, homes, and health; the list is innumerable.

There should be an element of praying for others, to pray by name for those around us, to include them in our conversations with the Lord.

There should be an element of supplication to God. This is where we ask for the things we need. Many people think prayer is only supplication, but it is not. Supplication should come after we thank God and after we pray for others.

Years ago, I made a simple formula for prayer that I use myself and that I teach others, especially those who are not in the habit of praying. It's called "The Rule of Five." We started teaching it in Sunday school so that our children would know how to pray. The rule of five is this:

After beginning prayer with an acknowledgment of the Lord, offer five things for which you are thankful. On a given day, I thank God for my health (that I'm alive), my wife, our son, the roof over our heads, and that I have a place to go (I thank God for my ministry, or on a rare day off, I thank Him for a day of rest).

The second list of five is five people I wish to pray for today. Usually, the list is a lot more than five, but at a minimum, five. They include my family (by name), people I know are sick or need prayer, healing, or God's mercy, close friends, co-workers, and parishioners. If I ever run out of specific people to pray for, I pray for "categories of people," such as teachers, doctors, those who are sick, those who take care of them, first responders, those who serve in the military, clergy, college students, those who struggle with addictions, and many more categories. The list of categories of people is innumerable as well.

Then I go to supplication, five things I need. There are two caveats here to keep in mind. The first is that what we think we need is not necessarily what God thinks we need. So an element of humility must kick in to ask God to grant us what He thinks we need. The second is that I limit my supplications to things I need on a particular day. I do not pray any further down the line than the needs of today, which are generally very few. On a given day, I pray for safety because I drive almost every day, so I hope for safe travels. I pray for patience because this is a consistent challenge for me. I pray for wisdom because on a given day, I have to make a lot of decisions, and I want to be wise in the decisions I make. I pray for efficiency because I need to focus and be without distraction as well as temptation to get my tasks accomplished and still have time for family, rest, socializing, and so on. I also ask God for the opportunity to laugh. Life is stressful, and on a given day, I hope to laugh, have fun, and enjoy something.

So there it is, the rule of five: five things for which I am thankful, five people for whom I wish to pray, and five things I need today.

Of course, you can make this list a rule of ten or twenty. The point is that it is to give some shape to your prayer, and also, the rule of five pray can be done in less than two minutes.

A couple of years ago, I added one additional thing to the rule of five. I started asking God to put one person in my path whom I can serve or encourage on a given day. And I have to say, God answers this prayer every time I offer it. God always provides someone who I can encourage or help on a given day. Sometimes it is someone I know is coming to see me. Sometimes it is a surprise visitor who I wasn't expecting or a surprise situation I didn't see coming. Sometimes it happens in the morning, and other times it doesn't happen until late in the day.

One day, I had spent virtually all day alone, writing and doing office work, and I had only minimal interaction with anyone. It seemed as if the prayer to help someone would not be answered. I stopped at a gas station on the way home about 8:00 p.m. that night. As I was pumping gas, a man came up to me, and noticing my black shirt and collar, asked, "Are you a priest?" I laughed inside, *I wonder what gave it away.* And I answered, "Yes, sir. I am." He asked if I would pray for him, that he had lost his job and wasn't sure how he'd tell his wife and kids and how he would provide for his family. Most immediately, he was just afraid to go home. So we sat on the hood of my car and talked, and I prayed for him. My prayer to help and encourage someone was answered, as it always does.

If you are not sure how to pray, remember 5-5-5-1: Five things for which I am thankful, five people I wish to pray for, five things I need today, and a prayer for God to place at least one person in your path today whom you can help and encourage.

Lord, thank you for (list five things you are thankful for). Lord, bless (five people that you wish to pray for). And Lord help me (list five things that you need God's help for today). Lord, put one person in my path today who I can encourage and help. As I strive to encourage others, help me to find encouragement through prayer and Scripture reading. Help my heart to stay filled with peace so that I have peace to give to others. Help my heart to be filled with joy so that I have joy to share with others. Help my soul to feel encouraged so that I will be inspired to encourage others. Amen.

Encouragement Challenge: Make sure to pray today, preferably at the beginning of the day!

Part Eight

GIVE THANKS

Give thanks in all circumstances; for this is the will of Christ Jesus for you.

1 Thessalonians 5:18

GIVE THANKS IN ALL CIRCUMSTANCES, NOT FOR ALL CIRCUMSTANCES

Give thanks in all circumstances; for this is the will of Christ Jesus for you.
1 Thessalonians 5:18

We often see the power of one word to change the meaning of something. In the instance we observe here, we see the difference between the use of the word "in" versus the word "for." Many people mistakenly quote 1 Thessalonians 5:18 as saying, "Give thanks FOR all circumstances," when, in reality, this verse tells us to "Give thanks IN all circumstances," a critical difference in meaning.

Many people in the world are suffering. Many people who are reading this message are suffering. Some of you have gone through a recent divorce, others have significant health challenges, and others have lost jobs, moved unexpectedly, had your children get in legal trouble, and so on. It would be unfair and unreasonable for you to say to God, "I'm so thankful that I have cancer," "I'm grateful that my marriage is over," or "How wonderful it is that my daughter is failing math."

However, it is possible to be thankful in all circumstances. It is possible to see at least some things for which we can feel grateful at all times. A person in the hospital can be thankful to the doctors and nurses who take care of him. The student failing math can be thankful for the teacher, tutor, or parent willing to take the time to make sure she learns.

Too often, we focus on what we've lost rather than on what we still have left. The highest goal and purpose in life is salvation. If you are alive to read this message, that goal is still on the table, no matter how bad your life might be at this moment. If everything is going wrong for you, and I pray that it isn't, we can comfort ourselves with the grateful thought that this won't last forever. At some point, life on earth with its sufferings and setbacks will end, and life in the kingdom of heaven will begin for the faithful Christian. I'm thankful for that. I'm also thankful that God focuses more on our efforts than our results. While success is something we cannot always control, we can control effort, and we definitely can control attitude.

We know that Christ's suffering was not in vain. In fact, because of His suffering, untold millions upon millions of people have found their salvation. Our sufferings need not be in vain either.

In Luke 2, we read the story of when Jesus was presented in the temple on His fortieth day. This was a law from the Old Testament, that male children were to be presented to God on their fortieth day of life, and the parents were to offer a sacrifice of turtle doves or pigeons. A priest named Simeon was in the temple and had been promised by God that he wouldn't die until he saw the Christ. On that day, when he saw the baby Jesus, he took him in his arms and offered the prayer: "Lord, now lettest Thou Thy servant depart in peace, according to Thy word; for mine eyes have seen Thy salvation which Thou hast prepared in the presence of all people, a light for revelation to the Gentiles and for glory to Thy people Israel" (Luke 2:29–32).

Mary and Joseph must have been very excited to see their Son given this honor. Then Simeon turned to Mary and said this, a line that most Christians seldom remember, if they know it at all: "Behold, this child is set for the fall and rising of many in Israel, and for a sign that is spoken against (And a sword will pierce through your own soul also) that thoughts out of many hearts may be revealed" (Luke 2:34–35).

Many times, when life gets really hard, my mind goes to these verses. As the sword seems to pierce my own soul, as I struggle, my thoughts go to the thoughts of other hearts that may be revealed; in other words, something good can come from something bad. And it may be a good that I will see, or a good that I will never know.

In John 11, Jesus is told that His friend Lazarus was sick. His response was "This illness is not unto death; it is for the glory of God, so that the Son of God may be glorified by means of it" (John 11:4). We know that Lazarus did end up dying, and that made his sisters, Mary and Martha, very despondent. We also know that Jesus used this occasion to raise Lazarus from the dead, and many believed in Him because of it.

Christ can be glorified in any and in all circumstances. And because the number-one goal in life is to glorify Him so that we can receive entrance into His heavenly kingdom, the spiritually mature thing is to be thankful IN all circumstances, even as we have sorrow FOR our circumstances. This is something to strive for. In our human frailty, it becomes hard to find thankfulness in all circumstances. It is much easier to talk about it than to do it. Christ has always presented us with the ideal. Ideally, we find a reason to give thanks IN all circumstances, even as we are frustrated FOR the circumstances in which we may find ourselves.

Lord, thank You for the dawning of another day. Thank You for the circumstances of my life that are good (list some of them). Please help me to be patient in the circumstances where I struggle (list them). While I may not give joy for them, please help me to find You in them, and by finding You in them, may I feel thankful, and may I glorify You in all circumstances. Amen.

Encouragement Challenge: Learn to give thanks IN all circumstances, as God is able to work through any circumstance, and any opportunity to grow in Christ or glorify Him is indeed a reason to feel thankful.

Our First Words Should Be Words of Thanks

I will bless the Lord at all times; His praise shall continually be in my mouth. My soul makes its boast in the Lord; let the afflicted hear and be glad. O magnify the Lord with me and let us exalt His name together!
Psalm 34:1–3

One morning, a group of school students complained loudly about having to be in school. They complained about their tests. They complained about their homework. They complained about their loss of freedom. They complained that they had to go to school, and they would much rather have been at the beach. I said to them that they should thank God that they were in school. And they looked back at me with expressions that said, "Are you kidding me?"

I pointed out to them that at the children's hospital, there were many kids who would love to be in school, who would love to take tests that didn't involve needles, who would rather wear any clothes besides a hospital gown, who would be glad to be able to walk outside, who would love to eat a meal and keep it down, and who would like to not worry about whether they will be alive in a year. Sometimes our thoughts are a matter of our perspective.

One of the things I have tried to discipline myself to do is to have my first words each morning be words of thanksgiving. I confess that in younger years, my first thoughts were usually negative, like, "that darn alarm, already!" Over the years, I have disciplined my mind so that the first thoughts every day are thankful ones. Before my feet hit the floor next to my bed, I say five words of thanks—

- Thank You, God, that I am alive to see another day.
- Thank You, God, for my wife, who is next to me.
- Thank You, God, for our son, who is down the hall.
- Thank You, God, for the roof over my head and that there is food in the house to eat.
- Thank You, God, that I have a place to go today.

Many people who die in their sleep. Every day, I thank God that He has shown me the light of another day.

Many people who are lonely. Every day, I thank God for my wife, and later on, I thank Him for other friends.

Many people who do not have children or are not happy parents. Thanking God for our son shows the Lord that I am grateful for His gift to us, and I am more motivated to be happy in my parenting because I bring the Lord into my relationship with our son before I interact with him each day.

Many people in the world who have no home or food. I am thankful to God that I am not one of them.

There are also people who have nowhere to go; they don't have jobs or can't find jobs, or they are unsure of who they are and who they want to be. I thank God every day that I have a job, which provides the means to have a home. And I recognize that my house, my job, and the financial benefit of the job that pays for the house, these are all gifts from God.

Now, I have bad days, just like everyone else. But no matter what is on my plate on a given day, no matter what circumstance I find myself in, I begin each day with words of thanks.

Thank You, Lord, for (name as many things or people as you can for which you are thankful). Amen.

Encouragement Challenge: Make thankful words to God the first words you say each day!

The Power of a "Thank You"

*And let the peace of Christ rule in your hearts, to which indeed
you were called in the one body. And be thankful.*
Colossians 3:15

The words "Thank you" are words we don't hear enough. I think in many instances, it is easier to get the words "I love you" out than "thank you" because to thank someone, you have to actually think of what you are thankful for. Good encouragers use the words "thank you" often. Why? Because it makes the person who gets thanked feel good, it makes the encourager feel good, and it often gets a behavior to repeat. Here is an example from real life:

At summer camp one year, the retreat center staff who provides our meals cooked ribs for the campers and the camp staff and priests. I love ribs, and so do many other people. Having been at camp for years, I can easily say it is the best meal I've ever had there, and that's saying something because, over the years, the food has been great. As I was carrying my empty tray to the place we clean them, I turned toward the kitchen and yelled as loud as I could, "That was the best meal ever!" The cooks in the kitchen all had big smiles on their faces. The campers who were standing close to me who heard what I had said started clapping. Here is the good that happened:

- ~ The kitchen staff felt good because they were acknowledged;
- ~ I felt good because I made them feel good;
- ~ It cost me not time to do this as I was going to put my tray up anyway. I didn't even break stride to thank them; and
- ~ The next week at camp, they served ribs again. The behavior repeated.

It was a win all around.

Unfortunately, this is not how we generally handle "thank you" in real life.

As I mentioned before, the food at camp is just about always good. I can count on one hand the number of bad meals I've had there in the thirty-six weeks (and counting) of camp I have attended. We're talking well over 600 meals, and maybe five of them were not great. That's less than 1 percent. Over 99 percent of the time, I have eaten a great meal.

In life, we usually only notice when someone does something bad or wrong, and we make a big deal out of it. When things go well, it's like we expect them to go well, and we fail to voice any thanks or encouragement.

Using the camp numbers, let's say that I complained for those five "not great" meals, less than 1 percent of the meals I have eaten at camp. And let's say that I never said any thank you for the other 99 percent of the meals I have eaten there, save for the ribs. The camp kitchen staff might think that they only make one out of six meals good since they got one thank you and five complaints. This might cause them to have doubts or feel discouraged when this isn't the case at all.

So we see there are positive outcomes when we are thankful and encouraging, and negative consequences when we fail to be thankful and encouraging. However, saying nothing is almost as bad as saying something negative. Think about it from the staff's perspective: Five meals were complained of as bad. One meal was complimented. And if the other 594 meals were not even worth a comment, perhaps they will think they were bad as well. Think of how the staff would feel if they thought that only one out of 600 meals was good! It would lower their self-esteem and self-confidence, and this would be completely unnecessary and wrong because the truth is, 595 meals have been great! I just didn't make a point of thanking and encouraging them.

We see the power of encouragement to make someone feel good. We see the power of encouragement to make us feel good. We see the power of encouragement to get a behavior to repeat. And we see that encouragement does not have to take much time at all. In this case, it took none.

We also see what can happen if we do not encourage. Indifference is just as much a negative as criticism. Perhaps even more. To criticize, you have to evaluate. To be indifferent is as if to say it wasn't even worth the time to evaluate.

I'm sure I have said thank you more than one time in all my summers of camp. However, I'm very sure I didn't say thank you even half of the time.

Many people are in our lives all the time—our spouses, children, co-workers, and friends. Do we make a point to thank them with any regularity? Or do we only make a point of being critical when they do something wrong? Encouragement is a great motivator. Not only does it make someone feel good, but it also gets good things to repeat.

It's not only those who you are related to or friends we should be thanking. Think of all the people who serve you in a day—a doctor, dentist, the person who delivers the mail, clerk at the store, server at the restaurant, police officer, your child's teacher, or a coach. Many serve us in relative obscurity, generally only recognized by us when they do something wrong. Let's make it a point of thanking those around us for all they do that is right.

When someone does something good for you, don't forget to thank them. You'll feel good. They will feel good. And they will be motivated to do good for you again. The best news of all—it costs nothing to say, "thank you." In fact, you can do it in less than a few seconds.

Heavenly Father, thank You for all the people who do so much for me in my life (list members of your family, friends, co-workers, others whom you are thank for). Thank You for the many people who serve me and make my life better (your doctor, dentist, accountant, police officer, teacher, coach, etc.). Help me to be more aware of those around me who make my life more full, who help me daily. Help me to have a heart that is filled with gratitude, and give me the words and opportunities to express my gratitude to them. Amen.

Encouragement Challenge: Make sure you make thanking people a daily part of your life!

Gratitude Spawns Generosity

We want you to know, brethren, about the grace of God which has been shown in the churches of Macedonia, for in a severe test of affliction, their abundance of joy and their extreme poverty have overflowed in a wealth of liberality on their part. For they gave according to their means, as I can testify, and beyond their means, of their own free will, begging us earnestly for the favor of taking part in the relief of the saints—and this, not as we expected, but first they gave themselves to the Lord and to use by the will of God.
2 Corinthians 8:1–5

Things tend to run in cycles. People who are optimistic tend to stay optimistic. People who are organized tend to stay organized. And people who are generous tend to stay generous.

Generosity means being plentiful when it comes to giving. One who is generous with money gives liberally to others. One who is generous with time offers it plentifully to others.

Generosity in giving doesn't really correlate to that amount of something one has to give. Those with riches are not necessarily the most generous when it comes to sharing them.

Generosity is more of a disposition of the heart. A generous person has a large heart when it comes to giving. A generous person sees a need outside himself or herself and runs to fill it. A generous person often thinks of others before themselves. A generous person thinks more about the joy of giving something than the cost of giving it.

How does one become generous? There is a correlation between gratitude and generosity. If I am always desiring more rather than being grateful for what I have, it becomes harder to be generous with what I have. If I am grateful for what I have, then it is easier to be generous with it.

What makes us more grateful? We become more grateful when we begin to see the good things in life as blessings from God. If I see today as a gift from God, and I am grateful for the gift, then it is easier to offer part of this day to helping someone else. If I see the ability to earn income as a result from a talent that came from God, then I am grateful for the God-given talent that allows me to earn an income, and then I'm more likely to be generous in giving to charity.

What stifles gratitude? The answer is entitlement. If I see every day and every dollar as things I am entitled to, then I will be less likely to give away anything that is "mine." If I see my talents as having been earned rather than having been entrusted to me by God, then I am less likely to share them.

Thus, gratitude and generosity go hand in hand. Those who are more grateful are more generous.

In the above verses from 2 Corinthians 8, St. Paul speaks of the witness of the churches in Macedonia, which were beset by poverty, people struggled to make ends meet and to put food on their tables. Yet, when the call went out for the churches to support the church in Jerusalem, it was the poor Macedonians who stepped up to the table first. Despite their "severe test of affliction" and "extreme poverty," they had an "abundance of joy" and "overflowed in a wealth of liberality on their part (2 Cor. 8:2). Ironically, it is often people who have the least who are willing to share the most, perhaps because they best understand what it is like to have nothing and to feel grateful for whatever little they have.

There are two memories that come to mind about generosity of people who were poor. I remember one Sunday, we asked for some help for someone who was very down on their luck and desperately needed some money. I put an envelope in the front of the church and told people to put whatever they wanted in the envelope on their way out and that I would give it to the person after church. Of course, the person who was going to receive this money didn't realize I was collecting for them (I've left the gender out intentionally). They thought I was collecting for someone who was really poor. They came up and put five dollars in the envelope for the "poor person." Others put in one dollar. When everyone had left, I found the person and gave them the envelope. Of course, they were surprised and very appreciative.

On another occasion, someone who was dressed rather poorly came to the office, asking "to see the pastor." Most of the time, it is someone who needs something, sometimes food and oftentimes money. While our church operates a food pantry, we have a policy that we don't give out cash, which upsets many people who come by looking for money. I assumed, looking at this person, that they were going to ask me for money. To my surprise, they said they were having a bad day and just needed some encouragement and prayer, which I was happy to offer. About a week after this encounter, I received a card from this person in the mail. It read, "Thanks for your help the other day. I wanted to give you a gift to thank you for your time. It's just a dollar, but it's all I can afford." I felt ashamed as I read this card because I had prejudged someone and because, realizing they barely had any money to their name, they would go buy a card, mail it, and put a dollar gift in it; this was a significant expense for them.

It's not necessarily those who have the most that give the most. Generosity is based more on what's in your heart than what is in your wallet. Gratitude spawns generosity. And God expect us to be people of generosity, to have hearts that are generous.

Lord, thank You for all that I have. Everything that I have that is good is a gift from You. Help me to be appreciative for all that I have. Help me to have a heart that is generous and eyes that recognize those who need some generosity. Amen.

Gratitude spawns generosity!

Generosity of Time

*Each one must do as he has made up his mind, not reluctantly
or under compulsion, for God loves a cheerful giver.*
2 Corinthians 9:7

The whole concept of generosity is based on two things—the joy of giving and the understanding that everything good that we have is from God, and so, in a sense, we do not give; we give back from what He first gave us.

Let's look at time. Today is a gift. Some people did not wake up today. Today is a gift that I have received from God. If every moment of this day is part of my gift, why wouldn't I want to give part of this day back to God or to my fellow man? If today is not a gift but rather seen as an entitlement, if today is MY day and not His, then I will greedily hold onto the moment of MY day rather than giving back to Him the moments of the day He first gave me.

We know that God loves cheerful giving. And why shouldn't we be cheerful in giving? In reality, we are not giving away what we have earned. We are giving back what He has blessed us with. That's why when God gives us a twenty-four-hour day, we should give some of that back to Him in prayer. When God gives us a seven-day week, we should give back some of that to Him in worship. And when God gives us a 365-day year, we should give some of those days back in service to others—offering volunteer work of some kind, giving without expectation of receiving anything. And going back to today, if you are going to be awake for sixteen hours of this day, this adds up to 930 minutes. Certainly we can give some of those away in prayer, reading Scripture, and going out of our way to show kindness to someone and offer words of encouragement as well.

Multitasking seems to be viewed as some kind of virtue worthy of emulating. The problem with multitasking, when it comes to how we give our time to other people, is that if we are multitasking, we are not 100 percent present with the person whom we are talking, and this is not generous with our time. For instance, if we are carrying on a conversation and texting or looking at stuff on our computers at the same time, we are not 100 percent present with the person we are speaking with. That's one reason why when I hear confessions or do counseling, I don't have my phone with me. How can I be generous with my time if I'm dividing it between two people at the same time? How can I be 100 percent present with someone if I am dividing my attention?

There may be a difference between putting away dishes while talking on the telephone versus having a serious conversation with your spouse or child while putting away the dishes. If you are gabbing on the phone with a friend, you can probably still have a good conversation being 90 percent on the phone and 10 percent with the dishes. However, if you are having a serious conversation, this merits 100 percent of attention being given to the person you are speaking with. So, in being generous with your time, I encourage you to seriously evaluate when multi-tasking is good and when it might be considered not only inefficient but insensitive and rude.

One final comment on giving time—no two people are equal on any metric, starting with the hairs on our heads. So equality is not something we should strive for in any relationship. Rather we want to strive for mutuality, for the mutual good of all parties involved. That means that all parties take turns giving. Generosity should flow generously between people. Ideally, everyone strives to do as much as they can. Everyone gives with joy. This is what generosity is. Acts 20:35 says, *"It is more blessed to give than to receive,"* which means that there is joy in generosity. It brings joy to give. So learn to be a good listener and a generous giver of time, and see the joy it will bring to your life.

Lord, thank You for the gift of this day. Help me to truly appreciate this day as a gift that I have been given rather than something I am entitled to. Inspire me to give generously of my time, spend time in prayer and Scripture reading, spend time helping someone today, and spend time encouraging someone else. Help me to give consistently and with joy. Help me to stay present and not be distracted as I offer myself to help others. Amen.

Encouragement Challenge: Give joyfully today!

Generosity with Money

And He sat down opposite the treasury, and watched the multitude putting money into the treasury. Many rich people put in large sums. And a poor widow came, and put in two copper coins, which make a penny. And He called His disciples to Him, and said to them, "Truly, I say to you, this poor widow has put in more than all those who are contributing to the treasury."
Mark 12:41–43

Imagine if someone "gave" you one hundred dollars a week just because. Every week, you'd get one hundred dollars. Would you keep it all to yourself? Would you share a portion of it with anyone else? What if, after a while, the person who gave you the money said, "I'm going to give you the same one hundred dollars a week, but I want you to give ten dollars of it back"? Would you be angry with him? Would you think, "Hey, once you've given me the hundred dollars, it's mine to do what I want with it."

Everything we have that is good ultimately has God as its source. That means that even every dollar we "earn" is actually a gift because if I have a job that nets me a salary, I have the job because I have a talent, and I have a talent because I was given that talent by God. God gives some the talent to be doctors, others teachers, others architects, and others athletes. Every person has a gift. And God expects each of us to use our gifts to His glory, and whatever we derive materially from our gifts, He expects that a certain amount will be given back. This is the concept of the tithe, and the tithe is 10 percent.

In Leviticus 27:32, we read, *"And all the tithe of hears and flocks, every tenth animal of all that pass under the herdsman's staff, shall be holy to the Lord."* What a beautiful image that paints, all of the people of Israel passing under the staff of Moses, receiving a blessing as they joyfully offered a tenth of their property each year in thanksgiving to the Lord.

We are conditioned in our society not to give but to exchange. To truly give means to offer, expecting nothing in return. When we expect something in return, then we are exchanging, not giving. This is why I will never understand in our churches when people "donate" something, but they get their name on it, why we consider that a gift. It is an exchange. Someone exchanges money for recognition. This is exchanging, not giving.

We also are conditioned to think of our things as OUR things rather than gifts from God. Every dollar we have we see as an earning rather than a gift. This is why it is hard for many to part with their earnings rather than joyfully offering gifts.

The story of the widow's penny quoted above shows how God views joyful and sacrificial giving. It is not how much you give compared to anyone else. It is how much you give back in comparison to how much you have been given.

Acts 20:35 says, *"In all things I have shown you that by so toiling one must help the weak, remembering the words of the Lord Jesus, how He said 'It is more blessed to give than to receive.'"* So giving brings blessing as well as joy.

In Matthew 6:21, Jesus says, *"For where your treasure is, there will your heart be also."* The heart of the widow in the above Scripture message was such that she gave everything she had back to the Lord. That is the ideal. Before we can reach 100 percent, let's try for 10 percent, and before we get to even 10 percent, let us give what we give rather than exchange. And let us give with joy. After all, we're not really giving at all. We're *giving back* a portion of what He first gave us.

Lord, thank You for the many gifts and talents with which You have blessed me (name them). Thank You that I can provide sustenance for myself and my family. Help me be a grateful steward of my treasures, seeing my treasure as a gift from You and joyfully sharing it with the church and with charity. Help me to also be a trusting steward, trusting that even as I divest myself of material things, I not only gain spiritual treasures but that You will continue to provide for my well-being.

Encouragement Challenge: Give today without expecting anything in return!

Would Anyone Describe You with This Word?

It is well with the man who deals generously and lends, who conducts his affairs with justice.
Psalm 112:5

On Christmas Eve, as part of my sermon, I read the children a Christian Christmas book. After reading the story, I asked them to describe Santa Claus. One of them said, "He wears red." Another said, "He has a big, white beard." And another said, "He's fat," to which I replied, "You shouldn't be fat-shaming Santa on the day he's supposed to bring you presents."

After a few more answers, I asked them, "Does anyone ever think to describe Santa as 'generous?' After all, he never seems to run out of gifts." One child answered, "Gosh, I never thought about it like that. That is so true. Santa is the most generous person ever!"

Well, we certainly can make the case that God is more generous than all of us put together. But leaving this on a human level, if someone were to describe you in five words, would one of those words be "generous?" How about if they described you in ten words? In fifty words? Does generosity even get on the list anywhere if someone were to describe you? And if someone wrote a list of dozens of descriptions of you, is the word generous more likely to be on the list, or the word stingy?

In Matthew 10:8, Jesus says to His disciples, "You received without paying, give without paying." In other words, we have received generously of God's blessings. He has blessed us with talents that allow us to reap material and monetary reward. Most importantly, He has blessed us with life itself. Since God is the Author of life, every day that I wake up and am alive is a blessing from God. My very life is a result of God's generosity. As we have discussed, when we look at things or at life itself as an entitlement, as something we are owed, it is easier to be stingy with our things and our time. If we see our things and our very lives as blessings, it is much easier to be generous with them. People who are thankful are generous because generosity is an important manifestation of gratitude and thankfulness.

Because we have "received without paying," we should be generous in giving "without pay." That's what generosity is. Generosity is about sharing, expecting nothing in return. If we give expecting something in return (which doesn't necessarily have to be money; it could be some kind of recognition), then we are exchanging, not giving.

The legend of Santa Claus involves a little exchange, as it is traditional to leave out cookies and milk. But nowhere in the legend of Santa Claus is this demanded, that is, no cookies and milk nets you a lump of coal. The legend of Santa Claus is a tradition that focuses on the generosity of Santa, that he travels throughout the world to give toys and gifts to all the boys and girls, returning to the North Pole only after every child has been visited.

A generous person gives freely and joyfully, and I dare say, almost tirelessly because the effort to be generous is more invigorating than taxing. Generosity renews us more than it exhausts us. People get exhausted earning, not giving. I know from personal experience that I get exhausted faster from working for a paycheck than I do from volunteering. Working as a volunteer re-energizes me because it just feels good to give. It feels good to be generous.

The above Scripture verse from Psalm 112 reminds us that "it is well with the man who deals generously and lends, who conducts his affairs with justice." There is something wholesome about it. Too many people in this world are self-serving. So much of peer pressure focuses on personal material gain rather than generosity. When someone is generous, it is like a breath of fresh air.

Generosity does not necessarily have to correlate with quantity. The hardest thing to be generous with is our time because it is so limited for all of us. I try to be generous with my time. I try not to overbook appointments (though it does happen occasionally). If I anticipate that someone will need more time, I'll block some extra time off. However, sometimes time is limited. If quantity is not possible, I make sure there is quality, meaning, I don't look at the phone, and we speak at a conference table where there are no computers or things on a desk to distract me. When there are distractions, I, like everyone, can be stingy with my attention.

There are other things we can be generous with as well besides time and money. We can be generous in patience, forgiveness, and assistance. And we can be generous with encouragement. We can be generous with compliments, with building others up. If it's ever a good thing to be stingy, it would be with criticisms and discouragement.

Lord, thank You for Your generosity towards me. This very day on which I am offering this prayer to You is only possible because of Your generosity. Please help me to be have a grateful heart and a generous spirit. Please help me to understand and appreciate my gift so that I can generously offer them to others. Amen.

Would anyone describe you as generous?

We're Supposed to Be Satisfied with How Much?

Jesus said "What man of you, having a hundred sheep, if he has lost one of them, does not leave the ninety-nine in the wilderness and go after the one which is lost, until he finds it? And when he has found it, he lays it on his shoulders, rejoicing. And when he comes home, he calls together his friend and his neighbors, saying to them, 'Rejoice with me, for I have found my sheep which was lost.' Just so, I tell you, there will be more joy in heaven over one sinner who repents than over ninety-nine righteous persons who need no repentance."
Luke 15:3–7

At some point in life, all of us get frustrated with our jobs. If we were to give ourselves a job-satisfaction rating, it is doubtful that any of us would score 100 percent. In fact, for many of us, that rating would be much lower. Many people strongly dislike their jobs. Is there an answer for how long you should stay with your job if you are not satisfied in it? Believe it or not, the Bible has an answer for us as to what percentage of satisfaction we should take away from our jobs, and the number is astonishingly low—it is 1 PERCENT! That's right, 1 percent.

Jesus said in the above Scripture that if one sheep is lost and the shepherd finds that one sheep, he will rejoice more than over ninety-nine sheep that never left. The other ninety-nine sheep may be compliant, or indifferent—perhaps they have made no impact on the shepherd, and he has made no impact on them. But when there is the opportunity to help one or save one, this is what brings the shepherd joy. The job of the shepherd is not just to herd the sheep around but to care for them.

The job of a teacher is not just to babysit students but to teach them. Many teachers lament that students today are apathetic and disinterested. Based on this biblical teaching on satisfaction, if you are a teacher, and one student out of one hundred really loves the class and wants to learn, you have to learn to rejoice in that even if nine-nine students are apathetic.

Lawyers have difficult clients, doctors have difficult patients, and we all deal with difficult people. If even 1 percent of the people we deal with are enthusiastic, we are supposed to take joy from that.

Most of us have much more than a 1-percent job satisfaction rating. Thus, if your rating is more than 1 percent, you've exceeded the standard Christ told us should bring us joy.

I can personally say that my job satisfaction rating is much more than one, though it is much less than one hundred. I am very joyful when a "lost sheep" returns to the fold. It is very encouraging to find lost sheep. However, as I have written before, I try to focus on effort and not necessarily the results because on a given day, I may not be able to find the lost sheep. But I can control my effort in searching.

So the message for today is, do your best. If you find the lost sheep, rejoice. If you can't find the lost sheep today, give your best effort and be satisfied with that. And if you have one star student, one star patient, one star client, or one star customer, do not have sorrow over why it is only one and not one hundred. Use the standard of Christ, and rejoice for the one.

Lord, thank You for the gift of (your job, or jobs). In my work, may I always give the best effort to those with whom I work, to those for whom I work, and I always give my best effort for You, my God for whom I work. Help me to be patient in the moments when satisfaction is hard to find. Help me to be grateful and joyful in the moments when I find "the lost sheep." Please put people in my path who will be joyful and enthusiastic. May I also be joyful and enthusiastic around those I meet as well. Amen.

Encouragement Challenge: Give your best today, and be satisfied with your best effort!

God Wants Us to Succeed

Yet among the mature we do impart wisdom, although it is not a wisdom of this age or of the rulers of this age, who are doomed to pass away. But we impart a secret and hidden wisdom of God, which God decreed before the ages for our glorification. None of the rulers of this age understood this; for if they had, they would not have crucified the Lord of glory. But as it is written, "What no eye has seen, nor ear heard, nor the heart of man conceived, what God has prepared for those who love Him."
1 Corinthians 2:6–9

Several years ago, I confided in a friend that I was nervous about a big day in our church community and that when the moment of truth came, I might not succeed. When the day came, before the service, my friend gave me a card with Philippians 4:13 on it: "I can do all things through Christ Who strengthens me." And my friend asked me "Do you think that God wants you to fail? Don't you think that He is going to be with you in the task that you are doing?"

Of course, my friend was right. God didn't want me to fail. He does not want us to fail. He wants us to succeed.

Like most of us, I've had many teachers over the years. I remember teachers who told us on the first day of class, "You all start with a zero and have to work your way up." And thankfully, I had a majority of teachers who said, "Everyone starts with one hundred, and it's yours to lose." It was these teachers who wanted us to succeed. And it is just like these teachers when it comes to God. He wants us to succeed.

We are currently raising a teenager. Our hope for him is that he will go to college, have a career, and hopefully have a family one day. While we can't control the outcome of any of these things, we can certainly create expectations, offer encouragement, and create an environment that models these things. We certainly are giving him every chance to succeed in this "plan." He may choose differently. He may choose to not do well in school. That's not our plan for him, but that may be his choice.

In a similar way, God has called each of us to something. He has given each of us unique talents, abilities, and opportunities. It is His plan for us to succeed in them. Not everyone will have the same success because not everyone has the same talents, abilities, and opportunities. God wants each of us to succeed in the unique set of circumstances that we are presented with. Like our son, we also have a choice to stick with the plan or go against the plan.

God didn't put me here on the earth so that I can fail, harm others, or end up in prison. He put me here so that I can succeed in some way. Because of His love for us, He has given us free will so that each of has a choice in following God's plan or going against it. If I harm someone and end up in prison, that's not God's plan to my life; that's my choice to go against His plan, which, for me, includes being a priest.

God's ultimate plan for each of us is salvation. We may have many failures and setbacks in life. God may even allow us to fail at things at times. Parents sometimes allow their children to fail so that they will learn something. Of course, there is a critical difference between allowing a failure and causing one. While I've never caused my child to fail, I have allowed him to fail. For instance, I didn't remind him to take his PE clothes to school one day, even though I knew he was forgetting them. He got a conduct cut and learned the value of remembering to take them. Likewise, I don't believe God causes our failures, but at times allows us to fail so that we can learn from our mistakes.

Again, God's ultimate plan for each life is salvation, and this is something that is very much on the table for everyone as long as they are alive, irrespective of how many times they have failed. God wants us to succeed in this. This is why He offers us innumerable opportunities to believe, work, and repent. We are ultimately saved by God's mercy. Salvation isn't something we bestow on ourselves. However, we play a critical role in our salvation based on our faith and works.

The above Scripture verses remind us of God's wisdom and power as well as the reward that "God has prepared for those who love Him" (1 Cor. 2:9). These are things that "no eye has seen, nor ear heard, nor the heart of man conceived" (2:9). Indeed God's plans for our salvation are too awesome to comprehend. His plan is for us to enjoy His rewards. It is our role to work in concert with God's grace through our faith and works. He has certainly blessed us with all the tools.

Lord, thank You for paving the way to our salvation through the crucifixion and resurrection of Christ. Thank You for the unique talents and opportunities that You have given me as well as the very life I enjoy today as I offer to You this prayer. Help me to make strides daily in my journey to salvation. Help me to make the right choices that keep me on track for salvation. Help me to have wisdom to see good choices and avoid bad ones. Please reassure me in my moments of doubt so that I know at all times that I can do all things through Christ Who strengthens me. Amen.

Encouragement Challenge: God's will is for us to succeed in our journey to salvation. Will we? It's our choice. Make the choice for God today (and everyday)!

The Highest Goal Is Holiness

But as He Who called you is holy, be holy yourselves in all your conduct; since it is written, "You shall be holy, for I am holy."
1 Peter 1:15–16

If you ask the majority of people what their number-one goal in life is, the answer is, "to be happy." How one defines what it means to be happy probably varies from person to person. To be happy might mean getting to travel extensively for one person, to be wealthy for another, to be famous for another, to have a great marriage for another, to have successful kids, a big house, lots of money in the bank, live a long time, being healthy, and many more.

There are a couple of problems with "happiness." The biggest one is that it is temporary. All of the things on the aforementioned list stop when life ends. We don't take wealth or travel or money or fame or family or house with us when we die. Happiness is fleeting. Thus, if happiness is the number-one goal in life, we are consigned to chasing something that we can never have. Because even if we "achieve" happiness, it is temporary.

The next problem with happiness is that it pits us against other people. It creates competition. Why? If my greatest goal is happiness, and YOU stand in the way of MY happiness, then you become the enemy; you become a threat to my happiness. Thus, you become my competitor, and my road to happiness is paved by defeating you.

The highest goal in life can't be happiness. So, what then is the highest goal in life? The answer is theosis (which can also be described as holiness or deification), to be "like God."[24] Theosis is not just a destination but a journey. And it is not a journey we can "achieve" in this life because if we could, it would be a competition to see who could get there first. To choose to live in cooperation with God is a daily choice; it is a choice we make multiple times day. When we have a situation where happiness is only possible at the expense of someone else's happiness, the journey to theosis dictates humility, putting someone else ahead so that we are not obsessed with our place in the line of other people, but that we are obsessed with being in the line of sheep waiting for the security of the sheep pen, which is the gate of heaven. (See John 10, when Christ talks about being the Good Shepherd.)

Christ came to change the world. He didn't come to take all the fun and happiness out of the world. Rather, He came to bring hope to the hopeless and bring purpose and focus. Instead of seeing the sand emptying out of the hourglasses of our lives as we get older and losing our sense of happiness as our earthly lives come closer to the end, living a Christian life should give us hope that as we get to our earthly end, we will reach our heavenly beginning.

This becomes possible when we change our goals from personal happiness to serving others (and securing their happiness). This becomes possible when we lead with humility instead of pride, when we self-empty instead of self-indulge. Jesus did not drive a fancy car. He rode on a simple donkey. He didn't lead by expecting others to bow down to Him. He led by bowing His head and dying for us.

What is your highest goal in life? Is it happiness or something even higher than that? I like being happy. There is nothing wrong with being happy. God doesn't tell us to be miserable. To the contrary, He tells us not to advertise our prayers and fasting so that these things don't become part of a pursuit of happiness through bragging on our spirituality. God wants us to be happy. Yet, He wants us to be more than happy. He wants us to be holy, as He is holy. That should be the greatest and most important goal for every human life.

In this study on encouragement, I encourage you to pursue holiness, not just happiness. When happiness is not possible in a situation, it is easy to become discouraged. Many times our happiness is affected by external forces we cannot control. The journey to holiness is something we can control because we can control how we react to even the most difficult of external forces. If we pursue holiness, we can make positive strides even in negative circumstances, which can leave us feeling encouraged spiritually, even when we might feel discouraged in other ways.

Lord, the heavenly, holy, and blessed one, shine Your Light in my heart and on my life so that I may be inspired to pursue holiness. Help me to set and meet spiritual goals, not just secular ones. Give me spiritual joy, especially in moments of unhappiness. Help me to turn to You as the source of encouragement during moments of discouragement. May I find joy in the pursuit of holiness today and always. Amen.

Encouragement Challenge: Make holiness your highest goal!

KEEP YOUR EYES ON THE PRIZE

For what does it profit a man, to gain the whole world and forfeit his life (soul)? For what can a man give in return for his life (soul)?
Mark 8:36–37

One of the most egregious (in my opinion) mistranslations in the Bible is in Mark 8:36–37. The word that is translated as "life" in the original Greek is *psihi* or soul. The correct translation is "For what does it profit a man to gain the whole world and forfeit his SOUL? For what can a man give in return for his SOUL?"

When you ask people, "What is the worst thing that can happen in life?" many people will say, "to die young." For the Christian, the worst thing that can happen in life is to die with a soul that is not ready to meet God. Think of all the bad things that can happen in life—financial troubles, dead-end job, difficult marriage, problem children, living in the wrong part of the country, illness, lack of friends, and the list goes on and on—which of these would you trade for if it meant that you'd lose your own soul? Would you trade in poverty for riches if it cost you your salvation? Would you trade lack of friends for popularity if it cost you the kingdom of God? Would you upsize your car if it meant downsizing your soul? I would hope the answer is no.

If you are struggling in life in material terms, but you are growing in spiritual terms, you are on the road to eternal riches. And if you are rich in material things but poor in spiritual things, you are on the road to eternal poverty.

I once gave a sermon where I laid a rope down the middle aisle of the church. I attached a paper clip onto the rope. The paper clip was so small that people only a few rows away could not see it. The rope represents eternity. The paper clip represents our life on earth in the span of eternity. If one has the best life but doesn't have a relationship with God, he is in for an eternity of misery. If one has the worst life but has Christ in his heart and truly loves God and serves God, then he is in for an eternity of happiness. Ideally, we have a good life in material terms and spiritual terms, but if you have to choose which one you'd prefer, I'll take the tough life and the eternal joy instead of the easier life and eternal misery.

The message today is to keep our eyes on the prize—which is not riches and fame on earth. The prize is the kingdom of heaven to those who are patient and willing to lose the whole world to save their souls.

I can stay encouraged when everything is going wrong in material terms as long as I am growing in spiritual terms.

Lord, thank You for the gift of my life because with life, I could not work toward eternal life. When life gets hard, when I don't achieve the material reward for which I had hoped, please help me always to meditate on the spiritual reward. Please inspire me to put the spiritual first and the material second. Please help me to have healthy relationships with other people. Please help me to have a healthy relationship with You. Yes, I hope to gain a portion of the world. I pray for material sufficiency. Whether I succeed in material terms, help me always to seek and find spiritual wealth. Protect, guard, and grow my soul toward You. Amen.

Encouragement Challenge: Keep your eyes on the prize today!

Remember Those Who Have Helped You

*Remember the days of old, consider the years of many generations; ask your
father, and he will show you; your elders and they will tell you.*
Deuteronomy 32:7

As I reflect on my life, I can recall people and conversations that changed the course of my life or were instrumental in helping me become who I am today. One such person was Frank Panezich, or Mr. P, as we called him. He was my high school English teacher my senior year. I wrote on him previously, but I'll mention him again. He was a hard teacher. He made our class do a ten to fifteen-minute timed writing to begin class each day. Many of us, including me, dreaded it. We had to sit down and write quickly because we would get a grade for each day. What I didn't realize at the time was that Mr. P was teaching me how to write quickly, how to quickly put ideas together and put them down on paper. Mr. P is as responsible as anyone for the Prayer Team, the daily writing I do, because he is the one who taught me the discipline of writing daily and writing quickly. I wish I could thank him. He passed away several years ago, so I'll never get my chance.

Then there was Fr. James Adams, my priest when I was in college, who told me to "be a survivor and not a victim" in life. A conversation I had with him in August 1991 remains one of the most profound and life-changing conversations of my life. I remember back in 2007, Fr. James came to visit me in Tampa, and we served the Divine Liturgy together. At the end of the service, I gave a sermon, and it was about how Fr. James had changed my life. I remember saying, "We usually save these kinds of comments for a eulogy, and we don't tell people in life what they really mean to us." I'm so glad I thanked him in person that day. He has since passed away.

George Reed was my scoutmaster. He taught me many things in Boy Scouts that I still use today in my life. I called him one day, after not talking to him in over twenty years, just to say thank you. It not only made his day, but it also made my day too. It was a great opportunity to reminisce about old times and also for him to know that his contribution in my life has not been forgotten. The thing that had been forgotten was that I hadn't gone back and thanked him.

Each of us has people like Mr. P, Fr. James, and Mr. Reed in their lives. Each of us has people who have changed the course of our life for the better, even though we didn't know it at the time.

Each of us has probably changed the course of someone else's life, even though we may not know it. In fact, we may not even remember it. When I told Fr. James, for instance, that our conversation in August 1991 changed the trajectory of my life, he didn't remember the conversation. And that's not a bad thing—it meant that he had that conversation to serve God and serve me, not for any kind of reward. Many of us will wonder as we go through life, "Have I made an impact on others?" Parents will wonder that about their children, spouses will wonder that about their spouses, lawyers will wonder that for their clients, doctors for their patients, teachers for their students, and so on.

One of the easiest and most rewarding things one can do is simply say thank you to someone. Whether that person is from your recent or distant past, everyone likes receiving a thank you. I think it is especially important to remember people from our distant past, people who are retired, who aren't on the front lines anymore. It is important to let them know that things they did really mattered in our lives. We don't say thank you enough to anyone but especially to those in our distant past.

I'll never be able to thank Mr. P in person. I wish I could. I'm glad I got to thank Fr. James when he was alive, and recently with Mr. Reed. There are others who come to my mind that I now feel motivated to track down and thank. If we are honest, we can all think of people like this from our distant as well as our recent past, who have had a profound impact on us, who we may not see often or at all.

Think of people you no longer see who have made an impact on you and write or contact them just to say thank you. It will make their day, and it will make your day as well!

Lord, thank You for all the helpful influences I have had in my life. Thank You for the people who have constantly impacted me, like my parents and siblings, and thank You for those who have impacted me in significant ways, even if they don't know they have (list some of these people). Help me also to be a good influence on others, whether I know it or not. Amen.

Encouragement Challenge: Thank someone from your distant past. Thank someone from your recent past. And thank someone who you see all time. Make thanking people part of your daily life!

Part Nine

LET THE SPIRIT LEAD

Do not quench the Spirit. Do not despise prophesying.

1 Thessalonians 5:19–20

The Holy Spirit—Let the Spirit Lead

Teach me the way I should go, for to Thee I lift up my soul. Deliver me, O Lord from my enemies! I have fled to Thee for refuge! Teach me to do Thy will, for Thou art my God! Let Thy good Spirit lead me on a level path!
Psalm 143:8–10

Most of us have had the experience at some point of being in a three-legged race. This is where two people have their feet tied together and have to move in sync to complete a race. In that moment, they have to share a will. They have to work together to go in the same direction. If they are independent with their thoughts and actions, they cannot succeed.

The mystery of the Holy Trinity is one of the most profound things in all of Christianity. There is one God in three persons, who each share the same will and move in sync: God the Father, God the Son, and God the Holy Spirit. Each has a distinct role in the Trinity. God the Father is the Creator and the creating energy. God the Son is the mouthpiece of the Trinity, who is also the redeemer of the fallen humanity. God the Holy Spirit is active in the world today, bestowing grace upon each of us to help us and comfort us in our Christian walk.

If God the Father is the Creator, and God the Son is the Savior, then the Holy Spirit is the Comforter, or we might even say, the encourager of the Holy Trinity.

The Holy Spirit bestows grace upon us. We hear that word a lot in Christian circles. What does it mean? The best definition I have found is an Orthodox Christian understanding of grace, which is an intangible quality that completes what is lacking and heals what is infirm in each person.[25]

For instance, let's say that two friends have an argument. They are separated and not friendly. When they reconcile and ask forgiveness from one another, it is the grace of the Holy Spirit that comes into play and is intertwined with forgiveness to create restoration of trust. What was lacking in the relationship—joy, trust, and so on—is now complete. What was infirm is now healed. Grace is what allows that to happen.

Grace not only fixes what has gone wrong, but grace also guides in what is going on and what is going right. Let's say that I am going to give a speech, and I am super nervous about it. The Holy Spirit, the Comforter, is the one who will provide the comfort and encouragement I need to calm my anxieties and perform at my best. His encouragement can come through prayer, through a feeling of calm that everything will be alright, or through the encouragement of a friend, who has been inspired by the Holy Spirit to encourage.

At summer camp, we (halfway) jokingly use the phrase, "leave room for the Holy Spirit" when we let the campers do one slow dance. That phrase is used as a loving reminder to the kids to not get physically close in a way that would be considered inappropriate. However, joking aside, this is a good motto for life—leave room for the Holy Spirit. What does that mean exactly? It means, leave room for grace to come into a situation. It means what we read in Psalm 143:10, "Let Thy good Spirit lead me on a level path!" If we are calling for the Spirit to lead, then we must be willing to follow. And if we are following, we don't exactly know where we are going, or else we'd lead on our own. When we trust the Holy Spirit to lead, we are open to the possibilities of where He will lead us. We also ask Him to lead us on a "level path," meaning a path that is ideally free of obstacles. In searching for the level path, we also play a role. We can't intentionally put ourselves on rocky ground and then ask for the Spirit to help us make it smooth.

It is important for us to ask for the grace of the Holy Spirit to come into us, guide us, inspire us, complete what is lacking in us, and encourage us. The prayer that accompanies this reflection is an Orthodox Christian prayer to the Holy Spirit, often used to begin Orthodox worship services.

Heavenly King, Comforter, Spirit of Truth, present in all places and filling all things, treasury of good things and giver of life; come, take Your abode in us; cleanse of every stain, and save our souls, O Good one. (Trans. by Fr. Seraphim Dedes)[26]

Encouragement Challenge: Leave room for the Holy Spirit to operate in your life. Allow (and ask for) His grace to complete what is lacking and complete what is infirm in your life!

Be a Follower, Not a Fan

Now when Jesus saw great crowds around Him, He gave orders to go over to the other side. And a scribe came up and said to Him, "Teacher, I will follow You wherever You go." And Jesus said to him, "Foxes have holes, and birds of the air have nests; but the Son of man has nowhere to lay His head."
Matthew 8:18–20

One of the most inspiring and sobering books I have ever read is entitled *Not a Fan* by Kyle Idleman.[27]. The premise of the book is that most Christians behave more like "fans" of Christ rather than "followers." What does that mean?

In the sports world, people are fans of teams. For instance, I am a fan of the Tampa Bay Lightning hockey team. I own a shirt, a jersey, a hat, and a sweatshirt. I go to a few games a year. I read about them in the paper. I am a fan.

However, I do not "follow" the Tampa Bay Lightning in the sense that this organization leads my life. When there is conflict between a hockey game and family, family wins. When there is a conflict between work and watching a hockey game, work wins. And when the team plays on the other coast so that they are playing until 1:00 a.m., and there is a conflict between watching them and sleeping, off goes the TV, and I go to bed and check the score in the morning.

Many people take the same approach to their Christianity. They are fans. They wear a cross or have a Bible on their nightstand. They even go to church when they can. But when there is conflict between Christianity and life, life wins. And that might mean choosing a baseball game over worship on a Sunday. Or it might mean choosing dishonesty over honesty because it's more convenient. It might mean succumbing to peer pressure rather than doing the godly thing for fear of losing status with your peers.

To be a follower of Christ is a lot different than being a fan. If you are a follower of anything, it means that there is a leader. And there is both obedience in following the leader and sacrifice in following the leader where the leader is going, which doesn't necessarily agree with where we may want to go.

When there is a conflict between what we want (or what our friends want) and what Christ wants, the follower of Christ goes with Christ. The fan doesn't.

The hockey team needs fans because fans fill stadiums and buy gear and allow a business organization (the hockey team is a business) to make money.

Christ doesn't need fans. He doesn't need us to buy crosses or Bibles or even fill churches. Christ wants us to go and change the world. Unfortunately, sometimes churches are so caught up with the "business" of the church (making enough money to keep the doors open) that they forget about the "mission" of the church, which is to spread the Word of God to all nations. Being a Christian is not about what we wear or the songs we sing. It's about how we behave and serve others. Being a follower of Christ is about loving Christ and serving Him by serving others.

In the above Bible verses, a scribe came up to Jesus and declared his desire to follow. And Jesus warned him, "Foxes have holes, and birds of the air have nests; but the Son of man has nowhere to lay His head." In other words, being a follower does not necessarily come with a lot of glamour or convenience. It's not about just putting on some Christian gear, knowing Christian songs, or even, I dare say, going to church. Being a follower can be like the fox who doesn't have a hole, or the bird who has no nest. Being a follower might cost you some friends if you choose Christ over the crowd.

I'm a hockey fan when the team is playing. During the "off season," I'm into a different sport, and I don't give hockey much thought. For followers of Christ, there is no off season, no day without a game. Following Christ is a continuous journey, where He is leading, and we are obedient. The journey doesn't stop, take breaks, or have an off season. Following Christ is not something we do only when it's convenient. As Jesus says in Matthew 8:20, being a follower might actually leave one materially poor. Imagine that Christ had nowhere to lay His head. He didn't hobnob in fancy hotels, restaurants, or enjoy a lavish lifestyle. His constant pursuit wasn't for money or fame. On the contrary, many times, He told someone He healed not to tell anyone.

Following Christ does not necessarily mean we will feel poor or oppressed all the time. However, to truly follow also means there will be difficult and challenging times when we will feel poor or oppressed. In encouraging one another to be better Christians, let's encourage to be followers, not fans, which means knowing there will be many difficult times to be a follower and encouraging one another especially in those times.

In this section of our study, we are focusing on letting the Spirit lead. It's not about letting our friends lead or popular media or the latest fashions. To let the Spirit lead means moving ourselves from fans to followers.

Heavenly Father, there are so many joys as well as challenges to being a Christian. Help me to be more follower than fan. Give me strength and wisdom in the times when this is difficult. I love You, Lord! Help me to love You and serve You more and more. Amen.

Encouragement Challenge: Be a follower, not a fan!

God's Glory Will Change You

Moses said to the Lord, "See, Thou sayest to me, 'Bring up this people'; but thou hast not let me know whom Thou wilt send with me. Yet Thou hast said, 'I know you by name, and you have also found favor in My sight.' Now therefore, I pray Thee, if I have found favor in Thy sight, show me now Thy ways, that I may know Thee and find favor in Thy sight. Consider too that this nation is Thy people." And He said, "My presence will go with you, and I will give you rest." And he said to Him, "If Thy presence will not go with me, do not carry us up from here. For how shall it be known that I have found favor in Thy sight, I and Thy people? Is it not in Thy going with us, so that we are distinct, I and Thy people, from all other people that are upon the face of the earth?" And the Lord said to Moses, "This very thing that you have spoken I will do; for you have found favor in My sight, and I know you by name." Moses said, "I pray Thee, show me Thy glory." And He said, "I will make all My goodness pass before you, and will proclaim before you My name 'The Lord'; and I will be gracious to whom I will be gracious, and will show mercy on whom I will show mercy. But," He said, "you cannot see My face; for man shall not see Me and live." And the Lord said, "Behold, there is a place by Me where you shall stand upon the rock; and while My glory passes by I will put you in a cleft of the rock, and I will cover you with My hand until I have passed by; then I will take away My hand, and you shall see My back; but My face shall not be seen."
Exodus 33:12–23

One of the most comforting stories in the Bible is the story of Moses beholding God's glory. As we know, Moses was leading the children of Israel out of Egypt to the "promised land." They didn't know how long the journey would take, and in the end, it took forty years. They were plagued along the way with various challenges—hunger, thirst, the elements, serpents, and disease. For Moses, it seemed like the journey would never end. The people got frustrated. He got frustrated. He had doubts. He probably even wondered if God still loved him if he had fallen out of favor with God. He even wondered aloud to God if he had found favor in God's sight.

God assured Moses that Moses indeed still had the favor of God. Moses, exacerbated, said to God *"I pray Thee, show me Thy glory,"* and God acquiesced to this request. He told Moses that he could not look upon the face of God but that He would put Moses into a cleft in a rock and let him see God's back, but not His face.

This experience did not change Moses's situation. He was still leading the people of Israel through the desert. He was still battling the elements and the strong will of the people. He wasn't transported from the desert to paradise in an instant. However, this experience changed Moses. He was never the same again. We are told in Exodus 34:29, *"that the skin of his face shone because he had been talking with God."* The people were not able to look at Moses because his face was so bright. He beheld God's glory, and it changed him. It didn't change his situation. It changed him.

We've all felt like Moses at times—exacerbated, frustrated, and wondering when our problem (or problems) will ever end. We've all had doubts. We've probably all wondered at some point whether we have fallen out of favor with God. The truth is that God loves each of us. He never abandons us. Sometimes the journey to the "promised land" (heaven) is a lot like the journey of the Israelites. It is fraught with challenges. It is long. It seems like it will never end.

One thing I do when I feel like Moses did, when faced with stress, uncertainty, or am just tired and wrung out, is to ask God, "show me Your glory." I ask God over and over again to let His glory shine in my life, in a situation, on that given day, or even in a given moment. I ask Him to show me glory, even in the midst of being sick, or before a difficult conversation.

This "glory" is not fame or fortune. It is not glory in the way we or I might define glory. It is "glory" in the way God defines it, in whatever way He reveals it. When Moses asked God to show him His glory, he wasn't specific about what he expected that to look like. He just asked God to show him glory. And God decided to show Moses what He looked like from the back. And that was enough to change Moses.

Meditating on God's glory (however He wants to reveal it) and His majesty helps me pass through difficult moments. It is a form of encouragement that comes from God and seems to come whenever I ask for it. The key thing is that it requires immense concentration. I work to block out the bad thoughts and focus on the concept of His glory. And then the time, or the test, passes. When I take my mind off of the glory and put it back on the worry, the worry comes right back. So, when you are anxious, think about God's glory, and ask for Him to show you His glory in some way, large or small, and continue to focus on this.

Lord, thank You for the gift of this day. Show me Your glory in some way, large or small today. Let Your glory cover over me, especially when I'm feeling challenged and overwhelmed. Give me confidence in the midst of doubt. Give me calm in the midst of anxiety. Give me peace in the midst of stress. Give me focus in the midst of confusion. And give me joy in the midst of any sadness. Help me focus on Your glory when I feel overwhelmed. And as Your glory changed Moses, please allow me to be continually changed as well. Amen.

Encouragement Challenge: Think about God's glory throughout the day today!

I Sin Most on Wednesdays

O God, be not far from me; O my God, make haste to help me!
Psalm 71:12

Is there a day of the week where you are more likely to sin? Or least likely?

My answer for the day I'm most likely to sin is Wednesday. Why Wednesday?

Every Sunday, I celebrate the Divine Liturgy (the Orthodox Eucharist Service) and receive Holy Communion. Holy Communion does several things for me. One of those things is it puts my antennas up as far as sinning goes. I'm less likely to use foul language on a Sunday right after Liturgy because I've just received Holy Communion. Something in my conscience reminds me, "Be careful what you say today; you've just received Communion." I'm less likely to use foul language on a Saturday night because I'm about to receive Communion the next day, and my conscience reminds me, "Be careful what you say today; you are going to receive Communion tomorrow."

I'm more likely to use foul language on a Wednesday because this is when I'm usually the furthest away from receiving Communion. Last Sunday is far in the rearview mirror, and next Sunday is too far over the horizon. And my conscience plays with me and says, "You don't have to be so careful today."

The week of the year where I sin the least is Holy Week (the week before we celebrate Easter, or as the Orthodox call it, Pascha). For this week of the year, I'm receiving Communion every day, and my conscience is on high alert at all times.

I don't know if other people have the same experience when it comes to Holy Communion, conscience, and foul language. But this is how it works for me. I can't imagine what kind of games my conscience would play if I only received Communion once a month or a couple of times a year. For me, frequent Communion helps act as a filter on behavior.

Holy Communion is the biggest spiritual event of the week but does not have to be the only spiritual event each week. Prayer should be a significant daily event in our lives. And it should, among other things, help act as a filter on our behavior. It would seem more difficult to go from being on our knees in prayer to yelling at a co-worker in the span of an hour. I would think that if one is praying, it would help us to act in a more Christian way toward others. Using the co-worker example, it will be harder to yell at the co-worker if they are included in your prayer each day.

When we don't pray regularly, it puts God out of view. He's either far in the rearview mirror or too far over the horizon. We forget about Him. And then we forget to act like Him. We forget to be loving, kind or forgiving.

This doesn't mean that because we pray, we do not sin. Everyone sins, no matter how much they pray. But when we pray more often, and I don't mean just checking a box and reciting some empty words, but when we pray often with a sincere and humble heart, it will slow down our sinful patterns.

It's like the person who eats healthy and exercises; they are less likely to have a heart attack. That doesn't mean they won't get sick because we all get sick. But the person who overeats and never moves is more likely to have a serious sickness.

The person who prays often still sins, but the sins will probably not be as serious. The person who never prays and never thinks about the Lord is more likely to succumb to temptation.

Often in counseling, I'll ask someone having marriage problems, "Do you pray for your spouse? Do you pray about these problems?" And the answer is usually no. Or the answer is, "I do now." If spouses, as an example, are in the habit early on in marriage of praying for each other, there is less likely to be a gulf between them later.

Prayer can do a lot of things for us, including closing gulfs between us and other people and closing the gap between sinful behavior and godly behavior. So, pray often so that God is the front and center in your life, not in the rearview mirror or over the horizon. And when He is there in the lead in your daily life, you will sin less.

One week is too long to go without a connection with God. And sometimes God can disappear from view even in the middle of a day. That's why we should pray often during the day to keep God in our view at all times.

There is no reason to sin more on Wednesdays. Prayer helps keep the focus every day.

Lord, I come before You today, placing You at the front of my life for this moment. Be with me today. Be front and center today. Help me to look at You before decisions and conversations. Help me to stay focused on You. And in the moments when You seem far away, bring thoughts of You to my mind. Stay close to me. Help me to stay close to You. Amen.

Encouragement Challenge: Pray today! And keep God in the front of your life today and always!

You Don't Do Stupid Things When You Feel Full

God did not give us a spirit of timidity but a spirit of power and love and self-control.
2 Timothy 1:7

One year at summer camp, after doing an activity where everyone encouraged each other, I asked the campers, "How do you all feel?" They said, "We feel really full." Then I asked them, "What if I suggested to you that we go drink or smoke weed right now? What do you think about that?"

They looked at me a little puzzled. Why would I be making a suggestion like that?!

One answered, "No, that would be really inappropriate." I answered, "Why? Because it's illegal?"

And the person answered, "No, it would be inappropriate because we all feel full. People do that stuff when they feel empty, to fill empty spaces."

One of the reasons why encouragement is so important is that it fills empty spaces. It makes people feel full, complete. And when people are full and not empty, they are less likely to go and do the things that fill the empty spaces—drinking, drugs, overeating, porn, and so on. When people feel discouraged, they feel empty, and they go to unhealthy places to fill those empty spaces.

When a person feels full of food, like after you've had a good meal at a restaurant, there is no desire for anything else to eat because eating more would make a person go from feeling full to feeling uncomfortable. When a person feels empty, they will go looking for food. And if they can't find food they like, they will go looking for food they don't like, just to have some food.

Many times, I have asked people, "Would you eat food out of a garbage can?" And the answer is always, "Heck no! That's disgusting!" To which I respond, "What if you hadn't eaten in a week?" And then the answer becomes, "The garbage can would look pretty good."

Most people can't conceive of eating out of a garbage can, but if they were hungry enough, they would.

Most of us don't think we're capable of robbing a store, but again, if you hadn't eaten in a while and were so empty and in need, you might cross that line and break the law, just to get some food.

When we are "hungry" in the sense that we need something that we can't get in an appropriate way, that is when we start doing inappropriate things. We go outside who we are to fill empty spaces. No one is born desiring violence. Violence is born out of a sense of emptiness—it might be caused by poverty, anger, or rejection. Something negative causes violence.

It is negative things that drive us to escape into food, alcohol, drugs, porn, watching too much TV, and so on.

Think about this—when you have had a very positive experience, you generally will not run to something negative, such as, "I just got a great grade on a test, so I'll run out and shoplift." You wouldn't do that. Negative things happen when we feel discouraged, that is, "I just got a bad grade, and I'm not thinking very highly of myself, so I'll go get high."

Even words of encouragement can help to stem a negative tide from rising. If someone says, "I'm counting on you," the response is generally not going to be, "Let me go get high" because when one is high, they can't be counted on. Words of discouragement make us feel empty and sometimes are even more harmful than a bad action, like a bad grade on a test. Because tests seem temporary, there will always be other tests to take. Words, however, seem permanent. Once they are said, they can't be unsaid, and they tend to haunt us. As encouragers, it is critical that we watch our words and use them to build up rather than tear down, to help fill people rather than empty them.

When we are filled with hope and positivity, things like anger and rejection and their consequences are harder to fall into.

It is important for us to feel full. It is important for us to feel encouraged. And we play an important role in making others feel full by encouraging them.

In closing off our small unit on letting the Spirit lead, it is important that we allow the Spirit to work through us as encouragers because encouragement will help fill us, and through it, we can help fill others. When one is full, there aren't empty spaces available that we generally fill with bad things.

If the Holy Spirit is the one who "fills all things," the Spirit is an encourager, and we, in tandem, work with the Spirit and in the Spirit to encourage others to fill their empty spaces.

It is such a great feeling to be satisfied, to not be in want. Seek out healthy ways to feel full, and make a conscious effort to fill others. There is enough "stupid" things going on in the world today. A little encouragement can go a long way to eliminating or significantly reducing some of them.

Lord, thank You for all the positive things that fill my life and my mind (list some of them). When I feel empty, let Your Spirit fill my empty spaces. And send people into my path who will encourage me and help keep my empty spaces filled. When I feel empty, help me to resist unhealthy temptations. Help me also to fill others. Bring people into my path today who feel empty and beat down so that I can encourage and fill them. Give me the thoughts and words to help fill others. Amen.

Encouragement Challenge: Seek out healthy things and healthy people so that you will feel "full." Help others feel full by encouraging others.

Part Ten
HOLD FAST

But test everything; hold fast to what is good.

1 Thessalonians 5:21

My Struggle Is too Ugly, so I Suffer in Silence

I said "I will guard my ways, that I may not sin with my tongue; I bridle my mouth, so long as the wicked are in my presence." I was dumb and silent, I held my peace to no avail; my distress grew worse and my heart became hot within me. As I mused, the fire burned; then I spoke with my tongue: "Lord, let me know my end, and what is the measure of my days; let me know how fleeting my life is! Behold, Thou hast made my days a few handbreaths, and my lifetime is as nothing in Thy sight. Surely every man stands as a mere breath! Surely man goes about as a shadow! Surely for naught are they in turmoil; man heaps up, and knows not who will gather! And now, Lord, for what do I wait? My hope is in Thee. Deliver me from all my transgressions. Make me not the scorn of the fool! I am dumb, I do not open my mouth; for it is Thou who has done it. Remove Thy stroke from me; I am spent by the blows of Thy hand. When Thou dost chasten men with rebukes for sin, Thou dost consume like a moth what is dear to him; surely every man is a mere breath. Hear my prayer, O Lord, and give ear to my cry; hold not Thy peace at my tears! For I am Thy passing guest, a sojourner, like all my fathers. Look away from me, that I may know gladness, before I depart and be no more!
Psalm 39

As a society, we tend to categorize and differentiate between struggles that are socially acceptable to discuss and those that aren't. Unfortunately, we know statistically that many people struggle with things that are seemingly unacceptable to discuss—pornography, infidelity, drug and alcohol abuse, suicidal ideation, and abortion, to name a few. It's not only these "bad" things that are kept in dark corners. There are things where there is no blame to be cast where people still think they have to suffer in silence—

A miscarriage is the first thing that comes to mind. A surprising number of women have had them. Surprisingly, few are able to talk about them. Menopause, intimacy problems, depression, anxiety, learning disabilities, and other things are other issues that many people struggle with that also stay hidden. Because we don't talk about these things, it is easy to pretend they don't exist, and the cycle of avoidance and discouragement continues.

I've come to the conclusion that everyone has something they struggle with. And that something might be a temporary something, and for some, their something is a permanent struggle.

I've also come to the conclusion that when we suffer in silence, our suffering is exacerbated because, in addition to the actual circumstance from which we suffer, we add loneliness and isolation to it. When we join others in the struggle, we benefit from encouragement, advice, and sometimes even useful help in managing or conquering our challenge.

Stoicism is viewed as a virtue by some. Some people will say it's not okay to cry or show weakness and will look down on those who do. It is interesting to note that even Christ cried on two occasions. When His friend Lazarus died, Jesus went to the tomb, and He wept there for His friend. Those tears were genuine sorrow over a friend who had died. Jesus didn't act stoic. He didn't say, "well, easy come, easy go." He genuinely mourned a friend whose life really mattered to Him.

In the Garden of Gethsemane, shortly before His crucifixion, again Jesus cried, and this time, He was meditating on His own death, and it scared Him. It made Him sorrowful. He took three disciples—Peter, James, and John—and He asked them to "watch" with Him. He didn't ask them to actually "do" anything, just to watch Him while He prayed so that He would know He was not alone. Of course, we know that they fell asleep. Watching proved to be difficult.

But there is a lesson here—If Jesus asked friends to "watch" with Him, why are we not doing the same? Why do we suffer in silence? We should ask trusted friends to help us, and if they are not able to help us, then at least "watch" with us, validate us, encourage us, and help us know that we are not alone in our struggles. The encouragement advice to be taken from this reflection is to make a decision to not suffer in silence and to consider asking others to help, and if not help, then to watch, to know your struggle so that they can encourage and validate and also go to the Lord in prayer over your struggle.

The second piece of advice is to tell your friends that you are there for them, that if they are ever struggling with something, you want them to bring you in so you can "watch" with them. You can't force anyone to lean on you, but you can create an environment in your life that will encourage those close to you to lean on you in their struggles. Create an environment where people will recognize you as a "safe" person, a person who will make it safe to confide in, who can hold a confidence, and who will not judge.

Lord, thank You for Your many blessings. Help me in my struggles. Bring people into my path who will lift me up and "watch" with me, who will accept me, struggles and all. Open my eyes so that I can see others who need encouragement and someone to "watch" with them. Amen.

Encouragement Challenge: Offer to "watch" for your friends. Ask them to "watch" with you as well.

Coming Out of the Dark: It Can't Happen Here. No, It Can and It Does

*Then they cried to the Lord in their trouble, and He delivered them from their distress;
He brought them out of darkness and gloom, and broke their bonds asunder Let them
thank the Lord for His steadfast love, for His wonderful works to the sons of men!
Psalm 107:13–15*

The was a mini-series when I was a child entitled *Blood and Honor*. It was about the Hitler Youth in Nazi Germany. In the story, there are two families, a German family and a Jewish family, living in a small town. News comes from the big cities that the Germans are persecuting the Jews. The Jewish mother says to her husband, "Let's get out of this town and out of this country before something happens to us," to which her husband replies, "It can't happen here. We are a small town; we are all like family." Later on in the movie, indeed the German family turns on their former Jewish friends.

This line, "It can't happen here," has always stuck with me. Many people think that just because we belong to a church and are active in a church community, we are somehow immune from all the problems in society that everyone else suffers from. The truth is, we are not. In many instances, we are batting the same average as the rest of society when it comes to smoking weed or looking at porn. Many Christian marriages end in divorce. Plenty of Christian spouses cheat. Drugs and suicide hit people in church communities as well. To think, and worse, to say, "It doesn't happen here," is simply an untruth. It does happen here.

In Tampa, where I currently serve, there is an annual charity walk for suicide prevention, which has as its title "Coming out of the Dark." The name comes from the idea that topics like suicide are kept in the dark. We don't talk about them. We pretend they don't happen in our communities. Except that they do.

Bringing issues from the "dark" of not being spoken about and into the "light" where they are spoken of is very important. In the area of encouragement, if we are going to encourage certain behaviors or just encourage in general, we have to be honest about the issues that discourage us, our peers, and our children. We have to be willing to tackle the hard issues instead of running away from them or pretending they don't happen in our communities, to our peers, or to our children.

In this unit, we will discuss issues like mental illness as well as how to create environments where people can feel safe to bring up things they struggle with. I do not pretend to be an expert on mental illness or suicide or any of the other societal problems. Many people are professionally trained in these areas, and I encourage you to seek out a professional counselor as appropriate. What I do know is how to listen as well as encourage those who need help to get it, but more importantly, to encourage people who have any kind of problem or struggle that you are not alone or hopeless, nor is your situation hopeless.

It's time that we come out of the dark and into the light with struggles that we have so we can deal with them, so that we can overcome them.

I once heard it said that, "If you are over age forty and don't wake up with a pain somewhere, you are dead." That's because virtually everyone over forty is struggling with some pain or ailment. The same is true for anyone who says, "I don't have problems." That person is either dead or lying. Everyone has some problem, some issue. Some problems we can solve on our own. Other problems may require medication. And other problems may be correctable through therapy. Thankfully, there are some that just require us to be more careful or change a habit.

Every human being is "fallen" in several ways. Each of us is fallen spiritually in that we all succumb to sin and temptation. But each of us carries some struggle. It may be something we are born with, like a health defect. It may be something we are prone to, that is, depression that tends to run in families. It may be something that comes from our life experience, such as a child who is bit by a dog as a kid and has a lifelong fear of dogs.

If we can turn a spotlight on issues we all have, we can all do a better job conquering the issues that can be conquered and managing the issues that cannot. And we can all do a better job encouraging one another as we each struggle with our unique issues.

Years ago, I had the opportunity to participate in the "Coming out of the Darkness" walk that was held in Tampa. I was there to support a friend whose son died by suicide. There were literally thousands of people who were there who had lost someone to suicide. Each person wore a different color of beads to represent the person they had lost—white was if it was someone's son or daughter, blue if it was a friend, and so on. It was sobering to see how many people know someone who has been lost to suicide. And yet, by and large, we stay quiet on this subject. From my work experience, I can tell everyone that it is coming up more and more often—people are either doing it, talking about doing it, or suffering from the struggles that lead to it. Clearly it is something we need to do a better job getting out into the light.

The next reflection will be specifically about mental illness, another issue that has come more into the light but still needs more attention. The point of this reflection is that we can't tell ourselves "It (suicide, mental illness, struggle, etc.) doesn't happen here (in our cultural group, neighborhood, or town)" because it does, it can, and it will.

As encouragers, we need to provide safe spaces to tackle the tough issues, and encourage one another to keep struggling with whatever cross we are carrying.

Lord, each of us struggles with something. (Name some of your struggles.) Help me in my fight against my struggles. Help others in their fight against theirs. Give me an eye to see others who are struggling and a heart that runs to help them. Be with all those who have lost someone to suicide, and give rest and mercy to those who have. Amen.

We can all do a better job of shining the light on struggles that have been kept in the dark too long and supporting and encouraging one another in our unique struggles!

**In memory of Alex Vukmer.*

Mental Illness

Cast all your anxieties on Him, for He cares about you.
1 Peter 5:7

One of our prayer team members asked me to write on how to live as a Christian while also living with mental issues like depression, anxiety, body image issues, and others. Again, I am not an expert in mental illness nor a medical professional. But here is my take on mental illness and Christianity.

Because of the fall of Adam, we all are subject to imperfections. We all sin. We all get tired. We all get hungry, angry, frustrated, and so on. We all get physical illnesses. They may be a cold, the flu, or a fever. We have bodies that break. Most of us have broken an arm or a leg. Many of us or our children need braces to fix imperfect teeth. And there is no shame in any of these things. No one has ever felt ashamed because their child needed braces. We might feel annoyed if we have a headache, but no one feels ashamed because of it. When we are physically sick, most of us are pretty quick to run to the doctor, eager to get the treatment or medication that will fix the problem so that we can go on with our lives.

There are two kinds of physical illnesses— acute ones and long-term ones. Examples of acute physical illness include a cold, flu, strep throat, and so on. Medication, rest, and some patience are needed, and these illnesses generally peter out, and we are back to restored health. Long-term physical illnesses include things like cancer, diabetes, stroke, dementia, and Parkinson's Disease, among others. These are illnesses that generally will not get better. Most of us know someone with at least one of these illnesses, and unfortunately, in our lives, many of us will suffer from one of these as well. Again, there is no shame there. They are generally a part of every life.

If the human being is composed of body, mind, and spirit, then we know that we get sick in more than just our bodies. At some point, most of us will suffer from some degree of "mental illness." While "mental illness" may seem like a word or term associated with some degree of stigmatism, I would argue, what else would we call it? We all have been afflicted with physical illness—headache, cold, broken arm, and so on. And likewise, we are all afflicted to some degree with mental illness.

A mental illness is a disease of the mind. It is not a disease of the body but of the mind. If the body can get sick, and we all know it can from experience, the mind can get sick as well. The sickness of the mind can be temporary—extreme stress, grief, and sadness might be due to a situation and can be temporary.

However, there are times when a condition of the mind is not temporary. While depression might be situational for all of us at times, such as when a loved one has passed away and we feel sad for a while, there are times when mental illness becomes chronic, something we deal with every day. There are people who have issues with depression and anxiety that are not situational but come up every day. Just as there would be with a chronic physical illness, there should be no shame associated with a mental illness. There still is shame in our society, and that is a sad thing. We should not have a stigma or a shame about mental illness.

How do we live as a Christian with mental issues? The same way as we live as a Christian with physical issues. We ask God for the strength to get through each day and each challenge. We realize that God cares more about our efforts than our successes because success tends to be defined by society. What society sees as successful, in the eyes of God, it might be a failure. For instance, a person who is financially successful who uses nefarious means to attain that financial success might be seen in a positive light by a society that praises fame and fortune, but at the same time would not be seen in a favorable light by God, who prefers us to be people of honesty and integrity.

We should also avail ourselves of the people and services that help deal with mental illness. Just as God doesn't expect us to go it alone with physical illness, He doesn't expect us to go it alone with mental illness. This is why He calls people to be physicians of the body as well as physicians of the mind.

If the human being is body, mind, and spirit, then people get spiritual illnesses also. Generally, the spiritual illnesses are a consequence of a physical or mental illness. Spiritual illnesses include doubt and despondency—that is, if God is so great, why has this malady befallen me? The "physicians" of the soul are the clergy. We go to the clergy for spiritual support. A priest or pastor will not heal a broken leg; a medical doctor does that. But a priest can work with someone to heal a wounded soul.

Encouragers need to recognize that illness is a part of life. We can't tell people to pretend they aren't sick or even tell them that all sicknesses can be healed because some cannot. We can all encourage people to go to the proper place—a doctor, mental health specialist, or pastor—to take care of whatever illness has come over them. We can all do our part to remove the stigma of illness—whatever kind it may be. We can also love people for who they are. I'm 100 percent certain that people don't want to be sick. Most sickness is not part of our own doing. We don't go out seeking to break a leg, catch a cold, or have a learning disability. Sickness is generally the consequence of living in a fallen world. We can validate those who are sick that sickness is difficult. We can help those who are sick, whether it is listening, encouraging, or helping with something specific like a ride or referral. The biggest thing we can all do is to accept others without judgment.

Spiritually, as we read in the Scripture verse from today, we should cast our anxieties before the Lord and know that He cares about each of us. We all have heard the phrase, "God doesn't give us what we can't handle." I actually think that is a bad phrase. Rather, I prefer the phrase, "God helps us handle what we have been given." Encouragers help those who are challenged to handle what they are challenged with.

Lord, You created each of us in Your image and likeness. The imperfections we each have are a result of a fallen world, which was not Your intention. As we work our way to Your kingdom, help us to remember that Your kingdom is a place where there will be no more pain, sorrow, or suffering. Help us therefore in the struggles we have in this life, whether they be physical, mental, or spiritual. Give healing and provide healers to treat our various maladies and wounds. And give comfort when healing is not possible. Give strength to those who suffer from any illness of body, mind, or spirit. And help me to be sensitive, encouraging, and helpful to anyone who is suffering from any kind of illness. Amen.

There should be no stigma about any kind of mental illness—we've all got to work to purge our society of the stigma surrounding mental illness!

Managing the Things That Cannot Be Changed

More than that, we rejoice in our sufferings, knowing that suffering produces endurance, and endurance produces character, and character produces hope, and hopes does not disappoint us, because God's love has been poured into our hearts through the Holy Spirit which has been given to us.
Romans 5:3–5

There are things in all of our lives that are not perfect, things we wish we could change. We can change many of those things. If one is not a good public speaker, there are classes one can take to improve, and experience will generally help one improve in this area and many others.

Some things in this world each of us are not good at, and that's okay. We don't have to be good at everything. I was a terrible student when it came to science. And while I struggled with that in my life as a high school student, it's not something that really matters in the big picture of my life because I earn a living doing something that isn't science. I was never very good at sports, so I didn't up as a professional athlete either. Even for those who excel in sports, most will not earn a living playing a sport.

Then there are things each of us struggle with that do make life a challenge. These are the physical and mental challenges that we mentioned in the last reflection. Some can be conquered. For example, it is possible for a person who struggles with being overweight to lose weight in a sensible way.

There are certain things, however, that we cannot conquer. And the operative word for these things is "management." We have to learn to "manage" some of our challenges.

Allow me to speak personally for a moment. I was born with a cleft lip and palate. I didn't choose to be born with these things. They just happened. I have had multiple surgeries to try to correct the issues that these things bring into a person's life, and they have been effective, but only to a certain point. There are some residual issues that cannot be corrected. So, they have to be managed. I get a lot of mucus discharge from my nose. Therefore, it is necessary to carry Kleenex with me at all times because after eating or after talking or singing for a while, I have to blow my nose. I've even built in a few seconds in the middle of our Sunday service to step away from the altar just to blow my nose. Because there is a hole in the roof of my mouth, things can sometimes go through it and come out of my nose. So, when eating ice cream, I have learned to flip the spoon over so the spoon is against the roof of my mouth so no ice cream can go up there. I can't amass any air pressure in my mouth, so blowing up balloons is impossible. When balloons need to be blown up, I make sure someone else can do that for me. I've had to wear expensive orthodontic apparatus in my mouth for virtually my entire life, so I've managed to make it without chewing gum or hard candy. And for nearly thirty years, I had to wear a steel plate over my palate, which prohibited me from eating or drinking anything that is too hot, so I learned to eat things lukewarm. When I don't drink enough water, mucus will get stuck in my throat, and I will cough or choke until it somehow gets out. Some people comment that it always sounds like I'm sick or have a cold, and that is not the case; it's just part of the cleft palate. When I was a teenager, people made fun of how I looked, and that was devastating, but thankfully, in adult like, very few people make comments about that. I had to do speech therapy until the end of seventh grade, and many people commented to me in those early years that I would have no future in public speaking. Thankfully, I didn't listen to them. As challenges go, I'll take a cleft lip and palate over other physical maladies.

The operative word in some struggles is "management." If we can't conquer something, we have to learn to manage it. And if someone has an issue they can't fix, then we've all got to learn not only how to accept it but embrace it. When we "accept" people for who they are, that sounds like a negative, such as, "I'll accept you despite your shortcomings." It would be better to embrace people for who they are. I didn't choose my physical and neurological challenges—they are part of who I am. Others have their own challenges—they are part of who they are. A person can't control if he or she is autistic, has a developmental delay, a learning disability, a stuttering problem, social awkwardness, or two left feet.

If we embrace people for who they are, we will quickly discover their strengths and gifts since we all have many of each. I have a cleft palate. It is part of who I am. I can't conquer it. I can only manage it. And I manage it so it doesn't manage me. If someone is going to embrace me, they are going to have to embrace those things because they are part of me. I hope that when people see me, they see my gifts and talents, not the things I struggle with. As we look at others, may we do the same.

St. Paul had it right in Romans 5:3–5. I used to not like these verses. I heard too much of "suffering build character" when I was younger. Suffering doesn't produce character, though.

It produces endurance, as St. Paul so correctly writes. (Patience is another word that can be inserted here.) Endurance and patience are the things that produce character. Character produces hope. And keeping our hope on God may occasionally disappoint us (as God occasionally disappoints us), but over the long haul, hope in God will not disappoint us.

The prayer that accompanies this reflection is the well-known Serenity Prayer by Reinhold Niebuhr[28] Most people know the first three lines. However, most are unfamiliar with the rest of the prayer. It is printed in its entirely below. Indeed, it reminds us that there are certain things about ourselves we will never change. It takes serenity to accept the things we cannot change. It takes management of them as well.

> *God grant me the serenity to accept the things I cannot change,*
> *Courage to change the things I can,*
> *and Wisdom to know the difference.*
>
> *Living one day at a time,*
> *Enjoying one moment at a time,*
> *Accepting hardship as a pathway to peace,*
> *Taking, as Jesus did,*
> *This sinful world as it is,*
> *Not as I would have it,*
> *Trusting that You will make all things right,*
> *If I surrender to Your will,*
> *So that I may be reasonably happy in this life,*
> *And supremely happy with You forever in the next.*
> *Amen.*

Encouragement Challenge: Learn to manage the things you cannot change. Encourage others to do the same. Learn to love people as they are and for who they are, including the things about them that they cannot change.

Empathy – Getting in the Sufferings of Others

On one of those days, as He was teaching, there were Pharisees and teachers of the law sitting by, who had come from every village of Galilee and Judea and from Jerusalem; and the power of the Lord was with Him to heal. And behold, men were bringing on a bed a man who was paralyzed, and they sought to ring him in and lay him before Jesus; but finding no way to bring him in, because of the crowd, they went up to the roof and let him down with his bed through the tiles in the midst before Jesus.
Luke 5:17–19

Jesus told us that the greatest commandments are to love God and love our neighbor. There are many ways to love our neighbor. Encouragement is certainly an important way to express that love. Encouragement comes in different forms. The easiest form, perhaps, is verbal. We offer words of encouragement to our neighbor. Listening can provide encouragement as well, as people need sensitive ears to listen to problems and challenges.

Many times, however, encouragement involves more than words. It involves actions. In the story of the paralytic who was healed by Jesus, his friends played a crucial role. They carried him to where Jesus was. He couldn't have gotten there without them. And when they got to the house where Jesus was, and they realized they couldn't get in, they got the man up on to the roof of the house, cut a hole in the roof, and lowered him to Jesus. Only then did the miracle of his healing occurred.

The miracle of our spiritual healing involves encouragement from others. Sometimes that encouragement is not only words but actions. Those actions require thinking and even risk-taking. Look at the friends who had to take a big risk lifting their friend onto the roof of a house.

Most people confuse the word empathy with sympathy. Both words include the Greek word *pathos*, which means "suffering." When one is sympathetic, they say, "I know what you are going through, and I am sorry." When one is empathetic, it means, "I'm going to get in there and suffer along with you." Empathy is putting yourself in the shoes of another. Empathy is what St. Paul refers to in Galatians 6:2 where he says, *"bear one another's burdens and so fulfill the law of Christ."*

Empathy involves DO-ing something to alleviate the suffering and provide healing. We all suffer in physical ways. This is why we have doctors. We all suffer in emotional and spiritual ways as well. While we have professionals like psychologists and priests who dedicate their lives to the emotional and spiritual being of others, anyone can offer assistance to those suffering in physical, emotional, and spiritual ways. For those who are physically sick, we can lend a hand or cook a meal and take it over to their house. We can drive people to doctor appointments or sit with their family in a waiting room during an operation. For those who are emotionally suffering, we can offer a kind ear, shoulder to cry on, and positive reinforcement. For those who are spiritually suffering, we can offer prayer and encouragement.

Empathy means picking up the phone or getting in a car and visiting, sacrificing some time, showing some vulnerability, and thinking outside the box. Yes, it is sometimes hard to be empathetic. But loving relationships are built when we allow ourselves to be vulnerable. Encouragement is a step that should lead to empathy, vulnerability, and love. Love for one another fills God's greatest commandment to us.

Lord, thank You for the many blessings in my life. Be with those whose lives do not have the blessings I enjoy. Help me to be a person not only of sympathy but one of empathy. Allow me to meet my responsibilities in life so that I have sufficient time to get my things done and still have time to serve others. Open my eyes and heart so that when there is an opportunity to show empathy, I am ready to do so. Amen.

Encouragement Challenge: Keep your eyes open for opportunities to show empathy and to help others! Make at least one unsolicited gesture of help today.

VULNERABILITY

Love is patient and kind; love is not jealous or boastful; it is not arrogant or rude. Love does not insist on its own way; it is not irritable or resentful; it does not rejoice at wrong, but rejoices in the right. Love bears all things, believes all things, hopes all things, endures all things. Love never ends.
1 Corinthians 13:4–8

The most basic building block of any human relationship is respect. Two people who don't know each other should operate at a minimal level with respect. No one should be physically or emotionally hurt. If I've never met you before, and you come to the office, you are guaranteed that I won't hurt or harm or threaten you. That's basic respect.

The next step in building a relationship is commonality, spending time together and finding things you have in common with someone else. If two people like baseball, maybe a friendship is built with an outing to a baseball game, or throwing the ball around the yard.

Over time, a rapport is built between two people, and trust begins to develop. The next step is crucial, and that is showing some kind of vulnerability. Where there is trust, there can be vulnerability. To move from trust to love, there has to be vulnerability. Love begins to take root the day that someone says, "I'm not doing so well," and the other says, "I'd like to help." Both people are then vulnerable. One becomes vulnerable in sharing. The other becomes vulnerable by listening and helping.

The problem in our society is that we are "plastic." Many relationships consist of only surface dialogue. "Hi." "How are you?" "Fine, how are you?" "Fine." And they don't get much beyond that. There is no vulnerability here, and thus there will never be love. Part of the reason we don't get to the vulnerable stage is because of what precedes vulnerability, and that is trust. Trust is hard to build, hard to maintain, and easy to break. And because we don't build environments of trust, we don't feel comfortable being vulnerable.

The other problem that we all have is that we are all prideful. We don't like admitting when we are wrong or when we feel weak. We don't trust that it won't be used against us in some instances. Or we're just plain stubborn in others. Or we feel like we can do it alone or have to do it alone. Christ told us not to be prideful, that it is okay to feel weak, to repent when we've done wrong, and work with the failings of others, not holding things against them. Most of all, Christ told us not to feel alone or allow others to feel alone.

Obviously, not every relationship in our life will allow for vulnerability. But we will have a hard time getting through life without any relationship where there can be vulnerability. Some relationships do not lend themselves to vulnerability. They might be classified as transactional relationships. For instance, at the bank I go to, I regularly see the same teller. She knows my name. She knows the amount of money in my bank accounts. And that's all she knows about me. Our interactions are friendly; we've never had a cross word, but there is no vulnerability there. There is some trust there—I trust that she will get the money into the account. But there is no need for her to trust me. It is a transactional relationship. The only time I interact with her involves a bank transaction.

An authentic relationship involves vulnerability. We need authentic relationships. Most of us crave authentic relationships. A big part of encouragement involves building authentic relationships.

If an authentic relationship is the goal in some (obviously it will not happen in all) of our relationships, then it starts with time in fellowship, laughing, and conversation. Spend this time, and you build rapport. Set boundaries and guidelines for what to do when you have conflict. Learn how to forgive when things go wrong. Then trust will form, and the environment has been created for you to go deeper in conversations, share honestly, and be vulnerable. This is how you build an authentic relationship with someone.

When a relationship begins to break down, to restore it, you go back to the foundation of time, rapport, and trust and work your way back to being vulnerable. Just because a relationship reaches the vulnerable stage doesn't mean you don't have to keep working at it or that there aren't occasionally steps backward. This holds true with our relationship with Christ and one another.

We ALL need work on authentic relationships—on building them and maintaining them. Authentic relationships are necessary to experience love as God created love. Love is a sense of oneness and unity, and this isn't possible when relationships remain strictly on the surface. So, while vulnerability is hard—no one likes showing vulnerability—this is the only way to authentic relationships, which we all need and crave.

If an authentic relationship is the goal in a relationship with Christ, it starts with time. It starts with time in prayer, Scripture reading, worship, and charity. Spend this time, and you build rapport and then trust. Vulnerability begins with honest prayer, confession, repentance. And these lead to an authentic relationship with Christ.

Lord, help me to know You better. Help me to trust in Your plan for my life. Let me bring my joys and struggles to You, confident that You hear my prayers. Help me to build an authentic relationship with You. Bring people into my life who will love, support, and encourage me. Help us create environments of trust, where it is okay to be vulnerable and easy to forgive. Give me the courage to be vulnerable. Help me build authentic relationships. Amen.

Time. Create the environment. Build trust. Be vulnerable. Build an authentic relationship. This works with Christ and your neighbor.

Creating Environments Where It Is Safe to Be Vulnerable

For who is God, but the Lord? And Who is a rock, except our God?—the God who girded me with strength, and made my way safe.
Psalm 18:31–32

In the last reflection, we discussed the concept of vulnerability. To have an authentic relationship, there needs to be an environment where one can be vulnerable. One of the reasons we struggle with vulnerability is that we live in environments of competition, where there are winners and losers. For example, in situations of employment, workers are commodities, and they are replaceable and disposable. The sad truth is that in many circumstances, it is not safe to be vulnerable.

Many people go through "crises of conscience." They have doubts about their careers, marriages, faith, abilities, or other things. Let's say, for example, that a teacher is struggling with doubts about whether he or she should continue teaching. Where can the teacher safely go to talk about these doubts? It's won't be the principal. If the principal doubts the teacher, the principal will want to replace the teacher. It can't be the students. If the teacher lets on to the students that he or she might not feel like continuing to teach, the teacher will lose his or her authority in the classroom. It can't be the parents of the students. If the teacher shares his or her doubts, he or she will lose the trust of the parents. What about other teachers? The problem in a competitive environment is that teachers may see other teachers as competition. Can other teachers be trusted with the secret doubts this teacher is carrying? If those teachers gossip, word will certainly get to the principal, other teachers, students, and parents.

What if the person with doubts is the principal? Who will he or she confide in? The school board? The subordinate teachers? Parents? Students?

What if the doctor has doubts about practicing medicine? Does he or she confide in the nurses? Patients?

You get the point. Because so many people are riddled with doubts and struggles and have no one to confide them in, they suffer in silence. It may be with something significant, as we discussed in a previous reflection, or it might be something mundane, such as the "midlife crisis" that hits many people as they approach middle age or get to the middle of their careers.

Everyone needs at least one (and probably more than one) relationship where they can feel safe being vulnerable, where it is safe and expected to be honest. Many people from all walks of life don't have this.

There are a couple of specific types of people I've met over my years in ministry who seem to feel the most alone. One of them is the "CEO" type. The person who is at the top of the company or organization still has the same need to show vulnerability as anyone else. However, because this person has only subordinates, they feel they cannot confide in anyone and must maintain a certain image or persona, whether it is true or just a façade. Another type of person who might feel alone is the affluent person. People assume that money equates to happiness. It doesn't necessarily. People who are affluent assume they will get no sympathy from those who are not and don't confide in affluent peers because, well, there is pressure also to keep up a certain image.

We perpetuate this cycle of dishonesty, image, persona, and façade because we haven't learned how to be vulnerable; we haven't managed to create environments where it is safe to be honest.

The first thing needed to have a safe environment is respect. That's the building block of any relationship. When I hear confession, in my ministry, for example, there is an implied rule, which many times I actually say to the person going to confession: "I love and respect you before you start. I will love and respect you when you are finished." This statement creates a boundary; it tells the person coming to confession that you can feel safe saying whatever you want to say and be assured that I won't think any less of you. Imagine if I said, "Well, you say what you want, and I'll think what I want," no one would feel safe to be honest, worried that I might lose respect for them. It doesn't matter whether we are priests hearing confessions or friends hearing the pains of other friends, we have to create environments where people feel they will still be respected even if they say something that is disappointing.

The second thing needed in a safe environment is confidentiality. Everyone struggles with keeping confidences. There are two reasons for this—first, when we have news to share, we are more relevant in our peer groups. When we don't have our own news to share, there is a great temptation to share the news of others, such as, "Did you hear about so and so?" It makes us relevant. Second, people are curious. We press each other for details about other people. And it is very hard, under pressure, to not want to share something that has been confided in us. There can't be vulnerability without trust, and there can't be trust if there is no ability to keep a confidence.

The third thing needed is commitment. This goes hand in hand with respect. If one is not sure a relationship will continue, it will be hard to be honest or to feel safe. If there is a commitment in a relationship, it will be easier to feel safe being honest. We can't feel committed if we feel like we are disposable.

The fourth thing (and there may be more, but I'll stop at four) that is needed is a mechanism to forgive and restore if, in being honest, one is also offensive. For instance, if I tell a friend that he has disappointed me, and that friend might be hurt, the relationship could get compromised. In another instance, in the context of being honest and trying to sort out feelings when a friend has wronged me, I might say the wrong thing or make a wrong step. It is critical in a relationship that if one person offends another, there is a mechanism for forgiveness and restoration.

Once one is assured that they won't lose respect (or a job, friendship, etc.), that what they say won't be repeated, that there is a commitment to the relationship, and there are mechanisms in place for forgiveness and restoration to take place, it will be easier to be vulnerable because a person will know that it is safe to be honest.

One additional key ingredient to keeping a relationship safe and honest is to keep it Christ-centered. When we pray for one another, forgive one another, and seek to love one another as Christ loves us, behaving in a Christlike manner to one another, it is much easier to maintain authentic, vulnerable, and honest relationships.

Everyone needs a place where they can be vulnerable, where it is safe to be honest. If we cannot be honest, that leaves us to living our lives and building relationships that are less than honest. And this is discouraging! To feel encouraged in our lives and relationships, we need relationships where it is safe to be honest.

Lord, thank You for relationships and friendships I have made in my life. (List the names of your closest family, friends, and confidants.) Help me to be respectful in my relationships, keep confidences, listen without judgment, and forgive easily. Please guide my family and friends to do the same for me. Help me to create and maintain relationships where it is safe to be vulnerable. Bring others around me who can do the same for me. Amen.

Encouragement Challenge: It is critical that we create relationships where it is safe and expected to be honest.

My Secret Heart

Behold, Thou desirest truth in the inward being; therefore teach me wisdom in my secret heart.
Psalm 51:6

Deep inside each person is something Psalm 51 refers to as "my secret heart." This is the place where a person has his or her internal battles, secret hurts, or most profound joys. The secret heart is our soul, our conscience. There are some people in society, I believe, who have a conscience that is for all intents and purposes, dead. These people are called sociopaths because they do wrong but believe they are right. And perhaps, to a degree, all of us exhibit sociopathic tendencies at times. However, for more people and most times, we know deep down what is right and wrong. And the battle is to stick with what is right, even when we are tempted by ourselves or others to do what we know is wrong.

There is nothing wrong with enjoying something. There is nothing wrong with having an ice cream cone or a beer and a pizza. There is something wrong with eating ice cream every day; it's not healthy. There is something wrong with having six beers with pizza if it makes one incapable of rendering aid to someone in need. There is nothing wrong with taking an afternoon off to watch a ballgame. There is something wrong with doing that every day.

There are some boundaries that have to be sacred, that can't be crossed no matter what. During college, I saw plenty of pot around. It was offered to me on more than one occasion. I never tried it. I felt pressured to drink until I stopped hanging around with those people. I've been with people who wanted to shoplift, and when they went to make their move, I ran out of the store. Not only did I not want to get caught with them, but I also didn't want to associate with them anymore because these people were willing to cross boundaries that were sacred to me. I got plenty of ridicule in college for going to church on Sundays, but that was a boundary for me. And I lost just about all my friends when I told them I was going to the seminary, that God's call was also a sacred boundary I could not ignore. In my professional life, there have been times I've been asked and even pressured to do things I knew were wrong, and I stood up and did the right thing (at least I hope I have), even though it came at a personal cost.

Everyone has their own secret heart, their own lines they draw between what they know is right and wrong. Certain things we are not sure on, and that's part of learning and growing, but most things we know what is right and wrong. If it is illegal, it is wrong. If it degrades ourselves or someone else, it is wrong. If it profanes God, it is wrong. If it hurts someone else, it is wrong. We all know that deep down.

Here's where it gets difficult. There is a definite boundary for when you are in my office. Once you cross the threshold and leave my office, you are not in my office. If you were sitting just outside my office, and someone called and asked where you were, most people would probably say, "I'm at Father's office," even though the correct answer is, "I'm just outside the office." If you were in the parking lot near the office, one might still be tempted to say, "I'm at the office." Same thing if one was down the street from the office—they might be tempted to say, "I'm at the office," knowing that they will be at the office momentarily or had just left it.

This is where we get in trouble because we all rationalize: "I'm almost 21," or "just this one time" or "just one more," or "everyone is doing it," or "no one will get hurt," or "it's not that bad," or "it's not like I killed anyone," to mitigate behaviors that we all know are wrong that we still want to do. Even worse than this is when we use these phrases to pressure or goad other people into doing things that we and they know are wrong because we want to do them.

This is why we need to continually pray for wisdom in our secret hearts, to know right from wrong, and stay the course for the right while steering away from the wrong. Some things have to be sacred, untouchable by anyone, and not taken away by peer pressure or even personal temptation.

One of my favorite all-time quotes comes from a Greek Orthodox priest named, Fr. Nicon Patrinacos, who wrote the following:

> *Whenever I think of a church Cathedral, I find myself thinking of the Cathedral of one's own soul in which he, in absolute solitude, and face to face with God, lives the most earnest and most decisive moments of his life. The Cathedral encloses within its splendid architectural line something more than a physical achievement. In fact, if the walls and the art of this edifice could speak, I am sure they would voice the presence here and now of the joys and sorrows of our hearts as well as the upward flying of our souls. They would attest to the fact that this building is a living entity, heart-beating and breathing, a treasure that is becoming constantly augmented as we grow in the life of Christ.*
>
> *~Fr. Nicon Patrinacos*[29]

Our secret hearts are where the battle is fought. We are aided when we are encouraged. We are tempted when we are pressured. No one can steal our secret hearts, though. They are ours. And we must guard them for the sacred entities that they are.

Lord, deep within me is my secret heart, my soul, my being, the place where there are certain things known only by You—my secret joys, my secret fears, my secret struggles. Lord, help me with these things with which I struggle. Help me to always know right from wrong. Help me to have courage of conviction to do right and avoid wrong. Bring people into my life who can support and encourage me as I carry my heavy burdens, even the ones I cannot share. Help me to define my boundaries and hold fast to them. Teach me wisdom in my secret heart. Amen.

Some boundaries we set must be sacred, unable to be touched by anything and anyone!

Test Questions

The name of the Lord is a strong tower; the righteous man runs into it and is safe.
Proverbs 18:10

Before we spend some time talking about holding fast to what is good, there is another important part of this verse, which is to test everything. The word test has several connotations. The first thing that comes to mind for most of us is the kind of test we take at school, to examine what knowledge we have on a certain subject. The second thing that comes to mind is a medical test, where we are examined to determine what kind of health we are in. Another kind of test is when we test equipment to make sure it will work. For instance, before doing a speech or concert, participants will test the microphones to make sure that they work. They will make sure the volume is adequate, the batteries (if used) are fresh, and their voice can be heard everywhere in the room. If there is something wrong, if the microphone will not work as it is needed, adjustments are made before the show goes on.

We make many decisions each day. And most of those decisions are inconsequential. For instance, if we have a chicken sandwich or a cheeseburger for lunch, it doesn't really matter. However, many decisions we make have consequences. Some of those consequences won't matter in a few days. The choice to stay up late watching a movie and not getting enough sleep will make one sluggish the next day, and that's about it. Of course, watching a movie and not studying for a test and failing it could have more long-lasting consequences. And some choices might matter for the rest of your life. For instance, the choice to drink and drive could result in the driver's death, the death of someone else, or an arrest for drunk driving.

It is important that we "test" things we are about to do; to see how they might play out. Here are some questions to consider:

1. *Is it safe?* Meaning, is there the potential for me or someone else to get hurt? Most of us have a survival instinct that kicks in to keep us safe. Peer pressure, being under the influence of drugs or alcohol, and inadequate sleep can inhibit us from answering this question correctly. What many of us don't think on enough is does a particular situation or decision make someone else unsafe? Most of us learned in pre-school that "hands are for helping," and "hands are not for hitting." Just as most of us have a survival instinct

for ourselves that kicks in to keep us safe, we should also work at cultivating a survival instinct that keeps others safe as well. If we are in a situation where someone is hurting someone else, there should be an innate instinct that motivates us to stop it. Because of peer pressure, and as some would call it, a *Lord of the Flies* mentality, we are sometimes slow to step in to prevent someone else from getting hurt.
2. *Is it smart?* There are certain things that are safe in the sense that they won't physically hurt us, but they are not smart, such as staying up until 4:00 a.m. and thinking one can function properly the next day.
3. *Is it in line with my character?* We spend our lives building a resume and reputation, which are shaped by our character. Unfortunately, it is very easy for one's character and reputation to be destroyed by one mistake. Getting caught in a lie is a great way to do this, so is committing a criminal offense. Because everything we do now is so public, we have to be even more careful and vigilant in what we do. A good rule of thumb is don't do or say anything you wouldn't want to read on the front page of a newspaper.
4. *Does it honor God?* As we've said before, we should test things not according to if they are moral (accepted by society) but if they are righteous (if they are right and true in the eyes of God).
5. *Does it get me closer to my goals?* Pornography doesn't get one closer to the goal of having a stable family. Neither does working too many hours. Overeating doesn't contribute to one's overall health (though an occasional feast probably doesn't hurt). Many people don't spend enough time setting and achieving goals so they don't necessarily think of this "test" question. When we make concrete goals and commit ourselves to achieving them, it becomes easier to use this question to keep us focused on doing the right thing.

Just as we wouldn't go on stage to give a speech without testing whether the microphone works, we shouldn't make important (or even small) decisions without testing whether they are a good idea.

Lord, thank You for the gift of this day and for the many opportunities it will bring. Along with opportunities, this day will bring many choices to me. Help me choose what is safe, to not only stay safe myself but to help others stay safe. Help me to make choices that are smart and think through my choices before I make decisions. Help me to not bend to pressure to be someone that I am not or do something that is not in line with my values. Help me to make decisions that will bring me closer to my goals. Most important, help me to make decisions today that will honor You. Amen.

Encouragement Challenge: Evaluate your choices today using these five test questions: Is it safe? Is it smart? Is it in line with my character? Does it honor God? Does it get me closer to my goals?

Hold Fast to Your Boundaries—
Drinking and Drugs

What agreement has the temple of God with idols? For we are the temple of the living God; as God said, "I will live in them and move among them, and I will be their God, and they shall be My people. Therefore, come out of them, and be separate from them, says the Lord, and touch nothing unclean; they I will welcome you, and I will be a Father to you, and you shall be My sons and daughters, says the Lord Almighty."
2 Corinthians 6:16–18

As we have discussed, it is important to create environments where it is safe and expected to be honest and vulnerable. One of the challenges to creating and maintaining these kind of environments is peer pressure to cross over boundaries. It seems that throughout life, there is a tension between identifying proper boundaries and then not falling to temptation to cross them. Over the next few reflections, we will discuss several boundaries that people will be tempted to cross. Today we will focus on drinking and drugs.

Through my ministry, I've watched many people go through high school and college. My teenage son is rapidly approaching these stages, and it scares me. I'm scared for him. We've raised him with certain morals and encouraged him to maintain certain boundaries. But he (and many others) is about to run a gauntlet that will test and tempt what we're raising him to know is right.

Drinking, drugs, and vaping are high on the list. He knows that these things are wrong. We've talked about them a lot in our home. And yet, many of his peers will be into these things in high school and college. While not every teen and young adult will fall into these things, they will ALL know people who will. There is no way that anyone gets through high school or college without being exposed to these things and people who are doing them.

Teens will have a hard time discerning what is right and wrong on their own. What will make it even harder is the pressure to do these things and the consternation that will come if one doesn't engage in them.

I remember back when I went to college in the early 1990s that I felt pressured to drink. I had no experience drinking before college. I had a great respect for the law, which said people under twenty-one were not allowed to drink. So, I had a conflict. Virtually everyone was drinking, had a fake ID if they were under twenty-one, and was drinking irresponsibly. Because I didn't have anyone I could confide in about this subject, I waded very cautiously. And after some minimal experience, I decided that this was not for me. Sadly, that did cost me some friends. I might take a sip of something just to be social on a very rare occasion, but I generally do not drink. And even now, I get occasional looks and comments like I'm doing something wrong.

For the teen who has gotten out of high school with little to no drinking experience, I almost feel sorry for them because they are about to run a gauntlet that will challenge and pressure them to conform to some kind of college norm. Some will learn to manage appropriately. Others will make critical mistakes. Will any of them have a safe environment, especially in college, to talk about this?

Drugs are rampant just about everywhere it seems. Illegal drugs, prescription drugs, opioids, drugs are everywhere. People take drugs to get high, sleep, stay up, escape, you name it. Because we don't feel safe to be vulnerable, authentic, or honest, there is a pressure to be someone that we are not, and drugs (and drinking) can aid in that.

Vaping is something that wasn't around when I was growing up. Vaping is advertised as the legal alternative to pot and the healthy alternative to smoking. In truth, it is neither. Vaping is a "gateway" to both of these things. It is addictive and carcinogenic. And sadly, it is everywhere.

The temptations and pressures don't end with college. There are plenty of adults who are abusing alcohol and drugs and pressuring others to do the same. There are plenty of people telling others about the dangers of alcohol and drugs, but are they lectures or dialogues? Are we providing safe spaces to talk about these things WITH our children rather than only talking AT our children?

There are two reasons why we shouldn't abuse alcohol and drugs, besides the fact that doing so isn't healthy or, in some cases, isn't legal. One reason is that using alcohol or drugs to alter our state of reality provides a commentary on our relationship with Christ. Imagine a group of friends get together—they can laugh, tell jokes, play a game, sing a song, watch a movie, eat great food, and the list seems endless. When alcohol or drugs must be introduced into a situation to make it go, it is like saying to God, "It is not enough; all the talent and personality you've given us is not enough. We need more." The second reason relates to God's commandment to love our neighbor as we love ourselves. If one is drunk, high, hung over, and someone cries for help, and we cannot respond, then we are failing to love our neighbor, which is a sin. We are supposed to love our neighbor and be ready to render aid to our neighbor at all times.

There is nothing wrong with having a drink. As long as it's not done excessively. There is nothing wrong with using medication under the direction of a doctor, but there certainly is something wrong with abusing medications.

We need to be talking about these kinds of boundaries, we need environments where it is safe to talk about them, we need courage to keep boundaries, and compassion and love to confront others who are stepping over boundaries and acting unsafe.

The next few reflections will examine other kinds of boundaries we should be setting and encouraging others to set as well.

Lord, You created us in Your image and likeness. Help us to see You in ourselves and in others. Help us to appreciate our unique talents and the talents of others. Help us to negotiate pressure to be things and do things that we know are wrong. Help us to know what is right and wrong. Give us strength to hold fast to what we believe, especially when we face peer pressure. Amen.

Encouragement Challenge: Define your boundaries and have the courage to stick with them!

Hold Fast to Your Boundaries—Honesty

And as for what fell in the good soil, they are those who, hearing the Word, hold it fast in an honest and good heart, and bring forth fruit with patience.
Luke 8:15

Another boundary everyone will encounter involves cheating. There are many kinds of cheating. Probably the most common opportunities to cheat include on tests, using work time for non-work things, cheating in sports, and cheating on financial things.

There is a common perception that everyone is cheating in some way. Cheating is something that is fairly normalized. If we are not cheating on taxes, we are certainly looking and reaching for every loophole. Cheating and shopping are connected. There are temptations to "buy" something we need to use one time, and then return it for a refund, having used it the one time we needed it. For instance, someone's heating goes out, they buy a space heater for a few days, then their heat gets fixed, and they return the heater. That's cheating.

Cheating is rampant in the work place. It generally occurs in one of two ways. The employees cheat their employer by doing non-work related things while being paid to work. If a person earns $50,000 a year at a job and spends 10 percent of the work day on personal calls or social media, that amounts to $5,000 essentially stolen from an employer over the course of a year. If someone stole $5,000 from another person, that would be a felony, and someone would go to jail. But we think nothing of "stealing" from employers for personal things.

There are also jobs where employees are almost "required" to cheat, specifically, doctors and lawyers who are required to bill for so many hours, even if it is hours they don't work. That is not to say that every doctor or lawyer is dishonest, but over the years, I have heard from many of them who feel pressured by their company to be less than honest in how they bill for their time.

Having worked with teenagers for my entire ministry, I know that cheating is rampant in school. Because there is so much pressure to get good grades to get in to college, many students cheat because they feel they have to. If they do what is honest and get a "B," and someone else cheats and gets an "A", the dishonest "A" student is more likely to get into college than the honest "B" student. So many people cheat because they feel they can't afford to be honest. This brings two thoughts to my mind. First, is anyone getting through school without cheating? And second, when, if ever, does the cheating stop? The problem with cheating is that it becomes a habit. The world won't change because an eighth grader cheats on a math test. But if that eighth grader is a serial cheater and cheats into college and graduate school, becomes an engineer and cheats on building a bridge, then that bridge can collapse and kill people, and cheating becomes a big deal.

I have always believed that in school and sports, it is better to lose with honesty than win by cheating. In sports, cheating is also rampant. There is the old adage, "If you aren't cheating, you aren't trying," and that is actually an abominable thought. Most of us have heard of the scandal with the Houston Astros baseball team cheating to win a World Series. Whether they strip the team of the title or not, it will have an "asterisk" by it forever. As the scandal unfolds, there are all kinds of cheating methods that are being uncovered. Despite warnings of severe punishments, we frequently hear of yet another athlete suspended for using performance-enhancing drugs. Can anyone make the major leagues without cheating and compromising? Are these really our best baseball players? It makes me seriously question why I would want to keep watching a league of cheaters. Even sadder is that people aren't just cheating on the top levels but at every level of sports. A few years ago, a little league team had a pitcher that was two years too old playing for them. He wowed the crowds, and the team was amazing—but it was all fake.

Where do you stand on cheating? Will you cheat to get ahead? What if you have to cheat just to keep up? Where there is no honesty, there can be no trust, and where there is no trust, there can be no love, vulnerability, or authenticity. We just continue the cycle of a fake society where people are discouraged rather than an honest society where people are empowered.

I'd rather fail at something by doing it honestly than succeed at something by cheating. Even if no one knows, I will know, and God will know. Any victory that isn't fully earned is a hollow victory. Hold fast to honesty.

Lord, thank You for the gifts You have given me. No one has every gift. Each of us has unique gifts. Help me to appreciate the gifts You have given me and use them to the best of my ability. Help me resist the temptation to be dishonest with my gifts or seek other gifts through dishonest means. Help me to have the humility to accept my limits. And help others to appreciate my gifts and strengths. Amen.

Encouragement Challenge: If respect is the basic building block of any human relationship, there cannot be respect if there isn't honesty. Encourage honesty!

Hold Fast to Your Boundaries—Truth

Jesus then said to the Jews who had believe in Him, "If you continue in My word, you are truly My disciples, and you will know the truth, and the truth will make you free."
John 8:31–32

In our last reflection, we discussed the subject of honesty as it relates to cheating. This reflection is closely related, as it relates to telling the truth versus telling a lie.

The best definition of a lie is that it is an attempt to rewrite history, either to make up for something that happened or embellish the truth for what we wish would happen. Let's say that a teenager is out at a party they don't want their parents to know about. When asked where they were, the teenager responds with "at the library." This is a lie, told to cover up a truth they don't want to be held accountable for. Here is another common example of a lie: someone doesn't finish an assignment for work because they were busy doing other things and didn't manage their time well. When the boss asks why the job isn't done, they figure they will blame it on a sick child at home. After all, who will be angry at someone for taking care of their child? We rationalize these small lies by telling ourselves, "Well, no one got hurt" or "What I did isn't that bad."

Then there is embellishing the truth to make one look good. We see this where people augment their resumes. I see it when high school students ask me for recommendations, and they present resumes that are so detailed and full that I think, *There is no way a person could actually do all this.* Then there are people who write, "I'm active in church youth group" when I know they come once a year.

A 2021 study by the University of Wisconsin-La Crosse found that the average person lies zero to two times a day.[30] That means that average people lie 730 times a year; that totals to 43,800 by the time a person is sixty. The most common lie is, "I'm fine."

When I was a child, I enjoyed watching the news on TV. I'd watch the six o'clock news every night. I hear stories about crime, achievement, the weather, sports, and consumer reports. There was very little editorializing on the news back then. Then came the twenty-four-hour news stations, and because there isn't enough news to fill twenty-four hours, the news stations became more opinion stations. Now we have news stations that are pretty much all opinion, more like political lobbies. Everyone editorializes with their opinion, so there is not much news, and one cannot trust that the news will tell the truth.

Complicating this culture of opinion is today's environment of political correctness, where feelings oftentimes get in the way of the truth. There is this idea that everyone should get a trophy in sports. This idea has now stepped in front of the truth that some people are better than others, and the trophies are rewards for excellence. The truth is that we can't all excel in everything. And the truth is we all need to learn how to handle failure as well as focus on the things we are good at. Giving a trophy to everyone doesn't help on either count.

Here is the other problem with placing feelings over truth. Feelings constantly change. Truth does not. When a person feels hungry or tired or sick, that "feeling" dominates all other truths. One doesn't feel successful or loved when the dominant feeling is being tired, when all a person can think of is going to sleep. That's why success and love aren't feelings. Success is a truth, and love is a choice. Truths do not change. And choices don't need to be affected by feelings. I can love someone, even when I'm tired. And hunger can't take away job success.

Society is allowing feelings to lead the way, and truth is somehow getting lost. Here is an example, a dialogue between Fr. Stavros and Evan (a made up name):

Fr. Stavros: Evan, what color is my black shirt (an obvious question)?
Evan: Well, it's black.
Fr. Stavros: You sure about that?
Evan (looks closely at the shirt): I think so.
Fr. Stavros: Ok, so now you are not sure. Would you put a hundred dollars on the fact that my shirt is black?
Evan (thinks carefully, and then answers, a bit unsure): Yes, I think I would do that.
Fr. Stavros: Ok, what if I told you the shirt is green (something it obviously is not).
Evan (looks again very closely): Well, I guess I can see that. But I think it's probably still black.
Fr. Stavros: Well, Evan, you seem like a nice guy, and we could probably be friends, but if you don't think the shirt is green, you are hurting my feelings.
Evan: Well, I don't want to hurt your feelings, so the shirt can be green or whatever you want it to be.

There you have an example of how truth and feelings get mixed up in our world today. We don't want to hurt the feelings of others, so we leave the truth—the shirt is black, I'd stake my life on that—and we change it so that no one's feelings get hurt. Try this exercise with people of different ages. Many people will end up like Evan in this exercise. They won't be able to stand on a truth with any kind of conviction.

Jesus says in the Bible, "I am the way and the truth and the life; no one comes to the Father but by me" (John 14:6).

Feelings are getting in the way of obvious truths. This is true on a practical level. For instance, we might say, "I feel like I want to buy that (something)." The truth is, "I can't afford it." Which wins more in your life in this instance, truth or feelings? Or, "I know this is wrong, but my friends are doing it, and I don't want them to feel disappointed that I'm not." Do we succumb to peer pressure, or do what we know is right?

We are faced with the choice to lead our lives with truth or with feelings. And we are each faced with the choice to live out our truth, or to rewrite our truth in the form of a lie. If we lead our lives with God's truth, loving one another, respecting one another, and respecting God's laws of righteousness, then it won't be necessary to rewrite history in the form of a lie.

Back to the lie we tell most often, "I am fine." There are several reasons we tell this lie so often:

1. We don't believe others care about our well-being;
2. We believe that others might use our misfortune against us, gossiping about it;
3. We're not sure how to handle our misfortunes;
4. We are ashamed to admit our misfortunes; and
5. We lack an environment where it is safe to be truthful.

When we think about it, answer #5 is probably the biggest reason we are less than truthful. Building environments where it is safe to be truthful as well as respecting rules and laws and letting truth guide us instead of feelings, all of these things will lead to a more truthful and honest life. Encouragement can play a big role in being able to live our individual lives in God's truth and being more comfortable in our own truth as well.

Lord, You have said that You are the way, the truth, and the life. Help me understand what that means. Help me to be secure in the truth of who I am and not desire to stretch the truth to be someone I am not. Help me to make good decisions so that there will be no need to rewrite my history. Help me to be an encourager of truth in those around me. Let the truth of Your love for me be my guiding light always. Amen.

Encouragement Challenge: Be truthful today! And help create environments that encourage others to be truthful, where it is safe to tell the truth!

Hold Fast to Your Boundaries—The Tongue

The tongue is a little member and boasts of great thing things. How great a forest is set ablaze by a small fire! And the tongue is a fire. The tongue is an unrighteous world among our members, staining the whole body, setting on fire the cycle of nature, and set on fire by hell. For every kind of beast and bird, or reptile and sea creature, can be tamed and has been tamed by humankind, but no human being can tame the tongue—a restless evil, full of deadly poison. With it we bless the Lord and Father, and with it we curse men, who are made in the likeness of God. From the same mouth come blessing and cursing. My brethren, this ought not be so.
James 3:5–10

There is another activity that we are tempted to engage in daily, and that is gossip, or negativity. At some point, probably all of us, or just about all of us, get sucked into the gossip circle or the negativity circle. It is important to recognize that we can't maintain healthy relationships like this and that we do not live up to our full potential when we consistently engage in gossip. As crazy as it sounds, if you said to your friends, "I'm not gossiping any more in our conversations," they might start gossiping about you. And so, many times, we bow to the pressure to gossip rather than standing on a firm boundary of being positive.

God gave us only one mouth. The same mouth that encourages people is also the same mouth that can tear people apart. As James points out in his epistle, the tongue is like a fire that can set a forest ablaze. It can set it ablaze with gossip and negativity, or it can set it ablaze with encouragement and positivity. The choice is ours.

Most of us have heard of the "telephone game." It's a game where multiple teams are assigned, where, let's say, each with ten people, and each team is put into a line. The first person in each line is shown a phrase or sentence. They are asked to whisper it to the person behind them, who whispers it to the person behind them and so on until it gets to the last person, who writes down the phrase or sentence that they heard. And just about every time, the phrase that the last person heard is significantly different from the phrase that was given to the first person. This is how gossip works. Whatever is said first might be true, but by the time the truth has made it around, what is being said is far from the truth. We obviously know what happens when what starts out is an untruth. Its results are even worse.

Why do people gossip? I would venture to say it is because people want to be relevant and noticed. If someone has something interesting to share, they are relevant. Thus, if a "less than truth," or a private truth that has been share in confidence will get one noticed, a person will be prone to gossip to be noticed, to be relevant.

What then, is the antidote to gossip? It's honesty. Sometimes we gossip about someone because we are afraid to confront them. We have to learn how to confront people in an honest and loving way rather than talk about them behind their back. The second antidote is just giving people some attention. The person who is on the margin of the social group many times feels like they can't get into the group unless they bring gossip about someone else into the group. Many people fight for their place in the social group by conspiring against others in the group with gossip. In other words, we work to build ourselves up by tearing others down rather than seeking to build ourselves up based on our own merits.

Another antidote to gossip is being comfortable with silence. By and large, we are not comfortable about silence. We tend to fill silence with noise. And when we don't have good noise, we fill it with bad noise. At times, we also don't know how to end conversations. Many times we keep conversations going, and they go to gossip rather than just saying, "Our business is concluded. Talk to you soon."

One of the Ten Commandments is "Thou shalt not commit murder" (murder is senseless killing). Most of us think regarding this commandment, "I've never killed/murdered anyone, so I haven't broken this commandment." When we gossip about other people, we murder reputations and kill self-esteem. Of all the commandments, the "thou shalt not kill" commandment is probably the one we all commit the most. We would all be well-served to heed the words of Psalm 141: "Set a guard over my mouth, O Lord, keep watch over the door of my lips!"

Lord, open my lips that I may praise You (Ps. 51:15) at all times and in all places. Help me resist the urge to open my lips to words of gossip. In my groups of friends, help us collectively to have conversations that are constructive, that do not destroy others. Thank You for the beautiful parts of my life. Help me to carry these forward in conversations. Bring people around me who will encourage and build me up, so that in my moments of temptation, I do not have to resort to gossip to build myself up. Amen.

If we need a boundary on anything in our life, it is how we use our tongue.

Hold Fast to Your Boundaries—Time

For everything there is a season, and a time for every matter under heaven.
Ecclesiastes 3:1

Many people have negative thoughts when they think of the words rules or boundaries. Rules and boundaries are there to help us feel freer. Where there are no rules or boundaries, there is no freedom. As we have previously discussed, if one sets up a boundary of respect, where it is safe to be honest without being judged, then there is freedom to discuss things in an open and genuine way. Another example of rules and boundaries are the laws we have that keep us free. There is a law that says someone can't come into your house and steal your stuff while you are gone. If we didn't have that law, none of us would feel free to leave our homes. Boundaries and rules are good things.

The boundary of this reflection relates to time. Time is our most precious commodity because we can't get any more of it. One can work an additional job and make more money if needed. One can take a class and get more adept at a certain skill. But there is nothing we can do to get more time or recover time that has been lost. Time is our most precious commodity because there is only a finite amount of it.

I once heard someone say that there is a reason the day has twenty-four hours. We are supposed to spend eight of them resting, eight of them working, and eight of them on other things, like family, chores, hobbies, relaxation, and spirituality. In twenty-first-century America, we've tinkered with this equation. Most adults get less than eight hours of sleep a night. Most working adults work more than eight hours a day and more than forty hours a week. Chores are chores. Things like shopping, cooking, and cleaning have to be done. So this pushes family, hobbies, relaxation, and spirituality to a back burner.

One of the Ten Commandments is to remember the Sabbath and keep it holy. This was not a suggestion but a commandment to preserve one day of the week for the Lord and for rest. Virtually none of us follow this. We may get to church on Sunday, but after church, it is back to chores, cooking, and shopping, not necessarily family or rest. As people are required to work more and more, work creeps into Sunday, even if it is working from home. Where Sundays (mornings at least) were respected as a day for worship and family, now extracurricular activities like sports or birthday parties are unashamedly placed on Sunday mornings.

Sports have become way more serious too. When I was a child, we played one sport for a season and then did a different sport or didn't do any sport at all at certain times of the year. Now, it seems that any commitment to play a sport is a year-round commitment. A local high school gives players ONE WEEK off in summer for a family vacation if they are on the football team. It is known that if one is going to play a sport, that sport has to be the priority. Of course, the irony is that for all this investment in sports, about 1–2 percent of people who play sports will actually play them in college, and of those who play in college, 1–2 percent will play professionally, and of those who play professionally, only 1–2 percent will really "make it big" in their sport. So for all the emphasis we place on sports, they won't have a significant impact on most adult lives, certainly not more than family or Christ.

Many people are able to work from home, even more so after the Covid-19 pandemic. I don't mean that they don't have to go to work at an office, but most people do some of their work from a computer, like a teacher doing lesson plans, a priest writing sermons, a lawyer preparing for trial, or a doctor doing charting. And because we have computers with us all the time, we get work in all the time. It never shuts off.

The final issue is with the phones. They never go off either. Everyone knows everyone has a cell phone, and everyone knows that everyone has their cell phone with them at all times. When I was a child, people only had phones at home and work. If someone wasn't home, we left a message on their phone, and they got back to us later or the next day. Now we expect instant answers to calls, emails, and texts, and we don't allow an excuse that "I am not available" because now with the mobile phone, everyone theoretically is always available.

This is where some rules and boundaries are needed. We need to set boundaries as it relates to time. Some boundaries are easier to set than others. But here are some thoughts. I know on many nights, I stay up later than I need to, doing mindless things like watching television. We need to be more vigilant on making sure we sleep enough.

Many of us do not work as "smart" as we should. We work hard, even long hours but could probably be more efficient. Some of us don't know how to be truly "off." We are either addicted to our phones, jobs, or feel guilty if we are not in perpetual motion. Make some things about your time sacred, such as not having a phone at the table when you are eating. Make that time sacred with your family.

Each of us has a choice to make when it comes to worship on Sundays. We've made it known that we don't go to birthday parties that are on Sunday mornings. On a very rare occasion, we will let our son go to a swim meet on Sundays, but we find ways for him to "make up" for not going to church, such as going to a weekday service. Again, it's not because worship is about "checking a box" but because we want to impress on him that worship is an important part of being a Christian; indeed, it is one of the great joys about being a Christian.

Keep sports in perspective. Even if your child is very good at sports, the odds are that he or she will not play in college or professionally. And even if they have the talent to play in college or play professionally, everyone is always one injury away from not being able to play sports. Don't let them put all of their future "eggs" into the sports basket. That's not smart for anyone.

We also must recognize that while only a small percentage of people play sports, everyone will one day stand in front of Christ to give an accounting of their lives. This is a 100 percent certainty.

Fight for your time off, whether that means fighting with a coach for a family vacation or making sure you take your allotted vacation time and personal days.

As much as you can, don't do your job after hours at home.

Finally, set some boundaries with your phone, email, and social media. Be patient if someone doesn't answer immediately, especially if it is at night or on the weekends. Try to keep work to work hours. And don't feel guilty about taking a few hours away from the phone.

Lord, thank You for the gift of time, for the years of life that I have enjoyed, and for this very day and moment in time that I am offering this prayer to you. Please Lord, help me to be efficient with my time, work smarter, and have wisdom and clarity when I'm working, and help me to have the discipline to minimize distraction. Help me to balance my time between work, family, hobbies, and rest. Most important, give me the discipline to give You the first of my time. Amen.

We all need to set boundaries when it comes to our time. As we read in Ecclesiastes 3, there is indeed a time for everything—a time to pray, a time to work, and a time to be off from work.

Hold Fast to Your Boundaries— What Is Purity?

Finally, brethren, whatever is true, whatever is honorable, whatever is just, whatever is pure, whatever is lovely, whatever is gracious, if there is any excellence, if there is anything worthy of praise, think about these things.
Philippians 4:8

I began to write the reflection that follows this one about how to remain pure, and as I was writing, I realized that we don't even know what purity means. We all know what gossip is, so writing a message on how to guard one's tongue didn't require a whole lot of definition; same thing with guarding our time or avoiding drug and alcohol abuse. We know what these things are, so we could get right to the point of discussing how to hold fast to what is right regarding them. Because we don't use the word purity much in our society, many of us don't even know what this word means. So before we discuss how to remain pure, let us first define what the word even means.

What do you think of when you hear the word pure? What images come to mind? I think of newly fallen snow that hasn't been walked through. It is pure white and unblemished by footprints. When the sun comes out and glistens off freshly fallen snow, it is one of the most beautiful sights for the eyes to behold. When the snow has fallen on grass, as the snow melts, the grass below emerges and is a brilliant green color. However, when the snow has fallen on the street, as it melts, it intermingles with the dirt, salt, tire tracks, and whatever else is on the street, and it becomes very ugly.

Pure water emerges from mountain springs. Unfortunately, it doesn't stay pure for long, as animal bacteria end up in the water so that even water from the mountain stream must be boiled before one can drink it. Even fruit that is picked from the tree (before it is packaged and shipped to a store) is not pure. Pesticides sprayed on trees and the impure air that the trees grow in necessitate a washing of the fruit before it can be eaten. It's hard to find things that are pure.

Philippians 4:8 connects purity with honor, justice, things that are lovely, graciousness, excellence, and praiseworthiness. If we are to recover the concept of purity, it is related to these things. Pure is a white piece of paper before anything is written on it. Does that mean that once we write something on the paper, it is impure? I would argue the answer depends on what is written on the paper. If a person writes a love letter to his or her spouse on the pure white paper, the paper is still pure. If a person paints a beautiful picture on the paper, it is still pure. When a person puts the same pen or paintbrush and authors a letter or a picture of hatred, the same paper, pen, and paint become impure based on their use.

Pure thoughts and actions go to things that are honorable. So honesty helps one stay pure.

Pure thoughts and actions go to things that are just. So when one is fair, when one learns the art of compromise, when one has the humility to forgive, purity is there.

Pure thoughts and actions go to things that are lovely. When we appreciate beauty in nature and others, their talents, their gifts, and when we encourage others and show gratitude, purity is there.

Pure thoughts go to things that are gracious. When we put others ahead of ourselves, when we appreciate others for who they are, rather than pressuring them to be something they aren't or labeling them, purity is there.

Pure thoughts go to things that are excellent. Excellence has more to do with effort than result. As an example, I can give my most excellent effort to paint something, and it probably won't be all that great because I am not an artist. When we learn to appreciate the strengths of others and recognize their strengths rather than just their weaknesses, purity is there.

Pure thoughts go to things that are worthy of praise. The one most worthy of our praise is God. When we praise God through prayer, song, worship, or actions of love, purity is there.

We don't think about purity very much, which is why it is not a priority action in the lives of many. Maybe we've become desensitized to the idea of purity, or we've become so busy that we've forgotten what purity is and why it's important.

There is one other area of purity, and that is our bodies—our bodies are composed of our physical body, minds, and souls. And this is what we will discuss in the next reflection. However, before addressing why we need to hold fast to purity, it is necessary to understand what purity is because many of us have never learned, and even more have simply forgotten.

Lord, I come before You today, asking that You put thoughts of purity into my mind so that I can bring them forward in my life, serving You and others. Help me to understand what purity is so that I can be pure in my body, mind, and spirit. Help me to rejoice in truth, honor, justice, purity, and things that are lovely. Help me to be gracious, give my best effort, rejoice in the excellence of others, and be quick to praise others and build them up. In a world that has forgotten what purity is, help me to learn what purity means and to practice it in my life. Amen.

Encouragement Challenge: Meditate on the concept of purity today!

Hold Fast to Your Boundaries— Our Bodies Are Temples

Do you not know that your body is a temple of the Holy Spirit within you, which you have from God? You are not your own; you were bought with a price. So glorify God in your body.
1 Corinthians 6:19–20

One of the best books I have ever read is entitled *It's Not About Me* by Max Lucado.[31] The basic premise of the book can be understood from the title. Life is either about me (us), or it is about God. Either God or me is at the center of my life. Either God or me is the focus of my life. There can't be two centers or two central foci. It's one or the other.

The eleventh chapter of that book is entitled "My Body Is About Him." And it talks about how we glorify God (or not) with our bodies. It also has the best case for sexual purity that I've ever read. The introductory paragraphs to this chapter are very powerful, and I want to share them with you:

> You're acquainted with house sitters. You've possibly used one. Not wanting to leave your house vacant, you ask someone to stay in your home until you return. Let me describe two of your nightmares.

> The house-sitter redecorates your house. White paint is changed to pink. Berber carpet to shag. An abstract plastic chair sits in the place of your cozy love seat. His justification? "The house didn't express me accurately. I needed a house that communicated who I am."

> Your response? "It's not yours! My residence does not exist to reflect you! I asked you to take care of the house, not take over the house!" Would you want a sitter like this?

> You might choose him over nightmare number two. She didn't redecorate; she neglected. Never washed a dish, made a bed, or took out the trash. "My time here is temporary. I knew you wouldn't mind," she explains.

> Of course you'd mind! Does she know what this abode cost you? Both house-sitters made the same mistake. They acted as if the dwelling was theirs. How could they?

(It's Not About Me, Chapter 11, pgs. 109-110)[32]

The body, mind, and spirit work as one cohesive unit to make up the human being. When one part is not honored, the others are dishonored. So when our eyes take in what is not pure, our minds and spirits go to impurity. And we are not just talking about sexual things. We overindulge in food, alcohol, movies, and many other things. And in so doing, we lose our sense of purity and replace it with a sense of gluttony, which then becomes a sense of entitlement.

Our bodies are gifts from God. They are temporary, just like life is temporary. The only permanent thing in our bodies are our souls. The souls are permanent. The body protects the soul. The eyes, ears, mouth, hands, all of them are supposed to be used to enrich our souls. God has placed a soul into each of our bodies at our conception. At our death, our souls will go back to God, where He will judge each soul worthy or unworthy to be with Him. This is our destiny. Each of us will face this at the end of our earthly lives. Our purpose then is to use our lives so that our souls glorify God, radiate God, and are ready to meet God and be with Him forever.

Because we are a combination of body, mind, and spirit (soul), all work in concert together. When the body overindulges in food and becomes uncomfortable, the mind becomes irritated and unfocused, and the spirit cannot reflect God. When the body overindulges in alcohol or drugs, the mind does not function properly, and the spirit cannot reflect God. As an aside, the sin that occurs when we overindulge in alcohol or drugs is that we are rendered incapable of loving our neighbor. If a person is inebriated to the point that they would be unable to render assistance to someone in need, they have now crossed the boundary where sin has occurred.

Because we are a combination of body, mind, and spirit, we have to work hard to honor all three, realizing that none of them belong to us. They are all essentially "on loan." There will come a time in each life when that loan is due or the lease is up, so to speak. What will we have to show God for His investment in our lives?

God gave each of us gifts and talents that we are to use to glorify Him and help one another.

Perhaps it is because we don't understand that our bodies are really the shells that protect our souls. Or we don't understand that our bodies are gifts from God, entrusted (loaned) to us. In terms of setting boundaries and holding fast to them, we've all got to do a better job with guarding how much we eat, drink (not too much alcohol, enough water), exercise, sleep, relax, manage stress, and how much we work, all of it.

St. Paul writes that our bodies are temples of the Holy Spirit. I know how meticulously we keep the church that I serve in. We often vacuum, dust, clean, and sanitize it. We always keep it in good repair. When something needs to be repaired, we fix it. The temple we worship in is not any more precious than the temple of our own bodies. The church I worship in doesn't contain my soul. My body does. So as we clean our churches, houses, and cars, we have to remember to keep our bodies in good shape, physically, mentally, and spiritually.

Lord, thank You for the gift of my body, my mind that thinks, my eyes that see, my ears that hear, my mouth that speaks, my hands that move, my feet that walk, and my heart that beats. Help me, Lord, to honor You with these gifts today and always. Help me to focus my mind on godly things, to keep my body in shape with proper food, drink, exercise, and rest. Help me to discipline what my eyes see, ears hear, mouth speaks, hands do, and where my feet walk. Help me to make my body and life more about You than about me. Amen.

Our bodies are not ours; they are His! So we have to make them more about Him than about us!

Hold Fast to Your Boundaries—
Sexual Purity

Blessed are the pure in heart, for they shall see God.
Matthew 5:8

There is one other area of purity, and that is our bodies—remember, our bodies are composed of our physical bodies, minds, and souls. The purity of each is a concept that is fast disappearing in our society.

I'm reminded of the story of the frogs in the boiling water.[33](Adapted from "The Story of B" by Daniel Quinn.) If you have a pot of boiling water and drop a frog into it, the frog will instantly jump out. However, if you put the frog into a pot of tepid water, the frog will relax. As the water heats up, the frog will continue to relax, the way we do when we take a hot bath, and eventually, without resistance, the frog will be boiled to death.

Let's change the story a little big, making the frogs a little more active.. A group of frogs jump into a pot of tepid water on a stove. Many of the frogs begin to relax in the warm water. A couple of the frogs decide to jump out, warning the others that the water will eventually boil, and they will die. The frogs in the water ridicule the ones who have jumped out, saying, "You don't know the fun you are missing out on; it is so nice in here." The frogs on the outside say, "We may be missing out on some fun, but we are saving ourselves in order to have a life. You are on the fast track to certain death." Eventually, the water gets warmer. The frogs in the water still relax. The ones outside of the pot continue to implore them to jump out. Eventually, the water boils, and all the frogs in it die. The ones who are outside now mourn the loss of the friends while rejoicing that they chose to leave and live.

The moral downgrading of purity matches the story of the frogs. The allure of instant and inappropriate sexual gratification has almost put to death the concept of sexual purity. Like the frogs in the pot of tepid water, almost everyone will begin the association with sexuality in a tepid way. Perhaps it is a scene in a movie, an accidental stumble on pornography, racy article in a magazine, or raunchy conversation with friends. This will happen to every young person probably as a pre-teen and certainly as a teen. A few teens will make the smart jump immediately out of the water. They will realize that hanging around scenes, articles, websites, and conversations like this will not end well if purity is the goal.

The problem is we become like the frogs in the tepid water. We become easily attracted to impure thoughts, sights, and actions. Because it seems like "everyone" is doing it, we become desensitized to how this is taking our society down. Pornography is everywhere. We can't take a ride around town without seeing it on a billboard ad. It is in college dormitories, behind the closed doors for our teenagers, on many screens in the workplace, and many other secret places. And besides secret places, it is in plenty of public places, the aforementioned ads, in many movies, and on magazine covers at the check-out in the grocery store. It's everywhere.

Practically no one seems to care about sexual purity. The concept of waiting until marriage to have sexual relations has all but disappeared. Practically no one marries as a virgin. Most couples live together for a long time before getting married. I stopped saying, "You may kiss the bride" at weddings after a brother priest pointed out to me how stupid that sounds when people have been living together before marriage. The biggest problem with sexual impropriety before marriage is that it leads to sexual impropriety after marriage. Because we haven't learned how to wait before getting married, once a dry spell hits marriage (either because we are fighting, someone is sick, we've just had kids, or whatever the reason), it doesn't take much for sex outside of marriage to occur.

Most people don't understand what sex is. Yes, sex is the way by which we create children, and as a bishop in our church told me after we had our son, we become co-creators with God. Many people think that the church demonizes sex; it makes it something that is dirty and shameful. To the contrary, sexual purity, restricting sex to within the confines of marriage but celebrating it within those confines, makes sex an expression of holiness.

To take it to an ever deeper level, sex is what allows the human being to feel what it was like in paradise before the fall, for as we read in Genesis 2:25, "the man and his wife were both naked and were not ashamed." Yes, one of the reasons God made sex is for us to feel like Adam and Eve did in paradise before the fall. It is the only place where we can be naked and unashamed. (As a funny aside, someone once challenged me on this and said, "What about when we are at the doctor; we can be naked and unashamed." To which I replied, "When I'm at the doctor, I'm naked and afraid!")

Because we do not understand either sex or purity, it is no wonder that both are slipping out of our society. There are a few, however, who are committed to purity before marriage, and thankfully there are still many who are pure in the context of marriage. They have discovered, like the frogs who jumped out of the pot, that impurity is like boiling water that can kill our minds and souls and is killing the moral fabric of our society. Much of society sits in the ever-heating-up water of immorality, either enjoying it or reasoning that it is not that bad. The collapse of families and the pervasiveness of sexual immorality and temptation are strong indicators that we are reaching the boiling point.

To young friends I have met who have said they would stay pure until marriage, I applaud you and pray for you. And I implore you not to give in to temptation. Set boundaries and stick with them. If you are not sure what appropriate boundaries are, find a trusted adult, pastor, or counselor and talk about it. If your partner says, "I only want you to do what you feel comfortable with," that actually means, "I'll do whatever you let me get away with." And when you've found someone who respects your desire for purity, that one might be a keeper.

To those who have fallen and have regret, there is no such thing as "secondary virginity," but you can start living right at any time. And to those who relish in sexual immorality, please don't tempt the ones who are trying to stay on course. To those who are planning a bachelor or bachelorette party that has a male stripper, does that seem like an appropriate way to celebrate with someone who is about to get married? To the college fraternity that is planning a porn night, is that really necessary to prove yourselves to be real men? To the guys and girls out there who think sex is the cornerstone of a relationship, it isn't. Christ is the cornerstone.

For those who are trying to pressure their mate into further sexual foray, that is not love. Love is patient and kind, not forceful and manipulative. For those who are dating in their thirties and think purity is just for teenagers, it isn't; it is for everyone. And for everyone who is doing it wrong and has guilt, read Genesis 2:25. When sex is done right, not only does it bring a sense of pleasure and deepen love, but it also brings a sense of holiness.

It is critically important for teens and young adults to understand that promiscuity not only leads to disease and unwanted pregnancy, but it also confuses us emotionally. To have your heart built up, then broken, and go through this cycle many times will cause you to bring emotional baggage into the marriage. Freely changing sexual partners also does not set up one to have one partner for life. This isn't a religious statement; it's actually common sense.

As for pornography, there are several problems with that. First, it degrades and devalues all of us, especially women. Second, it is fake. Third, our minds are like computer hard drives that register all images that we see. Those who have gone to summer camp will forever have the images of the lake and the trees embedded in their minds. It is the same with those who have been to the Grand Canyon or the beach. I can still see my dad in my mind even though he passed many years ago. Filling our minds with images of crap will confuse our brains, so that when there is an opportunity to intimacy, sexual or not, our minds will be confused based on the crap that fills them. Pornography is everywhere, from billboards to movies to ads in the mall. It used to be that one had to go to the store and sneak to buy a magazine. Now it's at the touch of a button. This is a big problem and only becoming bigger.

Many confuse sex with intimacy. Sex is an intimate act. But there can be intimacy without sexual activity. Intimacy is the ability to accept others as they are and share vulnerability, respect, and honesty without judgment or pretense. We crave intimate relationships. The concept of intimacy should not be restricted to marriage. Sex should be restricted to marriage—it is the physically intimate expression that makes a marriage different from other "intimate" relationships. But intimate, non-sexual relationships are important and necessary, and they are being lost in our world precisely because we've lost the ability to have intimacy without sex and continue to confuse the two.

I'd like to end this reflection with the story of a real person named Elizabeth, who I met many years ago at summer camp. She was probably fourteen when we met. She said to me with great conviction, "I'm saving myself for marriage," to which I replied, somewhat insincerely, "Good luck to you with that." Having heard this promise many times, and later having seen just about everyone break it, I had become jaded in my responses to promises like this. She looked me in the eye and said, "No really, I'm going to do it." And I said, "Good luck with that." Again, she looked at me and said with conviction, "I'm going to do it, and I want you to promise me right here and now that you'll be at the altar at my wedding and say to me, 'Congratulations, you made it.'" I said, "Okay." Unconvinced of my sincerity, she said, "Say, 'I promise.'" So I said, "I promise, if you make it pure until you are married, I will be at the altar to congratulate you."

Over the years, we kept in touch, and she would reiterate to me her promise to stay pure. One day, she met a man named Stone who shared the same desire as her. And a couple of years later, they married. She kept her promise. And I kept mine. I flew to her wedding, greeted them at the altar, and said, "Congratulations, you made it." I've told that story to many teenagers I have encountered to let them know that purity isn't dead. And I've even offered to them, "I'll come to every wedding of anyone who makes it to the altar still pure. And the reason I can offer that and not worry about going broke is that probably only about 2 percent of people will make it." I'd gladly go broke if it meant seeing more purity in our society.

Lord, help me to honor You in my sexuality. (For single people: Lord, please help me to remain pure in body. For married people: Lord, please help us to remain pure in our marriage.) Lord, if the goal is to walk with You in this life and for eternal life, help me come before You in a way that is pure and without shame. Help me to find the intimacy that Adam and Eve enjoyed with you before the fall. Amen.

Encouragement Challenge: It is a struggle to be sexually pure when sexual immorality is all around us. Keep your eyes on Christ and on things of purity.

**Dedicated to Elizabeth (Poulos) and Stone Hendrickson.

Hold Fast to Your Boundaries—The Faith

Let us hold fast the confession of our hope without wavering, for He who is promised is faithful.
Hebrews 10:23

One of the classes I was required to take my freshmen year of college was entitled "What Are Human Beings?" This class was mostly philosophical, designed to get us to learn about ourselves, ostensibly. One thing I vividly remember from this class was that we were forced to question every aspect of our lives. It started off with gender, and was I sure I was actually a man. The professor didn't seem satisfied with a simple yes or the answer that my gender was confirmed through my biology and appearance of my body. Eventually, I became annoyed with having to defend something I had and have known to be true my whole life. I am a man.

The class "progressed" toward other things I needed to defend, and one of them was my Christian faith. When it came to discussing religion, I was asked if I had a faith that I identified with. When I answered that I was a Christian, I was then asked, "Have you ever considered another faith or tried another faith?" And when I answered, "No, I hadn't, and I didn't feel the need to," I was told, "You are a close-minded person. Only close-minded people are unwilling to try new things."

I quickly realized that as much as colleges said they wanted us to have an "open mind," what they really wanted us to have was an "empty mind," a mind that had no conviction but was open to being completely changed on questions as basic as our gender and faith. I believe many colleges still operate like this.

There is a difference between an open mind and an empty mind. An open mind can have conviction but lack direction. An empty mind lacks both. What does that mean? I went to college positive that I was a man and a Christian. I knew I had some skills in writing and in public speaking. I liked the idea of being a teacher and a counselor. I had an open mind about career choices. While the priesthood was always tugging at my heart, I took classes in psychology, secondary education, history, and political science and considered careers in education, city management, and counseling before deciding to pursue the priesthood. To me, I went to college with an open mind as far as careers were concerned. I entered college certain that I was not going to be a scientist but open-minded to various careers in the humanities. I did not, however, go to college with an empty mind. I was very sure of my Christian faith when I entered college. I was very sure of my values and boundaries. And while some of these got tested and pushed and occasionally even crossed, I exited college with the same values and faith with which I had entered but with a more defined career path than when I had entered.

It's not just during college that our values are challenged when we are called upon to be open-minded or, in reality, empty-minded. Christians are being challenged as never before to defend our Christianity. Western society is quickly becoming anti-Christian. Perhaps because as Christians, we cling to values and beliefs that are quickly becoming unpopular. Just clinging to a belief is becoming unpopular.

We live in a disposable society. If a person is still clinging to a rotary phone they used thirty years ago, the world has passed them by. People would probably laugh at them. You can't be in a profession now without using the internet or email. If a doctor is still trying to practice medicine the way he did twenty years ago, he's probably out of a job. It seems that we have to adapt to many things in our world, or we get left behind.

There is a great pressure to adapt our faith to fit some societal contemporary norm of what faith is. Or even worse, for faith to be regarded like the rotary phone, something we no longer need or have a use for.

Faith is something that grounds us. Faith is not something that changes. We read in Hebrews 13:8, "Jesus Christ is the same yesterday and today and forever." As Christians, we are called to believe specific things and act in specific ways. To cling to those things and act in those ways shows conviction and faith. It doesn't show close-mindedness, which is seen as weakness.

In holding fast to boundaries, we need to cling to what we know is true as far as our faith goes, and practice what we know is right according to our faith. The challenge is to know the faith and practice it with consistency and conviction. Otherwise, when we are challenged as to what we believe, when we don't know what we believe, it will be very easy for our faith to be changed, even lost. We need to continually grow in our faith so that when a storm of criticism and questionings are leveled against us, our faith is strong enough to withstand them. And when we have a strong faith, we need to have the courage of conviction to stand with a mind that is confident, not open for influence away from our faith.

There have been a few occasions in my life (and most of them happened in college) when influences around me caused me to question my faith. Thankfully, my faith is strong enough that it has survived each barrage against it. We have to know as people of faith that there will be times when our faith will come under attack, and we have to have the strength of faith and courage to hold onto it in the face of opposition.

There is a difference between morality and righteousness. Righteousness is what is right and correct in the eyes of God. Morality is what is right is acceptable in the eyes of society. Morality changes. There are plenty of things that were immoral one hundred years ago or even twenty years ago that are perfectly acceptable today. And those who do not accept them are often criticized. Righteousness, what is right in the eyes of God, does not change. Faith should be tied to what is righteous, not what is moral. Righteousness doesn't change; faith shouldn't either.

Lord, help me to be Your faithful servant. Help me to understand what is righteous in Your eyes. Help me to cling to righteousness, even when I am tempted or encouraged not to. Help me hold fast to my faith. Surround me with people who will encourage me to be faithful to You. Amen.

Encouragement Challenge: Hold fast to your faith and what is righteous in the eyes of God!

Make a Mantra and Use It

I love Thee, O Lord, my strength. The Lord is my rock, and my fortress, and my deliverer, my God, my rock, in Whom I take refuge, my shield, and the horn of my salvation, my stronghold. I call upon the Lord, Who is worthy to be praised, and I am saved from my enemies.
Psalm 18:1–3

One of my most memorable experiences in all the years I have gone to summer camp occurred in the summer of 2021. I was assigned to a cabin of young men who were juniors and seniors in high school. Working with teenagers is hard. Trying to teach about the Christian faith and Christian morality is tough. I decided that the best approach with this particular group would be to appeal to their "manhood." The entire week, I was purposeful in calling them "men" instead of "boys" or "guys" or even "young men" or "teens." We ended up having some pretty amazing conversations—deep, personal, and emotional. I will not discuss them in further detail. We all agreed that part of what would get up to go deeper was a commitment that whatever was said in the room would stay in the room. And I will honor that commitment.

On what would be my last night with them, as our session was about to come to a close, I threw out a bunch of things for them to think about in a very rapid fire manner:

~Think about being a real man when you are objectifying women.
~Think about being a real man the next time you want to smoke weed.
~Think about being a real man when you are cheating on your homework.
~Think about being a real man when you are looking at pornography.

I told them the story of how my dad died. I also told them the story of another dear friend who passed away. And I told them that real men think about their salvation. I could see that it touched a nerve with several of them. The session ended, I left, and we all prepared to go to our next activity. A few minutes later, the counselor of this cabin called me back. He told me that all the men were upset and wanted to talk more. I came back to the cabin to find the men very emotional. One of them said, "We're not the men you are building us up to be. We aren't doing most of the things you are talking about." I could see that many them were very upset and in very deep thought. I felt bad for them. And I also wondered how we could end this now extra-session in a way that would make them feel encouraged rather than sad.

I suggested that they each come up with a mantra.

A mantra is a short statement that can be used as an answer for every question.[34] Think politicians. Most politicians have a five-line mantra that they use as the answer for every question. "We want to build the economy, make America stronger, stick up for the rights of citizens, create jobs, have the best schools," and so on. So when the politician is asked a question like, "How do you plan to make America stronger?" the answer will be, "We are going to create jobs, fix the economy, and fight for the American worker." And if the question is, "How are you going to fight for the American worker?" the answer will be, "We're going to build up the economy, create jobs, and make America stronger." You get the idea.

The mantra I was suggesting they write would be a fine-line answer they can give for every stupid question they receive. Here is a sample:

~I have value.
~I'm above stupid sh*t.
~I need people who are going to pull me up and not tear me down.
~I need more God in my life.

And now the mantra can be the answer to every stupid request:

- Do you want to smoke weed?
- Let's cheat on our homework together.
- You want to go to a party and get drunk?

Each of these three questions, and more, can be answered with the above mantra.

Here is a mantra for the person who is trying to maintain purity, to offer to their boyfriend/girlfriend/fiancé:

~I love you.
~But I love God more.
~I want it all.
~I want you and God, and I don't want there to be any conflict.
~I will work to honor both you and Him.

Here is a mantra for the newly-married couple whose parents complain they aren't seeing enough of them:

~I love you, Mom and Dad.
~We just got married.
~We are trying to figure it out.

The men of the cabin at summer camp seemed satisfied that writing a mantra would be a good first step, a good tool to have in their teenage toolbox. Several of these men have told me since camp that they have their mantras printed and up on the wall in their rooms—they look at them every day.

A mantra isn't the answer for every problem, but it is a good way to clarify things that are important to you.

Lord, thank You for the gift of my mind and its ability to think and to solve problems. Help me create in my mind mantras, short statements of what I believe, that I can offer with conviction when confronted with a challenge or temptation. Help me to put my faith in You as the thing I value most, so that whatever else I am flows first from my identity as a Christian. Give me the words to say in difficult circumstances. Help others to hear my words and respect the conviction and the faith that is behind them. Amen.

Encouragement Challenge: I encourage you to write a mantra for yourself so that you can clarify who you are, what you believe, and what's important to you, to everyone else.

**Dedicated to the men of St. Luke's Cabin, Week Two, 2021, St. Stephen's Summer Camp.

We Have to Know Him, Not Just about Him

Woe to you, scribes and Pharisees, hypocrites! For you tithe mint and dill and cumin, and have neglected the weightier matters of the law, justice, mercy and faith; these you ought to have done, without neglecting the others.
Matthew 23:23

Several reflections ago, I used the term transactional relationship. This referred to relationships that are based on a transaction, like the relationship we might have with a bank teller. We give the bank teller our check, and he or she sees that it gets deposited. There is a relationship of some trust in that we must trust the bank teller to get the deposit into our account, but the teller doesn't need to trust us in return. It's a transactional relationship. There is no emotion or intimacy in this kind of relationship. In fact, most customer service relationships are transactional. A service is offered, and money is paid.

Many people have a transactional relationship with Christ. Specifically, they have a good relationship with the church but not with Christ. Many people in the world teach Sunday school, sing in the choir, or serve on the Parish Council who have a great relationship with the church but don't have a great relationship with Christ. I dare say that many priests appear outwardly successful in their ministries but struggle in their relationship with Christ. I'm one of them. This is why I want to address this topic.

There is a great temptation to fill our church calendar with programs; youth group, men's group, women's group, small groups, all kinds of group. There is an inherent desire to have socialization in our churches and lives. And there is nothing wrong with that.

There is great temptation in the worship aspect of our churches. Just because the choir is beautiful and sings in key, just because the priest has beautiful vestments and gives a beautiful sermon, and just because the altar is filled with altar boys and the line for Communion seems endless, it is still possible to have all these things and still not have Christ.

There have been many a Sunday that I have put on beautiful vestments and given a sermon that I was told was meaningful, yet I still felt empty, guilty, or less than stellar about my relationship with Christ. There have been many times I have felt more like an actor than a priest, and I would venture to say that many of us have at times felt like actors, whether we admit that to someone else or just to ourselves.

Perhaps the greatest temptation is to treat church as a transaction. We write a check as if we are paying dues at a country club. A parish council member at the first church I served many years ago described the church as "an organization to which I belong," a description that could be ascribed to the Kiwanis Club or the Junior League. And we even faithfully attend programs like youth group, Bible study and even worship, but we don't internalize the substance of faith, salvation in Jesus Christ.

Our relationship with Christ is supposed to be intimate. We are supposed to pour out our souls to Him. We are supposed to let Him into our secret hearts. His Word should be our lighthouse, guiding us in our dark times. His Word should be our roadmap, guiding us each day.

Our relationship with the church should be like a tourist going to a resort. We should come to church to relax and recharge.

Our relationship with the church should be like a patient at a hospital. We should come to church for healing.

Our relationship with the church should be like a teacher and a student. We should come to church as students, eager to learn. And we should leave as teachers, filled with knowledge that we are equal to share.

Our relationship with the church should be like that of parent and child. We should come to church as children of God, eager to see our Father, confident of His love for us. We should leave eager to care for and nurture others the way a parent nurtures a child.

Nowhere in these images is that of a customer at a store. We do not come to consume things. The church doesn't exist to produce things, even if those things are beautiful services and nice programs. Christ came to save the world. The church exists to bring His saving message to all.

The above Scripture verse is a rather harsh one. It is Christ castigating the temple leadership as getting the transaction right but losing the essence of what was most important. There is certainly a need for order in churches. And there are many useful Bible verses to memorize. There is nothing wrong with charitable giving, and a great choir and a good Sunday school are important things. Yes, it is important to get good grades and have good behavior. There is nothing wrong with any of these things. However, the end goal of Christianity is not to know about Christ but to know Christ. Christianity is not about what we know but what we do. And the end goal of life is to serve Christ at all times and see Him in all people.

One of the most refreshing statements in the whole Bible comes from a man who wanted his son to be healed from an evil spirit. Jesus's disciples could not cast out the demon. And Jesus asked the man if he believed that Jesus could cure his son. The man said, "I believe; help my unbelief!" (Mark 9:24). In many ways, if we are honest, this statement describes all of us. Anyone reading this message has at least some belief. And anyone reading this message has had their faith tested with doubt. Thus, the statement that we believe but that we need help holding fast to faith when we feel doubtful with "unbelief" is actually a verse of encouragement in itself.

As we come to the conclusion on this unit of "Hold Fast," it is important that we not only hold fast to the church or to outward forms of Christianity but we hold fast to Jesus Christ, who is the centerpiece of Christianity. Many people stand around the center who never actually get to the center. It is critical that we all hold fast to form but to substance.

Church is one place where we practice faith; in fact it is a necessary place. However, the church is not faith. We place our faith in Christ. It's not just knowing *about* Christ that makes us people of faith. *Knowing* Christ is what matters.

Lord, Jesus Christ, help me to know You. I can't hold on to faith if I don't have faith. Help me to have faith. Help me to believe. Help me to believe when I don't believe. And help me to hold on to what I believe. Help me to grow the faith that I have. Give me the desire to deepen my faith. Make Yourself known to me. Allow me to feel the joy and hope that comes from You. Amen.

Encouragement Challenge: Hold fast to faith—Hold on to what you have. Strive continually to deepen your relationship with Christ.

There Is No Need for Self-Pressure

So when they had come together, they asked Him, "Lord, will You at this time restore the Kingdom to Israel?" He said to them, "It is not for you to know the times or seasons which the Father has fixed by His own authority. But you shall receive power when the Holy Spirit has come upon you; and you shall be My witnesses in Jerusalem and in all Judea and Samaria and to the end of the earth."
Acts 1:6–8

A previous reflection discusses how it is okay to be a "Smith" and not a "Jones," in other words, not feeling stressed out about "keeping up with the Joneses." There is definitely a palpable pressure to keep up with what others are doing as if we are in some kind of competition with them.

We are all familiar with peer pressure, which is when peers pressure us to do what they are doing. This pressure might be overt, like our peers actually demanding that we do something. Or it might be as in the case of "keeping up with the Joneses" and feeling our own sense of pressure to keep up with them.

This reflection talks about another kind of pressure, self-pressure. This is a pressure that we put on ourselves to be at a certain place at a certain time in our lives. Regardless of what others pressure us to do, we each have ideas in our own minds for what we want to accomplish by a certain point in life. For instance, a senior in high school might feel pressure to date, not from their friends, but from themselves because in their own mind, they think they should have dated before they finish high school. So they go ahead and force a dating situation to occur, even if it is not the right person. A freshman in college might feel pressure to drink, not because others are telling them to but because they think it is something college students do. So they go ahead and start down this road, even if it is risky or they aren't comfortable with it. A person in their late twenties might feel pressure from others to get married, but there might be a certain expectation from their own minds that people should be married by age thirty. So they go ahead and rush to get married, perhaps to the wrong person. The same can be said for the thoughts that one might have as to how many children they want, what part of the country they want to live in, what successes they hoped to have at work, how much money they have hoped to save, and all the other pressures and expectations we put on ourselves. We create goals and then pressure ourselves to achieve them, sometimes at our own peril.

There is a certain "logic" that permeates our minds, where we think certain things should happen in a certain order by a certain age. I often think of these verses from Acts 1:6–8. By this point, the disciples had loyally followed Jesus for three years. Many times, they were confused as to who He was and what His purpose was. They had their own sense of what they thought would will happen. After suffering through the terror of the crucifixion and experiencing the joy of the resurrection, the disciples turned to Jesus and asked Him a question that had been on their minds: "Lord, will you at this time restore the kingdom to Israel?" (Acts 1:6). They had lived under Roman oppression as well, and they were hoping that with the power Jesus had shown to rise from the dead, He would use that same power to give them political freedom. This was the next logical step in their minds. The answer Jesus gave to them must have seemed like a punch in the gut: "It is not for you to know the times or seasons which the Father has fixed by His own authority" (1:7). In other words, the kingdom would not be restored to Israel at that time. The plans and hopes that the disciples had for political freedom would not be realized, at least not yet. Jesus told them, however, that He had other plans for them. They were to "receive power when the Holy Spirit has come upon you; and you shall be My witnesses in Jerusalem and in all Judea and Samaria and to the end of the earth" (1:8). Jesus had plans for the disciples that were not contingent on whether they received political freedom. And stretching this a step further, perhaps Jesus didn't allow their request because it might have proven to be a distraction from what they were really called to do.

Many times our goals and plans for ourselves will not work out. And we won't understand this at the time. Sometimes what happens will not make any sense at all but will make sense later. Take, for instance, the senior in college who is devastated to break up with a boyfriend. At the same time, she gets accepted to a graduate school in a faraway city, decides to attend the school, and goes on to have an amazing career (and eventually gets married). Later on, she will look back and be thankful for the breakup, realizing that had she stayed with her boyfriend, she might have not gone to that school.

In Isaiah 55:8, we read, "'For My thoughts are not your thoughts, neither are your ways My ways,' says the Lord." Yes, we should motivate and pressure ourselves to achieve goals and excel in what we are doing. But when a goal can't be realized, or we feel pressured to do something we really don't want to do, we should back up and reflect on the possibility that God is using our situation to lead us to something different than what we are thinking, or perhaps even protecting us from making a mistake. In the instance of the person who didn't date in high school or who broke up with a boyfriend in the process of applying to graduate school, sometimes God allows these things to protect us from making a wrong decision.

When I was in high school, it saddened me that I wasn't dating. However, looking back now, it was a good thing to not have the temptations that go along with dating in high school. When I was younger, I had a desire to climb the career ladder and go to a very large parish. Looking back, I'm glad that I didn't get the transfer that I had hoped for because I'm very happy where I am. These "failures" were God's way of protecting me and have not only led to what He has desired for my life, but they have led me to be happier as well.

Sometimes we try too hard to do something or be something that we aren't. A wise person once told me, "If you are trying too hard to get a square peg in a round hole, you are probably doing the wrong thing." Another person told me, "The right decisions are the ones that bring you peace." And yet another person told me, "If you are thinking too hard about a decision you are making, it is probably the wrong decision."

There are times when we will make plans and goals and work hard, and we will achieve them. There are also times when we make plans and goals and work hard, and we will not achieve them. Sometimes there is no reason for this other than we won't succeed at everything. And sometimes there is a reason for this; we just won't realize it at the time. And many times, the reason is because God is protecting us from something or helping us become who we are really supposed to be.

While we should try to not succumb to peer pressure, we should also not succumb to self-pressure.

We should also remember that some peer pressure and some self-pressure can be good.

Mostly, let us remember that what seems logical to us in terms of the times and seasons of our life may not fit with God's plan for our lives. However, be assured at all times that God has a plan. For His disciples, that plan was not political freedom but to receive the Holy Spirit and spread the gospel to the ends of the earth. What higher goal in life could there be than that?

Lord, thank You for the many gifts, talents, and opportunities You have given to me. Help me to know Your plan for my life. Help me to stay true to who I am and who You created me to be. Help me in times of pressure and uncertainty to know what is the right thing to do. Help me to remember that if I am honoring You and serving others, not achieving other goals or expectations is not necessarily the end of the world. Help me to understand the best way I can honor You and serve others.

Give me wisdom to set goals, wisdom to achieve them, and patience when they work out differently that I had planned. Help me to trust You at all times. Amen.

Encouragement Challenge: Stay true to yourself and stay true to God!

Hold Fast to Your Boundaries—
Be (the Good Parts of) You

Do not be afraid of sudden panic, or of the ruin of the wicked, when it comes; for the Lord will be your confidence and will keep your foot from being caught.
Proverbs 3:25–26

I'm not ashamed to share some of my story through my writing. I've had triumphs and setbacks, just like everyone else. They are part of the narrative that makes me who I am. When I was in high school, I was very introverted and socially awkward. I didn't have many friends and felt lonely much of the time. It's interesting that in recent years, as I have communicated with high school classmates via social media, I find that many of them, especially the ones I looked up to and were envious of because I thought they had many friends, say that they were actually pretty lonely too. Just because they had friends or were popular didn't make them understood and didn't give them a place where they could just be them without pretending to be someone else.

One beautiful memory from high school was something someone wrote in my yearbook senior year. It said, "Stay the person you are, and one day, someone special will love you for it." In other words, just be you. Most of us spend a good deal of our lives trying to be someone we are not. Either we engage in risky or wrong behaviors to get approval, or we are motivated by jealousy to be someone else that we aren't. The "essential me" is probably pretty good for most of us. That's because each of us was created in the image and likeness of God, and God doesn't make people that are no good. The not good part of each of us is learned; we are not born with it.

In today's world, we've taken the phrase, "just be you," and used it to rationalize all kinds of stupid and unsavory behavior. That's not what "just be you" should mean. "Just be you" should refer to the best version of ourselves, the person who God created us to be. God did not create me to be a doctor or athlete. I don't have scientific skills, and I sure don't have athletic ones. In high school, I tried so hard to be an athlete because athletes were "popular," and if you wanted to be popular, this seemed to be the only way to do it. I pushed myself as an athlete to the point that I suffered a serious injury to my elbow. And then I hid the injury because I was determined to be an athlete and get a "letter jacket" (does anyone wear THESE things anymore?). In the process, I ended up having ulnar collateral surgery on my right elbow. Now, decades after graduating from high school, I no longer have the letter jacket, but I do have a right elbow that gives me issues, all because I tried to be something I really wasn't.

Pushing oneself to be popular has led to unwanted pregnancy, sexually transmitted disease, sexual assault, legal issues, bad grades, failed marriages, lost jobs, and health issues. "Just being you" might not make you popular, but it will probably keep you from getting seriously hurt. One of the many problems in the world today is the pressure to be someone we are not as well as frustration when we can't be something we are not. We aren't all meant to go to college, just like we aren't all meant to be athletes. God means for each of us to love one another, serve one another, and be kind to one another. Each of us will do this in a different way.

I was explaining to my teenage son recently that there are some careers that pay more money than others. For instance, a lawyer and a priest could work the same amount of hours, and the lawyer might make ten times more than the priest and the professional athlete ten times more than the lawyer. That doesn't make a lawyer ten times more valuable than a priest or an athlete ten times more valuable than a lawyer. God will not judge us based on popularity or pocketbook but rather on effort, on whether we were the best version of who He created us to be. God's call for my life is to be a priest, not a lawyer or athlete. Rather than mourn for what I cannot be, I can be grateful for what I can be, for what God created me to be, and for who and what I am.

Be the best version of you, stay away from things that cause destruction to you or others, keep God's commandments, and work your way to eternal life.

Lord, thank You for creating me and bringing me into this world. Thank You for (list things about yourself that you are thankful for). Help me to be the best version of the person You created me to be. Give me discernment to see who and what I should be. Give me gratitude for who I am and what I have. Help me to look at others not with jealousy but with joy so that I may encourage others to be the best version of themselves. Bring people around me who will encourage me to be who I am, not who I am not, who will encourage me to be the person You created me to be. Amen.

Encouragement Challenge: Do not mourn for what you cannot be. Be grateful for who you can be, for what God created you to be, and for who and for what you are. Just be you!

**Dedicated to the California High School (CHS) Class of 1990, many of whom I have connected with as adults in a way that we never did as teens.

Part Eleven
ABSTAIN FROM EVIL

Abstain from every form of evil.

1 Thessalonians 5:22

Stick with the Good, Stay Away from the Bad

Abstain from every form of evil.
1 Thessalonians 5:22

It seems that our world is dominated by negativity. The newspaper, news shows, and magazines are filled with it. So are our conversations. Life is like the scales of justice. Good competes with evil. Keeping the scales with more good than evil is hard, especially when the majority of voices are discouraging.

We have no choice in some of the evil that happens to us. We are all victims to the bad mistakes or ill-intent of others. However, some of the evil that befalls us is of our own making. For instance, we have the freedom to decide to use foul language or gossip. We choose to bring evil to conversations. We choose to make mistakes that potentially harm others. So staying away from evil is, to some degree, a personal choice. St. Paul reminds us to abstain, to conscientiously choose to go away from evil things.

I remember years ago, I went to confession. There was no need for a lecture from my spiritual father. The things I was doing wrong, I knew they were wrong. I didn't need him to tell me they were wrong. I remember his advice to me that day was very simple: "You know what's right, and you know what's wrong. Stop doing wrong and start doing right."

Most of the time, we know right from wrong. I supposed sometimes we come to a fork in the road and truly do not know what is the right thing to do. However, that is not the majority of the time. The majority of the time, we know right from wrong. We know which is the right fork to take in the road, and our choice to take the wrong road is just that, a choice.

We've addressed questions like, "Is it smart?" and "Is it safe?" when making good choices. Here are some other questions to reflect on as we think about choosing good and avoiding evil.

Will it unnecessarily hurt someone? We know that only good things come from God. Hurting someone is not a good thing. Not all kinds of hurt are bad. For instance, when we correct our children, it might hurt their feelings, but it is necessary to correct a wrong or dangerous behavior. If the intention is to correct, that is different than an intention to hurt someone. Most of us know when we do something if it will intentionally hurt someone.

Is it a sin? In other words, is what we are doing violating God's law? The Ten Commandments are pretty clear about not stealing, bearing false witness, murdering, committing adultery, coveting, and other things.

Does it show love? Christ's two greatest commandments were to love God and love one another. In other words, love. Sin can be described as failure to love. One can show love even when correcting another, such as correcting a child. We yell at a child not to touch a hot stove out of love and concern for their safety, not to destroy their sense of self-worth. If what we are doing is not showing love and concern, then it is probably not a good choice.

Will it have a negative consequence for me or someone else? Many times, we do not think out what we are doing. If what we do could have a negative consequence down the road for ourselves or someone else, it might not be the best choice. We'll explore this question more in an upcoming reflection.

First Thessalonians 5:22 reminds us to abstain from evil. That is pretty straightforward. The best way to abstain from evil is to make godly choices.

Lord, thank You for the many gifts that You have given to me. Thank You for the Holy Spirit, which is continuously at work in the world. Help me to allow the Holy Spirit to be at work in my life. Help me to be a good listener, see the good in others, and seek to do good on my own. Give me the discipline to abstain from evil. Help me to glorify You in all that I do today. Amen.

Encouragement Challenge: As you make choices today, ask yourself: Will it unnecessarily hurt someone? Is it a sin? Does it show love? Will it have a negative consequence for me or someone else?

What Do You Fill Your Empty Spaces With?

Fill me with joy and gladness; let the bones which Thou hast broken rejoice.
Psalm 51:8

In a previous reflection, we discussed the topic of empty spaces. Each of us has empty spaces in our lives, in other words, places where we feel deficient. Perhaps we lack something to do, so we are bored. Perhaps we lack money, and we are jealous for the things that others have. Perhaps we haven't advanced in our jobs, our marriages aren't going well, or even more common, we feel anxious, nervous, tired, or alone. Sometimes we just aren't having a good day. We discussed when people feel "full," when they feel very encouraged, confident, and content, that they don't generally do "stupid" things. People do stupid things when they feel empty, when they have a space they need to fill.

Today's reflection poses a question to each of us—what do you fill your empty spaces with? What do you go to when you feel empty?

Most of us go to some form of escape. Drugs, alcohol, pornography, and gambling are some of the destructive places some people go. Ice cream or candy are popular choices. They are not as destructive as the options given before, but they certainly aren't healthy if we go to them regularly. Some people will take their toxicity to friends in the form of complaint or gossip, which brings destruction into relationships. Others will take it out in the gym, which is one of the best places to go when we feel empty. Some will go to a therapist, which is a good outlet. Others will find a close friend in which to confide, another good outlet.

A great thing to do when we feel empty is to do something fun. Take an hour and go to the beach or read a good book. A mental health professional once told me that when we feel empty, we should find some time for some "inconsequential activity." So much of what we do has consequences, and these consequences cause stress and anxiety, and when we don't get something right, we feel empty. An example of inconsequential behavior is reading a book or magazine for pleasure. If we finish it, great. If we don't, there is no consequence. Watching TV or a sports game, taking a walk, or reclining in our favorite chair, these are great things that also carry little to no consequence.

Some people go to a hobby to fill an empty space. Hobbies are good things as long as they are wholesome, healthy things that don't cause us to not fulfill our obligations to family or work.

The mature Christian goes to the Lord to fill the empty spaces. The words of Psalm 51:8 and others like them are not just beautiful words. They can become lifelines and sources of strength. Ideally, the Lord doesn't just become a source of refuge in the storm; He isn't just the place we go to fill our empty spaces. Instead, He is the place we go even when we feel full. Filling the spaces in our life with the Lord—through prayer, worship, Scripture, acts of charity—is a good thing.

If we know that we all have empty spaces at times, the good encourager learns to sense when a friend is in an empty space. Here is a great place to offer some encouragement in the form of words of reassurance to build someone up. And when possible, it is a great time to offer some wholesome distraction, like inviting someone to lunch, going for a walk, a few hours at the beach, or even a good phone conversation.

Empty spaces are part of every life. There is no one who feels full all the time. Most of us have a place we "go" when we feel empty. The challenge is to fill our empty spaces with healthy things rather than destructive and sinful things. The challenge as encouragers is to be involved in the lives of people around us to the degree that we are in the position to help fill their empty spaces through our presence and encouragement.

Lord, thank You for the things that bring fulfillment to my life and make me feel "full" (list some of them). Lord, You know that there are times when I feel empty, there are challenges in my life that make me feel empty (list some of them). Fill me with joy and gladness so that my empty spaces are filled with the joy and hope that come from You. Give me the eyes to see and the heart to discern those around me who may feel empty today. Give me the words to help fill them with encouragement. In my low moments, keep me away from sinful and destructive thoughts and behaviors. Fill me with You at all times and in all places. Amen.

Encouragement Challenge: Fill your empty spaces with healthy things. And encourage those around you to do the same. Most of all, fill your empty spaces with the Lord!

WE'VE FORGOTTEN HOW TO ARGUE

Put on then, as God's chosen ones, holy and beloved, compassion, kindness, lowliness, meekness and patience, forbearing one another, and, if one has a complaint against another, forgiving each other; as the Lord has forgiven you, so you also must forgive. And above all these put on love, which binds everything together in perfect harmony.
Colossians 3:12–14

In the fallen state of our world, it is impossible for everyone to get along all the time about everything. There will be disagreements, arguments, and fights, even among the best of friends, never mind complete strangers. The word pandemic is now well known in our world, related to Covid-19. However, there are other kinds of pandemics in the world, and one very toxic one relates to our inability to argue properly and forgive sincerely. Wars have been started over petty arguments, marriages have been strained, friendships have been broken, people have left jobs, teams have fallen apart, and so on. There is a certain "art" in how to argue well, and in most corners of society, we've forgotten (or maybe never learned) how to do both. Part of being a good encourager involves learning how to argue.

Little children know how to argue. On the playground, they fight over a toy, they cry, they pout, and within minutes, they are playing again. All is forgotten. Adults don't argue like this. We quit. Or we get even. Or character assassinate someone. Or call an attorney.

Many arguments quickly get out of hand when a simple solution could have been found. And sometimes arguments don't happen at all because the fear of starting an argument makes one stay quiet. Until one day, they explode. Psychologists call this passive aggressive behavior.[35] Many of us are passive, absorbing all the negativity, until one day we explode, sometimes at the smallest of things, because we haven't dealt with conflict appropriately all the way along.

So, how does one go about negotiating differences of opinion? How does one avoid arguments? How does one get out of an argument once an argument has started?

There are a few things that are easy to say and write down, though harder to do. One of those things is creating an environment where it is safe to be honest. This is done by specifically saying that to the person, you have a difference of opinion with. Just say, "We have a difference of opinion. Let's come to the table with honesty and respect and work it out." That's not what politicians do. That's not what people who have signed contracts do. However, that's what friends should do, spouses, and co-workers who really matter to us.

The place to start an argument is not from the place of difference but from the place of similarity. At the beginning, find any points of agreement and start there. For instance, let's say that one spouse wants to buy a car while the other one thinks the desired car is too expensive. If both spouses can agree that a new car is needed, if they can come to a point of agreement on something, then the argument becomes about the means to the same desired end.

Having said that, when the desired end goal is the same, it is easier to negotiate the means of how to get there. Many times, there isn't unity on the end goal, so there is an argument about the means. Thus, another good place to start an argument is by stating the desire to a common end goal.

This may all seem like it's common sense, and it is. However, many times we are starting arguments or perpetuating them because we can't find common ground or common sense either.

Imagine you began an argument/heated discussion by reading today's Bible verses together with your "adversary." How amazing it would be to affirm that we are God's chosen ones, holy and beloved, and that we should act toward one another with compassion, kindness, lowliness, meekness, and patience. How wonderful it would be if we led with any ONE of these traits, to argue with kindness, patience, or compassion toward someone else. And when the "argument" is over, ask for forgiveness if you have offended someone or for another to ask forgiveness of you so that everything can be bound together in harmony. This is what love is. If God tells us that the greatest commandments are to love Him and love one another, learning to love one another in the midst of an argument, and learning how to argue by leading with love are two very crucial things. An argument that takes on the form of a good discussion rather than a heated disagreement can actually be encouraging. Creating a space where it is safe and expected to be honest can be reassuring and affirming.

It is increasingly frustrating in the political sphere when no one can reach across the aisle to work with the other party. Likewise, in our daily lives, it is sad when we can't reach across the aisle of difference to work with another person. Learning this skill and applying it with patience, compassion, and love would go a long way to making our world a more encouraging place to live.

Lord, thank You for making each person different. Thank You for creating different talents, personalities, and viewpoints. Help us all in those times when we have disagreements to come to the table with respect and safety. Give us wisdom and patience as we look for points of unity. Give us humility to work through differences. Help us to keep our focus on love for one another. Bring us peaceful resolution to differences, and when that is not possible, give us patience and help us to serve one another with humility, even when we don't see eye to eye. Amen.

Encouragement Challenge: Learn how to argue and find points of unity even in times of difference!

Relationships: Competitive, Cooperative, or Indifferent

Behold, how good and pleasant it is when brothers dwell in unity.
Psalm 133:1

We relate to one another generally in one of three ways—we are either cooperative, competitive, or indifferent in our relationships. A "competitive" relationship sees someone as an enemy to be defeated. There can be only one winner in a competition. So, when we compete with one another, there will be a winner and a loser. In the competition, there isn't much room for love because love is about giving rather than taking, building up rather than tearing down, about encouraging rather than beating someone. In a competitive relationship, there will be an emphasis on taking, tearing down, and beating someone because the goal of competition is to win, and to win, someone else has to lose.

A relationship of "indifference" is, in some ways, worse than a relationship of competition. In a competitive relationship, there may be respect for an opponent. We find the opponent worthy of our competition. To be indifferent to someone means that we don't even find them worthy to engage with in competition. If someone doesn't like another person, at least they have taken the time to evaluate the person to decide not to like him or her. In an indifferent relationship, a person isn't even worth evaluating.

In the theme of this section on abstaining from evil, we should try to avoid being competitive or indifferent in our relationships.

The healthiest way to relate to someone is through cooperation. In a cooperative relationship, people encourage one another, bring out the best in one another, and see the best in one another. Forgiveness is easier in a cooperative relationship, so is honesty, trustworthiness, and so many other things.

If the major thrust of our life is happiness that can only be achieved through competition, then we've lived a rather narcissistic existence. Of course, there are way to achieve happiness that do not involve competition. Sitting in front of the TV eating pizza with one's family produces happiness without competition. That is a wholesome expression of happiness. Getting home quickly from work when there is no traffic produces happiness. However, trying to get home quicker while driving like a maniac in heavy traffic produces happiness through competition and, ultimately, narcissism.

This is not to say that competitive sports or other types of competition are bad things. Competition can be a healthy thing, but we also don't generally have close relationships with members of the opposing team. There are certain things in life that are set up to be competitive to drive us to better ourselves at something. Relationships should not resemble sports teams. They are not meant to be competitive.

Our purpose in life, according to God, is to love God and serve one another. God has given each of us the tools to do both. These tools differ from person to person. The fallen world also gives challenges to each of us in using our tools to love God and serve others. We each have "handicaps" and limitations that inhibit us at times or, at the very least, challenge us. Our purpose in life is to live cooperatively with God and one another, bringing out the best in one another.

The same three metrics—cooperation, competition, and indifference—can also be applied to our relationship with the Lord. Many are indifferent. There is no relationship. There is no involvement in a church community. There is no thought given to God's purpose for our lives.

There are people, even people who faithfully attend church, who live in competition with God. They oppose Him all the time by the way they behave. Some may come to church as a way to "let God win sometimes" and keep the competition to a minimum, or even make it appear as if they are cooperative.

Those who relate to the Lord in a cooperative way work together with Him in worship, and most especially on days when they don't worship because it is easy to look cooperative when everyone around us is cooperative. It is a challenge to be cooperative when we are not in church and are surrounded by situations that beckon us to be competitive.

I remember a line that a bishop I used to work for used in his prayers: "Remember those who suffer because we are indifferent to them." We have three choices in all relationships, from the person we are married to, the person we work with, and the stranger in the car next to us on the highway—we can be competitive, indifferent, or cooperative. Psalm 133:1 tells us that it is a blessed thing when brothers live in unity. In other words, the godly choice in relationships is to be cooperative.

Lord, thank You for the many relationships I have. Thank You for the people who are closest to me, who I see all the time (name them). Thank You for the people around me who I do not know but who are helpful in my life (think of some of them, like your bank teller, the cashier at the grocery store, etc.). And thank You even for the people around me who I do not know, the complete strangers that cross my path each day. In each of these relationships, give me a heart that seeks cooperation. Help me not to size everyone up as a competitor. **And remember, Lord, all those who suffer because we are indifferent to them.** *Amen.*

Encouragement Challenge: Choose cooperation over competition and indifference!

**Dedicated to His Eminence Metropolitan Methodios of Boston.

Consequences of Positive, Negative, and No Input

Let us consider how to stir up one another to love and good works, not neglecting to meet together, as is the habit of some, but encouraging one another, and all the more as you see the Day drawing near.
Hebrews 10:24–25

The message of this reflection is straightforward. A positive input will generally result in a positive output. Generally, if someone pays you a compliment, you won't turn around and respond negatively to them. It just doesn't fit. A positive stimulus will generally result in a positive reaction. A positive input generally boosts confidence and performance in a job setting.

A negative input will generally result in a negative output. Insult someone, and they generally will react negatively. One big problem in our world today is that a small negative stimulus results in a large, negative reaction. For instance, driver A cuts off driver B in traffic. Driver B then takes out a gun and kills driver A. This is a complete overreaction. The appropriate reaction of driver B would be to just ignore driver A and drive along. A "normal" (not appropriate, just normal) reaction might be for driver B to cut off driver A or ride beside driver A and curse at him. People overreact to negative stimuli because we are a very angry society. Our primary emotion in the world is rage, which goes beyond anger. As we've discussed, we've forgotten how to argue and forgive. Thus, we've forgotten how to react appropriately to a negative input. We generally overreact to negative input.

Negative input, even justified negative input, lowers confidence and affects performance. If a person tells me, "You are doing a great job," I feel confident and want to work even harder. If a person tells me, "You are doing a bad job," my confidence suffers, and doubt creeps in.

Here is the thing that most of us forget. What happens when there is no input? The consequences actually are the same as if there is a negative input. If I am working hard, and you tell me I'm doing a good job, I'll feel confident. If you tell me I'm doing a bad job, I'll have doubts, and my confidence will go down. And if I work hard, and you tell me nothing, you give me no feedback, I will actually have doubts, and my confidence will go down. No input ends up having the same result as a negative input.

This is why encouragement is so important. When a person is doing something right, we have to recognize and celebrate that. That doesn't mean we have to throw a party or give out a trophy or award for every good thing we do. It means, however, that we have to recognize good things that people are doing because that will motivate them to do more good things. Saying nothing, even to people who are doing good, will cause them to lose confidence and have doubts. No feedback is almost as bad as negative feedback.

When someone does something right, recognize that. When someone does something wrong, react appropriately. We don't kill people who argue with us. We either argue back at them, or we walk away. That's appropriate.

The indifference and lack of input is really hurting our society. There are some people who have a mind to do bad things, and perhaps nothing can stop them. People who commit school shootings come to mind. While encouragement is not the sole antidote to violence, I very much doubt that people who are committing violent acts are receiving a lot of encouragement. They are probably not told daily that they matter or that they have talent. They are probably not being listened to. Of course, there are some serious problems with mental illness that lead people to do things that are out of character, they hear voices that tell them to do something violent, or there are people with sociopathic tendencies that are hard to correct. I have wondered for a long time whether these people suffer from either extreme negative input or no input at all.

Encouragement certainly doesn't hurt. An extra positive comment never hurt anyone. Negative comments hurt, even though they are necessary sometimes. And no comment hurt almost as much as negative ones. So when something goes right, don't forget to offer encouragement. And when something goes wrong, make sure that the negative input is appropriate and isn't an overreaction.

St. Paul says it well in Hebrews 10:24–25 that we should "consider how to stir up one another to love and good works." That would be encouragement. He reminds that we should be "not neglecting to meet together as is the habit of some." This would be indifference. But that we should be "encouraging one another."

Lord, help me to have eyes that see others appropriately. Help me to see the good works that others do and applaud and encourage those. Help me, when I see something negative, to react with a spirit of gentleness and not to overreact. Take away from me the tendency to be indifferent to others. Please help me to see the best in people. Amen.

Encouragement Challenge: Make sure that a positive input gets a positive reaction, not no reaction and that a negative input gets an appropriate reaction, not an overreaction.

BE THE SALT OF THE EARTH

"You are the salt of the earth; but if salt has lost its taste, how shall its saltiness be restored? It is no longer good for anything except to be thrown out and trodden underfoot by men."
Matthew 5:13

Salt is used for two reasons. First, it is used to bring taste to food. Second, it is used as a preservative. In Matthew 5:13, Jesus tells us that we are the salt of the earth. Like salt, we serve two purposes. We each have the ability to bring some "taste" to life through our personalities and talents. Each of us can bring some depth to the world. We not only add a person to the quantity of the population but we are supposed to add something to its quality, it's "taste" as well. Think of spices that are used in small quantity but add rich quality to food. This is how we are supposed to be, individual spices that bring quality to our world.

Like salt, we also have preservative qualities. We are supposed to preserve the fabric of God's righteousness from generation to generation. When our generation passes away, the Word of God should have been furthered. Goodness should have been expanded. We are supposed to leave the world better than we found it. Is that the case right now?

Encouragement is a lot like salt. It adds taste to a world that seems to be bitter with anger. While encouragement in itself will probably not cure anger, it certainly will make a difference. We've all had the experience of having a bad day, when nothing seems to be going right. We've all sat down at the computer exasperated, dashing to complete an assignment or send an email. Imagine turning on your computer and finding an encouraging email in your inbox. Imagine someone has written you a message that their life is better because you are in it. You would get a reprieve, even if only momentarily, from your frustration. Imagine if you found ten such emails in your inbox. Your anger might dissipate. Imagine if you found a hundred such emails. You might forget what you were angry about. And imagine if you found a thousand such emails. You would be euphoric!

Like salt, encouragement is also a preservative. In many cases, it preserves our good mood, even our sense of sanity. Encouragement might mean the difference between feeling crushed and having the strength to take another step. We can't underestimate its power.

One of my all-time favorite stories is *The Starfish Story* by Loren Eisley. It goes like this:

> One day a man was walking along the beach, when he noticed a boy hurriedly picking up and gently throwing things into the ocean. Approaching the boy, he asked "Young man, what are you doing?" The boy replied, "Throwing starfish back into the ocean. The surf is up and the tide is going out. If I don't throw them back, they'll die." The man laughed to himself and said, "Don't you realize there are miles and miles of beach and hundreds of starfish? You can't make any difference!" After listening politely, the boy bent down, picked up another starfish, and threw it into the surf. Then, smiling at the man, he said. . . "I made a difference to that one."[36]

We live in an angry and discouraging world. There is no doubt about that. If our world was compared to a pot on the stove, its contents would be described as bitter. Encouragement helps remove the bitterness. It helps to make what was bitter palatable, even tasty. If we each do our part, we can make a difference.

There are many cynical people, like the man on the beach who laughed at the boy. They think, *What possible difference can a few encouraging words make in the world?* You'd be surprised.

In the book entitled *Getting Together and Staying Together* by William Glasser and Carleen Glasser, the authors write about the "Seven Deadly Habits of Marriage."[37] These include criticizing, blaming, complaining, nagging, threatening, punishing, and bribing or rewarding to control someone. These deadly habits not only kill marriages; they kill relationships, and these deadly habits are, in large part, the culprits behind the bitterness of our society. Think about these seven bad habits. How many do we do each week or even each day?

The authors also switch gears and talk about "Seven Caring Habits of Marriage" (which can be extended to other relationships). These include listening, supporting, encouraging, respecting, trusting, accepting, and always negotiating disagreements. When we think about these good habits, one of the easiest to pick up is encouraging. These are the healthy habits that will give taste and depth to the world, which will crowd out the bitterness of society.

Be the salt of the earth as Christ called us to be. Being salt through encouragement will give depth and taste and preserve positivity and, in turn, godliness in our world!

Lord, thank You for the many things that are unique about me (think about some of these things and bring them into this prayer). Help me to use the things that are unique about me to make a positive difference in the lives of other people today. Help me to be "salt of the earth" today, to do my part to put away bitterness and be positive. Help me to preserve as well as to spread Your gospel by being salt in the world today. Amen.

Encouragement Challenge: Make a difference for someone in a good way today!

An Important Conversion for Parents

Who is like the wise man? And who knows the interpretation of a thing? A man's wisdom makes his face shine, and the hardness of his countenance is changed.
Ecclesiastes 8:1

I'm a parent. I'm a parent who makes many mistakes. I'm a parent who struggles to find the line between being an encourager and a disciplinarian. Discipline can be discouraging for the person doing it and the person receiving it. I also realize that a parent has to change their parenting style as their children get older.

When our children are babies, it is necessary at times to use an alarmist voice to "encourage" our babies, or perhaps more accurately, to discourage them from behavior that could be detrimental to them. For example, we scream, "Don't touch the hot stove!" at our toddlers because raising our voices reinforces for them that what they are doing is potentially dangerous. The alarmist voice comes out by necessity when our children are very young. Let's say, for example, this is the most effective voice when they are less than five years old. Once they become an age where they can reason and understand things, it is no longer necessary to use this voice as often, if at all.

It is a challenge to every parent, and I speak from experience, to learn to use a different "voice" of encouragement with their children. For people who have many children, there might be a child who is ten and another who is two, and the parent has the challenge of using different voices with different children. We can't yell at the ten-year-old with the alarmist voice we use with the two-year-old. Once a child goes to college, a parent can't speak with the same voice of daily director that the parent used when the child lived at home. Once a child becomes an adult, a parent become more consultant than director. And once a child gets married, the parent becomes more friend than parent.

One pitfall that parents fall into, which I am hoping to avoid, is that they don't move from alarmist to encourager. When our children were babies, many things became a cause for alarm, and it was necessary to raise our voice to make our point in the interest of safety. Once they become of rational age, we need to switch our discipline to something that is more thoughtful rather than alarmist. If we don't make the conversion from alarmist to encourager, we risk raising kids who are not only irresponsible but not confident. Encouragers learn how to motivate without constantly sounding like an alarmist and without killing the confidence of our children. They see their role as a confidence builder.

Of course, until our children become adults, discipline is necessary. There is a difference between discouragement and discipline. These can easily be confused. If I tell our child, "You can't have dessert if you don't eat dinner," that is not discouraging; that is good discipline. It encourages good eating habits. It is the same thing with, "You can't play until you finish your homework." That is good discipline and encourages healthy study habits. However, it's the way we say these things that matter. Discipline has to be infused with encouragement. For instance, if we say, "You did a great job on your homework, thanks for being so focused; let's play," that is encouraging. It is also encouraging to connect positive results with reward rather than threatening punishment with negative results. In other words, it's more encouraging to say, "Let's be efficient on your homework so we can do something fun" than to say, "If you don't get your homework done, you won't have time to do anything fun." It's better to encourage someone to work for reward than to avoid punishment.

One other important note to parents. Do we have a negative response when someone tells us, "I love you" or "I'm proud of you"? No, we don't. We all like to hear these words. They build us up and make us feel more confident. Our children like to hear these words too. While our role as parents is to discipline, and sometimes we have to do that with an alarmist voice, it is important not to forget to tell your children you love them and are proud of them.

Several times in working with teenagers, I asked them who had the biggest voice of discouragement in their lives. And the answer was resoundingly their parents. This made me kind of sad. Perhaps, in the defense of parents, the parents are the only voice of discipline in the lives of teenagers. They certainly don't get encouragement to be disciplined by their peers. However, this served as a wake-up call to me that together with the voice of discipline, we can't forget the voice of encouragement, and we can't be effective encouragers to rational children or teenagers if we are still using the (necessary at the time) alarmist voice we used when they were babies.

Lord, thank You for the gift of children. Thank You for the opportunity to be a parent. Lord, bless me as a parent. Help me to be not only a voice of discipline and direction but a voice of encouragement for my children. Help me to find the balance between the two and provide the tone of voice that conveys love, even in times of concern. Bless my children and help them to grow up with confidence. Bless our relationship so that as they grow up and become adults, we will always remain close. Help me to see the best in them. Help me to change as they change so that I can be an effective parent and encourager to them. Amen.

A good parent needs to know how to change between disciplinarian and encourager and learn to change the tone of voice and parenting styles as children grow up. We may be their parent and chief disciplinarians, but we need to be their chief encouragers as well!

Getting Rid of Guilt and Shame

Instead of your shame you shall have a double portion, instead of dishonor you shall rejoice in your lot; therefore, in your land you shall possess a double portion; yours shall be everlasting joy.
Isaiah 61:7

Very early on in this study, we discussed 1 John 4:18, which says, "There is no fear in love, but perfect love casts out fear. For fear has to do with punishment, and he who fears is not perfected in love." Fear and love cannot co-exist. Likewise, guilt, shame, and punishment cannot co-exist with love. And they can't co-exist with encouragement either, as encouragement is an expression of love. One cannot feel encouraged and shameful or guilty at the same time.

The movie *Mean Girls* debuted in 2004 as a film about social cliques among high school girls and how they are negatively affected by them. A sequel was made in 2011 as a TV movie. While the movie did well in the theaters, thanks to a star-studded cast, many girls (and boys too, for that matter) live this movie as part of their everyday life. They are either the mean girls (or boys) or the victims of the mean girls (or boys). And it doesn't stop once high school is over. There are plenty of mean women and men as well as victims of them in all pockets of society.

The notion that one is not good enough does not inspire confidence. Rather, it induces feelings of inadequacy, doubt, guilt, and shame. This can happen both objectively and arbitrarily, as bars are set so high that they can't be reached. Objectively, this happens when one doesn't measure up to an academic or professional standard. For instance, if one doesn't attain a certain grade point average or test score, they may not get into a certain class or college. While this may negatively affect a person's confidence, the fact is that we won't all receive get straight As or get into the college of our dreams. When there are many more applicants than openings for a school or a job, some very qualified people will be disappointed. That's life, and this kind of disappointment is almost unavoidable. We will all experience it at some point.

There are arbitrary bars, however, that are set high and can't be reached, not because one doesn't measure up to an academic or professional standard, but because he or she won't be allowed to reach the bar because of someone else's opinion. In the case of the mean girls, a clique may decide that a certain girl isn't pretty or popular enough to get in. That's arbitrary.

If a college says one isn't good enough to get in, a student can choose to work harder, improve grades, and try again. If a clique says you aren't popular enough or have the right look to be admitted, there is nothing one can do other than look in from the outside and wonder.

What does this have to do with encouragement? When we set subjective bars that cannot be reached or judge people with arbitrary measures, we are not being good encouragers. When we shame people because of how they look, an ability they lack, or an opinion that differs from ours, we are not being good encouragers. People who choose to be mean and strike fear in others will not be good encouragers. And shaming someone into doing something will not build their confidence. Rather, it will foster doubt and even resentment.

In seeking to abstain from evil, one great place to start is to not use shame as a motivator. Another place is to set bars that people have a chance of meeting.

The prophet Isaiah wrote about the exile of the children of Israel, foreshadowing a time when they would be taken from their land and held in Babylon. This would be a time of great shame for them as well as fear and oppression. Isaiah foretold that they would eventually return to their homeland, and their shame and dishonor would be replaced by a double portion of blessings and an everlasting joy.

In many ways, we can relate to the people of Isaiah's time. We feel shame and dishonor, we feel trapped, we can't seem to find sustained joy, and we wonder if things will ever improve. This is true for many teenagers, college students, adults, spouses, parents, and seniors. Lack of friends, money, health, confidence, bad choices, and other deficits combine to make us feel this way. Some encouragement can go a long way to restoring joy and lessening shame.

Encouragement, like love, is a choice. The choice to encourage is a choice to build up someone else. The choice to shame someone, give them a guilt trip, or raise the bar to an unreachable arbitrary level causes discouragement. If we are seeking encouragement and learning to be good encouragers, by necessity, these are tactics we need to change. We don't need mean girls or boys, mean men or women. The choice to encourage brings the "double portion" Isaiah spoke about to everyone. It brings joy to the encourager and confidence to the one receiving encouragement.

Lord, thank You for the good parts of me (reflect on your talents and positive characteristics). Help me to accept who I am and rejoice for what I can do rather than becoming discouraged by what I can't do. Help me to be a good encourager. Help me to manage thought and actions that could bring shame to others. Help me not to pre-judge people. Give others the eyes to not pre-judge me. Help me to accept things I cannot change. Help me to change things that I need the change. Help me to see the good in others and encourage others to see the good in themselves. Amen.

Encouragement Challenge: Work to remove guilt-tripping and shaming from your interactions with others!

Then What?

According to the grace of God given to me, like a skilled master builder I laid a foundation, and another man is building upon it. Let each man take care how he builds upon it. For no other foundation can anyone lay than that which is laid, which is Jesus Christ. Now if anyone builds on the foundation with gold, silver, precious stones, wood, hay, straw— each man's work will become manifest; for the Day will disclose it, because it will be revealed with fire, and the fire will test what sort of work each one has done. If the work which any man has built on the foundation survives, he will receive a reward.
1 Corinthians 3:10–14

Years ago, I heard a memorable sermon from a priest, which he entitled "Then What?" The story he told was about a college student who went to talk to his priest and had all kinds of anxiety about what his future held. The conversation went something like this:

Student: I'm anxious about my future.
Priest: What are you anxious about?
Student: Well, I want to find a good job.
Priest: And then what?
Student: I want to make a lot of money.
Priest: And then what?
Student: I want to get married and have children.
Priest: And then what?
Student: I want to have a successful career.
Priest: And then what?
Student: I want to retire and enjoy grandchildren.
Priest: And then what?
Student: I'll probably get sick and eventually die.
Priest: And then what?

The point of the sermon was to illustrate that without God and without faith, when everything else in life is over, then what?

I love this sermon not only because it was memorable and applicable to faith and life but because I found another way to use it as it relates to making good decisions and staying out of trouble. We previously discussed test questions before making a decision—Is it safe? Is it smart? Is it in line with my character? Does it honor God? Does it get me closer to my goals?

"Then what?" is a good test question to use when making decisions. Take any scenario, ask, "Then what?" and answer the question over and over again until the scenario plays out to completion. Here is an example from teenage behavior:

> I'm going to go to a party and drink.
> Then what?
> I'm probably going to get sick.
> Then what?
> I'm going to have to lie to my parents about where I was.
> Then what?
> They aren't going to trust me.
> Then what?
> I may permanently harm my relationship with them.

Going to the party and drinking doesn't play out to a good ending for a teenager. It's a bad decision.

Let's take this from an adult perspective.

> I'm going to a party and get drunk.
> Then what?
> I'm going to drive home.
> Then what?
> I might get caught drinking and driving.
> Then what?
> I will be embarrassed when my mug shot ends up all over the internet.
> Then what?
> I won't be able to get a job and will face a lifetime of embarrassment.

Drinking and driving is not a good decision. It doesn't play out to a good ending.

There is an innumerable amount of scenarios of things we are tempted with every day: flirting with a co-worker, fudging on a financial figure, driving recklessly, staying up too late, and the list goes on and on.

When we are confronted with these scenarios, we should ask ourselves the "Then what?" question and let it play out to all possible conclusions. Then we will avoid what is evil and cling to what is good.

Here is an example of a good decision:

> I'm going to exercise regularly.
> Then what?
> I'm going to get in better shape.
> Then what?
> I'm going to physically feel better.
> Then what?
> I'm going to have more strength and stamina to do more things.
> Then what?
> I'll probably live longer.

The decision to exercise, for example, is a good decision. It plays out to a good ending.

Encouragement, whether you are encouraging someone else or someone else is encouraging you, generally plays out to a good ending (unless bad behavior is being encouraged). It boosts self-confidence, lessens doubt, gets good behaviors to repeat, and brings people closer together. The choice to encourage is generally a good decision. It plays out to a good ending in the "Then what?" exercise.

"Then what" is an excellent test question in going to what it good and away from what is evil. It is also an excellent question to keep in mind when considering the primary importance of faith over the other things we may or may not achieve in life.

Lord, thank You for the gift of this day. I know that this day will be filled with choices and decisions that will affect my life and the lives of others. Give me the wisdom to meditate on the question "Then what?" as I make my decisions. Help me to understand that certain decisions do not play out to a good ending while others will play out to a good ending. Help me to have eyes to see the good paths and the courage and steadfastness to avoid the bad ones. Help me to have faith to know that the ultimate "then what" will be granted salvation and everlasting life. May my life and its daily decisions point me toward Your heavenly kingdom. Amen.

Encouragement Challenge: Ask yourself "Then what?" as you make decisions today!

**Dedicated to Fr. Dean Gigicos, in honor of his "Then what?" sermon.

The Signs Have to Match

Every athlete exercises self-control in all things. They do it to receive a perishable wreath, but we an imperishable. Well, I do not run aimlessly, I do not box as one beating the air; but I pommel my body and subdue it, lest after preaching to others I myself should be disqualified.
1 Corinthians 9:25–27

Another great sermon I heard years ago was called "The Signs Have to Match." The priest who gave the sermon had made a bunch of signs. As he gave the sermon, he would place signs around his neck. The gist of the sermon was that each of us wears a sign over our chests, which is an invisible report card. While the "sign" you wear might not be a physical sign that is visible to the world, what's written on that "sign" most certainly is.

If a person gets drunk and drives, for example, their sign says, "I'm irresponsible." If a person is abusive, their sign says, "Don't trust me." If a person is a narcissist, their sign says, "I'm all about me." If a person is always taking risks and putting others in harm's way, their sign says, "I'm stupid," and the list goes on and on.

Everyone who is a Christian wears a cross over their chest. When this priest gave this sermon many years ago, he put a large cross over his signs that said, "I'm stupid," "I'm irresponsible," and "Don't trust me." He said, "This cross is incongruent with the signs that are behind it."

We don't all wear a large gold cross on our chests, but whether we wear a cross or not, if we identify as a Christian, our identity needs to match our behavior. The invisible signs of our behavior have to match the invisible sign of the cross.

As encouragers, we wear a sign that says, "I'm an encourager." That sign also says, "I'm safe" and "I'll lift you up when you are feeling down." If we are going to be encouragers, our signs need to match. We can't wear a sign that says, "I'm going to lift you up" and a sign that says, "I'm a gossip-mongerer." We can't wear a sign that says, "I'm safe" and a sign that says, "I love risky behavior." We can't wear a sign that says, "I offer a sympathetic ear" and one that says, "I always get the first and last word in." The signs have to match.

The words of St. Paul from 1 Corinthians come to mind when we think of the signs we wear. Being an encourager involves many things, including self-control. If we are seeking to build people up, we can't make a habit of tearing others down at the same time. As Christians, we are not competing against others but racing with them to the kingdom of God. Earthly competitions, whether they are in the classroom, on the athletic field, or in business, are races for an earthly reward—a grade, trophy, paycheck. Christians compete with one another (as opposed to against one another) for the heavenly crown. Encouragers compete with others for things that money can't buy—confidence and joy. Fortunately, a person doesn't need to steal or win confidence over someone else. Confidence and joy are things we can all have, and they come in endless supply. There might be only one valedictorian in a class, one champion on the field, and one boss of the company. In the world of encouragement, everyone can be built up, and everyone can build others up.

St. Paul writes, "I do not run aimlessly. I do not box as one beating the air" (1 Cor. 9:26). His faith and work was purposeful, not chaotic. Encouragement follows the same path. It is purposeful and intentional.

St. Paul also wrote, "I pommel my body and subdue it, lest after preaching to others I myself should be disqualified" (9:27). St. Paul was intentional in writing that he lived a disciplined life, making sure that his signs matched, and making sure what he was preaching about Christ was congruent with all the other aspects of his life. This is important for us as Christians. It is also important for us as encouragers, that our encouragement is intentional, and we are disciplined to encourage others. It is important that the encouragement we offer is congruent with the rest of our lives. It is vital that the signs we wear match.

Lord, there is no doubt that life is a struggle. It is a struggle to make all the "signs" I wear in life match all the time. One sign may say, "encourager" while another sign says, "sinner." Help me to have the discipline to make the signs match. Give me the vision to see when they don't. Help me to be intentional and purposeful in both my Christianity and encouragement of others. Amen.

Encouragement Challenge: Make sure what is written on our signs all match.

**Dedicated to Fr. Steve Dalber, in honor of his "The Signs Have to Match" sermon.

Part Twelve
―――――――――
KEEP SOUND

May the God of peace Himself sanctify you wholly; and may your spirit and soul and body be kept sound and blameless at the coming of our Lord Jesus Christ.

1 Thessalonians 5:23

God and the Church Are Encouragers

May the God of peace Himself sanctify you wholly; and may your spirit and soul and body be kept sound and blameless at the coming of our Lord Jesus Christ.
1 Thessalonians 5:23

St. Paul wrote two letters to the Thessalonians. We have been studying the fifth and last chapter of the First Letter to the Thessalonians. Verse 23 makes a transition from words of instruction/admonishing/encouraging to words of farewell. Though we still have a lot to say on encouragement in this study, this verse also provides us an opportunity to transition from our individual need for encouragement and ability to encourage others and now shifts the spotlight to Christ and the church as sources of encouragement.

Years ago at summer camp, we did a study on the Ten Commandments. Over the course of the first few days of camp, we presented various moral lessons related to the Ten Commandments—do not commit murder, do not steal, do not lie, and so on. One of my brother priests pulled me aside after a couple of days and said, "You know you are presenting good lessons on morality but not on Christianity." He was right. Christianity is more than a bunch of dos and don'ts. It is more than being good. It is more than being moral. The same thing goes for encouragement.

Morality and encouragement are part of living a Christian life. They are not exclusive Christian ideas, though. To be Christian in our encouragement, we have to remember to encourage with Christ at the center of all that we do.

The verse that introduces this section of our study introduces us to the word sanctify. In 1 Thessalonians 5:23, the Greek word that is translated as sanctify is "agiase." The Greek word that is translated as holy is "agios." So, sanctification and holiness are closely related. Both mean "to set apart for God."[38] Holy people are those who set themselves apart for God, not in an egotistical way but in a way that is disciplined and focused. People who see their bodies as holy do not abuse them by over indulging in food or alcohol. People who see their mouths as holy use them as tools to build up and encourage others rather than to tear down and destroy them.

Thus, we don't encourage and build up others merely because it is a nice thing to do, it makes them feel good, or it makes life easier. We are supposed to encourage and build up others because it is a holy thing to do. Encouragement not only honors others; it honors God. It not only sets us apart in our interpersonal relationships. It sets us on the path to holiness, to oneness with God, to salvation.

First Thessalonians 5:23 acknowledges that we need God's help to be sanctified and made holy. In our fallen nature, this is something that none of us can do on our own. No matter how disciplined we are, how much we are encouraged to grow in Christ, and how much we encourage others to grow in faith, our sinful nature, sadly, will always cause us to fall short of holiness. Thus, we need encouragement not only from one another. We need it from God Himself. First Thessalonians 5:23 points us to our common destiny, which is that we will stand before Christ at His second coming. St. Paul prays for those reading his letter (the Thessalonians of the first century, and us today in the twenty-first century) to be sanctified with a spirit and soul that are sound and blameless and ready to stand at the awesome judgment seat of Christ.

Where do we receive encouragement from God? There are two important sources that we must regularly go to. First, the Scriptures. I heard the Bible described once as "God's love letter to us." Now, a given page of the Old Testament that talks about the misery of God's people in the wilderness, offers instructions on how to build the lampstand in the temple, or recounts yet another battle between Israel and its seemingly endless list of enemies may not sound like much of a love letter. However, the Bible, taken in its totality, is a history of God's love. And MANY (perhaps most) passages of the Bible bring into focus the mercy and love of God toward us. That's why it's important to read Scripture regularly. It not only gives us knowledge of God but encouragement for how to follow, live, prepare, and joyfully anticipate eternal life.

The second source of spiritual encouragement is the church. We all know the saying, "There is strength in numbers." A great number of people worshiping together is encouraging. Think of a bunch of people walking the same direction in a pool. They will create a current. If a person jumps into the pool, they will be caught in the current and go in the same direction, even if they don't make much of a contribution. It is easier to get caught in the current of faith and spirituality if we do it in the context of the church than if we try to go it alone. I dare say it is nearly impossible.

The end goal of life is neither to feel encouraged or be a good encourager. The end goal of life is to be sanctified and enter the kingdom of God with joy. A church community is a place where we will find encouragement for this end goal. It is a good place where we can spiritually encourage others because God doesn't just ask for us to encourage others and build them up professionally, socially, or even morally. He asks for us to encourage one another spiritually and build up faith in one another.

Lord, thank You for the gift of Jesus Christ, who came to earth to die for our sins and open for us the door back to paradise. Help me to remember my destination, which is to stand before You. May I come to that moment in a way that You will find me worthy to enter Your heavenly kingdom. Help me to take positive steps each day as I journey toward this moment. Help me to seek out and see opportunities for spiritual encouragement, from Your sacred Scriptures and Your holy church. Help me to take my place in a church community where I can also serve as a spiritual encourager, encouraging others not only in life but in faith as well. Amen.

Encouragement Challenge: Seek spiritual encouragement from the Scriptures and the church. Be a spiritual encourager!

Having Rules Makes You Free

I say this for your own benefit, not to lay any restraint upon you, but to promote good order and to secure your undivided devotion to the Lord.
1 Corinthians 7:35

We began our discussion of 1 Thessalonians 5:23 by reflecting on being sanctified until the coming of our Lord Jesus Christ. We will now pivot the discussion to focusing on the words "may your spirit and soul and body be kept sound and blameless." Our lives center around relationships, whether we are referring to our relationship with God or with one another. Thus, a goal and challenge in life is keeping our relationships sound as we make our journey to salvation.

One thing I have found helpful in some of my relationships is creating rules. Rules have the connotation of restricting things, but in reality, rules make us free. There is a rule that says we have to stop at a red light. If there wasn't this rule, or there weren't any traffic lights, none of us would feel safe driving. So, rules actually make us free.

The idea of rules making us free applies not only to society. It applies to personal relationships as well as to our relationship with the Lord. Let's begin there.

Many people criticize Christianity as a list of dos and don'ts and criticize churches as institutions focused solely on rules. It is true that we do not worship rules. We worship the Lord. However, some "rules" are good. They create order, and they make us free. It is a good that Scripture provides us with guidelines. It is good that church communities set traditions and expectations for their members. Again, we don't worship traditions and rituals. However, they provide us with a sense of order and freedom, which leads us to a sense of confidence and security.

If we have rules in society, why wouldn't we consider adding rules to relationships? Let me share a personal example. When I go to summer camp, it is an intense experience. The normal stress combined with lack of sleep and overall emotional environment can create a lot of fun but also make for easier arguments. The core staff and I stipulate before we go that at some point, we will have a disagreement. And so we agree on rules we will follow if and when we have a disagreement. We have rules on how to talk when there is a difference of opinion. We have a rule called the "is everything ok" rule so that if someone wonders if they've done wrong, they can just ask, "Is everything ok" and either know everything is alright or deal immediately if something is not.

There are rules on forgiveness—that if someone asks for forgiveness, they are not told, "Hey, don't worry about it"; they are told, "Forgiven." Forgiveness is given. We also have a rule that twice a week, we ask for forgiveness so that every few days, we make sure that everything is ok and there is no buildup of anything negative.

Rules like this can be applied to working relationships, friendships, and marriages. We KNOW that we will have disagreements, especially with the people we are closest to, who we see all the time. We KNOW that this will happen. So if we know things will happen, then we should establish rules for how to deal with things as they happen rather than letting them fester. And we should exchange forgiveness on a regular basis. Actually say the words, "Please forgive me" and offer the words "You are forgiven."

In school, we all did a fire drill once a month. The purpose for the drill was so that if there ever was a fire, people would respond in a calm and collected way rather than panicking. In life, we should set up contingencies in the form of rules so that when there is a "fire" in one of our relationships, we know how to put it out. Consider sitting down with your spouse, close friends, or co-workers and agreeing on rules that allow you to disagree and still be friends and that quickly bring you back to wholeness when things get off track.

Lord, thank You for the many relationships I enjoy in my life (list some of them). Help me to work together with those whom I love so that our relationships are safeguarded from harm. When we have disagreements, lead us back to wholeness. Help us to easily exchange forgiveness. Help us to develop mechanisms to easily resolve disagreements so that our relationships reflect the love and forgiveness that You have modeled for us. Amen.

Encouragement Challenge: Set some rules today in your relationships! Frame them specifically under God's "rules" that we are to love one another!

A Buddy to Keep You Accountable

Love one another with brotherly affection; outdo one another in showing honor.
Romans 12:10

We're all familiar with the term peer pressure; it's when you feel pressured by your peers to do something. Sometimes that thing is bad—like when people are in college and their peers egg them on to drink too much. Sometimes there is pressure to dress a certain way, and there is pressure to "keep up with the Joneses" when it comes to the latest technology and other fads.

There are instances where peer pressure, or, let's call it, "peer influence," can be a good thing. When your peers encourage you to do something good, that's a good thing. Today I want to connect the words accountability and honor to encouragement. Accountability is when you utilize another person to not only encourage you to do something but to make sure that you actually do it. For instance, let's say that I have a difficult time reading the Bible. In conversation, I speak to a friend who is having the same struggle. Neither of us makes the time to do it. We both know it is something we should be doing. So, we agree that each day, we will read the Bible, and we will take a picture of the passage we are reading and text it to one another. There is now accountability. Until I can get into the daily habit of reading the Bible on my own, I now have another motivation to do so. I'm accountable to someone.

Now you may wonder, why can't I just be accountable to my priest for spiritual things? The answer is, most people do not have daily communication with their priest. I'm speaking of finding a peer, friend, or fellow Christian and having some daily (or frequent) accountability for prayer, Scripture reading, or any other Christian discipline. There is something innate in each of us that wants to please other people. So, adding an "account-a-buddy" to your spiritual life can be very helpful because on the days you don't feel like praying, reading the Scriptures, or other spiritual disciplines for yourself, you have someone else that is counting on you to do them.

Years ago, someone I was close to was trying to kick the habit of smoking pot daily. This person asked me to keep them accountable and help them to try and stop. It was this person's idea to call me every day at 3:00 p.m. for thirty seconds and report on his last twenty-four hours of marijuana use. He thought that by having to admit it to me, the embarrassment would be enough to get them to quit. About once a week, he would slip up and call and tell me he slipped up. One day (and he told me this years later), he decided that he didn't want to feel embarrassed ever again by admitting this to me. So, for six months, he called every day and said he hadn't smoked. After six months, we decided to make the phone calls weekly instead of daily. After another six months, the calls became monthly. And now there is a once-a-year call on the anniversary of his last pot usage.

Most of us don't have problems we are trying to stop, so much as we have good habits that we are trying to form. A great way to create a new habit (or stop a bad one) is to get an account-a-buddy, someone you will have frequent contact with so that you can be accountable to someone and can receive encouragement from them. An account-a-buddy can be used for any habit you are trying to change—from praying more to reading Scripture more, diet, exercise, anything really.

Every bit of encouragement and accountability helps me in my spiritual life, and I encourage you to find a friend who can be your account-a-buddy when it comes to spiritual disciplines. This doesn't mean that you don't need a priest for spiritual direction and to hear your confessions. It means that you have an additional person(s) that you account to on a daily or frequent basis to strengthen areas of your life that need strengthening.

Lord, help me to be disciplined in my Christian life. Help me to have the discipline to pray, meditate on Scripture, and live a life of Christian virtue. Surround me with people who will encourage me and hold me accountable when I need it. Allow me to fill that role for others. May I seek to encourage others as they encourage me. Amen.

Encouragement Challenge: Consider who and how you can use an account-a-buddy in your life!

BE A LIGHT IN THE WORLD

Jesus said, "I AM the light of the world."
John 8:12

Jesus said, "You are the Light of the world."
Matthew 5:14

The concept of light plays an important role in the Bible. In Genesis 1:3, we read that light was the first thing God created. At the beginning of the Gospel of John, in John 1:4–5, we read, "In Him [the Word of God, Jesus Christ] was life, and the life was the light of men. The light shines in the darkness, and the darkness has not overcome it."

Light is not only the first thing God created. It is also the most powerful thing since nothing can overtake light.

In the gospel, Jesus reveals light as the one characteristic we share with God. In John 8:12, He says, "I AM the light of the world; he who follows Me will not walk in darkness, but will have the light of life." In Matthew 5:14, He says, "You are the light of the world." In Matthew 5:16, He tells us, "Let your light so shine before men, that they may see your good works and give glory to your Father who is in heaven."

In both becoming encouragers and feeling encouraged, remembering the concept of light is an important part of keeping sound and being sanctified. It is important to remember that light shines in darkness. Darkness is the absence of light, so even the smallest amount of light will defeat darkness.

It is important for us to remember two things. As long as we have the light of Christ in us (and we all do; it can't be taken out of us), darkness cannot overtake us. It cannot extinguish the light within us. Even in the bleakest of circumstances, the light of Christ is present in us.

Secondly, we are supposed to be the light. We are supposed to reflect Christ's light. How do people describe you? As fun? Mature? The life of the party? Dangerous? Sincere? Hopeful? Would anyone describe you as "light"? Would anyone say you radiate the light of Christ?

St. Paul writes in Ephesians 5:8–10, "For once you were darkness, but now you are light in the Lord; walk as children of light (for the fruit of light is found in all that is good and right and true), and try to learn what is pleasing to the Lord." In other words, we are to conduct ourselves as God's children, as children of light.

He continues in Ephesians 5:15–18: "Look carefully then how you walk, not as unwise men but as wise, making the most of the time, because the days are evil. Therefore, do not be foolish, but understand what the will of the Lord is. And do not get drunk with wine, for that is debauchery; but be filled with the Spirit."

Going back to Matthew 5:15, after telling His disciples (and us) that we are the light of the world, Jesus says, "Nor do men light a lamp and put it under a bushel, but on a stand and it gives light to all in the house." There are two meanings here. First, we are not to hide the light of Christ but put it on display for all to see and be inspired by. We are not putting on display for our own egos or recognition. Rather, we display the light of Christ to inspire and encourage others.

Second, by and large, we do not live in secret, who we are on display, like a light on a stand. Yes, there are pieces of our lives that are not shared and, to some extent, we all live a "double life" that is kept from others. However, plenty of our lives are on display for others to see—our language, work ethic, sense of respect for ourselves and others, generosity, and so on. When others see our lives as lamps put on stands for all to see, do they see a person of light? Or of darkness? Of all that is good and right and true (Eph. 5:9), or what is bad, wrong, and false?

Christ tells us that His Light is in all of us because He is the light of the world and has placed that light in everyone in the world. Christ also tells us that we are the light because we are the primary witnesses for the light of Christ. In John 12:36, He encourages us, saying, "while you have the light, believe in the light, that you may become sons of light." And in 1 John 1:17, we read, "if we walk in the light, as He is in the light, we have fellowship with one another, and the blood of Jesus His Son cleanses us from all sin." Thus, walking in the light, we will come not only closer to God but to one another.

Christ the true light, who enlightens and sanctifies every person who comes into the world, let the light of Your countenance makes its mark upon me, that I may behold Your ineffable light. Direct my steps in the way of Your commandments (adapted from an Orthodox prayer).[392] *Let Your light shine in me and help me to radiate Your light toward those around me. May I be a person of light and all that is good and right and true. Amen.*

Encouragement Challenge: Kindle Christ's light within you. Shine Christ's light toward those around you.

Preparing the Soil of Your Heart

Jesus said this parable: "A sower went out to sow his seed; and as he sowed, some fell along the path, and was trodden under foot, and the birds of the air devoured it. And some fell on the rick; and as it grew up, withered away, because it had no moisture. And some fell among thorns; and the thorns grew with it and choked it. And some fell into good soil and grew, and yielded a hundredfold."
Luke 8:5–8

In the introduction to his book, *Get Your Life Back*, author John Eldredge[40] writes about how the world has gone mad, citing specifically, among other things, that the internet is causing us to lose our ability to pay attention and focus for more than a few moments. Overall, the pace of life is moving too fast, and not only is this creating an intellectual problem but also a spiritual crisis. He writes: "God *wants* to come and restore our lives. He really does. But if our soul is not well, it's almost impossible to receive Him. Dry scorched ground can't absorb the very rain it needs."[1]

The words dry scorched ground call to mind the image of a desert where there is no water. The ground is dry and cracked. Nothing can grow on ground like this. The dry land craves water. However, when denied water for so long, when it finally rains, the water become a force of destruction rather than a source of refreshment. Have you ever noticed that most flash floods happen in the desert? Why is that? Because the dry, cracked ground is unable to absorb the water it desperately needs. When soil is healthy, when it is watered regularly and in an appropriate amount, the soil welcomes the water, and a healthy cycle ensues. When soil is deprived of water, it rejects the water it does receive, and the unhealthy cycle continues.

Our lives work in many ways like this. When we are "watered" regularly through our own sense of spirituality and with encouragement and positive reinforcement from others, the soil of our hearts is ready to receive God even more deeply, and encouragement is appropriately received. When the soil of our heart is like dry, scorched earth, our hearts are not ready to receive God, and encouragement is also inappropriately received. One who is not regularly encouraged may crave any kind of encouragement, even encouragement to do bad things. He or she might also develop an insatiable desire for encouragement, which can manifest itself as narcissism or greed.

In Luke 8, Jesus tells the parable of the Sower. In the parable, He is the sower. In the interpretation of the parable, the sower is Christ; however, in some ways, we are all sowers. The seed is the Word of God in the parable. It can also be encouragement or any way that joy and purpose are sown in our own hearts and the hearts of those around us.

Jesus tells us that the sower threw seed into various kinds of soil. Some was rocky, some had no moisture, some had thorns that choked it, and some fell into good soil. The soil is what is in our hearts. If our hearts are being watered with Christ and with encouragement, the soil will be healthy and ready to grow even deeper in Christ, love, faith, and purpose. If our hearts are so devoid of moisture, they don't have Christ, and they receive no encouragement, then the soil will become dry and cracked, unable to grow much of anything, and in a dangerous place if Christ or encouragement is poured out of upon them.

In many instances, we are becoming unable to appropriately worship or receive a compliment or encouragement because the interval of time between worship or encouragement is becoming too great. Worshiping once a year will not keep our soil moist and ready to receive seed. One might argue that even once a week is not enough. A daily walk with God through prayer and Scripture reading, added to frequent worship, will keep our souls read and glad to receive Christ. When someone is continuously put down and discouraged, when encouragement or a compliment finally comes, it isn't appropriately received. Thus, as individuals, we should seek nourishment for our souls through daily contact with the Lord. And we should hope for daily encouragement to keep our minds nourished and confident. To facilitate this, each of us has to look for daily opportunities to encourage others. In so doing, we not only help the health of their hearts, but our hearts benefit as well.

In 2 Corinthians 1:8, St. Paul wrote, "For we do not want you to be ignorant, brethren, of the affliction we experienced in Asia; for we were so utterly, unbearably crushed that we despaired of life itself." In other words, the soil of St. Paul's soul was so dried and cracked that not only could he not see a better day in the future, but he also despaired of his very life; he didn't want any days in the future. Many of us have felt like this at some point (or points) in life. We feel like we are in the desert and there is no water or hope for any oasis. We are parched, faint, and feel like we don't have the strength to take another step. The answer is not a deluge of spirituality or even encouragement. It is taking small sips of spirituality and receiving small sips of encouragement so that the soil of our hearts is appropriately cultivated, and then spirituality and encouragement are received in soil and ready to receive them.

We all play a role in this process. First, we can't absent ourselves from God for any amount of time and still think the soil of our souls will remain healthy and balanced. This, we control.

Second, we can't be absent from encouragement for any amount of time. This is the gift we offer each other to encourage and build up those around us, frequently, not necessarily in magnanimous gestures, but in small, consistent ones so that as we fight the battle to focus on the important things in this world that continuously distracts us from them, we can go into the battle with hearts and souls that have been nourished and can handle either a sudden storm or a short drought and not become dried, cracked, or scorched because of it.

Lord, there are times in my life when my soul feels like a parched desert—dried, cracked, and scorched. In these times, send rain into my soul to reassure and strengthen me. In the times when my soil feels watered and healthy, give me the wisdom to reach out to You so that my soul may continue to feel full. Give me the eyes to see others who are in despair and the wisdom to know how to minister to them, words to encourage them, and "water" to satisfy their thirst. Give me the strength to walk when I can't find my own strength. And give me the strength and insight I need to help carry others. Amen.

Encouragement Challenge: Seek comfort from Christ in prayer. Keep walking, no matter what!

Go for Excellence, Not Mediocrity

But above all, my brethren, do not swear, either by heaven or by earth or with any other oath, but let your yes be yes, and your no be no, that you may not fall under condemnation.
James 5:12

And as you wish that men would do to you, do so to them.
Luke 6:31

Many of us have had the experience of ordering fast food and having the food come out as if it was literally thrown into the bag—hamburger disassembled, burger half off the bun, and so on. Many of us have the experience of ordering a large sandwich, only to see the person making it put on one tomato slice or only a few pieces of meat. How about the double scoop ice cream cone that cost nearly five dollars and looks like half a scoop? On more than one occasion, I've wanted to ask the person behind the counter, "Would you each the sandwich or the hamburger you just made for me?" or "would you pay five dollars for that ice cream cone?" If you wouldn't eat or buy it, why would you expect me to?

Many times we feel simply underwhelmed by a sense of mediocrity of those around us. There doesn't seem to be enough drive for excellence anymore. Standards, it seems to me anyway, have been lowered so that what we are becoming more satisfied with mediocrity and are less focused on getting or giving something with excellence.

Part of the challenge is that so many people in the work force are in it for what they receive, not what they give. Many are working only for the paycheck; they put no joy or pride in their work. That's why coming in ten minutes late, leaving ten minutes early, and checking social media all day in between coming in and leaving has become almost the "norm." I used to think that if you threw enough money at someone, you could "buy" effort from them. I no longer think that. I'm not sure there is a correlation between money and effort. Those who work hard don't work for the money (yes, they need money to survive; we all do). They work for the value of being productive. Those who don't give much effort, I'm convinced, won't up their game for more money. They may ask for (or even demand) more money, but it won't translate into more effort.

There are two verses that accompany this reflection. The first one is from James 5:12: "But above all, my brethren, do not swear, either by heaven or by earth or with any other oath, but let your 'yes' be 'yes' and your 'no' be 'no', that you may not fall under condemnation." Many times in life, we either answer "yes" when in our hearts we know it's a "no," or we answer "maybe" to avoid a commitment. There is no excellence when we answer this way. For example, imagine if you are planning an event and invite twenty people. Imagine if all twenty tell you that "maybe" they will come. There is no way that this event isn't mediocre because as the host of the event, you have no idea how many people to plan for, and you don't even know that the event will happen if none of the twenty people come. When we are non-committal, we endorse mediocrity. Twenty answers of "no" means no event and, therefore, no excellence. But twenty quick answers of "no" give the host time to rethink and perhaps repackage what is being done so there can be excellence after all. The same holds true if someone is running a company with twenty employees. If the employees tell you they can't come to work, perhaps there is time to replace them with temporary workers or fire them and get different workers. However, if the employees say they will come and then don't, this leads to a mediocre outcome at best.

The second verse is from Luke 6:31, where Jesus gives what is known as "the golden rule," which says, "and as you wish that men would do to you, do so to them." When we are the customer, patient, or the client, we want/expect/demand excellence. If we demand excellence, it stands to reason that others will want/expect/demand excellence from us.

A company or customer that hires us will tell us how much we are worth. That's how our hourly wage, salary, or cost of product is determined. God tells each of us that we are of infinite value in His eyes. So, who do we work for? Do we work for our boss? Our customer? God? If we work for God, and God sees infinite value in each of us, this calls us to a sense of excellence and away from a sense of mediocrity. In Philippians 1:9–10, St. Paul writes, "It is my prayer that your love may abound more and more, with knowledge and all discernment, so that you may approve what is *excellent* and may be pure and blameless for the day of Christ." Imagine if we replaced "excellent" with "mediocre" in this verse so that the verse reads ,"so that you may approve what is *mediocre* and be pure and blameless for the day of Christ." It doesn't seem the "mediocre" is congruent with the idea of being pure and blameless for the day of Christ. If this is where our destiny lies, that we will meet Christ for a judgment on our lives, then our hope for a favorable judgment lies in excellence more than it lies in mediocrity.

Lord, each day I will be faced with a choice to be excellent or to be mediocre, to give my best effort or to just get by. Give me the wisdom and the mind that desires excellence. Give me the physical and mental stamina to be at my best today with all that I do and with all who I encounter. Amen.

Encouragement Challenge: Treat others as you wish to be treated, whether it is making them a sandwich or giving them a compliment. Strive for excellence. Avoid mediocrity.

Course Corrections Are Important

*All Scripture is inspired by God and profitable for teaching, for
reproof, for correction and for training in righteousness.*
2 Timothy 3:16

The earth and the moon are 238,855 miles apart.[42] In the late 1960s and early 1970s, when NASA was sending astronauts to the moon, it took approximately seventy-six hours from lift-off until the time the spacecraft was in lunar orbit; in other words, it took approximately seventy-six hours to span nearly 240,000 miles.[43] On the second day of the historic Apollo 11 flight, which would be the first mission to ever land on the moon, Commander Neil Armstrong fired the service module engines for three seconds to correct the course of the spacecraft so that it would reach lunar orbit two days later.[44]

One could argue that those THREE SECONDS were the most critical of the entire mission because had the astronauts not corrected their course ever so slightly, they would not have reached lunar orbit, and they probably would not have returned safely to earth. Three seconds out of seventy-six hours is almost nothing. Yet, it meant the difference between success and failure, between triumph and tragedy. This course correction was just that, a correction. It wasn't a "we've screwed this up and have to start over," and it wasn't a "we've messed this up and need a totally new course." It was a "we need a small modification to reach our goal."

The ability to make "course corrections" is critical to success in any aspect of life. There is no one who doesn't need some "course correction" at some point in life. This might be a slight correction in a marriage or friendship, between a parent and a child, in school, at a job, or spiritually. If someone is unable to see the need for any correction in their life, they probably won't have a successful life.

As with the Apollo missions, we aren't talking about "I've completely screwed up my life and need to totally start again" or "I'm totally unhappy with how life is going and need a new plan." Some people do need this kind of correction, but not most. Three seconds over the course of a three-day journey to the moon is hardly noticeable; it's just a blip of time and yet those three seconds determined the success of the whole mission.

Over the course of our lives, that's the equivalent of a few appointments with a therapist, a couple of trips to a marriage counselor, or an occasional confession with your priest. Yet these occasional corrections can make all the difference in the world in our life's mission. (There are people who can benefit or need to work with a therapist on a regular basis, just like there are marriages that are in serious trouble and need serious intervention.) We're talking here about even the best of marriages can stand a check-up, marriage retreat, or appointment with a counselor, just to see if any "mid-course correction" is needed. Even the most faithful of Christians should go to confession occasionally to see what spiritual "mid-course correction" may be needed.

Imagine if Neil Armstrong had argued with Mission Control about the need for a course correction. Imagine if he said, "The course I charted when we left earth was perfect—no correction needed." He wouldn't have landed on the moon, and he would have become famous as one of the first astronauts (along with his two crew members) lost in deep space. He was the commander of the mission, but he was also wise in listening to advice from Mission Control, which requested a very short burn of the engine to set things right.

Imagine if we all resisted any kind of correcting. Imagine if we all argued, "The course we've set for our life (education, marriage, career, parenting, etc.) is perfect—no correction is ever needed." We would have a world full of failed people, relationships, and lives. We are the "commanders" of our lives, but it is wise to listen and seek advice from others outside of ourselves as well as to look deep within ourselves to see where we might benefit from any kind of course correction.

Not every piece of advice is profound. Not every conversation with a priest or therapist will be life-changing. I can say, for certain, that there are a few conversations (and I can remember them, three of them in particular) that changed the trajectory of my life and helped me correct things that needed correcting. I'm also keenly aware that I need to periodically modify my course, whether it is how I approach prayer or worship, how I approach time management, relationships with family and friends, management of my emotions, or even managing my physical health. I know that without any correction, I am destined for catastrophe. Accepting and making slight corrections can and does make made a big difference in my life.

In seeking to encourage people to be the best version of themselves, it is important that each of us be open to occasional "course corrections" because that three-second course correction on Apollo 11 was the difference between success and failure and triumph and catastrophe. Short course corrections in our lives will make the difference as well.

Lord, thank You for the journey of life that You have created for me. Thank you for the years I have had, and bless me in the years to come. Help me to stay the course that honors You while serving others. Help me to see the need for periodic course correcting on my life journey. Lead my heart to consider who can be helpful with this. Lead me to people who can help correct me. Bring those people into my path. Give me the wisdom to understand how I can better serve You and others and the strength and courage to implement the corrections that will lead me to Your heavenly kingdom. Amen.

Encouragement Challenge: Think about where you might need a course correction in your life. Consider some outside help to assist you in identifying and implementing occasional course corrections.

Part Thirteen

GOD IS FAITHFUL

He who calls you is faithful, and He will do it.

1 Thessalonians 5:24

GOD KNOWS YOUR STORMS

Then He made His disciples get into the boat and go before Him to the other side, while He dismissed the crowds. And after He had dismissed the crowds, He went up on the mountain by Himself to pray. When evening came, He was there alone, but the boat by this time was many furlongs distant from the land, beaten by the waves; for the wind was against them.
Matthew 14:22–24

In the gospel passage above, Jesus made His disciples get into a boat and venture to the other side of the lake. Then He went up by Himself on a mountain to pray. The boat holding the disciples, meanwhile, was caught in a storm, beaten by the waves. It must have been a terrifying scene for the disciples.

If Jesus knows everything and knows events before they happen, He knew that there would be a storm. He didn't tell the disciples to stay on land to avoid it. He allowed "nature to take its course," Jesus, however, did two things for the disciples during this scary time. He prayed for them. Then He visited them. He walked on the water and came to them.

There are storms in every life. Sometimes the storms are quick, and sometimes they last a long time. Sometimes the storms are a little annoying, and sometimes they are really damaging. There are two things to remember in the storms of life. First, the Lord looks down on us from heaven. He knows our storms. And secondly, because He loves us, He visits us in various ways. He is not necessarily going to come to us like a ghost walking on water. However, He comes to us in other subtle ways—a burst of confidence, an extra bit of strength, a clear mind that can see things it otherwise wouldn't see. I've definitely been in situations that are stressful and chaotic, and all of a sudden, a calm will come over me, and I'm able to see and know exactly what to do. I attribute that to God visiting me in a storm.

Sometimes God comes to us through other people, who not only bring encouragement but also bring answers to problems that plague us. Examples of this include firefighters who come to the rescue, doctors who come with a good diagnosis, or teachers who take that extra time with our child.

When praying to God during a stormy time in life, the prayer isn't necessarily for God to take away the storm but to walk with us in our storms. There are certain things that plague each life—it might be a medical condition, an insecurity, worry about our children, challenges in our marriages, or the stress of trying to get it all done. If God takes every challenge away from every life, then we are reduced to robots. This is why God doesn't solve all the problems of the fallen world. In the things that plague each life, we can invite the Lord to walk with us, to strengthen and comfort us, and we can ask for God to send the right people into our lives to help us in the storms. We can be assured that He will watch over us in our storms and give us the strength to endure them.

Lord, thank You for walking with me in my life, in good times and in bad ones. In the good times, help me to always remain humble and glorify You with gratitude. During the storms, help me to always trust that You will watch over me and protect me. Help me not to get discouraged. Surround me with people who can help me in those times of need and sadness. Help me to know that Your will governs all, and that even when I'm not sure of what is happening, there is a divine purpose for my life. Continually reveal Your purpose to me. Watch over me in my storms, and smooth the waters of the seas of my life as it is Your will. Amen.

Encouragement Challenge: If you are in a storm today, trust God. If you are on calm waters, help someone else who is in a storm.

Walking on Water Is Possible with Encouragement and Faith

And in the fourth watch of the night He came to them, walking on the sea. But when the disciples saw Him walking on the sea, they were terrified, saying, "It is a ghost!" and they cried out for fear. But immediately He spoke to them, saying, "Take heart, it is I; have no fear." And Peter answered Him, "Lord, if it is you, bid me come to You on the water." He said, "Come." So Peter got out of the boat and walked on the water and came to Jesus; but when he saw the wind, he was afraid, and beginning to sink he cried out, "Lord, save me." Jesus immediately reached out His hand and caught him, saying to him, "O man of little faith, why did you doubt?" And when they got into the boat, the wind ceased. And those in the boat worshiped Him, saying, "Truly You are the Son of God."
Matthew 14:25–33

We are all familiar with the story of Peter walking on the water. We've just discussed how Jesus went to the mountains to pray, knowing that the disciples in the boat on the lake would be caught in a storm. In fact, He allowed the storm to happen. Understandably, the disciples were afraid. A massive storm befalling a small boat is a scary proposition. There were no motors on boats back then, no fancy navigation equipment. With clouds and rain, there was probably no moon, stars, or light by which to see or navigate, a truly scary time.

In the midst of this, Jesus came walking on the water. In addition to the terrifying waves and wind, the disciples had to contend with an unexplainable, ghost-like figure walking on the water. Jesus reassured them that it was Him and that they should have no fear.

Peter had his moments of doubt, to be sure, but he also had his moments of faith. He didn't say, "I don't believe it's you, Lord." He said, "Lord, if it you, bid me come to You on the water." Jesus encouraged Peter to do the impossible, to come out of the boat and walk on water. He didn't encourage Peter to do something he would fail at but something at which Jesus knew he could succeed. Jesus knew that with enough faith, Peter could walk on water.

Peter walked on water. He did something amazing. And he was doing just fine until he took His eyes off of Jesus and started looking at the situation around him. He lost focus. He lost trust. He starting having concerns for material things like his health and momentarily forgot about the faith that was allowing him to do what seemed impossible. It was in this moment that he began to sink.

He still, however, found faith in Jesus. He didn't curse Him, like, "Why are you letting me sink" or "You set me up to fail." He said, "Lord, help me." "You are still my Lord and in this situation. You can still help me." Jesus immediately reached out to grab Peter.

The Bible doesn't say what tone of voice Jesus used when He said to Peter, "O man of little faith, why did you doubt?" It doesn't say if He raised His voice or was disappointed or upset. One of the reasons I read the Bible is for some encouragement. If you imagine Jesus speaking in a calm and reassuring voice, you can almost hear His comment as words of encouragement: "You've got this. I've got your back. There is no need to doubt."

There are storms in every life. Sometimes Jesus asks us to walk through them. Sometimes it seems like He is asking us to do the impossible, to walk on water, or, in many cases, to have faith and not doubt, to stay strong and focus on Him. Like Peter, the goal in the storm is to stay focused on Him. Like Peter, we need to listen to His voice of encouragement—"Don't doubt. You've got this. I've got your back."

Lord, be with me in the storms of my life. Help me to trust in You even when the waves are big and I feel scared. Help me to step out of my comfort zone, my boat, and walk to You. Help me to know and trust that You've got my back. Help me to trust and keep focus on You and not on the waves. Bring me safely to You. Amen.

Pray. Focus. Trust.

WHEN GOD FEELS ABSENT

When you pass through the waters I will be with you; and through the rivers, they shall not overwhelm you; when you walk through fire you shall not be burned, and the flame shall not consume you.
Isaiah 43:2

Several years ago, we had the opportunity to vacation in Wyoming and Montana, to places where there is a lot of natural beauty. Majestic mountains, jagged rocks, roaring waterfalls, rushing rivers, grand lakes, beautiful natural colors, elevations that were so high that there were no trees growing, snow still on the ground in the middle of summer, and animals in their natural habitat provided relaxation, rejuvenation, and wonderful memories. Many times my mind drifted to Psalm 104:

> *The trees of the Lord are watered abundantly, the cedars of Lebanon that He planted. In them the birds build their nests the stork has her home in the fir trees. The high mountains are for the wild goats; the rocks are a refuge for the rock badgers. Thou hast made the moon to mark the seasons; the sun knows it's time for setting. Thou makest darkness, and it is night, when all the beasts of the forest creep about. The young lions roar for their prey, seeking their food from God. When the sun rises, they steal away and lie down in their dens Man goes out to his work and to his labor until the evening. O Lord, how manifold are Thy works! In wisdom hast Thou made them all (Ps. 104:16–24).*

It is always an amazing thing to experience nature in its fullest sense—how everything just seems to fit. I continually thought of the majesty of God—that there must be a God because no way can all of this stuff purely happen by accident. It is by a divine design that the earth is as it is. I definitely felt small and insignificant beholding His handiwork. Going out into nature is, for me at least, a faith-building experience. Just seeing the creation bolstered my faith.

Of course, there is another side to the Christian life, the rough parts of life that still affect even the most devout of Christians, when everything seems to be going wrong, when God feels distant, and we wonder if He is really there at all. In contrast to the words and images of Psalm 104, we have the story of Job.

Job was a devout man, *"blameless and upright, one who feared God and turned away from evil"* (*Job 1:1*). He had ten children and thousands of animals as well as servants. *"This man was the greatest of all the people of the east"* (Job 1:3). Satan came before God one day and challenged God regarding Job. He said that Job only served God because God had been so good to him. Satan said that he wanted to afflict Job, certain that Job would curse God if all of his possessions and people were taken away. God gave permission to Satan to afflict Job but not to kill him. And Satan afflicted Job in a big way. In very short order, Job lost his animals, his house, and his children.

> *Then Job arose, tore his robe, and shaved off the hair of his head; and he fell to the ground and worshiped, saying, "Naked I came from my mother's womb, and naked shall I return. The Lord gave, and the Lord has taken away. As it seemed good to the Lord, so also it came to pass. Blessed be the name of the Lord." In all these things that happened, Job did not sin against the Lord or charge God with wrong (Job 1:20–22).*

Now, for sure, Job is a better man than me. I'd like to think that I would have his faith and his patience. I can't say that if half of the things that happened to Job happened to me, I wouldn't fall away from God. I hope I never find out. It is very easy to say that I would be steadfast like Job, but the truth of the matter is, my faith has never been tested like his faith. My faith has been tested, for sure, but not like his.

There are times in my life that I feel as I did on vacation—I'm just a small part of God's vast creation. There must be a God because only someone greater than us could have created all of this natural beauty. There are times I feel like Job—everything is going wrong, and it's one bad thing after another; there is no break, no joy, and I confess, I sometimes wonder, is there even a God? I have wondered that in my life. I have wondered that even as a priest. There are times I have celebrated the Liturgy pondering on this question—is there a God, and if there is, why does He feel so distant from me? There are times I have wanted to stay away from church, where I have not had the desire to receive Holy Communion, when, I confess, I have come because this is not only a calling but it is a job; I had to be here.

Most of my life, I sit in the middle of two extremes—I don't feel the awe of God like that vacation in Montana, nor do I feel the despair of Job. I am somewhere in the middle. I confess that for much of my life, I do feel closer to Job than to the majesty of God.

I know there is a God. I know that He is great and supreme, and I know that on some very deep level. I know that He loves people. I know that He loves me. I know that He has blessed me with gifts and talents. I also know that He has allowed me to struggle and have deficiencies as well. I know that no matter how intelligent I think I am, no matter what I do, and no matter what I know, I will never be able to comprehend Him because He is God, and I am not. That means there are complicated and complex things in life that elude my grasp. There are hardships and challenges that I just don't understand. There are bad things that happen to other people and bad things that happen to me, and I wonder: why? Why the tragedies that have happened in the parishes I have served? Why the tragedies we daily hear about in the news?

This is where faith comes in. Faith is not fully knowing or fully comprehending but still believing. There are two aspects to faith: showing up and growing. There are times when I feel God's presence very strongly, where I am very motivated to grow. These are the times when I take big strides in my faith and my journey to salvation.

There are times when I feel that God is absent, or at very least distant, when I am not particularly motivated to believe or grow. If I've done anything right in my life, I've continued to show up. My spiritual father says that 80 percent of life is about showing up. One can show up and not grow, but one cannot grow without showing up. And I don't mean just showing up for church, I mean showing up for God—being obedient to His commandments, praying, and making some effort to love and serve.

When life gets hard and when unspeakable tragedy strikes, it takes a person of strong faith to keep moving forward. However, I will humbly suggest that it isn't necessary to keep moving forward at all times. It is necessary to show up, though. It is necessary to tread water in the faith, even if we can't swim strongly toward God. It is necessary to eventually move forward in the faith, but on a given day, one doesn't have to make great strides. It's like showing up for school or a job—each day won't have a breakthrough—we know that, but there won't be any breakthrough if we stay at home. So we show up, and on many days, we have breakthroughs, and on many more, we just go through the motions, thinking we haven't really accomplished anything, which sometimes is true, and sometimes we've actually accomplished something without even realizing it.

I know there will never be a day that I will be able to say, "I have it all together" as far as my Christianity goes. That is neither fatalistic or pietistic. It is true. I will never master God. I can grow in faith, I can allow Him to grow in me, but I will never master Him, nor will I ever master faith. I will seek as many glimpses of Him as I can and hope to witness His majesty not just in the natural beauty I saw on vacation but in the beauty of people and things that are part of my everyday life right here. There will be times in life that I will undoubtedly feel like Job; I will have setbacks and tragedies. I hope and pray that they won't be to the degree I have seen some of our parishioners suffer. I will keep showing up for God and others, even if all I can do on a particular day is just show up.

Undoubtedly, there are people who are reading this message who are hurting—people who have suffered the loss of a child, a parent, a spouse, a job, or a dream. There are people who have a challenging health issue, marriage, child, job, or financial situation. There are people who are feeling the majesty of God and people who are feeling the despair of Job and everything in between. There are people who are growing in faith and people who are just showing up. And all of that is fine. Keep showing up.

There are two things we need to offer each other—one is encouragement. Encouragement give us hope, and we all need that. Sometimes encouragement can be the validation of feelings of loss or hurt. Sometimes encouragement is simply being present with someone, listening and saying nothing.

The second thing we need to offer each other is grace—what happens when we meet someone who is full of God's majesty on the day that we are having the despair of Job? We can be angry at the person who is filled with God and lash out because we feel empty. They can dismiss us as being a downer to their good feelings about God. When we give each other grace to fill and complete the space between us, then we can be in the presence of God's majesty through another person. even in our moments of despair, and the one who is filled with God will be patient during our moments of suffering and doubt; they will show up and not judge.

Here is a quote from a beautiful prayer that is part of the Divine Liturgy:

> *It is proper and right to sing to You, bless You, praise You, thank You and worship You in all places of Your dominion: for You are God ineffable, beyond comprehension, invisible, beyond understanding, existing forever and always the same; You and Your only begotten Son and Your Holy Spirit. You brought us into being out of nothing, and when we fell, you raised us up again. You did not cease doing everything until You led us to heaven and granted us Your kingdom to come. For all these things we thank You and Your only begotten Son and Your Holy Spirit; for all things that we know and do not know, for blessings seen and unseen that have been bestowed upon us (Divine Liturgy of St. John Chrysostom, Translation by Holy Cross Seminary Press, 1985).*[45]

This prayer affirms that God is incomprehensible and beyond our understanding. It affirms that when we fall, He will raise us up again. He wants us to attain His kingdom. There are blessings, seen and unseen, known and unknown that He bestows upon us. The day Job lost everything, God gave him the blessing just to get through the day. God gave Him patience. He gave Job patience to endure everything that happened. At the end of Job's story, Job was rewarded more than any person who had ever lived because his faith had been tested as no man's had ever been tested, and Job still showed up.

We can't grow if we don't show. Just because we show doesn't guarantee we will grow. But faith starts off with a commitment to show up, not only when His majesty is obvious, but most especially when it isn't. It didn't take much faith to appreciate God when I was on vacation in Montana. I was surrounded by His majesty. It takes faith to believe in Him when I'm home and in the drudgery of everyday life, and even more so when that drudgery is marred by tragedy.

Let's focus on giving one another encouragement and grace—so that majesty can meet despair without judgment, and despair can once again find majesty.

Lord, thank You for all that is good in my life. On the days when I feel that nothing is good, give me the eyes to see Your goodness in others and myself. Help me to see You in creation and other people. Give me patience to endure setbacks and losses. Give me the strength to show up for You and others, even when I don't want to. When I can't carry myself another step, send encouragers to make sure I don't give up. Help me to notice those around me who are struggling, and provide the confidence I need to go and help them. Amen.

Encouragement Challenge: Keep showing up!

Yes, But What about My Crosses?

Jesus said "I have said this to you, that in Me you may have pace. In the world you have tribulation; but be of good cheer, I have overcome the world."
John 16:33

Ok, ok, we got it, we need to be encouraging. But what about the things that perpetually discourage us? What about the crosses we carry that never seem to go away? What happens when we are consistently praying to God for something, and that thing never happens?

In the midst of our desire to be encouraging and have a positive outlook is the reality that there are certain crosses that some of us bear that seem like they will never go away. And in some cases, perhaps they will never go away.

I wrestle with this one. There are times when I pray fervently for months and even years for certain crosses to be lifted, and they aren't. I sometimes wonder if I've lost favor with God. I know many people wrestle with the same thing because I've talked to many frustrated people over the years, including many people who are faithful in their Christianity.

We're all familiar with the scales of justice. There are two scales, and in the case of the scales of justice, the goal is to have them balanced. In our lives, we hope to live in balance, if not tilted toward joy and God. There are bad things that happen in every life that tip the scales in favor of the negative. If this is the case in your life, there are two ways to balance the scales—remove the negative or add the positive.

Sometimes we can work to remove the negative. A failing grade in a class can be reversed with studying more. A bad day at work can be made up with two good ones. But what about the big ones that aren't so easily removed—losing a job, illness, a difficult marriage, challenging children, or consistent financial challenges?

There are two things that can keep the scale balanced. One comes from God, and one comes from our neighbor. From God, we get "grace," the mystical but strong quality that completes what is lacking in us. Grace heals spiritual wounds and provides spiritual strength. Grace is found in prayer, worship, and the sacraments. It is our greatest expression of God's love toward us, continual grace. Grace is what keeps us going when we are frustrated. Grace is what gives us the strength to meet big challenges. Grace heals the soul even when a life situation cannot be healed.

Grace is our greatest expression of how we love God. We trust Him and keep leaning on and receiving His grace. The weight of God can balance a scale that is out of balance. God doesn't necessarily take away the bad things of our lives, but His grace is enough to offset them.

The second thing that keeps our scale balanced comes from our neighbor, and that is encouragement and empathy. Encouragement to keep carrying the crosses and sometimes offering help to carry someone else's cross. We've all had moments in our lives where we wanted to give up on something. Without some empathy and encouragement, it is much easier to give up. With support and encouragement, it is much easier to keep going. When the scales of life are tilting to the negative, even a little encouragement can tip them the other way.

This is a very serious subject. Some people reading this message carry very heavy crosses. One short reflection cannot give all the answers. This encouragement is to continue seeking God's grace, even when the crosses are heavy and the road is difficult.

Lord, I thank You for Your blessings in my life (name some of them). Lord, there are also things I struggle with in my life (name them). You know these struggles. You know how they affect me. You know how they discourage me at times. Give me the strength to carry whatever crosses I bear. Give me the grace to carry them with dignity. Give me grace so that they are manageable. Let me continually be defined not by my crosses but by how I carry them. Give me strength to bear whatever challenges come my way today. Give me the strength to meet them in ways that show my own dignity and witness for Your glory. Amen.

Encouragement Challenge: Don't get discouraged if your crosses are heavy. Ask for grace from God. Seek help from others.

The Lord Is My Shepherd

The Lord is my shepherd; I shall not want; He makes me lie down in green pastures.
He leads me beside still waters; He restores my soul.
He leads me in the paths of righteousness for His Name's sake.
Even though I walk through the valley of the shadow of death, I fear no evil;
For Thou art with me; Thy rod and Thy staff, they comfort me.
Thou prepares a table before me in the presence of my enemies;
Thou anointest my head with oil, my cup overflows.
Surely goodness and mercy shall follow me all the days of my life;
And I shall dwell in the house of the Lord forever.
Psalm 23

One of the places I run to in Scripture when I need encouragement is the 23rd Psalm. In a mere six verses, it paints such vivid images in my mind. When I read about the *"green pastures"* and the *"still waters,"* I see a beautiful natural setting. I imagine sitting in the grass overlooking a gentle stream on a warm spring day. Hopefully we've all experienced one of those moments of perfection in nature. I have experienced them. I don't experience them often, unfortunately. This verse reminds me that the Lord is the author not only of creation but of perfection itself. When I want one of those perfect moments, I can find them in nature, but I can find them any time in prayer.

"He restores my soul" makes me think of the scenes in movies where people who are parched with thirst kneel down by a river, cup their hands, drink the water, throw some over the heads, and their thirst is quenched. There are so many ways in which the Lord can restore our souls. However, we take part in the process. Like the scene I described from the movie, He provides the water, but we have to bend down and drink of it.

"The path of righteousness" reminds me of two roads—the simple dirt road and the interstate. Most of us have traveled both. Which is better? It depends on what your goal is. Quick and efficient travels favor the interstate. Solitude and reflection leads to the dirt path on which we can walk. The path to righteousness requires both. Sometimes it requires something that is direct and efficient. Sometimes it requires something more contemplative. We have to learn to walk both paths. The Lord, through the church, gives us a path to both.

"*The valley of the shadow of death*" makes me think of an apocalyptic scene in a movie. Gone are the tranquil waters described above. They are replaced with rivers of lava. Darkness replaces the light. An overall feeling of foreboding has erased the beauty. Yet with the Lord, even in a scene like this, one can take comfort. We've all been in this valley. It might be an illness, sense of loneliness, intimidating situation, or person who makes us feel uncomfortable. Whenever your life looks like an apocalyptic scene instead of a tranquil river, you have to remember that the Lord is still walking with us, comforting us.

Who would want to have a meal in the presence of enemies? Yet even in this instance, when the whole world seems against us, the Lord anoints us, and our cup overflows. The anointing with oil was the way that kings were chosen. The Lord has chosen each of us to be His children. He has "anointed" us with His "*goodness and mercy.*" The "*house of the Lord*" refers to both the church and the kingdom of God. We find restoration for our souls and the path to righteousness through the church. We prepare to live forever in God's kingdom through the church. Those who have the Lord as their shepherd, leading in the green pastures and the valleys of life, will one day inherit a place in the house of the Lord in heaven. The 23rd Psalm is really a psalm of encouragement, a go-to treasure from Scripture that I use both beside the still waters and dark valleys of life. I encourage you to do the same.

Lord, thank You for the beautiful images that are painted for us through Scripture. Thank You for the comfort of the pastures and beauty of the waters. Thank You for always restoring my soul when it is troubled. Please be with me in the valleys of life. Help me not to fear evil. Give me courage during difficult times. Help me stand strong in the face of enemies. Please comfort me when life is hard, and please send Your goodness and mercy on me all the days of my life so that one day, I may dwell in Your heavenly kingdom forever. Amen.

Encouragement Challenge: Pray the 23rd Psalm today!

God Rewards Effort

And He told them many things in parables, saying: "A sower went out to sow. And as he sowed, some seeds fell along the path, and the birds came and devoured them. Other seeds fell on rocky ground, where they had not much soil, and immediately they sprang up, since they had no depth of soil, but when the sun rose they were scorched; and since they had no root they withered away. Other seeds fell upon thorns, and the thorns grew up and choked them. Other seeds fell on good soil and brought forth grain, some a hundredfold, some sixty, some thirty."
Matthew 13:3–8

The parable of the Sower is told in the Gospels of Matthew, Mark, and Luke. We have discussed the parable of the Sower from the Gospel of Luke, and in this reflection, we will discuss it from another angle, referring this time to the account from the Gospel of Matthew.

One day, early in my priesthood, I called my spiritual father because I was feeling discouraged. I felt like whatever I was doing wasn't really making a difference. I wasn't seeing the reward for my efforts. I guess I thought that I would see people grow in their faith in dramatic fashion right before my eyes.

In a way that was reassuring and encouraging, my spiritual father discussed with me the parable of the Sower. He said:

> Imagine that you have a big bag of seeds. You walk down a long road each day, scattering the seeds. At the end of the day when you are tired, you set the bag down, sleep, and then wake up again the next day and continue down the road. Here is the thing—the road is a one-way street, so you will never come back on it. And secondly, you aren't even allowed to look over your shoulder as you are throwing the seed. You have to be content to just throw the seed. Where it lands and how it develops is not for you to know. God will reward your efforts, not necessarily your results. After all, you can't control the kind of soil your seed lands in, only throwing the seed. So stop concentrating on how many people come to services and focus on how many services you offer because God will not count how many people came to things but how many opportunities you gave them.

Sound advice indeed.

We are obsessed with results. So much so that if we don't get results, we feel as though we are failures. Sometimes so much so that we are willing to cheat just to get the results we want. We have to remember that God rewards effort. As parents, we teach our children to behave well. However, we do not go to school with them to make sure they behave. So, we have to concentrate on what we can control—which is what we teach them when they are in our presence.

Teachers naturally want their students to learn. However, some students don't want to learn. So, if a great teacher has a class of students, and only 50 percent of them want to learn, should the teacher feel like a failure? I would say no because the role of the teacher is to create an environment that encourages learning. The desire to learn is on the student. The teacher controls the environment and whether the environment encourages learning.

Let's look at doctors or medical personnel. The job of the doctor is to heal. Yet, part of the healing is on the patient. If the patient doesn't work with the doctor in developing a healthy lifestyle, the doctor can't be blamed if the patient is perpetually sick. The role of the doctor is to create an environment that encourages healthy living. Some of this involves treating acute sickness, and that is something only a doctor can do. When the sickness is cured, the doctor can encourage healthy living. The decision to follow through is up to the patient.

Many of us are frustrated with our jobs or other roles we play because we are obsessed with results. God is interested in effort. So, focus on creating environments that encourage certain kinds of behavior rather than on the resultant behavior, and you'll be less frustrated. The job description for just about any job involves encouragement. It involves "creating an environment that encourages" learning, teaching, healing, spiritual growth, and so on.

Lord, thank You for the opportunities I have each day. Help me to focus on my efforts and not results. Help me to create environments of encouragement in whatever role I am playing today. Help me to encourage others to be successful, but help me not to be discouraged if success doesn't come right away for them or for me. Help me to continually give a good effort. Amen.

Encouragement Challenge: Give a good effort today! Create an environment of encouragement in whatever you are doing today!

**Dedicated to my spiritual father, Father Aris Metrakos.

The Parable of the Talents—The Best I Can with What I Have on a Given Day

"For it will be as when a man going on a journey called his servants and entrusted to them his property; to one he gave five talents, to another two, to another one, to each according to his ability. Then he went away. He who had received the five talents went at once and traded with them; and he made five talents more. So also, he who had the two talents made two talents more. But he who had received the one talent went and dug in the ground and hid his master's money. Now after a long time the master of those servants came and settled accounts with them. And he who had received the five talents came forward, bringing five talents more, saying, 'Master, you delivered to me five talents; here I have made five talents more.' His master said to him, 'Well done, good and faithful servant; you have been faithful over a little, I will set you over much; enter into the joy of your master.' And he also who had the two talents came forward, saying, 'Master, you delivered to me two talents; here I have made two talents more.' His master said to him, 'Well done, good and faithful servant; you have been faithful over a little, I will set you over much; enter into the joy of your master.' He also who had received the one talent came forward, saying, 'Master, I knew you to be a hard man, reaping where you did not sow, and gathering where you did not winnow; so I was afraid, and I went and hid your talent in the ground. Here you have what is yours.' But his master answered him, 'You wicked and slothful servant! You knew that I reap where I have not sowed, and gather where I have not winnowed? Then you ought to have invested my money with the bankers, and at my coming I should have received what was my own with interest. So take the talent from him, and give it to him who has the ten talents. For to every one who has will more be given, and he will have abundance; but from him who has not, even what he has will be taken away. And cast the worthless servant into the outer darkness; there men will weep and gnash their teeth.'"

Matthew 25:14–30

One of my favorite passages of the Bible is the parable of the Talents in Matthew 25:14–30. There are so many lessons and life applications to this parable that we will discuss it over the next four reflections.

In the parable, a landowner entrusted "talents" to three servants—to one, he gave five, to another, two, and to another, one. At the time Jesus told this parable, a "talent" represented an amount of money, the equivalent to what one might earn over the period of ten years. The five talents represented the amount of money one would make in fifty years, the entire amount of money he would earn for his lifetime. That's a lot of money. The two talents represented twenty years of earning. Even the one talent represented ten years' worth of earnings. Before we pity the man who only had "one talent," we have to remember that even his one talent was worth a lot.

It is important to recognize that the master "entrusted" the talents to the servants. He didn't give them to them for eternity. It was clear that he entrusted them, and at some point, he would come back and see what they had done with what he had given them.

The one who had five talents made five more and ended up with ten. The one who was given two talents made two more and ended up with four. The one who was given one talent did nothing with what he was given.

When the landowner came back to settle up accounts with his servants, he was angry and disappointed with the one who had done nothing with his one talent. However, he was equally pleased with the other two. He didn't evaluate them against each other because the one with ten would have been more pleasing than the one with four. Rather, he evaluated them according to how much they had done with what they had been given. The one with the two talents wasn't expected to make ten with them. Likewise, had the one with five made only seven, he would have been seen as a failure. As for the one who buried his one talent, the master was disappointed because surely the man could have done something, even if it was putting the money (a talent was an amount of money in the story) in the bank and getting the interest on it.

One lesson from the parable is that God expects us to do our best with what we've been given. No one can give better than their best, but we can all give our best. One of the mottos I use in my life is, "the best I can with what I have on a given day." I can't do my best with what I don't have. I can't do my best with what someone else has. I can't do my best if I am complaining about what I don't have. On any given day, I will be short of something, usually time. So, if I give my best with my time, then that is all I can do. On other days, I lack the opportunity. For instance, what if I offer a program, and only a handful of people come? We've all planned things and had disappointing attendance. If I'm focused on giving my best, then I give the best to the handful of people because that is what I have.

Another lesson for us to learn is that the only moment we truly have is the moment we are in. We do not have what is passed, and we are not guaranteed the future. I could make plans for tonight and be killed in a car wreck on the way home—that happens to someone in America every day. The only thing we truly have is the moment we are in. So we must make the most of that moment. In Christian terms, the most important day of your life is the day you die because how you die sets up where you will be for eternal life. The second most important day is the day you were baptized because that sets in motion the journey to everlasting life. The third most important day of your life is TODAY because today is what you have. The day I got married and the day our son was born were great days in the top ten days of my life when I look at the totality of my life. But those days were years ago. Can those days possibly be more important than today? Those days are memories; I can't relive them. I can live today and do my best today. Today is what you have, so make the most of it. If you've given your best, you've pleased God. If you truly give your best, then you've done all you can to please your neighbor.

Lord, thank You for the gift of today. Help me to see every day as a gift. Help me to use my gifts and opportunities to the best of my abilities each day. Help me to make the most out of each conversation and experience. Help me to glorify You and give You my best today. Amen.

Encouragement Challenge: Do the best with what you have today!

The Parable of the Talents—Don't Be Discouraged If You Only Have One Talent

He also who had received the one talent came forward, saying, 'Master, I knew you to be a hard man, reaping where you did not sow, and gathering where you did not winnow; so I was afraid, and I went and hid your talent in the ground. Here you have what is yours.' But his master answered him, 'You wicked and slothful servant! You knew that I reap where I have not sowed, and gather where I have not winnowed? Then you ought to have invested my money with the bankers, and at my coming I should have received what was my own with interest. So take the talent from him, and give it to him who has the ten talents. For to everyone who has will more be given, and he will have abundance; but from him who has not, even what he has will be taken away.'
Matthew 25:24–29

Years ago at summer camp, we did a session on this parable. Each cabin group that participated had approximately eighteen campers. For an icebreaker, we gave each cabin a fifty-piece puzzle to do. We gave each camper a random number of pieces—some got five, some got three, some got two, and one camper got one piece. No one really knew who had received how many pieces. We quietly asked the camper with the one piece to sit quietly by and put his piece in last.

The campers then got to work on the puzzle. Those who had more pieces thought they had more power, more say in how the puzzle would come out. However, they quickly realized that no one had more than 10 percent of the puzzle to contribute. It then became more of a collaborate effort, which was good to see. The camper who had the one piece sat off to the side, mostly unnoticed by his cabin mates. Perhaps they assumed he's already put in his pieces. Perhaps they just lost track of him in their enthusiasm for getting the project done. Perhaps they just forgot about him because he was quiet, and they were not.

Eventually, the campers had forty-nine of the fifty pieces of the puzzle. Before they could become excited for what they had accomplished—98 percent of the puzzle was done—they quickly became concerned about the missing piece. They wondered if it was lost. They worried they wouldn't finish the puzzle. They were frustrated because this one piece was the most beautiful piece in the puzzle—they could even tell that before the piece was put in.

We asked the person who had the missing piece to put it in. It was the most beautiful piece of the puzzle. It made the puzzle complete. Without it, there would have been a gaping hole in the middle of the puzzle. Everyone cheered on the camper as he put that final piece in, and the cabin rejoiced together, every camper equally, it seemed, that the task had been accomplished. We then had a discussion about the experience.

The camper who had the one puzzle piece said that he felt alone and isolated during most of the icebreaker. He wasn't included in the conversation or the planning. In the end, he held the piece that made the whole thing come together. No, he didn't have five pieces, no he wasn't loud, no he wasn't included. But without him, the puzzle could not be complete.

In God's plan of salvation, everyone has at least one piece of the puzzle to put in. It may be large or small. It may be a corner or an edge or a middle piece. It may be colorful, and it may be plain. However, no one did not receive at least one piece of the puzzle to contribute.

We cannot fixate on what we don't have. We can't let jealousy and envy about what we don't have impact how we use what we do have. Of the three servants in the parable of the Talents, there was no one who received nothing. Everyone received something. In our icebreaker of the puzzle pieces, there was no one who received nothing.

Everyone needs to contribute what they have for the good of the puzzle. Everyone who contributes and everything that is contributed is important because without all the pieces, even the seemingly plain ones, the puzzle would be incomplete. And everyone needs to contribute because everyone has something to contribute. We need to celebrate and encourage everyone because we need all to do their share so that the puzzle is complete.

In the Talents parable, the man who had received the one talent did nothing with it. He claimed to have been afraid of the master. Maybe he lacked confidence; maybe he didn't think the master had much faith in him because he only entrusted him one talent. Maybe he was angry that he had only received one talent. The lesson of that man is that fear is not an excuse, nor is anger, jealousy, or laziness. There is no excuse to not use the talents God has entrusted us with.

This parable is especially meaningful in my own life. For many years of my childhood, I felt a call to the priesthood. At first, it was a very pleasant thought. I dreamed of wearing vestments and doing services. I was an altar boy, I went to many services, and I got to wear altar boy vestments. The priesthood, for a young child, was like the dream job. As I got older and considered the ramifications of becoming a priest, it started to seem like a nightmare. There was a lot more to being a priest than just going to church on Sundays. Taking a bit part serving in the altar was a far cry from leading a congregation. The worst part of the whole thing would be the separation from family, first going to the seminary in Boston, and then being sent wherever the church needed a priest to serve. I began making up a list of reasons to not be a priest, to not answer a call that I knew I had. I realized which piece of the puzzle I was holding and spent a long time wishing I was holding something else.

I had never read the Bible all the way through until I was in college. When I stumbled on the parable of the Talents, it actually frightened me. I read it over and over and over again. I started reading it daily. I realized that I had a call, a talent entrusted to me to be a Greek Orthodox priest. What would happen if I didn't follow it? Certainly the master would be angry and disappointed. If the ticket to salvation is in part how we've used our talent, not answering the call could cost me my salvation. And for what? Being afraid of the cold winters in Boston, being afraid of where I might get sent to serve? This parable was definitely the passage of Scripture that helped me answer my call to use my talent to serve as a priest.

What is your talent? What is the piece of the puzzle that you hold? Are you eager to put it into the puzzle of society? Hesitant? Afraid? Angry that it isn't another piece? Think your piece isn't important?

God gave everyone at least one talent. Each person holds at least one piece to the puzzle. Fear is not an excuse to not put it in. We should have an incentive to honor and encourage all people because each person has at least one piece to contribute to the puzzle. It might seem like an inconsequential piece, like the guy who delivers the food to the market. But remove that guy who gets us our food, and we would all die. Some quiet and shy person sitting in the corner of the lunchroom with no one to talk to might be the one who will eventually cure cancer. But if they are too lonely, they might withdraw and not do much, thinking they have nothing to offer. This is why it is vitally important to encourage and include everyone because we don't know which pieces each of us hold.

One more comment on puzzles. The puzzle of our society and puzzle of our salvation are so big that we can't possibly see all of it. I gave the example on time of a puzzle covering the grounds of our church. Some of the puzzle would be in the church sanctuary, some in the hall, and some on the back field. If one is in the church, he or she cannot see the back field. Just like in our world, we do not see all facets of everyone's life. I'm not familiar with water treatment plants, for example, but they are very important in my life. Without clean water, I'd die in a few days. The guy who works at the water treatment plant doesn't see the cancer surgeon, who does not see the priest, who does not see the scientist, who does not see the teacher, and so on. Each of us needs to place his piece(s) in the puzzle of humanity to make the big picture, which God sees, complete. So instead of wondering why we received one piece and not another, why we have one piece and not five, and why we can only see the puzzle in the church but not on the back field, let us do our best with the piece(s) we've received, trusting that God will reward us for what we have done and what we see.

Lord, thank You for the talents You've entrusted me (list them.) Help me to be a good steward of my talents, using them to Your glory and to help my fellow man. Help me not to be afraid to use what I've been given. Help me to be content with what I have rather than wishing for talents I do not have. Even though I can't see the whole picture of Your plan for salvation, give me the strength to do my part to contribute to the good of all people. May I honor You this day and always with what You've given me.

Encouragement Challenge: Use your talent, whatever it is, to the best of your ability. When we all do this, the puzzle of salvation will be complete!

The Parable of the Talents—
Be Careful What You Wish For

*"For it will be as when a man going on a journey called his servants
and entrusted to them his property; to one he gave five talents, to
another two, to another one, to each according to his ability."*
Matthew 25:14–15

Another memorable icebreaker concerning the parable of the Talents was the year we gave each camper a small rock at 7:30 a.m. and told them they had to carry it in their hand until lunchtime. At any point in those hours, a priest or member of the staff could ask to see their rock, and it had to be in their hand. This means they had to figure out how to do all their tasks while carrying around their rock, again in their hand, not in their pocket, not on the table next to them, not taking turns with a friend where one could hold two rocks while the other had his hands free. This means they had to eat while holding a rock, carry their tray to the counter, tie their shoes, pick up their backpacks, and whatever else was being done for those five hours they were carrying their rock.

When it came time for the exercise to end, we asked the campers for their rocks. And we found that some had lost their rocks. Some had the rocks in their pockets, and some had the rock on the table next to them. Very few actually had the rock in their hand as we instructed.

In this case, we said that the rock represented not only our talent but our souls. At any moment, our souls have to be ready to meet God. We can't forget our faith or leave it home while we are out; we can't ask someone to be faithful in our place. We have to be faithful on our own. We have to be ready at all times to "show the rock" to God. It was a powerful lesson.

We asked the campers, what if, instead of handing out rocks, we handed out denominations of money? We gave some campers fifty dollars, some twenty dollars, and some ten dollars? We asked how they would feel if they received fifty dollars or ten dollars. Some of the fifty-dollar recipients said they would feel privileged and powerful. Some of the ten-dollar recipients said they would feel cheated and jealous.

Turning to the parable of the Talents, we then changed the question to, "What if we gave some of you five rocks, some two rocks, and some one rock to carry around for several hours?" We asked how many people would want to carry around the five rocks. Each camper said, "I'd rather just carry one rock; that is hard enough."

Many times we look with jealousy and anger at those who have more than we do. We don't often realize that just because a person has more doesn't mean he has better. Perhaps the person with more struggles more. You might counter with, how does a super-rich person with so much money struggle? Perhaps they struggle to find meaning. Perhaps they will struggle at the awesome judgment seat of Christ as they try to explain how they hoarded and frivolously spent money and weren't more generous with what they had been given.

One story that always encourages me is entitled "The Cross Room." It goes like this:

> *A young man was at the end of his rope. Seeing no way out he dropped to his knees in prayer "Lord, I can't go on," he said. "I have too heavy a cross to bear." The Lord replied, "My son, if you can't bear its weight, just place your cross inside this room. Then open that other door and pick out any cross you wish." The young man was filled with relief. "Thank you Lord," he sighed, and he did what he was told. Upon entering the other door, he saw many other crosses, some so large the tops weren't even visible. Then he spotted a tiny cross leaning against the far wall. "I'd like that one Lord," he whispered. And the Lord replied, "My son, that is the cross you just brought in." (The Cross Room, Source unknown*[46]

Sometimes we are so busy looking around at what we don't have that we don't appreciate what we do have. Sometimes we are so busy dreaming of a life we don't have or talent that we didn't get that we don't realize God has provided exactly what we need. And sometimes we look around at those who have five rocks and wonder, *How come I didn't get the privilege of getting five* rather than being grateful that we only got one rock to be responsible for because carrying around five rocks would probably require two hands, making it impossible to do much else.

Lord, thank You for the things that I have. Help me to find contentment with them, not always wishing for more or different. Help me to see the good in the things You have given me. Help me to count my blessings. May I multiply my blessings on others. Amen.

Encouragement Challenge: Be careful what you wish for. Be more grateful for what you have!

The Parable of the Talents— I Want to Die Exhausted

"And he who had received the five talents came forward, bringing five talents more, saying, 'Master, you delivered to me five talents; here I have made five talents more.' His master said to him, 'Well done, good and faithful servant; you have been faithful over a little, I will set you over much; enter into the joy of your master.' And he also who had the two talents came forward, saying, 'Master, you delivered to me two talents; here I have made two talents more.' His master said to him, 'Well done, good and faithful servant; you have been faithful over a little, I will set you over much; enter into the joy of your master.'"
Matthew 25:20–23

The goal of any sports team is to win. That goal is not always achieved. On a given day, one team may compete against better competition, and lose. What can always be controlled is the effort one gives on the field. And so athletes have coined a phrase, "to leave it all on the field." This means to make every effort possible in the game, win or lose. I don't believe in winning at all costs because winning at all costs has led some teams to cheat just to win. I believe in going all out to win. If the effort is good and there is a win, that is great. If there is a win but the effort is poor, that is luck and not something to be proud of. However, if there is a loss and the effort is good, I'd rather take the loss with good effort than the win that involves cheating or less than the best effort.

I once heard a priest give a sermon on this parable of the Talents. He talked about how the talent is not just an amount of money, and it is certainly more than a talent in the modern way we think of the word—a talent to write, or to speak, or to sing, and so on. The parable, the priest said, is about stewardship. It's about being a good steward with the things that God has entrusted you. This stewardship starts with the stewardship of your life. The length of life is unknown for any of us. All we truly have, as we have previously discussed, is this day, this moment. So, are we being a good steward of this day, and even this moment that we are in?

We cannot possibly be working at all moments—there must be a moment of rest, times of fellowship, and time to sleep. We also can't be resting at all times either. There is nothing wrong with a vacation—that's part of regular rest. There is nothing wrong with resting while recovering from illness. That's also part of regular rest. I would hope that when I retire from ministry, I will still find ways to work and contribute because I might be retired for many years, and I wouldn't want the stewardship of those years to consist of just rest and fun. If God entrusts me with years after I retire, I need to have something to show for whatever He gives me.

In the aforementioned sermon, the priest said, "I want to die exhausted; I want to leave everything on the field when I die. I want there to be nothing left, no ounce of energy that I didn't use to serve God and others. I want to die exhausted."

This was a very powerful sentiment. I've long forgotten the name of the priest or the occasion of the sermon, but I didn't forget his words. Occasionally, people ask me why I write. And the answer I give is, "I write because I'm going to die one day, and I want to stand before God and tell Him I gave every effort to get His word out." When I think this way, I don't think about how many people buy my books or read my messages because the thought is more on the effort I'm giving than the results it is producing. Just like the athlete on the field focuses more on his effort and less on the scoreboard because many times, he can't control what is on the scoreboard, only the effort that he is making.

Sometimes it actually feels good to be exhausted, to know that one has done everything possible in a given situation. If we are never exhausted, we'll never know how much effort we held back and didn't give.

We have to see our very lives as gifts entrusted to us by God. This day that we are working is not a right; it is a privilege. It is not an entitlement; it is a blessing. If we learn to see our time as a gift and a blessing, it will be easier to offer the time to others. Jesus says in Matthew 10:8, "You received without paying, give without pay." In other words, we have received a gift when we woke up today. We didn't have to pay God for this day. He gave it freely and lovingly to us. What will we do with this day? Will we hold back on offering it back to Him? Will we leave everything on the field? Will we go to bed exhausted?

When I walk off the field one last time at the end of my life, and hopefully into the arms of God, I want to die exhausted. I want to meet God, knowing that I did the most with what He entrusted to me.

Lord, thank You for the gift of today. Thank You for whatever gifts and talents You've entrusted me. Help me make the most of this day. May I honor You in all I do today. Help me to give all that I have to You and others, to leave it all on the field today and each day. Between now and the time

You call me home, help me to learn to leave it all on the field so that on the day I walk off the field one last time, I can walk off exhausted and into Your heavenly arms. Amen.

Encouragement Challenge: Focus on effort, not necessarily on results. Being exhausted isn't necessarily a bad thing. It's a great feeling to walk off the field exhausted. It will be a great feeling to walk off the field of life exhausted as well!

Filling the Gap between the Life We Want and the Life We Have—The Rick Ankiel Story

"Praise the Lord! For it is good to sing praises to our God; for He is gracious, and a song of praise is seemly. The Lord builds up Jerusalem; He gathers the outcasts of Israel. He heals the brokenhearted, and binds up their wounds. He determines the number of the stars, He gives to all of them their names. Great is our Lord, and abundant in power; His understanding is beyond measure. The Lord lifts up the downtrodden, He casts the wicked to the ground."
Psalm 147:1–6

On a crisp October afternoon in 2000, twenty-one-year-old pitcher Rick Ankiel of the St. Louis Cardinals stood on the pitcher's mound against the Atlanta Braves in game one of the League Championship Series. He had not allowed a run in the first two innings of the game. He had debuted the year before at age twenty, the second youngest pitcher in Major League Baseball. Before that, he had shined at every level of baseball he'd ever played. Major League scouts said that he was a once-in-a-generation talent and had a Hall of Fame caliber-pitching arm. He was a phenom, a couldn't-miss star.

Except in the third inning of that game in October 2000, the "couldn't-miss" star unexplainably couldn't throw a strike, something he had successfully done hundreds of thousands of times, something he did better than almost anyone else on the planet.

The meteoric rise of Rick Ankiel was followed by a swift and precipitous fall. He only pitched in a handful of games before being sent to the minor leagues and didn't ever recover his pitching form. Someone who had never had trouble throwing strikes could suddenly no longer throw them.

Thankfully, the story of Rick Ankiel didn't end in failure. He switched positions. He stopped pitching and started playing the outfield. He stopped throwing and started hitting. He worked his way all the way back to the major leagues as a home run-hitting outfielder. He eventually hit seventy-six major league home runs and played eleven seasons in the major leagues. Only a small percentage of baseball players will ever make it to the major leagues, and only a fraction of players will ever make it at more than one position.

Rick Ankiel authored a book entitled *The Phenomenon* (co-authored with Tim Brown, published by PublicAffairs, NY, 2017).[47] It tells the story of his life as an abused child, chronicles his career as a phenomenal pitcher, describes in painful detail his meteoric fall, and gives an account of his impressive return and his now very solid life. Currently married with two children, Rick Ankiel presently works as a sport analyst.

There are three sentences in his book that really stand out:

> See, there is the life you want.
>
> There is the life you get.
>
> There is what you do with that[481]

Most of us won't succeed to the degree Rick Ankiel did. Most of us won't be sports stars, famous, or wealthy. Most of us won't fail on national TV or have our fall documented and dissected publicly. However, all of us will have successes and failures and gaps between the two.

There will be the marriage we want and the marriage we get, the job we want and the job we get, or the health, success of our children, income, travel, any number of other goals that we want, and the actual things we get. We will all have successes, failures, and gaps.

Our character and overall success in life will depend in large part on how we react and respond to the gap between our successes and failures, between the life we want and the life we get.

The story of Rick Ankiel is inspiring and encouraging, which is why it is included in this study. It's inspiring because he didn't let his failure define him. His dream of playing in Major League Baseball took a major detour, but he made it back and fulfilled his dream. It's inspiring because at a moment when he could have just stopped and faded away, he didn't. He kept fighting. He kept trying.

Encouragement certainly plays a role in this story because the day that Rick Ankiel decided to change his focus from being a pitcher to being a hitter, the St. Louis Cardinals organization didn't tell him "no." They encouraged him, remained patient with him, and stuck with him until he worked his way all the way back to contribute to the team as an outfielder.

There are many times when we will have to refine or redefine our goals and dreams. During these times, it is important that we stay focused and positive, and it will be necessary that we have people around us to encourage us as we work to fill our gaps between what we hoped for and what we end up with so that we define our gaps rather than letting our gaps define us.

We will meet countless people like Rick Ankiel in our lives, people who have a gap between what they wanted and what they have. We will have opportunities to make those gaps wider or narrower. Our choice to encourage can and will certainly make a difference.

Lord, thank You for what I have. There are many things that I want and don't have. However, help me to be thankful for what I have and to use what I have to the best of my ability. Fill my gaps with patience, reassurance, focus, and the encouragement of others. Help me to see others who are struggling between what they hoped for and what they have, and allow me to be an encourager, especially to those who are struggling to fill their gaps. Amen.

There is the life you want. There is the life you get. There is what you do with that. May we each have the strength to do good with that and to encourage others to do the same.

God Is Faithful, Even When We Are Not

*Create in me a clean heart, O God, and put a new and right spirit within me.
Cast me not away from Thy presence, and take not Thy Holy Spirit from me.
Restore to me the joy of Thy salvation, and uphold me with a willing spirit.*
Psalm 51:10–12

Most of us have heard something about King David in the Old Testament. If we know about him, it's probably because we remember the story of David and Goliath, how David, a young shepherd boy, killed a giant named Goliath, with a slingshot. In fact, in sports, it is very popular to use the image of David versus Goliath, when one team seems unbeatable and then somehow gets beaten, when one team seems like it can't possibly win, and then it does.

David was the youngest of eight brothers. No one thought he would ever be king. His brothers were all brazen soldiers. David was a simple shepherd. But he was favored by the Old Testament King Saul and was good friends with Saul's son, Jonathan. Saul became paranoid that David might one day take his throne, and Saul turned on David. After Saul and Jonathan were killed in a battle, David was anointed as king.

David had it all, it seemed. He had the favor of God and of his fellow man. He was a king. He was powerful. But David was not satisfied. One day, he saw from his palace window a beautiful woman named Bathsheba sunbathing on the roof of her house. She was the wife of a man named Uriah. David committed adultery with Bathsheba, and she became pregnant. Now David had a problem. He had gotten another man's wife pregnant. He decided to solve the problem by having Uriah sent to the front lines in battle so that he was sure to die. When he was killed, he took Bathsheba as his wife, and they had a son. However, what David did displeased God.

In 2 Samuel 12:1–7, we read the story of a prophet named Nathan, whom the Lord sent to David. He told David a story:

> "There were two men in one city, the one rich and the other poor. The rich man had exceedingly many flocks and herds; but the poor man had nothing except one little ewe lamb, which he had bought and nourished; and it grew up together with him

and with his children. It ate of his own food and drank from his own cup and lay in his bosom; and it was like a daughter to him. And a traveler came to the rich man, who refused to take from his own flock and from his own herd to prepare one for the wayfaring man who had come to him; but he took the poor man's lamb and prepared it to the man who had come to him." So David's anger was greatly aroused against the man, and he said to Nathan, "As the Lord lives, the man who has done this shall surely die! And he shall restore fourfold for the lamb, because he did this thing and because he had no pity." Nathan said to David, "You are that man!"

After Nathan left, David was heartbroken, and he realized the only way his soul could mend was to turn it over to the Lord. David wrote most of the 150 psalms, and they captured his sorrows and repentance as well as his joys and later-restored confidence.

He wrote in Psalm 51:6, *"Behold Thou desirest truth in the inward being, therefore teach me wisdom in my secret heart."* In other words, we all keep secrets, feelings that are too ugly to share with others, and shame that is too embarrassing to even say out loud, even to ourselves. To relieve our shame, we need God to put His wisdom into our secret heart, the dark places where we won't let anyone go, the dark places that so desperately need to be filled with light, the light that can only come from God.

He continued in verse 10, *Create in me a clean heart O God, and renew a steadfast spirit within me.* Let me be cleaned of my sins so that, as we read in verse 51:7, *"that I shall be whiter than snow."* That is hard to conceive of, a soul whiter than snow, especially when we feel that our soul is like a black cloud. Yet God has the power to put the new and right spirit within each of us and make our souls whiter than snow at any time.

Verse 11: *Cast me not away from Thy presence, and take not Thy Holy Spirit from me.* Here, David is in fear and lamenting, wondering if he will ever be again in God's presence, if he will ever have the fervor of God's spirit in him again.

Verse 12: *Restore to me the joy of Thy salvation, and uphold me with a willing spirit.* This is a plea that is actually made with some boldness. David, despite his heavy sin, asks God to restore joy to him and asks that this joy and new found restoration be upheld with a generous spirit because he knows there is no way he can uphold it on his own. He prays that God's spirit will be generous, gracious, and merciful to him.

Psalm 51 is the psalm of repentance. When we have failed at something, when we are failing at life, and when we feel like we are failing in faith, this is the psalm we should pray. We should pray it with a broken and humbled heart because this is the heart that God accepts in repentance.

Like David, we are God's chosen ones. And like David, we have all missed the mark. However, like David, God's restoration is still very much on the table. Despite all of his faults, David is still honored as a holy figure, and of all the Old Testament figures, Christ is mentioned as a descendant of David. David may have screwed up a lot of things, but in the end, he repented and made it right. And in the end, God is faithful to us, even when we haven't been faithful to Him.

One of the best things about Christianity is that a new start is literally possible at ANY time. So much of our life has a "record" that follows us around. For instance, if a student is having a bad semester in class, he can only improve so much and is stuck until a new term begins. Some people are stuck in jobs and other ways. Criminal records follow people forever. Even traffic tickets show up on a background check years later. The Christian, however, should never feel stuck in sin or spiritual sadness because the opportunity for a clean heart and a renewed spirit are on the table at all times. If you are reading this message at the beginning of the day, go for the "clean heart" today. And if you are reading it at the end of a bad day, go to bed with the clean heart on your mind and make your renewed start fresh tomorrow.

It is important to pray for and encourage others. It is also necessary to pray for oneself and continually ask God for strength and encouragement to have the clean heart and renewed spirit.

As much as we'd sometimes like to, we can't control others. The only heart that you can control is your own. So, focus on having a clean heart today. Ask God to keep YOUR heart pure and clean today.

> *Have mercy on me, O God, according to Thy steadfast love; according to Thy abundant mercy blot out my transgressions . . . Purge me with hyssop and I shall be clean; wash me and I shall be whiter than snow. Fill me with joy and gladness . . . blot out my iniquities . . . Create in me a clean heart, O God, and put a new and right spirit within me. Cast me not away from Thy presence, and take not Thy Holy Spirit from me. Restore to me the joy of Thy salvation and uphold me with a willing spirit . . . Lord, open Thou my lips, and my mouth shall show forth Thy praise. Amen. (Psalm 51: 1, 7, 8, 9,10-12, 15)*

God is faithful, even when we aren't!

Part Fourteen
PRAY FOR US

Brethren, pray for us.

1 Thessalonians 5:25

We Do Not Exist in Isolation

> *But when the Pharisees heard that He had silenced the Sadducees, they came together. And one of them, a lawyer, asked Him a question, to test Him. "Teacher, which is the great commandment in the law?" And he said to him, "You shall love the Lord your God with all your heart, and with all your soul, and with all your mind. This is the great and first commandment. And a second is like it, You shall love your neighbor as yourself. On these two commandments depend all the law and the prophets."*
> Matthew 22:34–40

There is a saying, "one Christian is no Christian." This is because Christians do not exist in isolation. To be a Christian is to be part of a community. The two greatest commandments on which all of the law and the prophets rest are the commandments to love God and love our neighbor. We can't love God and ignore our neighbor because the two go hand in hand. And we can't experience love without the presence of "another" because to love only oneself is narcissism. It is not love. Love is a choice that is extended from one to another. Even if one says he extends love toward God, there still needs to be the presence of another person because to love God is to serve others. We do not exist as Christians in isolation.

Love is experienced in two ways. We either are giving it, or we are receiving it. One needs to exist in some "community" to do both. That community can be a family, church community, group of friends, or anywhere where two or more people exist.

We must love our neighbor. Love is a choice to serve someone else with patience and kindness, even if they don't deserve it, especially if they don't deserve it. We also need love from our neighbor. Everyone needs to feel loved by someone else. Not everyone has the same need. There are some who need this more than others. However, no one can survive well in isolation without receiving love from others.

When Jesus Christ came to earth, He taught His disciples that they needed to exist in community. They weren't expected to make the journey through life alone. They would be part of a community, where they could learn together, worship together, and serve together. They could serve within the community (their fellow community members), and they were to serve outside of the community as well (serving complete strangers who were not part of the community).

One of the things that is supposed to occur in a community (not just in a church community, but in any community—family, group of friends, etc.) is that members of the community are both responsible for one another and accountable to one another. If a member of the community starts to slip away, the rest of the community reins him or her back in. Members are also accountable to one another. They check in with one another.

Responsibility and accountability are also supposed to be foundational to a church community. The church community is supposed to keep itself together by being responsible for all members, keep members together, run to serve when one member has been wounded (by grief or loss or illness), and add to the number of members through evangelism and outreach. The church members should also be accountable to one another, again that example of "safe and expected to be honest" so that the environment is set, where members can "*bear one another's burdens and so fulfill the law of Christ*" (Gal. 6:2).

At the center of the church community is worship, where members gather together as one body to worship the Lord. While most of this section will focus on praying in smaller groups, it is central to each church community to pray as one large group, to come to God as one body to worship and praise Him. This reinforces for the entire community at one time, the purpose and the destination of life—to glorify God and serve one another as we work our way to salvation in the kingdom of heaven. This message is not always simple to understand, nor is it easy to do. However, it is easy to state and necessary to repeat, which is why the community gathers so often for worship.

As Christians, it is nearly impossible to exist without a church community because the church community provides instruction, accountability, and encouragement to live a God-centered life. It is nearly impossible to do these things alone. If you are not a regular member of a church community, seek to change that. If you are a regular member of a church community, continually seek to strengthen that relationship with your church community.

Christians do not exist in isolation. They exist in community. They exist in small communities like families and friend groups, and they exist in larger communities, churches. Worship is the primary activity of the church community. Prayer should ideally be part of every small community, and service is how we express love in any "community" we belong to.

Lord, thank You for the "communities" to which I belong, my family, friendships, and church community. Help me to strengthen my bonds within each community. Help me to serve in each community with love, kindness, patience, and consistency. Help me to have eyes to see members of each community that need encouragement. Help others to see when I need encouragement. Help us all to keep our eyes on You, love You, and express love for You in service to others. Help me to have eyes to see people who feel isolated and bring them safely into a community. Amen.

Encouragement Challenge: Seek constantly to strengthen your bonds with your "communities"—your family, friendships, and church community.

INTERCESSORY PRAYER

Brethren, pray for us.
1 Thessalonians 5:25

In our study on encouragement, I don't specifically refer to Orthodox Christian concepts often because encouragement is something that crosses all denominations of Christianity. Hopefully, all Christians agree that one important job of each Christian is to encourage other people. Each denomination has a different way of worshiping, and some even have a different understanding of foundational precepts of Christianity.

One thing that is part of Orthodox Christianity is the concept of intercessory prayer. We invoke the intercessions of the saints in our prayers. In other words, we ask the saints to pray for us, and the saints are people who have universally been identified as people who lived extraordinarily God-centered lives. Perhaps they were martyred for the faith, or the Holy Spirit spoke through their sermons or writings in an extraordinary way. Over the two millennia of Christianity, the church has given the title of "saint" to pious people who have given extraordinary witness for God, a witness that "sets them apart." In fact, the word that is translated as "saint" is the word agios, which means "holy," and holy means "set apart for God."[49] We are all called to be holy. The saints are those who the church recognizes as extraordinarily holy in their life and witness for Christ.

Contrary to what some believe, we do not pray "to" the saints. Rather, we pray through the saints. We ask the saints for their prayers. We ask the saints to join us in bringing our needs before God.

In 1 Thessalonians 5:25, St. Paul asks for the "intercessions" of all who are reading the letter. His request is simple. "Brethren, pray for us."

Many people have had the occasion to ask someone else to pray for them. Perhaps one is going on a trip or having a serious surgery and asks others, "Please keep me in your prayers." That is intercessory prayer. When you ask someone to pray for you, you are not asking them to pray instead of you, so that they pray for you and you don't pray for yourself. You are asking them to also include you in their prayers before the Lord.

That leads to the question that if we can ask others to pray for us, people who are still in their spiritual struggle, why would we not ask the saints to pray for us? If we can ask others to pray for us, why would not we ask the Virgin Mary, St. John the Baptist, the angels, and other known holy figures to pray for us?

Another way to look at intercessory prayer is like asking someone we don't know well for something by using an intermediary who knows them better. For instance, let's say that Joe and George are friends. Michael knows George but doesn't know Joe. Michael needs something from Joe, so he asks George to intercede with Joe on his behalf, to ask Joe for something because George knows Joe better. Ultimately, Michael is the one in need, the one who is asking Joe for something. However, he is going through George to take his request to Joe.

Perhaps Michael does know Joe, but he knows that George knows Joe also and asks George to put in a good word for him in addition to the good word he will put in for himself.

Asking the saints for intercession doesn't replace going to Christ on our own, just like asking someone to remember us in prayer doesn't replace us praying on our own. Intercessory prayer bolsters individual prayer because it brings individual prayer into the context of a community. Asking a friend to pray for you brings individual prayer into the context of a community of friends. Asking the saints to pray for us brings individual prayer into a community of holy people.

The most important part of intercessory prayer is that it helps us now that we are not isolated. Many times, we are praying out of need, even out of sorrow. Joining others in our prayers helps us not to feel isolated and alone. Rather, it helps us feel encouraged that we are not alone.

Lord, thank You for the gift of life, and of this day of my life. Each day brings the opportunity for both joy and challenge. Allow me to share both in the context of communities—in the community of friends and in the community of holy people, saints, who have lived their lives centered on You and who now have made their way to salvation in You. May the community of saints around You also join my prayers with theirs, and may those who are already standing in Your presence in heaven pray for me also as I work my way there. Lord, I ask these things of You, but I also ask for the intercession of Your saints and angels, through the Virgin Mary, St. John the Baptist, the archangels, and all the saints (you can list specific saints like your patron saint). Amen.

Encouragement Challenge: Pray for others. Ask others to pray for you. Ask the saints to pray for you.

I'm Going to God for You

I do not cease to give thanks for you, remembering you in my prayers.
Ephesians 1:16

Perhaps the best gift one can give to someone is to pray for them. The most encouraging thing to hear from someone is, "I'm praying for you."

The most important and most intimate thing we do is to talk to God in prayer. What can be more intimate than a conversation with the Almighty God?! What more beautiful image can there be than to think that someone is on their knees in prayer, and while praying to God, they offer your name and your needs? That is so powerful. We definitely don't do this or talk about this enough. We can all do a better job praying for one another. Imagine how it could change relationships if people talked openly about praying for one another.

Earlier I shared the story of when I had sinus surgery, and about my lifelong fear of IVs. The day before the surgery, I posted on social media that I was having surgery the following day and asked people to pray for me. I got over 300 messages from people that they would be praying for me the morning of the surgery. I also received a lot of messages of encouragement. When I started thinking about 300 people actually pausing in their busy day, in their busy lives, and talking to God about ME, it was actually pretty humbling.

When I was laying on the hospital bed, I asked God to give me a thought that would take me far away from my anxiety about the dreaded IV and impending surgery. I closed my eyes and got lost in my thoughts. The first thought was me running on the old dirt track at my high school. I wondered why God had brought this thought to my mind. I didn't like high school, running, or the track. In the next moment, I heard a voice that said, "You got this." And I thought, *Well, at least one person cares about my suffering while running on this track.* A few seconds later, there were now hundreds of people in the stands cheering for me. And the effort to run felt lighter. Then the dream shifted to the streets of my town, where hundreds of thousands of people lined the sidewalks cheering for me while I was running in front of them. The running now seemed completely effortless because I was so inspired by all the encouragement. Then I thought, *I'm still the only one on this bed. I'm the only one who is having surgery.* However, somehow I didn't feel alone.

Perhaps for the first time in my life, I understood the value of intercessory prayer, whether it comes from the saints or my peers. Even though I was alone in my situation, in the sense that no one else was going through it or could take it away from me and do it for me, I was not alone. I was surrounded by the prayers and encouragement from many, which made my situation somehow easier.

Most of us don't like running. However, imagine if your whole town came out and lined the streets for you to run. It would somehow be much easier. And when people come out to say they are praying for you, that they are going to God for you, it doesn't change the roads on which you have to run, but it somehow makes them smoother and more tolerable.

There is a tangible closeness that occurs between people who pray for each other. There are people I have prayed for over the course of many years, even people that I don't see for years. And then when I see them, it was like we were together only yesterday. I can honestly say to them, "I was just thinking about you" or "I think about you every day" because in my prayers, I do.

One of the most encouraging things you can offer someone is your prayers, to take their name and their needs to God in prayer, and also to tell them that. It always makes me feel good when someone says, "I am praying for you."

Make a list of five people to pray for each day. If each person does that, all of us will end up on at least five lists. Tell your five people that you are praying for them. This will keep you accountable to pray for them and will give you a solid bond that won't be broken even if they are people you do not see often.

Everyone is going to run down an "empty street" someday—it might be a health crisis, job loss, death in the family, or some other trauma that will make each of us think that we are running alone. Each of us has the ability to go to God for someone, to be that person on the sidewalk cheering and praying, which will not necessarily mean a person won't have to run down a difficult road, but that they won't have to run it alone.

Encourage others by praying for them. Going to God for someone else is the most beautiful gift you can offer them.

Lord, thank You for the gift of friends that I have (list five friends you are praying for). Please be with these people today on whatever road they are walking. Give to them wisdom, patience, health, and peace. Lord, be also with the people who don't have friends and who feel alone. Lead them to others, and lead others to them. Help me to see those who don't have enough people around them, and move my heart with compassion to not only see them but to embrace them as well. Amen.

Encouragement Challenge: Make a list of a few people you want to pray for. Tell those people you are praying for them daily, that you are going to God for them. And then see how this not only improves your prayer life but your relationships as well.

Praying with Someone

Jesus said, "For where two or three are gathered in My Name, there am I in the midst of them."
Matthew 18:20

One of the greatest gifts I have ever received was many years ago. After the resurrection service on Easter (which finishes at 2:00 a.m.), one of my parishioners asked to pray with me. This person asked to stand next to me and pray, to offer my name to God in my presence. There were two reasons why this was so powerful. First, as an Orthodox priest, when I am offering services, I never say my own name; that is part of our liturgical tradition. So in services where the name of every congregant is offered, mine is absent. It was indeed refreshing to hear my name in a prayer in our church. Second, there is power in offering someone's name in prayer, as we just discussed, going to God on behalf of someone. However, it is even more powerful when we go to God on behalf of someone else in their presence.

This concept is familiar to some Christians. I've been in many contexts where people (two, three, or a small group) "have prayer," meaning that a person or people who are not necessarily priests or ministers pray for the others who are present.

It is important to note that praying with someone else in no way diminishes the need for ordained clergy or corporate worship. Corporate worship does not happen daily, nor are clergy present everywhere—in homes for meals, heavy conversations between friends, and so on. Learning to pray with others is a beautiful gesture that can be offered in addition to corporate clergy-led worship.

Many people are uncomfortable with the idea of praying with someone else because they are not sure how to begin. If you are not sure what to say in prayer, start off by praying about the context in which you are in. For instance, if you are visiting someone in the hospital, these are things that can be included in prayer:

- ~ Thanksgiving to God that you are able to visit with your friend who is in the hospital;
- ~ Prayers for the doctors and nurses who are caring for your friend;
- ~ Prayers for your friend to be free from pain and anxiety; and

- ~ Prayers for needs specific to that day—maybe someone is having surgery, is starting to walk after surgery, or just needs to keep food down.

When I pray with my Bible study group, I start off by thanking God for the group and the opportunity to gather with them. Then I move to praying for God to guide us in our study, to open our minds and our hearts to comprehend what we hear and apply it to our lives. Then I pray for people who are in the group, and if anyone has any specific needs, those can be brought up as well.

Two important things to note about praying with others. First, God doesn't grade our prayers. If you stumble and say, "um" a few times, God will not stop listening. Second, I have never prayed with someone who wasn't appreciative of the prayer. People love to receive the gift of prayer.

Several years ago, a young child in my parish passed away suddenly. I went to the house where the death had occurred. It is standard procedure that when a child dies suddenly, law enforcement is sent to the scene to make sure that there was no foul play involved. I went to the home, interacted with the bereaved parents and the law enforcement officials, and it was quickly determined that there was no foul play involved, just a sudden, tragic illness.

As the two women detectives were leaving, I followed them out and asked if I could pray with them. I asked if they were Christians. One answered that she was Catholic. The other said she didn't believe in God. When I asked if I could pray for them, it was the non-believer who grabbed my hand and said, "Go for it." When I finished, the detectives told me that they had worked together for fourteen years in a unit that investigates the deaths of children, this was the second dead child of the morning for them, and in all of their years working together, no one had ever offered a prayer with them.

I never saw them again, but they appreciated what I did that day. And who knows what happened? Maybe it strengthened their faith. Maybe for one, it started a faith journey, or maybe it didn't. However, at least for the moment, on a dark day, each felt somehow encouraged, even for a few moments. And that is one of the greatest results when we pray with someone else—they feel encouraged, and their burden is lightened even if for only a little while.

Today's prayer is for you, the reader of this message, offered in the context of me writing and you reading what I write.

Lord, thank You for the opportunity and the wisdom to write these daily messages. Thank You for the people who read them. Be with each person who is reading this message today and bless them with health, joy, peace, patience, and whatever it is they are needing today—stamina, safety, encouragement, efficiency, whatever it may be. Help each person to become a better encourager and more intentional in offering encouragement. Give each a deeper understanding of the faith. Lead each to salvation. Thank You, Lord, for the privilege of serving these people, some of whom I know and most of whom I do not. As it is Your will, allow me to continue writing and sharing You through these writings. Amen.

Encouragement Challenge: Pray with others. It is a beautiful gift to give. It is a beautiful gift to receive.

There Is No Shame in Asking for Help

Where there is no guidance, a people falls; but in an abundance of counselors there is safety.
Proverbs 11:14

Not all help comes through prayer. Some come through conversation. Friends help friends talk through problems and solve dilemmas. Sometimes, however, conversation with friends about challenges might not be helpful because friends sometimes have a hard time being objective.

I see a therapist. I have been seeing one for years. If that is some kind of stigma, well, it's not a stigma for me. Why do I see a therapist? I don't think I'm crazy. I explain it like this. Many of us have had the experience of filing mail in a mail room. You go into the mail room with a stack of mail and a big box with slots that have names on them, and you file the mail into the proper slots. However, what if those slots didn't have names on them? You'd have a stack of mail and wouldn't know where it should go. My therapist helps me to figure out what should go where in my life. He helps me figure out what is a big deal and what isn't, what need to be worried about right now and what can wait. He helps me to understand who I am and perhaps the reason I am how I am. We do this through talking about my past and my present. Yes, I sit on a couch, but I don't lay on it. I go about every two weeks, which is the right interval for me. Some people go once a week, others multiple times a week, and some once a month. He just helps me figure out how to file the complicated things that comprise my life.

In addition to a therapist, I have a "spiritual father," an Orthodox Christian term that defines the person who helps guide one spiritually and also the one who hears your confession. My spiritual father is also a person I go to for spiritual help and objective advice. Because he is a priest, he is better able to understand the unique challenges of my job since he shares in the same job.

Between an Orthodox priest who serves as a mentor and a non-Orthodox therapist who is completely objective, I have the help I need to talk about my challenges and get help to get things to fit where they go.

There is another scenario for which we all need help. It's when we are confronted with something we don't know how to do or something we don't have. Here is the analogy:

You are invited to go for a twenty-mile bike ride with some friends. You know it will be fun to be with friends, and some outside time would do you some good. The problem is that you never learned how to ride a bike. So, if you go, you are likely to get hurt and embarrassed. What do you do? There are four options.

1. You can go with the friends and likely get hurt and embarrassed. So that really isn't an option;

2. You can tell your friends you can't go. But they will be disappointed;

3. You can tell your friends you were once a biking champion but got hurt and can't go bike riding anymore. This is the option that most people choose because it gets you out of going and saves face; in fact, it may even impress some people. We call this option the big lie; or

4. You can grab a friend and tell the truth, that you don't know how to ride a bike but would like to learn. Perhaps the friend could get you a bike with some training wheels, which is completely embarrassing for an adult, and go to some secluded parking lot and help you learn. What's involved here is honesty, patience, and humility. The person who wants to learn must be honest and humble about not knowing how to ride. The person who has been asked to help must be patient and non-judgmental in teaching. They also need to keep a confidence that their friend needs help and not share what could potentially be embarrassing to the person who is just learning to ride a bike. Option four is the best option here because there is truth, there is growth, and ultimately, there is success.

Going back to that idea of creating an environment where it is safe and expected to be honest, when we have that environment, people are more likely to choose option four, which is the best option. Absent of that kind of environment, people will continue to choose option three and go nowhere.

We know that in the Bible, even Jesus needed help carrying His cross to Golgotha. A man named Simon of Cyrene was conscripted to do this. We should not wait to be conscripted to help. We should offer help freely and without judgment, and we should feel confident in asking for help that we will not be judged. Proverbs 11:14 says it perfectly: *Where there is no guidance, a people falls; but in an abundance of counselors there is safety.*

Lord, there are times in my life when I know I need help. Help me to have the courage to ask for it. Surround me with people who can help me without judgment. Most of all, Lord, I need Your help to be the person You created me to be. Give me strength and wisdom and patience and all the things I need to serve You, using the talents You have given me. Help me, save me, have mercy on me, and protect me, oh God, by Your grace. Amen.

Encouragement Challenge: Don't be afraid to ask for help. Look to help those who need help and do so without judgment. In my humble opinion, many people could really benefit from seeing a therapist.

****Dedicated to my therapist, Dr. Timothy Evans.*

I Need Help to Get to Christ—
I Can't Get There Alone

Help me, O Lord my God! Save me according to Thy steadfast love!
Psalm 109:26

One of the best ways to teach people is incorporating something called "experiential learning." This is where the teacher provides an experience so that the students will remember not necessarily what the teacher said but what they did. There are many lessons about Christianity that are conveyed much better through experience than sermon. Here is one of them that demonstrates why we need the help of others to get to Christ. See if you can envision this activity in your mind.

Take a large open space, like a basketball court and several people. Put a chair at some random place on one end of the basketball court. On the chair, put a small icon (picture) of Christ. A couple of people are asked to remain out of sight of the basketball court, so they won't see the beginning of the activity. Then a couple of others who are still on the basketball court (at the opposite end of where the icon is) are blindfolded. They are each asked how many sins, on a scale of one (few) to ten (many), they've committed in the past year. Most will say ten. Each will spin around ten times (or whatever their number was), and each will be instructed to walk toward the icon. No one else who is present is allowed to talk. Of course, there may be the 1 percent chance that one of those people is a gymnast who can still walk a straight line being dizzy, but most people who try this exercise fail miserably. They walk into walls, get impatient, or just quit. They can't find the icon. The message is that if we try to get to Christ without some kind of help, we are much more likely to get hurt, discouraged, or quit. Having help and encouragement to get to Christ is essential.

Now the activity is repeated with the two people who didn't see what has happened so far. They do it one at a time, and the second one does not watch the first one. There is a reason for this, and that is so each person does this differently. Choose two people, and get two different outcomes.

One person is blindfolded before coming to the basketball court. They haven't seen the chair or the set up. The facilitator asks them several questions. The first is, "Do you trust me?"

Most people will answer yes, they trust the facilitator, even if they don't know them well. The second question is, "Is there someone else you trust?" And they will choose someone from the group to help them. They are told, "There is a chair with an icon of Christ on it on the other side of the basketball court." They are then asked, "Do you believe this?" They will most likely answer "yes," figuring that the facilitator will not lie to them. The question of "how many sins have you committed in the past year" will be asked as it was asked to the previous people. Most will say "ten." Then they are told to spin around that number of times to then go find the icon, but if they need help, they can ask for help. The person they have chosen, when asked for help, is allowed to turn the blindfolded person's body toward the icon and then let go. The exercise begins.

Here is what inevitably happens. The blindfolded participant walks around, crashes into things, and doesn't ask for help for at least two to three minutes. Usually, as the facilitator, I have to ask them how they are doing and repeat the directions several times until they get the hang of that they need to ask for help. Once they figure this out, they find the icon rather quickly. The problem is that they don't figure it out quickly. They crash into things and get discouraged. One time when I facilitated this exercise at summer camp, the person doing it said, "I'm walking around aimlessly. I think you are goofing on me. I don't think there is an icon. I want to quit." That was a dramatic teaching moment. I told this person, "You can quit if you want, but if you quit and find out there really is an icon on this court, you can't restart," to which they responded that they'd continue. They weren't really sure there was an icon there, but they were more afraid to quit than to continue. How many of us feel like this at times?!

The lessons of this exercise are several. The most important question in setting this up is, "Do you believe there is an icon of Christ on a chair on this court?" If the answer is no, then the facilitator can't very well tell the person to go find it. Believing something is there without seeing it, believing there is an icon on a chair that you haven't seen, in this case, is what faith is. It takes faith to believe. It takes faith to start walking. It takes faith to continue walking, and it takes faith to ask for help.

The second thing that becomes very apparent every time I see this exercise is that people are hesitant to ask for help. Is that because we've been conditioned to go it on our own? Have we been taught that asking for help is a sign of weakness? Or have we asked for help and been hurt instead, so now we are afraid to ask? (Whether it is to get to Christ or with anything else in this life.)

The parameters of this exercise mirror real life. We are all at a distance from our salvation. This is why we need constant work on it. The blindfold represents sin, the thing that keeps us from seeing God clearly and clouds our path to Him. These parameters are the same for everyone. The variable parts of this exercise is who the participant chooses to help and how often they ask for help.

If a person asked for help every step of the way, they'd literally walk in a straight line to God, and if a person was really astute, they would ask for help from everyone and would be less likely to veer off the path.

The person who provides the help can represent our friends who encourage us to go to Christ or other goals we have in life. The more friends we have like this, the easier it will be to get to Christ.

This person also represents the church—the teachings of the church, clergy, Sunday school teachers, youth group, Bible study, and any other way the church is helpful in getting us to Christ. One critical thing about the helper in this exercise as well as with the church, the helper can only get the blindfolded person pointed in the right direction. They can't take them by the hand and lead or force them to go to Christ. They can't force the person to ask for help either. The church gets us pointed in the right direction. It doesn't take us by the hand and force us to go to God. It is our choice to walk the way we are directed. It is our choice to decide how often we ask for help.

One other thing about this experience is that the instructions are pretty easy: "Ask for help when you need it." Yet, I often have to explain the directions three to four times within a few minutes. I've seen an acronym for the Bible—Basic Instructions Before Leaving Earth, and people have complained that church is the same Sunday after Sunday. Well, we need these basic instructions over and over again because it takes us years and sometimes a lifetime to figure out that we need help, decide that there is indeed an icon on the court (or a God in heaven), and keep walking in the times we think we're never going to get there.

Back to that critical question, "Do you believe there is an icon you haven't seen on this basketball court?" Most people will say they do believe because they trust the facilitator not to lie. This is why we have to trust our "facilitators"—our parents, priests, ancestors, saints, and those who came before us because others can see what we can't see yet.

This exercise is only done successfully in the context of community with the humility to ask for help and the faith to follow the direction provided.

Lord, sometimes my life feels like this exercise. I can't seem to see You clearly, I don't know that path I should walk on, I'm lost and am afraid to ask for help, or I don't know who to ask for help. Sometimes I want to quit. Sometimes I wonder if You are even there. In my times of doubt, give me the strength to keep walking. In the times I'm not sure, surround me with people who will give me spiritual confidence. In the times when I'm lost, put the thought in my mind and heart that I need to ask for help. And in the times when I ask for help, provide someone who will get me in the right direction. Help me know that You are real. Help me to work my way toward You in this life so that I may be with You for eternal life. Amen.

Encouragement Challenge: When you feel lost in your spiritual journey, don't be afraid to ask for help. If someone asks you for help, point them in the right direction. If you feel like the person who wanted to quit, don't. Ask for help and keep walking.

**Dedicated to Connie Simopoulos.

You Can Ask for Encouragement

Finally, brethren, pray for us, that the word of the Lord may speed on and triumph, as it did among you, and that we may be delivered from wicked and evil men; for not all have faith. But the Lord is faithful; He will strengthen you and guard you from evil.
2 Thessalonians 3:1–3

Most people will ask for help with a difficult task, like carrying a heavy object. Most people don't have a hard time asking for help there because it is obvious that the task is too hard. However, there are some people who would rather go it alone and risk throwing out their back because they don't want to ask for help.

No one is expected to go it alone. That's why Jesus told us that the most important commandments are to love Him and to love one another, to serve one another. If we never serve someone else, we are not keeping this commandment. If we never let another serve us, we are not allowing others to keep this commandment in us. If everyone refuses help, then no one can love their neighbor. Thus, it is important that we freely offer help but also feel we can freely ask for help, that we freely and joyfully (and willingly) accept help from others.

This idea of asking for help also applies to encouragement. We are to encourage one another. We should expect to receive encouragement from one another. We should realize that everyone needs encouragement. We should realize that we need it as well. When there is an opportunity to offer encouragement, we should. When someone wants to encourage us, we need to say, "thank you" and accept encouragement, not shy away from it.

Ideally, we have eyes to see those around us who need encouragement so that we don't have to ask, "Do you need some encouragement?" When you encounter someone who you perceive needs encouragement, it is okay to encourage them and also tell them that this is your intention. You can say, "I'd like to offer some encouragement." (You don't have to add, "because I see that you need it.")

On the other side, when we are down and discouraged, it is okay to ask for encouragement. We ask for help in doing tasks we don't know how to do—we'll call someone to help us change a flat tire. We ask for help in tasks that we need help with, like carrying a big box. So, we should also be able to ask for encouragement in the times when we feel discouraged. This is the ideal. In a group of friends or co-workers, when one is feeling down, he or she should be able to say to others in the group, "I need some encouragement."

Again, it's the environment where it is safe and expected to be honest. It is not unsafe to ask for help lifting a heavy box. That need for help is obvious. And there is a fine line in asking for encouragement when one feels discouraged and asking for a compliment to feed an ego. When encouragement flows properly, there is less discouragement and less need for ego because people are built up in an appropriate way, leaving no one feeling either empty or prideful. This is why encouragement, in its essence, is very simple, but in creating environments where there is an appropriate amount of encouragement is more of an art form, we might say.

In 2 Thessalonians 3:1–3, St. Paul specifically asks for prayers (and asking someone to pray for you is a way to ask for encouragement) because he had some specific concerns. He was worried about wicked and evil people who might harm him or thwart his ability to further the message of Christ. He asked for encouragement in the form of prayer. He didn't say, "I got this," but rather expressed concern about his ability to speed on and triumph with the Word of the Lord.

When we are feeling discouraged, we should not be hesitant to ask for encouragement. It can be asking for a prayer. It can be asking for feedback. It can be a cry that we feel down in the dumps and need some reassurance. We should feel free to ask.

When we hear from someone who has asked for prayer or encouragement, we should freely give it. This is part of fulfilling God's commandment to love our neighbor as ourselves. We all need encouragement. We all need to be generous in encouraging others.

Finally, when we hear words of encouragement from other people, we should not shy away and put on some front of false humility or even genuinely feel that we are unworthy of encouragement. Receive encouragement with a simple thank you. This acknowledges the encourager and allows us to accept something we all need.

Lord, help me to find the humility and honesty to ask for encouragement when I need it. Surround me with people who will encourage when I feel down. Give me eyes to see those who need encouragement, ears to hear requests for encouragement, and words I can use to help build up others around me. Amen.

Most of us wouldn't hesitate to ask for help lifting a heavy box. It is okay to ask for help in carrying a heavy burden, which can be lightened through the encouragement of others.

YOU ARE WORTHY

To this end we always pray for you, that our God may make you worthy of His call, and may fulfill every good resolve and work of faith by His power, so that the name of our Lord Jesus may be glorified in you, and you in Him, according to the grace of our God and Lord Jesus Christ.
2 Thessalonians 1:11–12

Many people don't feel comfortable asking for help. Perhaps they were taught that to ask for help is a sign of weakness. Perhaps they feel that their ego will take a blow if they ask for help. And perhaps some even feel unworthy of help, inadequate with themselves, like they are burden to others.

At the ordination of a priest in the Orthodox church, the congregation screams and sings, "Axios!" which means "worthy!" to the new priest. They do this many times. They do this as the new priest is vested with each piece of his priestly garments. I felt God's call to the priesthood many years before I was ordained. I studied at the seminary for four years. I was ordained, first as a deacon, then as a priest, and I heard the cries of "Axios!" from many people.

I've had the opportunity to watch several priests offer their first service. Even though the new priest will usually celebrate his first service alone, there is almost always an older priest in the building to help out and encourage. For my first service as a priest, there were no other priests in the building, I was by myself. I remember feeling like I was stealing from a candy store. I knew what I was doing; that wasn't the problem. It was just that I wished there had been someone there telling me, "It's ok, you are worthy to be here doing this stuff."

For those who don't think they are worthy of help and encouragement, you are. We are all worthy of this. We all need this, and we are all worthy of this.

Christ summarized all the commandments into two commandments—to love God, and to love our neighbor. Imagine if every neighbor refused help and encouragement from his or her neighbor. This commandment to love our neighbor could not be kept. In accepting encouragement, we actually help others by allowing them to love us. One might argue that an egotistical person is always looking for help, and in some sense, that might be true if a person is always using others. On the other side, though, it is a proud person who will not ask for and accept help and encouragement from others.

It is interesting in Matthew 10:8, where Jesus tells His disciples, "You received without paying, give without paying." In other words, you received blessings without paying for them or possibly even deserving them. We should, therefore, bless others and help others without expecting anything in return. He not only mentions giving without pay. He mentions receiving without pay and receiving first.

Ideally among people, there is an "equal" exchange of help and encouragement. However, there is no such thing as equality. If we keep score about encouragement in our relationships, it will likely lead us closer to insanity than equality. Rather, we should freely encourage one another and be quick to help one another. And we should be grateful when others encourage and help us.

If you feel like you don't deserve any encouragement, you are wrong. We all need it, and we are all worthy of it. Part of the challenge in the area of encouragement is not only to be able to offer it but to receive it as well. We all need to become good encouragers and good helpers as well as to become good receivers of encouragement and help.

Many people are hesitant to accept encouragement and help because they think they are a bother. This goes back to creating a safe environment where people not only are safe to be honest but safe in the knowledge that they are valued so they can accept encouragement that is offered at the same time that they are encouraging others.

The proper response to encouragement for the one who is not comfortable receiving it is not to run away and hide but to simply say thank you. This shows humility and grace on the part of the receiver and shows gratitude to the encourager. Part of encouragement is not only learning how to offer it but how to receive it as well.

Lord, thank You for gestures of encouragement that I receive. Help me to not only be a good encourager of others but to be a good receiver of encouragement and help. Help me to put aside my own pride that I can do everything on my own so that I can accept love and encouragement from others. Bring people into my path who will encourage me, and give me the humility to accept encouragement. Amen.

You are worthy to be encouraged by others!

Part Fifteen

GREET ONE ANOTHER

Greet all the brethren with a holy kiss.

1 Thessalonians 5:26

Are Our Churches Places of Encouragement or Discouragement?

For I want you to know how greatly I strive for you, and for those at Laodicea, and for all who have not seen my face, that their hearts may be encouraged as they are knit together in love, to have all the riches of assured understanding and the knowledge of God's mystery, of Christ, in Whom are hid all the treasure of wisdom and knowledge.
Colossians 2:1–3

St. Paul framed his words in 1 Thessalonians 5:11–24 around general Christian encouragement. In verses 25–28, he connects encouragement with the life of the church. In verse 25, he asked the faithful to "pray for us," and we discussed intercessory prayer, praying for others, and praying with others. We concluded with the idea that everyone is worthy of encouragement.

Verse 26 brings our thoughts to the spiritual intimacy that a church community is supposed to have. This study on encouragement has focused a lot on feeling encouraged and giving encouragement in everyday life. This section will focus on encouragement as it relates to the church. Our connection to the church is supposed to be part of our everyday life as well.

Greeting one another with a hug is a cultural norm in social situations. In some cultures, the greeting is done with a kiss. In Greek culture, people exchange a kiss on both cheeks, while in the Arabic culture, three kisses are given. In a business context, a handshake is used. In other countries people might bow to one another. When one goes to eat at a restaurant, the restaurant staff will not hug you or shake your hand, but there is a verbal welcome. The point is that being greeted denotes a sense that one belongs. Imagine if you go somewhere, and no one notices you, greets you, or welcomes you. You would feel like you don't belong.

The questions we are reflecting on today is this—are our churches places of encouragement or discouragement, places where people are welcomed or made to feel that they don't belong? One of the significant aspects of encouragement is not only helping others feel confident in themselves but assuring them that they belong and are wanted. We've probably all had the experience of going somewhere and not being noticed. It leaves one feeling like they are invisible and unimportant. And this might be the norm at a large store or sports stadium. However, it can't be the norm when it comes to church communities.

We don't think of shoppers at a supermarket as being "close-knit." Maybe the employees are, but the customers are not. They are a large group of individuals who share the same space and purchase the same food but do not converse. They do their business and leave. St. Paul, in his letter to the Colossians, encourages members of church communities to be close to one another, "that their hearts may be encouraged as they are knit together in love" (Col. 2:2). It is only when they are knit together in love that they can come together to "have all the riches of assured understanding and the knowledge of God's mystery, of Christ" (2:3). When a church community is not knit together, when it resembles a supermarket rather than a family, people will loosely come and go and will never find "the treasure of wisdom and knowledge" of Christ that comes only when one has a deep-seeded understanding of Christ rather than a superficial one.

Intimacy with Christ is certainly helped by intimacy in a church community.

That leads to the question, can one be a Christian and not be connected to a church community? In today's world, we have many people who identify as "spiritual but not religious." In other words, they seek to find God (or their "higher power") on their own, outside of the confines of a community.

That doesn't really work, and here's why. If a person has no contact with anyone regarding their Christian journey, how can they know they are on the right track or believing the right things? Where does a person who has no community go when they are feeling discouraged in their faith or have a setback in their faith? Who will notice if a person is falling away from the faith if they are not part of a community? There obviously is the connection to a church community that provides opportunities for worship, learning, fellowship, and service.

There is so much discouragement already in the world today that if a church is a source of discouragement, people will be turned off from that church and the idea of belonging to a church community in general. This is why our churches need to not only be places of worship and learning, but they also need to be environments of encouragement because encouragement is an attraction while discouragement is a turn-off.

If you are part of a church community, ask yourself, "Is my church a place of encouragement or discouragement, and what am I doing/what can I do to bring more encouragement into the community?" We know that from the two-thousand-year history of the Christian church that the church community is a foundational unit. We also know that creating an encouraging environment is foundational to any social unit—family, workplace, friendships, and so on. Thus, as we build church communities to spread the message of Christ, we must be cognizant of making them environments that are encouraging.

Lord, thank You for sustaining the church for the past two thousand years. Thank You for those who have served as encouragers in communities, who have served to draw people to You. Help my church community to be a place of encouragement, which draws people to know and serve You. Help me to be an encourager in the context of my community. May I serve You, and through me, may others be drawn to You. Help Your light to shine through me so that others may come to know and love You. Amen.

Encouragement Challenge: Do your part to create/maintain an encouraging environment in your church community!

Encouragement to Serve

And Mary said, "Behold, I am the handmaid of the Lord; let it be to me according to your word."
Luke 1:38

To serve means to offer help in whatever way help is needed. If a person comes to a church community or to any other context and says, "I'm here to serve," that literally should mean, "I'm here to do whatever is helpful."

Unfortunately, while we may say, "I'll do whatever is helpful," we don't always mean that. What if you said, "I'll do whatever is helpful," and someone told you, "Go empty the trash, and then clean the bathroom"? How many of us would either say, "I don't clean bathrooms" or "Is there something else I can do instead"?

Today's verse is the response the Virgin Mary gave to the archangel Gabriel when she was told that God had called her to carry His Son in her womb. The Virgin Mary was certainly surprised by the visit of the angel. She had some questions, like how can this happen since she was not married? The archangel answered this question by telling her: "The Holy Spirit will come upon you, and the power of the Most High will overshadow you; therefore, the child to be born will be called holy, the Son of God" (Luke 1:35).

Then Mary said "Behold, I am the handmaid of the Lord; let it be to me according to your word" (Luke 1:38). She, thankfully, didn't say, "I can't do that" or "Can you please choose something else for me to do?" God had a specific plan for her, and she willingly and obediently went along with it.

God has a plan for each life. That plan might be something large, like a calling to a certain career, or it might be something small, like a circumstance or opportunity to serve on a particular day. Circumstances, some of which I believe are provided by God, give us opportunities to serve on given days in specific ways. For instance, someone drops their groceries in the parking lot of a store, and circumstance has us standing nearby. There is now an opportunity to serve. God tells us that we are to love our neighbor, and our neighbor is the person who is next to us at a given moment. Did God allow the groceries to fall to the ground so we could help pick them up? Or was the person who dropped them just clumsy? In either case, God calls us to serve, and in that circumstance, in that moment, we are supposed to help the neighbor by helping to pick up the dropped items.

There are many ways one can serve. We can choose any of them. When the call comes out for a volunteer baseball coach, if you don't know how to play baseball, it's okay to pass on that one. However, what if no one stepped up to serve as a baseball coach, and a team of kids had no one to coach them? Maybe this is a call to learn something about baseball and serve as a coach because that's what is needed.

This is probably an extreme example that will not happen to any of us. A more common example is at a church festival or school carnival, there is a call for volunteers. We eagerly step forward as a parent or church member and offer to serve. We are handed a mop and told to mop up spills on the floor. Our reaction is, "I don't do mopping; can I be a cashier?" If there is a call for cashiers, and one wants to be a cashier, then it is very appropriate to step up to serve in this way. However, if there is a general call to serve, and one steps up to answer it, one has to be prepared to serve in whatever way is needed.

Sometimes there are specific calls, like the call to be a baseball coach or sing in the church choir. And we have specific skills or interests to answer them. We not only get to serve, but we also get to serve doing something we like. However, many times there is a call to serve in a way that perhaps stretches our comfort zone or calls us to do something we'd rather not do (like taking out garbage or mopping a floor). To truly serve is to do whatever is needed, whether that is answering God's call for our lives or answering the call to serve in a temporary situation.

In a church community, there are many opportunities to serve and needs to be filled. Some of those are more attractive, like singing in the choir or serving on the church board, and some are less attractive, like washing dishes after coffee hour. Each of us needs to understand that service is whatever is needed in a given circumstance, and to truly serve, one must step up, eager to help in whatever way is needed at a given moment.

When the angel visited the Virgin Mary and told her God's plan for her life was miraculous, unbelievable, incredible, and hard, she didn't say, "Choose someone or something else," or "Find something easier for me to do." She said, "I'll do it." We are not likely to be presented with something as heavy as she was presented with. However, whenever opportunities to serve present themselves (whether in a daily circumstance or life calling), our answer should mirror that of the Virgin Mary, "I am here to serve, according to Your will," not mine.

Lord, thank You for the gift of another day. Thank You for the possibilities that this day will bring. Each day brings an opportunity to serve You, according to the talents You have given me. And each day brings an opportunity to serve, according to the circumstances I will encounter. Give me joy in using the talents with which You have blessed me. And give me the eyes to see the opportunities to serve others in whatever circumstances I find myself in today. Help me to always see myself as Your servant, and let my life today be lived according to Your will. Amen.

Encouragement Challenge: Be open to serving others as they need, not necessarily as you want. Seek to serve God in every circumstance that arises today!

Fellowship with Others

Let us consider how to stir up one another to love and good works, not neglecting to meet together, as is the habit of some, but encouraging one another, and all the more as you see the Day drawing near.
Hebrews 10:24–25

The concept of small groups was introduced to us by Christ Himself. Christ's church was the whole world. His congregation was everyone He met. He preached to thousands of people on occasions like the Sermon on the Mount. Crowds constantly gathered around Him and followed Him from place to place. It's safe to say that Christ knew many people.

We know, however, that when Jesus was not among the masses, He had a small group, twelve disciples (in addition to some women) with whom He had consistent fellowship. He ministered to them, and they ministered to Him. He prayed with them, ate with them, laughed with them, and cried with them. Christ took strength from personal and private prayer. He also received strength from His small group.

In a church community, many gather for worship each Sunday. Many do not know each other by name. In fact, it is probably not realistic to know every person in the congregation by name—you'd have to spend significant time with each of them. Even more difficult would be to know each person by circumstance—who is struggling, sick, just moved, or scared. While I know most people in the church I serve by name, I do not know all by circumstance.

How can we help one another if we don't know one another? How can we minister to one another if we don't know one another's circumstance? The answer is small groups.

In a typical parish, there are many small groups or subsets of the whole congregation. The choir, Sunday school teachers, Sunday school parents, youth group, Bible study, philanthropy group (Philoptochos), sports teams, and Parish Council (and more)—these are all examples of subsets within a church congregation.

Each ministry group has two purposes, one that is known and one that is often overlooked. The known purpose is that each ministry serves a need in the parish—the choir sings, the

Parish Council administers, the Sunday school teachers, and so on. So, each group has a purpose, and each member works to support that purpose.

The overlooked aspect of these groups is the ministering to members within the ministry. Each of us has not only strengths but also struggles. Where can we take those struggles? In front of 300 people at a worship service, we may not even know. At a recent meeting of our Sunday school teachers, I made a comment that I wouldn't have made in front of the entire congregation, but in this small group, in a retreat setting, I felt comfortable making a certain comment and being vulnerable.

Being part of a ministry as a subset of the larger church congregations is so vital because it allows us to be more real and vulnerable. It allows us to encourage one another more specifically. It also allows us to be more encouraged on a more personal level.

Small groups in Protestant churches are actually a ministry of the church. This concept of small groups as well as traditional ministries of the church will be discussed over the next two reflections.

Lord, thank You for my church community. Thank You that I have a place to go and worship. Help me to branch out in different ways in my community, to meet new people and become more involved in the ministries of the church. Help me to find a niche where I can glorify You by serving others. Help me to find people who will lift me up and encourage me. Help me to always lift up and encourage others. Amen.

Encouragement Challenge: If you are in a ministry already, pray for the members of your ministry today. If you are not already in a ministry, consider joining one.

One Body with Many Members

For as in one body we have many members, and all the members do not have the same function, so we, though many, are one body in Christ, and individually members one of another. Having gifts that differ according to the grace given to us, let us use them: if prophecy in proportion to our faith; if service, in our serving; he who teaches, in his teaching; he who exhorts, in his exhortation; he who contributes, in liberality; he who gives aid, with zeal; he who does acts of mercy, with cheerfulness.
Romans 12:4–8

St. Paul describes the church (and, by extension, all of society) as one body with many parts. Comparing the church to a human body, there are many parts, and when all work in unity, the body is successful in its work. The hand doesn't function independent of the brain. The heart must constantly beat. Without our eyes, we would miss 90 percent of our sensory input. Take away the ability to speak, and it would be hard to express ourselves. We need our legs for moving around, ears to hear, all of our fingers and toes, our elbows and knees, our noses, eyelids, teeth, and tongue. Each part has a purpose. Each part is necessary for the whole body to function at its best.

The church community is the same—we need a choir, parish council, ushers, greeters, community outreach, Sunday school teachers, and all kinds of other volunteers. These are ministries where people are called to serve, to provide labor for the work of the church. There are other ministries like youth groups and Bible studies where people go to learn, for fellowship, and to be ministered to.

Ideally, everyone should belong to two groups: a group where one can do the work of ministry and a group where one can be ministered to. There are other groups that are also needed in a church community, such as a group for people who are grieving, divorced, or coping with illness.

There is an infinite number of needs as well as possibilities in a church community. There is also a diverse group of people with different talents in each community. When each person steps up to offer their particular talent, they allow for the possibilities to become realities.

In the community where I serve, a woman came to me one day and asked if she could start a support group for people who are grieving. She had lost someone, had participated in a similar group, and had really benefited from it. Her stepping forward led to the creation of a "Griefshare" group in the parish, which would never have come into existence had she not stepped forward to volunteer.

Many churches have found great success with the concept of small groups, groups where members share something in common—that is, they are divorced, single, dads, cancer survivors, or parents of high school students. The possibilities are infinite. People go to their small group, and it is a place where they feel accepted, loved, and free to be vulnerable. These groups become support groups in spiritual and other ways.

Groups like these also keep members accountable. There is a commitment to the group, to attending, sharing, speaking, keeping confidences, and so on. Groups members keep tabs on each other. They offer spiritual support and social fellowship.

Small groups are, unfortunately, not part of the culture of every church community. In these days when people feel scattered and not together, small groups can be an anchor that keeps people united and potentially a lifeline to those who feel isolated. This is certainly a subject worthy of thought and development in every community.

Lord, thank You for my unique and special gifts (bring those to your prayer and thank God specifically for them). Help me to realize how I can use these gifts in my church community to grow my faith and encourage the faith of others. Inspire me to be someone that others can lean on. Help me to find others that I can lean on as well. Amen.

Encouragement Challenge: Consider what kind of small groups can be established in your church community!

No One Should Ever Feel Alone

Rejoice with those who rejoice, weep with those who weep. Live in harmony with one another; do not be haughty, but associate with the lowly; never be conceited. Repay no one evil for evil, but take through for what is noble in the sight of all.
Romans 12:15–17

Small groups are really at the heart of any strong church community because the members of the body of Christ are supposed to strengthen one another, and this can only happen in small numbers. Where there are small numbers, there is opportunity for dialogue, debate, vulnerability, support, and growth. The large group, the entire congregation, gathers for worship. Worship is where all the small groups come together to pray and to commune.

The communal worship of the large group is the essential thread that ties the whole community together. You can't have the small groups apart from the large group. That's why it isn't appropriate to go to Bible study or youth group or even do philanthropy without being a regular worshiper.

At the same time, you can't get individualized encouragement and support in a very large group. I know from experience that when you are speaking in front of a group of a hundred people, the only way to position them is in theater-style seating, with the speaker up in front. An intimate discussion is impossible. A presentation to one hundred people is a lecture with a few questions. In a small group, the spacing is intimate, like a small circle. People know each other's names. Everyone has a chance to talk and contribute.

Ideally, small groups are actually small; ten to twelve people is the ideal small group. Some of our small groups are larger than that. The small group is supposed to offer encouragement, empathy, and a sense of accountability. When someone in the small group has a need, the other members are ready to jump in and help.

There is a sense of group identity and, with it, a sense of mutuality and unity. While the small group may have a leader, it doesn't have a hierarchy, and it certainly doesn't have cliques and factions. And even the leader of the small group needs encouragement and support from group members.

Many times in the Bible, we read about Christ seeking help from His disciples. He asked them to see if anyone had any food before the miracle of the feeding of the five thousand (Matt. 14; Mark 6; Luke 9; John 6). He asked them to go and find a donkey for Him to ride on into Jerusalem on Palm Sunday (Matt. 21; Mark 11; Luke 19). He asked them to prepare a room for the Passover meal (Matt. 26; Mark 14; Luke 22).

When He was about to be betrayed, and His soul was sorrowful, Jesus asked His disciples to just watch Him while He prayed (Matt. 26). He didn't ask them to **do** anything, just watch with Him so that He wouldn't feel alone. Many times, the help we offer involves **doing** something. And sometimes it just involves being present. That is encouragement enough.

One specific goal in a small group is that no group member should ever feel alone. Keep tabs on one another. Work together, have fellowship together, and make sure that all group members feel part of the together, that no group member feels alone. And encourage your group leader. By virtue of them being the leader, they may feel alone at times.

The obvious benefit of belonging to a ministry is to have a place to use your talent for one of the church's ministries—the choir is a place for those who sing, Sunday school for those who teach, and so on. Belonging to a group gives you a place to be ministered to—Bible study is a place to learn. The other important, and overlooked/under-utilized benefit of belonging to any group, whether it is a ministry or small group, is that when you are "falling down" in your life, the group is there to pick you up. And when you are doing well in life, you come to the group so that you can pick up someone else who is falling down.

If the community is divided into smaller groups, then these small subsets serve as smaller communities within the larger community, and they help encourage people in a personal way. When hundreds of people gather to worship on Sundays, it is sometimes hard to feel a connection to others. Indeed, we feel a connection to Christ and may even feel that connection with others because others are present. But a ministry or small group will connect us to others who can help support and encourage.

I encourage you to join a ministry or start a small group in the church. Be it the choir, Bible study, or a committee, there are many ministries to choose from. If there is a group that you think the church needs, ask how you can help to implement such a group. And inside of already established groups and ministries, we need to seek to change the paradigm from a group of people that we not only work with, but a group of people that we can also lean on for support, who can lean on us for support as well.

Lord, thank You for the many gifts that You have given us. Thank You for the opportunities to laugh and make memories with special people. Thank You for the many opportunities to enjoy positive and wholesome activities. Lord, be with those who feel alone today and comfort them. Help me to recognize those who need some encouragement or help and always soften my heart so that I not only see a need but that I can step forward and meet it. Comfort me in the times I feel alone, and send people into my life who will encourage and help me as well. Amen.

Encouragement Challenge: Call or text someone from your ministry or small group today and offer words of encouragement!

BE the Church!

So Peter was kept in prison; but earnest prayer for him was made to God by the church.
Acts 12:5

Several years ago, I scheduled a prayer service (Paraklesis) on a random Wednesday night in October. There was no reason in particular other than I looked at the calendar for October, which is a light month for weekday services (we celebrate services every Sunday and also on certain weekdays according to a liturgical calendar) and decided I wanted to have an additional weekday service. I didn't know if anyone would come or if anyone would offer names of people to be prayed for at the service.

Interestingly enough, in the several days before this service, I had several prayer requests from outside of my church community—from a young man in college whose fraternity brother had died by suicide, a young woman who was having an important interview, someone who had been called upon to help a victim of a sexual assault, and a family whose father was having a serious surgery. By the time the service began, I had a list of people to pray for. Surprisingly, there was a large number of people in church who all brought not only names but specific needs to be prayed for.

Just about every week, someone calls me and asks me to pray with them over the phone. I used to actually think this was awkward, as if God couldn't hear prayer over a phone.

Like many people, I'm part of several text groups. In some of those groups, people feel comfortable asking the other group members when they need a prayer. When such a request comes in, within minutes, several texts of encouragement and prayer come for this person.

My friends, this is the work of the church. When there is a need, the church must respond in three ways—first with prayer, second with encouragement, and third with tangible help. And who is the church? The church is the people. When a person has a need, the people must respond with prayer, encouragement, and help. It is not the priest alone who does these things. The church building doesn't do these things. The by-laws of the church do not offer prayers.

I often become discouraged because we obsess about DO-ing church rather than BEING the church. We are good at lighting candles, having food festivals, and arguing about our rights as parishioners. The church, however, is not by-laws, buildings, budgets, and bureaucracy. The church is the people—praying, encouraging, and helping.

I have actually recorded voice memos on my phone of the various people I prayed for who are not from my parish. I have texted them the audio files of these prayers so that people could hear them in their far-flung cities. And then I received messages back saying that these gestures meant a lot. I'm not saying this to brag, so please don't read it that way. Whatever I did didn't change the situations I was praying about. What it did was let people know that they were not alone, that God is watching over them, and the church, the people, are praying for them. This in itself is a powerful thing, the knowledge that one is not alone. This is one of the reasons Christ gave us the church. He said in Matthew 18:20, *"where two or three are gathered in My name, there am I in the midst of them."*

Pray. Encourage. Help. This is what the church is all about. We need to shift the paradigm from "doing church" to "being the church."

Lord, thank You for the gift of the church. Thank You for giving us a place to grow in faith. Help us to include the people of the church community so that no one feels alone. Help us to reach out to those in need. Give us the courage to ask for prayer from others. Give us the courage to answer that call to pray with others, and give us the words to say to offer comfort. Help us to understand what it means to be the church and give us the courage to be the church rather than to just do the church. Lord, be with people who are in urgent need of prayer today—those who grieve the loss of people who have died by suicide, victims of sexual assault, people who are nervous about exams and interviews, and people who are facing serious medical crises. Be with all those who need You. Send ME to those who need You. Bring those who need You into my life. And give me the wisdom, love, and compassion to be the church to them. Amen.

Be the church!

Consumers versus Producers, Cruise Ships versus Battleships

And Jesus came and said to them, "All authority in heaven and on earth has been given to Me. Go therefore and make disciples of all nations, baptizing them in the name of the Father and of the Son and of the Holy Spirit, teaching them to observe all that I have commanded you."
Matthew 28:18–20

Several years ago, I was blessed to go on a four-day cruise with my family. There was no particular program or schedule on the ship. Passengers could eat whenever they wanted, use the pool at all hours, and it was buffet-style meals, so we could eat all we wanted since that had been included in our ticket. The only things on the schedule were docking at ports of call and movies and shows on the ship. What a great concept—pay your fee, enjoy yourself as much as you can, and no responsibilities whatsoever. Wake up and sleep as you will.

A military battleship is the exact opposite of the cruise ship. On the battleship, the objective is not relaxation but a life-and-death mission. Everyone on the crew has a job, everyone must work together, and their ability to do so is not only crucial to a successful mission but also fundamental for their very survival.

The church, in many instances, resembles a cruise ship. The priest becomes something akin to the cruise director with those who help becoming activity coordinators. Much of the work falls under the job description of the paid staff or core volunteers, so there is no responsibility other than church attendance (and for many occasions at that) borne by the members.

The health parish needs to resemble a battleship because the mission of the church is life and death. When members of the community work together, the message of salvation spreads and leads those who are within the community and those outside of it to eternal life. When members of the church community do not work together, when the community resembles a cruise ship rather than a battleship, not only is the work of the church in jeopardy, but so is the salvation of the members of the church who do not spread the good news and the people outside the church who don't hear the message.

People on a cruise ship are relaxed, tanned, and well-fed. Soldiers on a battleship are sleep-deprived, grungy, and edgy. No one would consider time on a battleship to be a vacation.

The life of a church is also not meant to be a vacation. It's life-or-death combat with the evil one. The life of a Christian is also not meant to be a vacation. It is a life-or-death battle for eternal life or eternal condemnation.

In the words of Fr. Aris Metrakos,[50] "There are few things as satisfying as being part of a focused, disciplined, hard-working team that knows its mission, understands and fulfills its responsibilities, is well-trained, and strives constantly to improve its knowledge and skills."

People on a cruise ship are consumers. They consume the food, drink, sun, and fun the cruise line provides. Sailors on the battleship are producers. They work together to protect and defend freedom. There is no one who is along for the ride. Everyone has a job, and everyone's job affects the success or failure of the mission.

If a Christian is to live out his or her role as an apostle, one who helps spread the message of salvation, he or she must identify more with a sailor on a battleship than a tourist on a cruise ship. If a church is to fulfill its mission to baptize all nations and to seek and save the lost, then it must resemble a battleship, not a cruise ship.

When a soldier completes basic training, they are given a commission, a specific job in the military—whether it is on a ship, plane, base, or on the ground; whether it is as a fighter pilot or aircraft mechanic. Everyone gets a commission, and every job must be done well for the military to succeed.

When each person is baptized into the body of Christ, they also receive a "commission." It is called the Great Commission. This commission was first given to the apostles by Jesus Christ. And this commission is to "go and make disciples of all nations, baptizing them in the name of the Father and of the Son and of the Holy Spirit, teaching them to observe all that I have commanded you" (Matt. 28:19–20). This is not a great idea or suggestion. It is a great commission. And it is a commission given to every Christian and every church. We are soldiers in the army of God. We are sailors on a battleship. We are to be producers of disciples. The mission is a matter of life and death for all of us.

Lord, thank You for dying on the cross for me. Thank You for opening for me a path to paradise. Help me to remember that I am a soldier in Your army, that my role is to spread Your saving message to all people, both by my words and actions. Help me to recognize that this is an awesome responsibility, but that You have given me gifts and tools that I can use to be successful in fulfilling it. Take away from me any tendency to be lazy or complacent when it comes to my spirituality. Help me to have a sense of purpose and urgency in all that I am doing. Protect me in the "fight" and lead me to salvation. Help me by Your grace to lead others to You as well. Amen.

The church is a battleship, not a cruise ship. Its members are sailors, not vacationers. Our primary role is to be producers, not consumers. The objective is eternal life for all. The battle is real.

***Much of this reflection was adapted, with permission, from an article entitled "Is Your Parish a Cruise Ship or a Battleship?" by Fr. Aris P. Metrakos, written in 2006.*

THE CHURCH SHOULD BE A SAFE ENVIRONMENT

I appeal to you, brethren, by the name of our Lord Jesus Christ, that all of you agree and that there be no dissensions among you, but that you be united in the same mind and the same judgment.
1 Corinthians 1:10

Churches should be safe environments where we can be vulnerable, not only places where we, ourselves, can feel safe being vulnerable, but places where it is safe to discuss the issues that make us feel vulnerable, the issues we don't feel safe discussing.

Several years ago, our church had a mom's retreat, and even though I'm not a mom, I was invited to the retreat in my role as the parish priest. A dozen moms got together for fellowship, learning, and sharing. There wasn't one mom that day who didn't feel vulnerable, not one who didn't cry or get emotional, and not one who didn't take a benefit away from the experience. We don't have ENOUGH of this in our churches.

At a recent GOYA (teenage youth group) meeting, we discussed the topic of suicide. Yes, that's a heavy topic. I felt vulnerable sharing thoughts. Others felt vulnerable sharing thoughts. People left the meeting grateful for the opportunity to have talked about a subject we don't talk enough about. If we stay away from topics like these in church, where exactly will we deal with them? The fact is, we won't.

Many other topics need addressing, where people need to feel support, encouragement, empathy, and to know that they are not alone in their suffering. If you had a suicidal thought or felt like a failure, where will you take that? To your boss? Your clients? Your students? Your young children? Where do we put the difficult things? The fact is, we don't put them anywhere, which makes us feel inauthentic and fake and begins a vicious cycle that lacks authenticity with both our friends and with our Lord.

No one can force anyone to do anything, I know that. I also know that creating an environment where it is okay to be authentic and vulnerable is something we can all take a part in cultivating, especially in our churches. Most of us who attend a church belong to a small group—not necessarily a Bible study or ministry. Most of us have a small group of friends we sit with at coffee hour each Sunday. We eagerly catch up on the news of the week; we probably all exchange in our share of gossip. Does this small group of friends ever go to a vulnerable topic? Do members ever shed tears? Does anyone feel it is okay to be vulnerable in front of others? Are these small groups fostering authentic relationships or just providing idle chit-chat?

Many people aren't in a small group at church. They sit alone at coffee hour, or they leave church immediately since they have no one to sit with because they've been part of the "worship circle" but haven't been invited to the "fellowship table." Do we make a conscious effort to invite them? Do we even notice? Do we think that is a responsibility we share as Christians and members of a church community?

These are some difficult questions. However, if we want our church to be what Christ intended for the church to be, we have to make authentic relationships an important priority in the life of the community. We have to create environments where it is safe to be vulnerable.

St. Paul wrote his epistles to the early churches, encouraging certain behaviors and gently correcting others. His writings are as applicable to today's church of the twenty-first century as they were to the church of the first century. In 1 Corinthians 1:10, the verse for this reflection, he pleaded that *"all of you agree and that there be no dissensions among you, but that you be united in the same mind and the same judgment."* In almost every service, we pray first for peace, then for the peace of God, and then for peace in the whole world and the unity of all. We pray for the unity of the faith and communion of the Holy Spirit. In other words, we pray for authentic relationships between us and Christ and us and one another. What is the upshot of authentic relationships in our church community? It is what we read in Acts 16:5, *"So the churches were strengthened in the faith and they increased in number daily."*

Lord, thank You for my church community. Remember all the people in my church community who are sick or struggling. Remember all those who don't have anyone. Help me to do my part to make my church community a safe environment, where it is okay to be vulnerable and authentic. Help those around me to foster authentic relationships with each other and with me. May I do the same for them. Amen.

Encouragement Challenge: Think seriously about how you can contribute to creating a safe environment in your church community where people can be vulnerable and grow to be authentic.

Part Sixteen

READ WITH ALL

I adjure you by the Lord that this letter be read to all the brethren.

1 Thessalonians 5:27

The Importance of Scripture

I adjure you by the Lord that this letter be read to all the brethren.
1 Thessalonians 5:27

The last two sections of our study have focused on prayer, which is the most essential practice of the Christian life, and the church, which is the base where we gather to worship and learn as well as a place from which we spread God's Word and work to serve others. This section of our study will be about the spiritual practices of Scripture reading, worship, and the sacramental life. For those who are not Orthodox who are reading, the reflections on the sacraments will be specific to the Orthodox church.

We know that prayer is the essential and preeminent way that we communicate with God. We can pray with others or alone. We can pray anywhere and at any time, for any length of time and for anything.

Reading Scripture is an essential way that we allow God to speak to us. We hear His voice in sermons in church. We may hear His voice coming through the encouragement of others. However, the Bible is a way that we can hear His voice at any time and hear it most completely. A sermon is on a specific passage of Scripture and is heard in church. A word of encouragement requires another person's input. The Bible is something we can pick up at any time and place to hear God's voice.

For many people, the Bible is intimidating. It's so long. We don't know where to start. We may not understand everything we read. If we try to go through the Bible reading from cover to cover, there will be passages and even entire books that may not hold our attention or feel relevant.

There are several ways to read the Bible. One can, of course, read the Bible from cover to cover. One can read a selected book or even a random passage.

The Old Testament contains a lot of history. It begins with the creation of the world, the fall of mankind, and includes the establishment of the Jews as God's chosen people through a covenant with Abraham. It recounts the history of the Jews as they moved to Egypt and then journeyed through the wilderness and settled in the land of Canaan. It recalls stories of battles, judges, priests, and kings. It includes times of prosperity and exile for God's chosen people. And it includes the writings of many prophets who foretold of a coming Messiah that would redeem God's people. The book of Psalms is a collection of poems, songs, laments, and joys that are attributed in large part to David the king. Every emotion comes out in the Psalms. The book of Proverbs is a book where nearly every verse offers some solid advice for life and faith.

The New Testament begins with the four Gospels, which recount the earthly ministry, teachings, miracles, passion, death, and resurrection of Jesus Christ, the Incarnate Son of God. The book of Acts recounts the establishment of the early church in the years following the resurrection. The Epistles are letters from St. Paul, St. James, St. Peter, and St. John to the early church. Most are to specific churches, others to individuals. The New Testament ends with the book of Revelation, which is the vision of heaven seen by St. John the Evangelist.

The message of the Bible is timeless. The history of God's people doesn't change. Our Christian ancestry has its roots all the way back to the covenant with Abraham and back to the creation of the world, for as Genesis 1:27 recalls, "God created man in His own image, in the image of God He created him; male and female He created them." In other words, every person who has ever come into being was created in the image and likeness of God, so we indeed trace our roots as human beings and as Christians all the way back to the creation.

The message of salvation given in word and deed by Jesus Christ is also timeless. Christ walked the earth at a specific time in history. Yet what He did is significant for everyone who has lived in the two thousand years since that time. For as long as there are churches, there will be problems and challenges. In fact, the same problems that challenged the early church are still present in contemporary times. This is why we continue to read the Epistles because their advice is timeless as well.

Everyone should make a plan for how to read the Bible. There are daily readings for the Orthodox church that can be found (and subscribed to) on the website of the Greek Orthodox Archdiocese of America website (www.goarch.org). There are several apps that one can use to read the Bible in one year or hear the Bible as an audio book.

If you've never read the Bible, I suggest you begin with the four Gospels. Read through the Gospels several times so that you have a grasp on the ministry and teachings of Jesus Christ since they are the foundation of the Christian life. The book of Acts almost functions like a fifth Gospel, as it recounts the establishment of the early church. Once you've read through the Gospels and Acts, then proceed with the rest of the New Testament.

As for the Old Testament, begin with Psalm and Proverbs. Then a suggestion is to read one chapter of the Old Testament and one chapter of the New Testament each day. This way, if one reading or the other is tedious and doesn't get your attention, hopefully the other one will. Yes, there are parts of the Bible like Leviticus, Numbers, Deuteronomy, and some of the prophets that are somewhat tedious.

Another helpful hint is to get an annotated Bible, a Bible that has a lot of study notes to help you understand what you are reading.

St. Paul, in 1 Thessalonians 5:27, told those to whom he wrote his letter that it should be read by all. By extension, we are all brethren, as we are all members of the body of Christ. This letter, as well as the rest of Holy Scripture, the Bible, should be read daily by all of us.

Thank You, Lord, for the gift of the Bible, for those who have been inspired by the Holy Spirit to write what they have heard and seen so that not only our history has been preserved but that Your voice speaks through their writings to us today. Kindle in me a desire to read the Scriptures. Help me to understand what I read. Speak to me through these sacred words and open my heart to accept the guidance they offer. Amen.

Encouragement Challenge: Make a habit of reading the Bible every day!

Encouragement from the Bible

For whatever was written in former days was written for our instruction, that by steadfastness and by the encouragement of the Scriptures we might have hope.
Romans 15:4

A couple of years ago, I received an unexpected package in the mail. It was unexpected because it had come from someone I hadn't spoken to in a while. As I opened the package, it was a mason jar filled with thin strips of paper. The lid had a beautiful cross on it. As I took out the pieces of paper, I was surprised to find that each one had a Bible verse on it, and not only that, but my name had also been inserted into each of the Bible verses. Needless to say, I was surprised that someone had taken the time to do all of this. The accompanying letter told me that there were hundreds of verses in the jar and to take out one each day and read it, or to pull out one when I needed some encouragement. To this day, this is one of the most thoughtful gifts I have ever received.

The gesture of putting my name into each verse is actually how we should read the Bible. In a way of speaking, the Bible is God's personal love letter to each of us. First, it is a letter, albeit a very long one. It recounts how God created us to be like Him and how He created us out of love. It talks about how when we fell away from God, God's love made a plan to redeem us. It also relates how that plan came to completion in the person of Jesus Christ and how His salvific work has been built on through the church, beginning two thousand years ago on Pentecost and now continuing through today.

We know that Christ summarized all the commandments of the Old Testament into two—to love God and to love our neighbor. He told us that there is no greater love than to lay down one's life for His friends (John 15:13) and that He then did just that. If we were to summarize the entire Bible in one word, it would be the word love.

The Bible should also be read in a personal way. What does that mean? If one hundred people were to sit in a church and write about what they see, someone will comment on the stained glass windows, someone else will comment on the size of the building, and someone else will notice a spot of the wall that needs repainting. And they'd all be correct. That's because when we look at someone, even if it is the same something, we will all take something a little bit different away from it.

The Bible, in some sense, works in the same way. When we read it with an open heart and a soft soul, God will speak to us through its words. I can't tell you how many times I've read a passage that I have read many times and still take a new thought away from it that I hadn't had before. If a person were to read the Bible and take notes about the things that come to his or her mind, those notes would be the best book one could ever read because it would be the thoughts that God brings to the mind.

Back to this gift, allow me to share a few verses that I randomly selected from the jar. I will write your name in place of mine in the verses. See how these read when you put your own name in them and how encouraging and comforting they are.

> *But now thus says the Lord, He who created you, O Jacob, He who formed you, O Israel: "Fear not, for I have redeemed you (insert your name); I have called you (insert your name) by name, you (insert your name) are mine. When you pass through the waters I will be with you (insert your name); and through the rivers, they shall not overwhelm you (Isa. 43:1–2).*

> *Be strong and of good courage (insert your name); be not frightened, neither be dismayed; for the Lord your God is with you (insert your name) wherever you go (Josh. 1:9).*

> *Hearken to me, O house of Jacob, all the remnant of the house of Israel, who have been borne by me from your birth, carried from the womb; even to your old age I am He, and to gray hairs I will carry you (insert your name). I have made, and I will bear; I will carry and will save (insert your name) (Isa. 46:3–4).*

> *I (insert your name) can do all things in Him Who strengthens me (Phil. 4:13).*

That brings me to the verse of the day, Romans 15:4: *For whatever was written in former days was written for our instruction, that by steadfastness and by the encouragement of the Scriptures we might have hope.* We know that encouragement from those around us builds us up. It can turn a bad day into a good one or a hopeless situation into a more hopeful one. That is the kind of power encouragement has. If this works among peers, imagine how encouragement works from Scriptures. When we can personalize Scripture, it is as if we are receiving encouragement directly from God. This is yet another reason to read the Bible, to receive encouragement.

Lord, thank You for loving me more than I deserve and more than I know how to love others and even myself. Thank You for the love letter that is the Bible that speaks to each of us in such a personal way. Help me to read its message and accept it as Your personal encouragement and guidance for my life. Guide me to use it to help encourage others in their lives. Amen.

Encouragement Challenge: Learn to read the Bible in a personal way. Put your name in passages. Hear God's voice calling you through Scripture because that's exactly what He does!

**Dedicated to Lygia Karagiozis, with gratitude for that gift which I still use to this day when I need spiritual encouragement.

Getting the Full Experience—Worship

Therefore, let us be grateful for receiving a kingdom that cannot be shaken, and thus let us offer to God acceptable worship, with reverence and awe.
Hebrews 12:28

The saying goes, "You only get out of something what you put into it." This applies to many things in life and applies specifically to worship. Our worship experience in the church is meant to be a "work of the people." In fact, that is the meaning of the word liturgy. The Divine Liturgy in the Orthodox church is meant to be an empowering and encouraging exercise. We are encouraged and prompted through the words of the service to both sing and do actions that bring us closer to Christ.

One of the most frequent lines of the services is the response, "Lord, have mercy." Mercy means to give someone something they don't deserve. In asking the Lord to have mercy on us, we are asking for Him to bless us with many things, even things we don't deserve. We pray for peace, safety, our church, and those who are in the church. The priest offers the petitions. The people offer the responses. Do you respond, or do you stand stoically disconnected?

At a birthday party, when everyone sings, "Happy Birthday" to the guest of honor, we all sing, whether we have a good voice or not. This is a moment of joy. No one is stoically silent. In worship, WE are the guests of honor. Christ is the host of the gathering, and WE are the guests. We sing not only to honor Him, but to also honor ourselves and one another because even if you don't need the mercy of the Lord regarding a particular petition, there is undoubtedly someone in the church who does. So, we sing for them.

Proper worship begins with getting to church on time. The habit of some people to come casually late to church affects their experience and the experience of the community as a whole. The opening line of the liturgy says, "Blessed is the Kingdom . . . NOW and forever and to the ages of ages." This means that in the Divine Liturgy, the kingdom of God is present in the here and now. It is not a far-off destination but a present reality. When that call is made to begin the Divine Liturgy, the entire community should be there to enter together.

"Let us love one another so that with one mind we may confess."[51] "Let us lift up our hearts."[52] "Let us give thanks to the Lord."[53] "Remember those whom each of us calls to mind."[54] "And grant that with one voice and one heart we may glorify and praise Your most honorable and majestic name."[55] "And make us worthy, Master, with confidence and without fear of condemnation."[56] These lines should prompt our bodies (lifting up our hands as well as our hearts when we hear, "let us lift up our hearts") and souls to action. Worshiping is an act of empowerment and encouragement for us. But you only get out of worship what you put into it.

This Sunday, when you go to church, come on time, sing, participate, get the full experience, and encourage others to do the same. For as we read in Hebrews 12:28, the acceptable worship we offer to God is when we come with reverence and awe, and also when we come with joy, when we offer the best version of ourselves in our worship of God.

Lord, thank You for the gift of worship. Thank You for this service which encapsulates everything I need in my life. Inspire my heart and mind so that I come to worship with a greater and greater sense of understanding. Open my lips that I may sing Your praises in worship. Bring me to Your temple continually with a greater sense of joy. And during the week, keep that joy alive in me. Amen.

Encouragement Challenge: Plan to sing in church next Sunday and encourage others to do the same.

The Divine Fellowship—Holy Communion

In the year that King Uzziah died, I saw the Lord sitting upon a throne, high and lifted up; and His train filled the temple. Above Him stood the Seraphim; each had six wings: with two he covered his face, and with two he covered his feet, and with two he flew. And one called to another and said: "Holy, holy, holy is the Lord of hosts; the whole earth is full of His glory." And the foundations of the thresholds shook at the voice of him who called, and the house was filled with smoke. And I said: "Woe is me! For I am lost; for I am a man of unclean lips, and I dwell in the midst of a people of unclean lip; for my eyes have seen the King, the Lord of hosts!" Then flew one of the Seraphim to me, having in his hand a burning coal which he had taken with tongs from the altar. And he touched my mouth, and said: "Behold, this has touched your lips; your guilt is taken away, and your sin forgiven."
Isaiah 6:1–7

I'm always looking for practical ways to help others understand Scripture and theology. In our church, we speak of Holy Communion as a way that we touch Christ and a way that Christ touches us. While preparing to teach a lesson on this at summer camp, I had a thought go through my mind that I never had before, and I used it as an icebreaker to introduce this idea of Holy Communion being a place where we touch Christ, and He touches us. (This is why we continually read the same passages of Scripture and meditate on the same things because each time we do, God sends us a different message. That doesn't mean a cursory reading. That may not accomplish much of anything, but a careful reflection often results in seeing something we never saw before.)

I walked into the cabin to teach the morning Orthodox Life class However, before doing anything, I asked people how they were feeling. Some said they were tired, some still felt some stress even though they weren't at home, some were anxious about the day, and so on. I told everyone to get up and give a hug to the other people who were in the room. The people were all cabin mates and friends, so this was something they got excited about. After two minutes, everyone sat down. I asked how everyone felt. Without exception, everyone felt good. That's the power of physical touch. That's why studies on prisoners who are held in solitary confinement shows significant mental anguish because they have no "touch" in their lives. For those people in the cabin, they were still tired, perhaps some were still anxious, but that hug brought some renewed energy, confidence, and comfort.

We have all experienced the warmth of the sun. We can't look directly into the sun for more than a second or two. It is powerful and blinding. If we traveled in a spaceship toward the sun, we would burn up. We can't experience the essence of the sun. But we can experience the energy of the sun. We can enjoy its warmth. Even with that, we have to be careful to use sunscreen if we are out in the sun for too long.

Christ gave us a way to experience Him in a way that we can handle. We can't handle the essence of God. If Christ walked into a room, as much as we'd like to think we'd run and embrace Him, most likely we'd duck and cover. Holy Communion gives us a way to experience Christ in a way that we can handle.

The verses from Isaiah 6:1–7 foreshadow the Eucharist, how Christ is like a live coal that touches our mouths but does not burn us. Rather, it should warm us, reassure us, comfort us, and encourage us. Just like the exercise with the hugs, the Eucharist is not a cure-all for every problem we have. It won't get someone a job or do better on a test. Rather, the Eucharist provides divine encouragement to keep going through life, on the way to everlasting life. In 1 Corinthians 11:26, St. Paul writes regarding the Eucharist, "For as often as you eat this bread and drink the cup, you proclaim the Lord's death until He comes." The Eucharist helps us to remember what Christ did for us. It also helps us to remember where we are going. Our end point is not a job, paycheck, or even friendship. Our end point is salvation in the kingdom of God.

We know when we are not encouraged, we become indifferent if not saddened. When we frequently partake of the Eucharist, it should provide some spiritual encouragement that will lead to spiritual confidence, which is what is needed to, in the words of 1 Timothy 6:12, "fight the good fight of the faith; take hold of the eternal life to which you were called."

Lord, thank You for the gift of the church and the gift of the Holy Eucharist. Thank you for giving us Yourself as a means of spiritual sustenance. Thank You for giving us a community in which to grow closer to You. Help me to commit myself more and more to You in faith each day. Help me to inspire others to be more committed in theirs. Amen.

Encouragement Challenge: Receive Holy Communion frequently for spiritual sustenance, spiritual encouragement, and an opportunity to touch Christ and for Him to touch you!

Confession as Encouragement

And if he has committed sins, he will be forgiven. Therefore, confess your sins to one another and pray for one another, that you may be healed. The prayer of a righteous man has great power in its effects.
James 5:15–16

I bet you've never thought of confession as a form of encouragement. The thought of going is so discouraging for some people that they rarely, if ever, go for this sacrament. As we're discussing encouragement and the encouraging aspects of our faith, I want to attach the word encouragement to the sacrament of confession.

When Christ commissioned His apostles to establish the early church, He knew that to be a faithful Christian would be difficult. He knew that despite people's best efforts and intentions, they would still fall through sin daily. He knew that this would discourage some from continuing on in the Christian journey. After all, when we sin a lot, we feel like God is far away and that we don't deserve His love. We carry a weight of shame, and it is hard to feel love when one is burdened by the weight of shame.

In John 20:21–23, Jesus said to His disciples: *"Peace be with you. As the Father has sent Me, even so I send you." And when He had said this, He breathed on them, and said to them, "Receive the Holy Spirit. If you forgive the sins of any they are forgiven; if you retain the sins of any, they are retained."* With this, He gave to them a gift and responsibility to loose and forgive sins.

Speaking now not as a priest but as a struggling Orthodox Christian (who happens to be a priest), I am really glad that our church has a mechanism by which I can be loosed of sin and the associated feelings of guilt and discouragement. Not only do I hear confessions as an Orthodox priest, but I also go to confession as an Orthodox Christian. I don't go to feel bad. I go to feel good, cleansed, renewed, and hear what is among the most encouraging things a person can hear: *"Have no further anxiety about the things you have confessed; go in peace. The grace of the Holy Spirit through my unworthy person has loosened and forgiven your sins."*

I can't honestly say that I look forward to going to confession. I actually still get nervous every time I go. It's no fun to own up to sins. Actually, sometimes I feel embarrassed and ashamed.

But when I finish, the priest offers the prayer, and I hear those words, *"go in peace,"* that God still loves me, it always makes me glad that I went. It always makes me feel encouraged and empowered. It is like God saying to me, "I know what you've done, and I still love you." Or as I once heard in a sermon, "I've given God a million reasons not to love me. None of them changed His mind."

Hand in hand with confession of our sins is repentance, a plan to change our sinful ways. We may not always be successful in keeping the plan, which is why we will need to confess and repent throughout our lives. However, we leave confession with an intention to repent of our sins. And God leaves with us, telling us not to worry about what we confessed but to go in peace as we strive for repentance.

Our sins are not forgiven by a priest. They are forgiven by the grace of the Holy Spirit. However, the priests in the Orthodox church are empowered by the Holy Spirit to listen to confession and offer the prayer of absolution, the words of encouragement that God still loves us despite our sins, and that whatever we have done can be washed away by His grace and mercy. What could be more encouraging than that! So, when you need some spiritual encouragement because you are feeling guilty and discouraged over your sins, contact a priest and go to confession.

Lord, thank You for the many gifts that You have given us. Thank You for the church You have given us as a spiritual home. Thank You for the sacraments that give us glimpses into heaven and sustain us through our life journeys. And thank You for the sacrament of confession that You have given us to encourage us when we have fallen through sin. Help me to always have the courage to come for this sacrament. Lead me to sincere repentance. And help me to feel encouraged through this sacrament that not only are my sins forgiven, but that You also still love me as one of Your children. Empower me through this sacrament to live a more focused and committed Christian life. Amen.

Encouragement Challenge: When you need some spiritual encouragement, schedule an appointment for confession!

The Sacraments

He appointed the priests to their offices and encouraged them in the service of the house of the Lord.
2 Chronicles 35:2

The dictionary defines encouragement as "to inspire with courage, spirit or hope."[57] The church provides encouragement through worship, prayer, and the sacraments. However, the key ingredient for encouragement is that it can only occur in the context of a community. There is no encouragement outside of community. You need at least two people for encouragement to happen—the one being encouraged and the encourager.

The church is here to primarily offer encouragement to us as we fulfill our purpose (to glorify God) on the way to our destiny (His awesome judgment seat). It helps us to remember where we came from and helps us to remain focused on the good and on God. When life gets hard and we just want to quit, the church community is supposed to be our "pick me up" so that we can continue.

The sacraments and services of the church help provide encouragement in all of life's important moments. When a new life comes into the world and we baptize a child, the baptism is done in the context of the community. The community joins together to pray for the life of that child. We have a tradition of a sponsor at a baptism—this person (or people) is supposed to offer spiritual encouragement to both the child and his/her parents through his/her life. Unfortunately, many sponsors do not fulfill that role, but that is the intended role of the sponsor.

Weddings also occur in the context of community. Family and friends come together to pray for and encourage the couple getting married. A sponsor is also part of the marriage sacrament. The role of the sponsor is to encourage and model good marriage for the couple. That is why (unfortunately, we do not always practice this tradition) the sponsor is traditionally an older couple who can mentor and encourage the younger couple.

A funeral is not a sacrament, but it marks the end of earthly life and also occurs in the context of community. The purpose of the funeral is actually encouragement. We are encouraged to remember that there is a life after death, and we are encouraged to prepare for that life for ourselves. The presence of others provides comfort and encouragement so that those who are mourning know that they are not alone.

The next time you attend a baptism, wedding, funeral, memorial service, or any other service that marks one of life's milestones for someone else, go not just to attend but to encourage. And if you have served as a godparent or sponsor at a wedding, stay in touch with your godchild or Koumbari (people whose wedding you sponsored) and offer regular encouragement to them.

Lord, thank You for the gift of the sacraments of the church. Help me to fulfill my baptismal pledge to continually grow in my faith and keep my baptismal garment spotless and pure. Inspire me to encourage others to do the same. Open my eyes and heart to be an encourager at important moments of other people's lives—whether it is joy or sorrow, use me as an encourager. And when I come to one of my important moments, surround me with people who will encourage me as well. Amen.

The opportunities to encourage both inside and outside of a church community seem like they are limitless. Any milestone, whether happy or sad, can be an opportunity to offer encouragement!

Part Seventeen

THE GRACE OF OUR LORD

The grace of our Lord Jesus Christ be with you.

1 Thessalonians 5:28

What Is Grace?

For by grace you have been saved through faith; and this is not your own doing, it is the gift of God—not because of works, lest any man should boast. For we are His workmanship, created in Christ Jesus for good works, which God prepared beforehand, that we should walk in them.
Ephesians 2:8–10

The last verse of this encouragement chapter from 1 Thessalonians 5 introduces us to the word grace. St. Paul tells us in Ephesians 2:8, "For by grace you have been saved through faith, and this is not your own doing, it is the gift of God, not because of works, lest any man should boast." So grace is something that comes from God. It is a gift, not entitlement. It is something that He offers us, not something we can earn. It is something that we need on top of faith and works.

There are several ways to understand grace.

One is to take a cup, some rocks, and some water. The cup is a structure that holds something. The cup is useful when it is filled. An empty cup is useless. The cup represents our faith. It is the structure of what we believe. If there are no works to compliment the faith, then the faith is empty, or as St. Paul writes in James 2:17, "So faith by itself, if it has no works, is dead."

The rocks represent the works that we do in our life. If we do works for the sake of works, the ultimate beneficiary of our work is ourselves, which is narcissism. Rocks poured out on a table have no structure and no point. When the rocks are put into the cup, they have some order to them. Similarly, when we combine our faith with works, our cup of faith starts to fill.

Fill the cup with rocks, and there will still be empty spaces. This is where grace comes in. Grace is like taking water and pouring it over the rocks. Once the water gets to the top of the cup, the cup is truly full. Grace fills the empty spaces. It fills what is empty in the cup and completes what is lacking in our lives. We need faith, works, and grace to get to salvation.

Another way of defining grace is to say that grace takes what is ordinary and makes it extraordinary. We take ordinary people, and through the sacrament of marriage, they become a family, they become what they were not before, and they become extraordinary. We take ordinary substances of bread and wine, things we can buy, things we can make, and we call the grace of the Holy Spirit on them, and they become extraordinary; they become the Body and Blood of Christ. We take ordinary people, intertwined in our sinful habits, and put the extraordinary Eucharist into them. And then we are supposed to be extraordinary.

Grace also comes through prayer. We bend our knees before God and ask Him to give us wisdom or patience to to help us come at a problem and find resolution. These answers to prayer, these times when an ordinary (but big) problem has an extraordinary resolution, this is God's hand at play. God's grace calls us to be extraordinary. The challenge is for us to react to it in the extraordinary way we are called to respond rather than receiving what is extraordinary and remaining content with being ordinary.

In signing off on this letter, saying, "The grace of our Lord Jesus Christ be with you" (1 Thess. 5:28), St. Paul is praying for the Thessalonians of the first century, and by extension, for the Christians of the twenty-first century, that he hopes we experience God's extraordinary grace, we allow it to transform us from ordinary into extraordinary, it completes what is lacking in us, and it fills the empty spaces in our cup of faith that our works cannot fill. It is God's grace that allows us to walk through this life, and it is ultimately God's grace that will get us to everlasting life.

Lord, thank You for the gift of grace and for every time that something ordinary in my life has become extraordinary, for every time that an empty space has felt full. Please continually send Your grace on me so that whatever is lacking in me may be completed, and whatever is empty will feel full. Help me to receive Your grace with a motivation to be extraordinary. Help me not be content with being ordinary but to meet your extraordinary grace with extraordinary faith and extraordinary effort. By Your grace, lead me to salvation. Strengthen my faith, bless my work, give me Your grace in this life, and place it upon me at the end of my life so that I may enter by Your grace enter into Your heavenly kingdom. Amen.

Encouragement Challenge: Be extraordinary in your Christianity today—in faith, works, kindness, generosity, patience, forgiveness, and love.

Let Him Lead

Trust in the Lord with all your heart, and do not rely on your own insight.
Proverbs 3:5

One very effective team-building activity is called a trust walk. This involves two people being paired together. One of the two is blindfolded and is the follower. The other one can see and is the leader. This activity can be done in a variety of ways—It can be done where the leader and follower may speak to one another but are not able to touch one another. It can be done where they are allowed to touch one another but not speak. They go on a walk together. This walk might be a walk on flat ground, or there may be obstacles to get around, under or over. After ten minutes or so, the partners usually switch roles so that both have a turn leading and following.

The activity is then debriefed. Participants are asked which is easier in this activity, being the leader or being the follower? Some will say it is easier to be the leader. These will admit that it is hard to cede control to someone else. They prefer being in charge, being in control, and knowing where they are going at all times. Some will say it is easier to be the follower. These will say that the leader has more responsibility, and it is easier in this activity to just follow along and not have to think.

In life, we actually rotate between the two roles. We follow the directions of parents, teachers, bosses, the law, and many more. We lead as parents, in work situations, as coaches, and many more. As Christians, we are followers of Christ (be disciples). We are also supposed to lead others to Christ (be apostles).

Let's focus, however, on our role as followers of Christ. If we are the followers, He is the leader. I once saw a bumper sticker that read, "God is my co-pilot." The problem with that is that in an airplane, the pilot is in charge, and the co-pilot is subordinate. The pilot can overrule the co-pilot. Having God as co-pilot means that we can overrule Him. God is supposed to be at the wheel of our lives, not in the passenger seat, back seat, or in the trunk.

Going back to the trust walk, we do this as part of our summer camp program. We do it during staff training in many years as well. We each take the role as leader and follower. One year, when I was in the role of the follower, there were several thoughts on my mind. The first thought was actually relaxation and ceding control. I knew the person I was paired with. I trusted that person. I knew ostensibly that I would not die or get seriously hurt doing this exercise. While I did not exactly know where we were going or how we were going to get there, I found that once I had allowed myself to cede control, it was actually really relaxing. The second thought was enjoying being "off." I spend so much of my time leading and being "on" as far as having responsibilities that having no responsibilities for a few minutes was also a big positive. The third thought was a focus on being present in the moment. I conceded that not only could I not see, I also couldn't do anything else in the moment other than follow. All the other responsibilities of directing camp or leading a parish or being a dad, all the roles that I have couldn't be fulfilled in that moment. So rather than stressing about what I couldn't be doing, I embraced what I was doing, which was just following. And the fourth thought was that this exercise is a metaphor for life and how there are many times when we have to just back off of our own thought and just LET HIM LEAD US!

We know the God we are paired with in life. He is not a stranger. He is not mean. We should trust in God. This is not a blind trust. A blind trust would be being paired with someone you don't know in a place you've never been. We don't follow God blindly. We follow Him with the knowledge that many others have followed Him, and it has enhanced their life and led them to eternal life. We follow based on our own experience of Him. Second, following God should be relaxing. Rather than wondering, "What must I do to follow God or get to heaven?" He's laid the path out plain and simple. We are to love Him. We are to love one another. When we lead with love, we will not go off the path. We only veer off the path when we do not lead with love. Third, following God involves being in the present. We have to be present with God. He is omnipresent with us. He never leaves our side. Yet, rather than walking hand in hand with Him, we put Him in the background, we listen to other voices, and our own voice becomes louder than His. Being present with God requires us acknowledging that God is present with us. Fourth, we have to let Him lead. There are two ways to get hurt on a trust walk. One is if you are paired with an irresponsible leader. And the other is if you do not cede control and overrule the leader, going your own way. We know that God does not hurt us. We know that God is not irresponsible. We also know that the path is not easy, and the route to where we are going is unknown. I do not know, for example, how long I will live, whether I will move, where my child will end up, or whether I will get sick at a young age. I don't know any of these things. What I do know is that I believe in God. I believe that if He leads and I keep on walking, I will end up in the kingdom of heaven. Do I believe that all the time? Yes. Do I follow His lead and not try to go my own way all the time? No, I don't. Every time we sin, it's like saying we know better than the leader.

Going back to the experience of the trust walk, some people have a hard time relaxing and doing this. It becomes easier if you have a good leader, if you cede control, and if you can get out of your own head that you will get hurt and just "go with it." There are times I have a hard time relaxing in being a Christian. It seems like the walk goes on forever, the terrain isn't easy, or I'm tired and want to stop walking. There are times when I'm not satisfied with how life is going, wondering where God is leading me or why He had led me to a certain point. There are times when I struggle to feel His hand holding mine and wonder if I'm just wandering around aimlessly. This is where faith comes in and also prayer. The prayer is to ask God for the strength to keep walking. The faith is when we just "go with it" and let go and let God do the leading.

Lord, teach me the way I should be walking. Help me to cede control and trust You in the times I want to do my own thing. Help me to keep walking in the times the path feels long or scary. Help me to always feel Your hand holding mine. Lord, I do not know at all times where the path is taking me. But I will let go and let You lead. Amen.

Encouragement Challenge: Let go and let God lead!

**Dedicated to the clergy, staff and campers of St. Stephen's Summer Camp of the Greek Orthodox Metropolis of Atlanta.

God Is Rooting for Us

I write this to you who believe in the name of the Son of God, that you may know that you have eternal life. And this is the confidence which we have in Him, that if we ask anything according to His will, He hears us.
1 John 5: 13-14

I mentioned earlier in this book that teachers have different schools of thought when it comes to students and their grades. There are teachers who tell their students, "Everyone starts with a zero and has to move their way up." And there are other teachers who say, "Everyone starts with one hundred, and it's yours to lose." I personally prefer the second kind of teacher mentioned here, the kind of teacher that wants you to succeed and starts everyone off by telling them that success is theirs to lose.

In many ways, God works in the same manner. God is rooting for us. He wants us to attain salvation. He wants us in His kingdom. He wants us to follow after Him. He wants that so much that He was willing to die for us for that to happen.

There are many verses of the Bible that point out God's role as our cheerleader and encourager. He wants us to feel confident about following Him, about where the journey is leading us, and even about the journey to get there.

In 1 John 5:14, John writes, "and this is the confidence which we have in Him, that if we ask anything according to His will, He hears us." If we spend our lives asking for God's mercy and asking to inherit His kingdom, we should have confidence that He will answer that prayer. The Bible is a book written to boost our confidence. Prayer builds us up; it is not meant to tear us down. It is the same thing with worship. Even when it seems like the whole world is against us, God is still rooting for us. We've already written about grace completing that which is lacking in us. On the day when we are so tired and down that it takes energy to move in any direction, it's then that we need to remember the words of Romans 8:31, where St. Paul writes, "If God is for us, who is against us?" And continuing on in Romans 8:38–39, he writes, "For I am sure that neither death, nor life, nor angels, nor principalities, nor things present, nor things to come, nor powers, nor height, nor depth, nor anything else in all creation, will be able to separate us from the love of God in Christ Jesus our Lord." By extension, not having money, fame, possessions, or a college degree can separate us from the love of God. Neither can a divorce, criminal record, bad grade on a test, or getting fired from a job. Yes, all of these things have human consequences. There are definitely things that will keep us from getting a job or staying married, but there is nothing that can separate us from the love of God. He is rooting for us.

Here are some other encouraging verses from the Bible:

> Be strong and of good courage. Do not be afraid or dismayed before the King of Assyria and all the horde that is with him; for there is one greater with us than with him. With him is an arm of flesh; but with us is the Lord our God, to help us and to fight our battles (2 Chron. 32:7–8).

In other words, there is no greater ally than the Lord.

Psalm 20:7 reads:

> Some boast of chariots and some of horses; but we boast of the name of the Lord our God.

There may be people who boast about their resume, possessions, or pedigree. None of these things have much meaning if one cannot boast about a relationship with God. If one has a relationship with God but is lacking in other areas, there is consolation that at the end of life, all that will have mattered is the relationship we have with God.

Another source of comfort is reading how God has called people, in the Bible and throughout history, who were not educated or even faithful, and how He called them anyway, in their state of sinfulness and failure. Simon Peter is an example. In Luke 5, we read of how Jesus encountered Simon Peter at the fishing dock. Simon was a fisherman. Jesus came aboard Peter's boat and asked him to put down the net to catch fish. Peter told Jesus that he and his partners had worked all night but had caught no fish. At Jesus's word, though, they put down the nets. When they did so, they caught so many fish that their nets were breaking.

> When Simon Peter saw it, he fell down at Jesus' knees, saying, "Depart from me, for I am a sinful man, O Lord." For he was astonished, and all that were with him, at the catch of fish which they had taken; and so also were James and John, sons of Zebedee, who were partners with Simon. And Jesus said to Simon, "Do not be afraid; henceforth, you will be catching men" (Luke 5:8–10).

Jesus called Peter. Jesus wanted Peter, even in his state of sinfulness as well a professional failure. Jesus wanted James and John, Peter's partners in professional failure. Jesus didn't care about their background. He saw their potential.

Likewise, Jesus wants us. He doesn't care how much we've failed in the past. He sees our potential. He is all about our future, not our past. This is what His grace does for us. It heals our past and inspires our future if we just accept it. It doesn't heal the past for us to have a failed future. It heals our past so that we can work toward a better future.

Lord, thank You for accepting me in my sinfulness. Thank You for giving me Your grace, even though I do not deserve it. Help me to remember in those times I feel alone that You are rooting for me. Help me to remember in the times when I am bogged down by past failures that You care more about my future than my past. Help me to remember in those times when I feel invisible that You see me, and You see the good in me. Help me to see the good in myself and to use that goodness for Your glory. Amen.

God is rooting for us! God is rooting for you!

Easy to Entreat, Easy to Forgive

> *As far as the east is from the west, so far does He remove our transgressions from us . . . But the steadfast love of the Lord is from everlasting to everlasting upon those who fear Him, and His righteousness to children's children, to those who keep His covenant and remember to do His commandments.*
> Psalm 103:12, 17–18

I saw a meme recently, which said, "I've given God a million reasons not to love me. None of them have changed His mind." If we really think about how many times we sin against God, we'd probably wonder why God would still love us. Because God is full of mercy and compassion, He still loves us despite all of the sins we commit against Him and against one another.

The Bible is full of examples of God's grace and mercy extended toward us. One example comes from Psalm 103. Psalm 103:12 reads, "As far as the east is from the west, so far does He remove our transgressions from us." We've all had the experience of looking over the horizon, which stretches out farther than the eye can see. On top of a mountain on a clear day, we might be able to see a hundred miles in the distance. Looking around in a complete circle, we might see an area of 400 square miles in total. This view would be majestic and incredible by itself. And yet, even 400 square miles (which is a lot of land) is a fraction of the land on the earth. Imagine looking at 400 square miles of God's mercy, grace, and forgiveness. That would be amazing, and yet it is still a drop in the bucket of how much God has of these things for us.

Not only is God easy when it comes to forgiveness, but He is also easy when it comes to entreating Him, to speaking with Him. We don't have to make an appointment to speak with Him. We can speak to Him at anytime, anywhere. We don't need to feel bad if we haven't spoken to Him in a while. He isn't going to chastise us and make us feel guilty. He isn't going to demand, "Where have you been?" God will embrace us in the same way the father embraced the prodigal son. Even though the son had wasted half of the father's wealth and returned in shame, the father still received him with joy, grace, and mercy.

As God is easy to entreat and forgive, we should be the same. Many of us have people we know that if we see their name come up on the phone, our blood pressure goes up. In some relationships, the question, "Can we talk?" strikes a chord of fear because "Can we talk?" means an argument will probably ensue. Perhaps there are people out there who don't care if they strike fear in others. Most of us do care. We would be absolutely mortified if someone's blood pressure went up because they saw our name come up on their phone.

"The steadfast love of the Lord is from everlasting to everlasting" (Ps. 103: 17). That means that it has no beginning and no end, and thus it also has no conditions. If we are really to imitate the Lord, then we must learn to love without beginning or end and without conditions. We must offer forgiveness in the same way. We must offer grace in the same way. This is a pretty tall order—to be limitless with love, forgiveness, and grace. Oftentimes, when we are severely wounded, we feel entitled to withhold love, forgiveness, and grace until the person who has offended us has earned these back to our satisfaction.

We are reminded in Psalm 130:304, that "If Thou, O Lord, shouldst mark iniquities, Lord who could stand? But there is forgiveness with Thee." In any relationship that lasts for a significant period, there will be bumps in the road, many of them. Without forgiveness, no serious relationship would be possible. It would be impossible to love a spouse, parent, child, or good friend if there is no forgiveness. In a close relationship, iniquities can pile up quickly. So we need to be easy to entreat and forgive if we hope to have lasting and loving relationships.

To become better encouragers, we need to follow the example of the Lord—to be easy to entreat and forgive. The grace we show toward others ideally is like the grace of God, "as far as the east is from the west." If we are expecting the grace of Jesus Christ to be with us, as St. Paul wishes for it to be in 1 Thessalonians 5:28, then we need to gift that kind of grace amongst ourselves.

Lord thank You for the gift of forgiveness that You offer so easily and freely to everyone. If You were to mark my sins, I would have no chance before You. Thank You for meeting my sin with Your mercy. Help me to do the same for others. As it is so easy to entreat You, may I also make it easy for others to entreat me. Thank You for the gift of Your grace and mercy, which I do not deserve. Help me to be generous with grace and mercy toward others, even those who have hurt me deeply. Amen.

Encouragement Challenge: The Lord is easy to entreat and forgive us. May we offer the same grace to each other.

Authenticity Starts with Christ

> *In this you rejoice, though now for a little while you may have to suffer various trials, so that the genuineness of your faith, more precious than gold which though perishable is tested by fire, may redound to praise and glory and honor at the revelation of Jesus Christ. Without having seen Him you love Him; though you do not now see Him you believe in Him and rejoice with unutterable and exalted joy.*
> 1 Peter 1:6–8

Throughout this study on encouragement, we have used the word authentic. Authentic means "genuine," "real," and "true." [58] Authenticity and encouragement go hand in hand. Placating someone is not encouragement. Encouragement needs to come from a place that is authentic, genuine, real, and honest. To be authentic with others, one has to be honest with himself or herself. Before one can be honest with oneself, one has to be authentic and honest with God. One reason why we have a hard time being authentic with others is because we are not authentic with God. One reason why we have a hard time extending unconditional love to others is that we don't understand the unconditional love of God. Or maybe we understand the unconditional love of God and just don't feel worthy of it.

I once asked a group of teenagers how many of them liked peer pressure. The answer was NONE of them liked peer pressure. I asked them how prevalent peer pressure was in their lives, and they all said it was something they dealt with almost daily. I then challenged them that if peer pressure is something that everyone has to deal with and no one likes, why couldn't they collectively work to eliminate it? If only half of them dealt with it or if half of them liked it, that would be one thing. However, if all of them deal with it, and none of them like it, it would seem that they could find a way to collectively eliminate it.

We all crave, or at least I would like to think we all crave, authentic relationships. Yet, there are significant challenges to making them, the greatest of which is you need other people who are also interested in having authentic relationships. As they say, it takes two to tango.

Before looking at authentic relationships with others, start with your relationship with Christ. He desires an authentic relationship with you and me. After all, what could be more authentic than to be willing to die for someone and then going through with it? There was nothing pretentious there. He laid down His life for us. He didn't just inconvenience Himself for a day or two or dig into his wallet and take out some money. He didn't just do us a favor or offer something out of guilt. He lovingly laid down His life for us. He wants an authentic relationship with us. He desires that authentic relationship from the garden of Eden, which is why, through His death on the cross and resurrection, He opened up a path back to that first relationship we enjoyed. He has opened the path; all we have to do is follow it.

If the two greatest commandments are loving God and loving our neighbor, the path to an authentic relationship begins with these two things. In loving God, in creating an authentic relationship with Christ, it will lead to more authentic relationships with our neighbors. In establishing more authentic relationships with our neighbors, it will lead us to a more authentic relationship with Christ.

Let's start with Christ—to make an authentic relationship takes time. So, are we investing time with Christ? Invest time speaking to Christ through prayer and listening through Scripture. If I say that God has "spoken to me" through prayer and the Scriptures, some might say that it is arrogant to think that God speaks to ME, to which I would say, "God speaks to all of us; the challenge is, are we listening?" In prayer, we don't just "give God His due," but we open our hearts to God. We cry to Him, take our pains to Him, take our joys to Him, involve Him in our decisions, obey Him, and many times surrender to Him, to His will, even when it contradicts ours.

What made the relationship of Adam and Eve become inauthentic with God is that they stopped loving Him and started following their own desires. They stopped trusting Him and went their own way. The foundation of an authentic relationship with Christ is based on love and trust. This is the same way we lay a foundation with others.

Encouragement and authenticity go hand in hand in building relationships with others. Encouragement can help to build or solidify a relationship. Authenticity will inspire encouragement.

When we are authentic with God, we will feel encouraged in the relationship. When others encourage us toward God, it will be easier to be authentic. God's grace comes in all kinds of ways. His grace gives us the courage to be authentic with Him and others. His grace strengthens relationships that are already authentic.

Lord, thank You for the gift of another day. Thank You for the gift of offering another prayer. Lord, fill me with thanksgiving for blessings, large and small. Help me to build an authentic relationship with You and others. Help me to have the courage to take down walls of pretense and pride and replace them with honesty and humility. Amen.

Encouragement Challenge: If an authentic relationship is something we all want, why can't we all agree to guide our relationships that way? A good first step is going to Christ, building our relationship with Him, and asking Him to help authenticate our relationships with one another.

If I Could Be like Christ

Jesus said, "Come to Me, all who labor and are heavy laden, and I will give you rest. Take My yoke upon you and learn from Me; for I am gentle and lowly in heart, and you will find rest for your souls. For My yoke is easy and My burden is light."
Matthew 11:28–30

Many of you reading this message remember Michael Jordan, the famous basketball players. I remember one of his many commercials had a theme song, which repeated over and over again, "If I could be like Mike, if I could be like Mike." Of course, many kids wanted to be like Mike. They wore his Air Jordan shoes, bought the products he endorsed, and pretended to be him in backyard basketball games. They flocked to the TV when he was playing. In fact, if you have a few minutes, go to YouTube and search for "if I could be like Mike Gatorade commercial" and listen to it. Get the tune stuck in your head. Then continue reading this message.

The motto of the Christian is, "If I could be like Christ," or more correctly, "I want to be like Christ." Imagine if you had this tune playing in your head. Go to the Michael Jordan commercial, get that song in your head, and then change the words to "If I could be like Christ, if I could be like Christ."

Isn't that the goal of the Christian life—to be like Christ? To live as He lived. To love as He loved. To forgive as He forgave. To trust as He trusted. To die in faith, as He died. We all had dreams when we were kids of which athlete or actor or actress or princess or superhero we wanted to be. Well, as teens and adults, we should have dreams of being like Christ. We should dream of all the good things we can do. We should dream of all the kindnesses we can offer. We should dream about loving more perfectly. And then, unlike our fantasies of being a superstar athlete or actor, which didn't come true for most of us, we should make these dreams come true by striving every day to be like Christ in some way.

Christ personified not only love but kindness and grace. He had time for the losers of society, outcast leper, despised blind man, hated tax collector, and the accursed harlot. To be like Christ means to look out for those who are forgotten. It also means to not forget those who are right next to you. It means not to neglect your spouse, even when kids, work, and activities drain all of your energy. It means not to neglect your children, even when they've worn out your last nerve. It means not to neglect your relationship with Christ, even when life gets hard and you start having doubts.

In today's Bible quote, Jesus said, "My yoke is easy and My burden is light." Sometimes I wonder if that is true. It is hard to be a Christian. It is hard to be like Christ all the time. But then I think, it would actually be harder to not be a Christian. I can't imagine life without an ultimate goal and purpose—salvation. Without Christ, I would just become older and sadder, watching the sand pour out of the hourglass of my life.

If I am trying to be like Christ, then every day has a purpose and focus, and because of that, even a bad day has joy. As the sand empties from the hourglass of life, there is not sadness but joyful expectation because the days of "being like Him" will soon become days of "being WITH Him."

When you are "heavy laden" with stress or sadness, be like Christ, and you will find rest. Focus on being "gentle and lowly in heart," and your soul will be comforted.

As we conclude this section on "The grace of our Lord Jesus Christ be with you" (1 Thess. 5:28), we are reminded that we want to be like Christ, and we have to extend grace and mercy as He did, without limits. If we are with Christ, we can be comforted that His grace and mercy will be limitless with us as well.

Lord, be with me in the times when my soul feels heavy. Bring rest to my soul. As I take up Your yoke, please walk with me in my stressful yoke. Help me to be gentle and lowly in heart. Help me to be humble. Help me to live for You, with You, and in You. Give me the discipline to work to be like You. Allow me one day to live with You. Bless me as I strive to be like You in my life today. Amen.

Encouragement Challenge: "If I could be like Christ. If I could be like Christ. If I could be like Christ." Let these words play in your head today!

CONCLUSION

THE RIDDLE

Greater love has no man than this, that a man lay down his life for his friends.
John 15:13

One of my favorite songs is called "The Riddle" by Five for Fighting.[59] If you've never heard it, I encourage you to take four minutes on YouTube and listen to it. The beginning lyrics are:

There was a man back in '95
Whose heart ran out of summers but before he died
I asked him, "Wait, what's the sense in life?
Come over me, come over me."
He said
"Son why you gotta to sing that tune?
Catch a Dylan song or some eclipse of the Moon
Let an angel swing and make you swoon
Then you will see, you will see"
Then he said
"Here's a riddle for ya
Find the answer
There's a reason for the world—
You and I."

At the heart of encouragement are some basic questions that we will uncover in this concluding part of our study. To be an encourager and to receive encouragement, there are some fundamental truths one must understand and accept. The song "The Riddle" states one of them; well, it states it in part. The song says that the reason for the world is "you and I." This is true in part. The reason for the world, the reason why God created the world was out of His love. No one who hates life would ever want to have a child. On some basic level, a person who chooses to have a child loves life and wants to bring a child into the world to share life and love with. Of course, this is sadly not true in every instance, but ostensibly, most who want to bring a child into the world love life.

God created us because of love. He is love. He created us out of love. He created us to love, to love Him, for Him to love us, and for us to love one another. The reason for the world is a collaborative one. It's not just about me. It's about God, you, and I.

The song reminds us that life is not about individuals. It's not about individual successes or even failures. Seeing the world as "you and I" as opposed to just "I" means that we have the capacity to celebrate the success of someone else, encourage someone else to success, and help encourage and pick up the one who is failing.

At summer camp, there is a rule that every cabin goes everywhere as a group. If it is time to go somewhere, and one cabin mate can't find his shoes, the others do not continue on and hope he catches up later; they stop, help him find the shoes, and then go together to their next activity. In the ideal world, this is how it would work. Of course, the world is far from ideal, as some neighbors don't want help, and there are other neighbors we feel unsafe around, so we are hesitant to help. Ideally, though, we help our neighbor. Life is about collaboration and cooperation rather than constant competition.

"You and I" sounds good. However, even that is not the end goal. It's you and I and God. It's you and I growing toward God. It's you and I encouraging one another to grow toward God.

There is nothing wrong with encouraging oneself. Positive self-talk is a good thing. Many of us engage in negative self-talk. Thinking positive thoughts about ourselves is a good thing. But it can't be the only thing.

Encouraging someone else to be the best version of themselves is a good thing. Encouraging someone else will help build their self-confidence. However, to what end are we encouraging? So we can get along better with others? So others can feel good about themselves? So that we can feel good about ourselves? So that others will return the favor and encourage us?

The ultimate encouragement goes beyond "you and I" and points all of us to God. There is a reason for the world—it's you and I and God. It's you and I encouraging one another to grow toward God.

Many people spend a lot of time pondering the meaning of life. If we are honest, like the song, we may look at life like we are trying to decipher a riddle or solve a mystery. The mystery is not what life is about—it's about you and I and God and getting you and I to God. The mystery is how to get us all going in that direction.

Lord, there is a lot of confusion in the world today. Help me to remember the simple truth that this life is about You first and foremost. It is about loving you and serving my neighbor. Help me to remember that today and always. Give me the eyes to see the neighbor who needs help. Give me the heart that desires to serve my neighbor. Give me the eyes to see You in my neighbor. And give me the heart that desires to serve You. Thank You for loving me and bringing me into this world. Please continue to love me and lead me through this life so that I may one day experience eternal life. Amen.

Encouragement Challenge: Love God today. Demonstrate love for someone else today. Do both every day, and you'll be well on your way to living out the reason for the world—you and I and God!

Who Is the Loudest Voice in Your Life?

And now, my sons, listen to Me: Happy are those who keep My ways. Hear instruction and be wise, and do not neglect it. Happy is the man who listens to Me, watching daily at My gates, waiting beside My doors. For he who finds Me finds life and obtains favor from the Lord.
Proverbs 8:32–35

There is a Cherokee Indian legend entitled "Two Wolves." The story goes like this:

> An old Cherokee is teaching his grandson about life. "A fight is going on inside me," he said to the boy. "It is a terrible fight, and it is in between two wolves. One is evil—he is anger, envy, sorrow, regret, greed, arrogance, self-pity, guilt, resentment, inferiority, lies, false pride, superiority, and ego." He continued, "The other is good—he is joy, peace, love, hope, serenity, humility, kindness, benevolence, empathy, generosity, truth, compassion, and faith. The same fight is going on inside you—and inside every other person too." The grandson thought about it for a minute and then asked his grandfather, "Which wolf will win?" The old Cherokee replied, "The one you feed."[60]

Many voices compete for our attention. They might be voices of positive or negative encouragement. They might be voices of joy or anger, optimism or pessimism. They might come from other people or from within ourselves. The question to ponder is this: Which voices are you listening to? Which voices do you feed into?

The voices change throughout our lives. When we are babies, the only voice we hear is the voice of our parents, maybe our grandparents. Whatever is happening in our home sets the tone. I remember when our son went to pre-school for the first time, and I mentioned to someone how nervous I was—not about him enjoying the experience or being safe, but the fact that up until that point in his life, the only voices he heard were those of his parents—we controlled the tone of voice and content of what was being said, and now someone else would have an influence and voice in his life.

In childhood, we primarily hear the voices of parent, teachers, and friends. Hopefully, children also hear the voice of God through parents reading the Bible to them, praying with them, and taking them to church. This is an important warning to parents—PARENTS are responsible for making sure that God's voice is present in the lives of their children. A young child is not going to drive to church on his or her own. Even if a parent gets a child to church and Sunday school each week, if there is no praying in the home and if the Bible is not being read in the home, then the voice of God will be drowned out by the other voices on the other six days of the week.

As children become teenagers, the voices of friends and media become the loudest voices they hear. Many times in working with teens, when I ask them which voice is loudest for them in their lives, they will rank friends and media first and second, then parents, teachers, and God. The influence of friends and media dominate the other voices. One problem with this becomes the fact that the ideas of the friends and media constantly change, and so listening to these voices while ignoring the stable voices of parents and most, especially the voice of God, leaves teenagers without a sense of stability. Everything seems to be constantly shifting.

Teens become adults, and the voices shift again. The voice of a boyfriend or girlfriend or spouse becomes the loudest voice. The voice of parents becomes one of friend or consultant rather than director. At some point in adult life, the voice of parents stops as they pass on. The voices of their own children become significant, but these are not voices of advice. Friends continue to have a voice. It's probably safe to say in the world today that the media has perhaps the most influential voice in shaping our thoughts and opinions. The loudest voices in life, for many years, have been angry voices. It has become virtuous to be angry (not even passionate because it goes beyond healthy passion) about something. And we continually go to sources to feed our anger, which primarily becomes the news outlets. Sadly, the voice of the media used to be for information. Now it is for influence. And because anger is seen now as a "virtue," if one isn't outraged about something, it seems as if one is lacking something.

The only voice that can be consistent throughout life is the voice of God. My parents have both passed away. I hear their voices only in my memories. I, thankfully, have a few mentors, but I no longer am a student who hears the voice of a teacher every day. I have a few very close friends, but they are not full-time in ministry. I hear the voice of my spouse every day but not while at work. I have some close friends who are priests, but they don't live in my city, so I don't see or hear from them every day. The competing voices in my life, the ones that are present everywhere and at all times in my life, are the media and God. Family, friends, and co-workers are not always in my office. However, the media is always a click away on the computer, and God is always available through prayer and Scripture reading. So, I have to soberly ask myself, do I spend more time clicking away on the computer or on my knees in prayer? Which voice in my life gets fed the most? And which voice feeds me the most? Is it the voice of the wolf (the media) or the voice of the Lamb (Jesus)?

Voices of optimism or pessimism affect us, so do voices of encouragement or discouragement. It is much harder to feel optimistic or encouraged when the voices around us are pessimistic or discouraging. It is important to ask ourselves what kind of voices we are surrounded with and what kind of voices we choose to surround ourselves with.

Our voices can also be influential—as parents, co-workers, and friends. Are our voices ones of encouragement or discouragement, do they bring peace or anger, and do they reflect God? These are all sobering questions.

Which is the loudest voice in your life—parents, teachers, friends, spouse, media, or God? The one you feed the most become the loudest voice in your life. And what kind of voice do you bring into the world? Will people hear God in your voice?

Lord, in prayer, I raise my voice up to You. As I pray, Lord, please help me to hear Your voice. There are so many competing voices in my life. Help me to lead with the positive ones and drown out the negative ones. Help me to hear voices of encouragement over the voices of anger so that I can bring encouragement rather than anger to those around me. Most importantly, help me to always listen for and hear Your voice, and may Your voice be reflected in my voice and in what I say in the world. Amen.

It is crucial for our salvation that God's voice is the leading voice in our lives. It is critically important to not let God's voice be drowned out by the other voices in our lives. That only happens when we spend time with God so that we can hear His voice of love and hope in a world that has somehow tried to silence both.

The Paralytic—Who Are Your Go-To People? Are You a Go-To Person?

And when He returned to Capernaum after some days, it was reported that He was at home. And many were gathered together, so that there was no longer room for them, not even about the door; and He was preaching the word to them. And they came, bringing to Him a paralytic carried by four men. And when they could not get near Him because of the crowd, they removed the roof above Him; and when they had made an opening, they let down the pallet on which the paralytic lay.
Mark 2:1–4

One of the many miracles Jesus performed in the Gospels was the healing of a paralytic. This healing is unique because for it to happen, it required the participation of other people. Jesus was in a house preaching. There were so many people in the house that no one else could get in. They couldn't even open the door. Four men came carrying their paralyzed friend. When they saw there was no way to get into the house, they got the paralytic up on the roof of the house, cut a hole in the roof, and let down the bed on which the paralytic lay. Jesus then healed the man.

The four friends were critical to the story. We don't know whose idea it was to carry the paralytic to Jesus. Maybe it was his idea, and he summoned four friends to carry him there. Maybe it was the idea of one of the friends, who gathered the others, and they went to the paralytic to offer to take him to Jesus. Maybe the paralytic went willingly and enthusiastically. Maybe he needed some encouragement. Maybe he didn't want to go, and the friends took him anyway. What we know for sure is that he was carried to Jesus by four men.

The other thing we know is that when the friends got the paralytic to Jesus, their path to Him was blocked. They needed some creativity to get their friend to Jesus. Imagine the four friends brainstorming how to get a bed up the wall of a house and onto the roof or how to make a hole in the roof and lower the man down to Jesus.

The lesson of this story is that to get to Jesus and through other challenges of life, it requires the help of other people. When we feel paralyzed, hopefully, we have four people who will carry us where we want to go. That might mean carrying us to Jesus. Or it might mean carrying us through a challenging time. Like the friends in this story, sometimes we might need encouragement. And sometimes we might need something more bold, even forceful. We might be hesitant to let someone carry us, and someone may come and carry us anyway, recognizing that carrying us is the only way we will get where we need to go. Do you have people to carry you when you feel stuck?

There is no ideal number of people we need to help carry us when we are paralyzed by life. Some people might get by with one other person. Ideally, we have several people, like the paralyzed man. If we hope to have four people to carry us, then we should expect to be willing to help carry four others.

I am thankful that I have a few go-to people who carry me to Christ when my faith is shaky and who pick me up when I feel down. I hope that those people know I am willing to carry them as well.

I encourage you to reach out to the people in your life who are your go-to people and thank them for carrying you when you feel stuck and paralyzed. Please let them know you are willing to be one of their go-to people as well.

One thing is certain. No one can go it alone. Even though Jesus is the one who ultimately healed the paralytic, that miracle would not have happened without the loving concern and help from that man's friends. This is why we need friends. This is why we need mentors. This is why we need encouragers. This is why we need to be part of church community. We all need help to get to Jesus as Christians, and we all need help as people just to get through life.

Lord, thank You for the gift of friends, especially for those special friends who help carry me when life gets challenging (list their names). Help me also to be a good friend, to see those who need help to be carried through their challenges. Help me also to bring people closer to You and bring people into my life who will encourage me to get closer to You. Be with all the people in the world who feel "paralyzed," trapped, and alone. Bring Your angels to carry those who feel like they have no one to carry them. Open our eyes to see them and carry them. Amen.

Encouragement Challenge: Build a community of people who can help carry you. Look for people you can help carry. Let your people know who they are. Pray for them. Thank them. Look out for them. Remind and encourage them to look out for you.

We Are Called to be Barnabas

There was not a needy person among them, for as many as were possessors of lands or houses sold them, and brought the proceeds of what was sold and laid it at the apostles' feet; and distribution was made to each as any had need. Thus Joseph who was surnamed by the apostles Barnabas (which means, Son of encouragement), a Levite, a native of Cyprus, sold a field which belonged to him, and brought the money and laid it at the apostles' feet.
Acts 4:34–37

What's in a name? Depending on the name you have, it could be quite a lot. We all have a family name that can often be traced back many generations. It reminds us of where we come from. On my father's side, our family name reminds us that we are Greek, more specifically Cretan (from the island of Crete). This shapes us culturally, with our values, and religion, Greek Orthodox. On my mother's side, generations back, our ancestors were Lutheran missionaries. Perhaps spreading the Word of God as my life's work is in my genes. Our first names often mean something. We may be named for someone, a grandfather or grandmother, or someone else who had significance to our parents when they were naming us. I was born on a prayer. My name Stavros means "cross," and I'm named for the holy cross.[62] It is certainly an appropriate name for someone who is a priest. My middle name is Nicholas, my father's name. I always sign my name with my middle initial because it reminds me of him, especially now that he is gone.

I share this because a name helps shape who we are. It might even give us expectations to live up to.

In some countries, it is not uncommon for people of wealth or nobility to have many names—a first name, family name, and a few names in the middle. In 1 Peter 2:9, we read, "But you are a chosen race, a royal priest, a holy nation, God's own people." According to God, we are royalty. As God's chosen people, imagine if we each added another name to our names. It should be the name Barnabas because Barnabas means "Son of encouragement" (Acts 4:36). Imagine adding this as a middle name, and more importantly, imagine adding this name as part of our identity.

In Acts 4:34, we read that none of the people of the church were needy. In this context, they were speaking about communal living. What is described is akin to a monastery, where everyone lives together and gives away what they have for the good of the community. Barnabas also sold what he had and brought it to the apostles. Barnabas later become an apostle and accompanied St. Paul on his journeys. While Paul might be considered "the front man"—after all, it is his Epistles we read, and we talk about him as the paramount of the apostles—Barnabas was his "wing man," his helper, and probably, in many instances, his encourager.

Going to Acts 4:34, many people in the world are "needy" when it comes to encouragement. Unfortunately, "needy" is sometimes translated as "high maintenance." The opposite of needy is self-sufficient, one who doesn't need anyone or anything. We all have a need for encouragement and positive reinforcement. Without at least some of it, we are all prone to self-doubt and even self-destruction. In Acts 4:34, we read that "there was not a needy person among them." We have an obligation to help those who are in need around us. That might mean offering food to places that distribute it to the hungry or offering money to help fund places that provide shelter for those who are without a home. Even more practical and something we daily encounter are those who need encouragement.

Barnabas offered encouragement in two ways—he offered it specifically to St. Paul, and he offered it in general through his contribution to the community. We are called to do the same. We are called upon to be positive voices in our communities, our large groups—whether it is a neighborhood, church, team, job, or family. We can all provide encouraging voices in our communities. We are also called upon to be encouragers to individuals the way that Barnabas was for St. Paul. These individuals include our spouses, children, parents, closest friends, and anyone we walk in tandem with. To walk in tandem with someone doesn't necessarily mean you do it for life, such as with a spouse. We might walk in tandem with someone for only a few minutes or only a few feet, like the random person who crosses the street with us or who we pass on the sidewalk. A "good morning" and a smile are forms of encouragement. We should be offering them to everyone.

My names (first, middle, and last) shape my identity. I think about them every day. I try to honor each of them. Let us each add a name to our names, the name Barnabas, son (or daughter) of encouragement. And let this adopted name also daily shape our identity. Let us make sure that we fill the need for encouragement that people around us have.

Lord, thank You for the gift of my name and the people and expectations associated with it. May I always remember where I come from and the meaning of the name given to me. Please help me to see myself also as a Barnabas, as a son/daughter of encouragement. May this role daily become part of my identity. May I glorify You through encouraging others each day. Allow me to see those who are need encouragement. And please send people to me in the moments when I am most need encouragement. Amen.

Encouragement Challenge: Attach the name Barnabas to your name. We were all born to be sons/daughters of encouragement!

A Summary of Four Existential Questions

> *Now there are varieties of gifts, but the same Spirit; and there are varieties of service, but the same Lord; and there are varieties of working, but it is the same God who inspires them all in every one. To each is given the manifestation of the Spirit for the common good. To one is given through the Spirit the utterance of wisdom, and to another the utterance of knowledge according to the same Spirit, to another faith by the same Spirit, to another gifts of healing by the one Spirit, to another the working of miracles, to another prophecy, to another the ability to distinguish between spirits, to another various kinds of tongues, to another the interpretation of tongues. All these are inspired by one and the same Spirit, who apportions to each one individually as he wills.*
> 1 Corinthians 12:4–11

I heard a sermon where an Orthodox priest posed four existential questions: a) Where did I come from? b) What is my purpose? c) Why is there a difference between good and evil? and d) What is my destiny? These four questions are very profound if you think seriously about them.

Today I want to focus on the question, "What is my purpose?" Take a snapshot of any moment of your life and ask God, "Is this my purpose?" Take a snapshot of you sitting in traffic, mowing the lawn, standing in line at the supermarket, helping your kid with homework, arguing with your spouse, reading the Bible, helping someone, and as many other "pictures" as you want to take of your life. As you put together this mental scrapbook of your life, write a caption under each picture that says, "Is this the purpose for which I am here?" Did God put me here to mow the lawn? Argue with my spouse? Help my child? Read the Bible? Help someone? You will quickly conclude, I hope, that the things in our lives that glorify God honor the reason He put us here, and clearly there are things in our lives that do not.

God didn't put us here so that we could argue with our spouses, drive like maniacs, or overeat or drink too much. None of these things glorify God. In fact, these things dishonor God and dishonor us as well. Our purpose, plain and simple, is for us to glorify God in this life while preparing to glorify Him in His presence for eternal life. This is whole purpose and meaning of life.

As you evaluate the snapshots of your life, and you come across snapshots that do not glorify God, know that these go against the purpose of your life and try to eliminate them. If you work at a job, for instance, that requires you to cross over moral boundaries like honesty, and you might want to reevaluate your job. If you have a marriage where you are perpetually at odds with your spouse, ask yourself, "Does this marriage glorify God? Are we realizing God's purpose for bringing us together in marriage?" If you have a marriage that radiates love but doesn't necessarily radiate riches, you still have a marriage that pleases God. God doesn't bring people together for material success but for emotional closeness and spiritual oneness. That is the purpose of marriage.

In life, the purpose is to prepare for the kingdom of God. So, if a person does not have a "great" job but glorifies God on a regular basis, then he or she is on the right track to the ultimate spiritual success, salvation. This is the purpose of why we are here.

As for the other questions, the origin of life is from God. God co-creates life with us in the institution of marriage. Our souls come from God—this is our origin. Our purpose is to glorify God in some way—some do it as parents, teachers, engineers, truck drivers, bank tellers, and so on. The difference between good and evil is the difference between doing what is pleasing to God and doing what isn't. If something is good, it is from God, the giver of all the good and perfect gifts. If something is not good, it is not from God because God only gives what is good and perfect. While we seem to redefine what we think is pleasing to God (the constant shift in morality), what is righteous in the eyes of God does not change. And as for our destiny, we will all one day stand in front of the Lord at our Last Judgment to answer to how we fulfilled our purpose using the talents we had been given.

Each of us is called on to glorify God in a different way—some will do it as parents, some as teachers, some as lawyers, some as business owners, some as athletes, some as students, and many will have a combination of different ways. If you are glorifying God and doing what is pleasing to Him, then you are fulfilling your purpose. Don't be discouraged if your career isn't glamourous or your bank account isn't flush; take encouragement that your glorifying of God in your work puts you in good stead at the Last Judgment and puts you in line for a place in God's everlasting kingdom.

Surround yourself with people who will help encourage you in living out your purpose, who will encourage you toward that which is good and godly and away from that which is not, and who will help you in making your way to salvation as your destiny. Encourage others to live out their purpose, encourage them toward the good, and offer help and encouragement to them as they make their way to salvation.

Lord, thank You for the gifts and talents You have given me (name them). Allow me to use them today for Your glory. In the moments of my life when I am tempted to not glorify You, give me the strength and discipline to maintain focus on Your glory at all times and in all places. Amen.

Encouragement Challenge: Focus on glorifying God in all situations today—even the mundane ones. This is our purpose.

**Dedicated to Fr. John Bociu, whose sermon provided the inspiration for this reflection.

For Whom Do We Exist?

"If you love Me, you will keep My commandments . . . He who has My commandments and keeps them, he it is who loves me; and he who loves Me will be loved by My Father, and I will love him and manifest Myself to him."
John 14:15, 21

Some Christian theology is very hard to interpret. There are entire books of the Bible that I've needed annotated notes to understand. There is, however, a good amount of Christianity that one might classify as common sense. This reflection is one of those things that one might classify as common sense. The question is, "For whom do we exist?" There are two possible answers—we either exist for ourselves, or we exist for one another. God either created us to serve ourselves, or He created us to serve each other. Or, I suppose, there is a third option, which is to believe that there is no God, and we find ourselves randomly here.

Let's say that we believe God made us to serve ourselves. This would mean we should have as much fun as possible, make as much money, and do as much for ourselves while we can before life is over. If this truly is our purpose, then as life goes on, we will become more and more sad because there will be less and less time to get things for ourselves.

If there is no God and we are randomly here, then life has no purpose. We either serve others to "go along to get along." Or we serve ourselves because if there is no higher purpose, we might as well look inwardly. Or we live in between the two in a state of confusion and eventual disinterest. If there is no purpose, then it's like there is no point to anything.

This brings us to the idea that God made us for one another, that God made us to serve one another. And in serving one another, we serve God. Either we serve God through serving others, or we serve ourselves. There doesn't seem to be other possibilities.

If life is all about us, then it is really pretty shallow. Let's think about how the world addresses this topic. Does the world tell us that life is more about us or more about others? Think of how we are raising our kids. We encourage them to get good grades so that they can get good jobs so that they can earn good salaries so that they can buy nice things and have a good life. In a sense, we are "breeding" our kids to be good so that *they* end up good, not necessarily others. Advertising on TV is all about our own material gain.

There is nothing wrong with relaxing and having fun. There is nothing wrong with owning a nice home or wearing nice clothes. However, life has to be about more than just having fun. It has to be about more than just us.

We've all had the experience of going to a restaurant and eating a meal that has been haphazardly prepared. This is especially true in some fast food restaurants. I know I've eaten many a hamburger that was prepared so quickly that it was falling apart. I presume that is because the boss tells the employees to work fast and get the people in and out quickly as opposed to serving the PEOPLE. This is what happens when we see people as dollar signs. It becomes more about us and less about them.

We exist either for ourselves or for others. If we understand our primary role as existing to serve others (and serving God in the process), then offering encouragement will become much easier and more frequent for us. After all, encouraging others is among the *easiest* ways to serve others. We've discussed many times already how it brings big reward (to others and to ourselves) with very low cost. If we are thinking, "I exist for you and not for me," then it will be much easier to see our role as encouragers because encouragement is all about building up others. When we want to see others do well and we want to help them, encouragement becomes our almost natural response to every person and situation that involves another person.

In the home where I currently live, we have a pool. There are three things that are controlled by the pool pump—the suction in the main drain, the suction in the skimmer, and the suction to the pool vacuum. These three controls can't all be at 100 percent. When I want to vacuum the pool, I open that suction more and put the others less. Because I don't have the time or attention to do this every day, the main drain get very little suction, the skimmer gets a little more, and the greatest suction is reserved for the vacuum that keeps the floor of the pool clean.

We can't put 100 percent attention on ourselves and 100 percent attention on others at the same time. That adds up to 200 percent. The total percent for our attention is 100 percent. It can't be higher than that. (There is no such thing as giving 110 percent—logically, someone can't give more than everything). So in our lives, we should reflect on what is receiving the majority of our attention and effort. Is it things that benefit us or things that benefit others? Reflection on this question is the best way to answer the question, "For whom do we really exist?" The correct answer is that we exist for others, and in serving others, we serve God. The challenge is to live a life that supports this correct answer.

Lord, thank You for creating me. Help me to always remember that You are the Creator. Whatever I may create in my life is possible first because You created me. Help me to recognize the greater purpose for my life isn't to be all about me but to be all about You, and in serving You, I will serve others. Help me to remember this daily. Help this knowledge to motivate me to serve others. May I look for every opportunity to build up other people. And knowing that encouragement is one of the easiest ways to do this, help me to be a strong encourager, so that in encouraging and serving others, I may honor You. Amen.

Encouragement Challenge: Remind yourself daily that we don't just exist for ourselves. We exist to serve God by serving others. There are many ways to serve others. The one that comes with the lowest cost in terms of time and effort is encouragement.

It's Not Goodness but Godliness We Are Aiming For

A ruler asked Him, "Good Teacher, what shall I do to inherit eternal life?" And Jesus said to him, "Why to do you call Me good? No one is good but God alone. You know the commandments: 'Do not commit adultery, Do not kill, Do not steal, Do not bear false witness, Honor your father and mother.'" And he said, "All these I have observed from my youth." And when Jesus heard it, He said to him, "One thing you still lack. Sell all that you have and distribute to the poor, and you will have treasure in heaven; and come, follow me."
Luke 18:18–22

The Bible doesn't tell us all of the settings where Jesus's conversations took place. Nor does it always tell us His tone of voice. I've always imagined that this conversation with the ruler took place under the shade of a tree, and that the tone of voice Jesus used was very calm and soothing, not animated. Many people "hear" this conversation between Jesus and the ruler as Jesus being somewhat harsh with the man, telling him that all the things he had done were not enough and that he needed to sell everything he had. On face value, this might have seemed like an unreasonable request. After all, who, reading this message, is willing to sell everything they have to follow Jesus? I know I'm not.

Each of us has something that keeps us from being the best version of ourselves, the whole person that God created us to be. For this man, it was his riches. I imagine Jesus looking into the man's heart and speaking to him with encouragement, like, "You've got so much going for you. Tweak this one thing, and you will be where you and God wants you to be." What is the one thing that keeps you from being the best version of yourself, the whole person that God created you to be? Each of us will answer that question differently.

One thing we will all struggle with is the difference between goodness and godliness. For example, I would say that I am a good driver. I don't have many tickets or accidents, I drive at a safe speed, and so on. However, I would not classify myself as a godly driver. I often get irritated that people around me are driving too fast or too slow, or there are too many people on the road. My motivation in being a good driver has nothing to do with the other drivers on the road. I want to avoid paying a ticket or wrecking my car; that's why I drive well. To be a godly driver means to actually care about the people in the cars around you, to care about their well-being, to hope that they get home safely, not to see them as people who are just clogging the road and slowing us down. I confess, that's the way I see them most of the time.

Jesus told the man in the story that the good things he had done were indeed good things. However, these things mostly benefited him. They were not godly things. If he was to truly glorify God in his life, he would need to take a godly approach, which, for this man, was to get rid of his riches because he was more concerned with them than he was concerned about his relationship with God. His riches were his stumbling block. For some of us, our stumbling block might be anger, it may be that we can't get off of our phones, it may be that we gossip too much, or any number of things. Most of us like to see ourselves as good, to think of ourselves as good. Jesus is telling us that good is *good*, but good is not enough. Godly is where we should be setting our sights because the usual beneficiary of our goodness is ourselves, which can make goodness by itself into something that isn't good—narcissism. Godliness is what leads to salvation.

As we wrap up our study on encouragement, the message here is to not have goodness as the highest goal but godliness. To do that, we have to see Christ in those around us and not see the people around us as a bother, as in the example of how most of us relate to other drivers on the road. We have to care about the well-being of those around us; it's not enough merely to be nice to them. Whether this is being a more patient driver, thanking the person at the register at the store rather than just having a silent transaction, offering encouragement to someone in addition to paying them for a service, and so on.

Jesus told the man in the story, "You are good, and that is good, but the goal is to be godly, and if you want to be godly, you have to remove the thing that keeps you from God, in this case, riches." What is the thing that keep you from going all in on God? What is the one thing you still lack? I encourage you to go after that!

Lord, thank You for the many things that I do well (list them). Help me use my time and talents to not only be good with what I have but to also use my talents in a godly manner. Help me to see You in those who are around me. Help me to understand that goodness is not the ultimate goal, but the ultimate goal is godliness, walk in step with You, see You in others, and bring You into everything that I do. Amen.

Encouragement Challenge: It's godliness, not goodness, that should be our goal each day.

Positive In-Positive Out, Negative In-Negative Out, Nothing In-Negative Out

Fathers, do not provoke your children, lest they become discouraged.
Colossians 3:21

One of the most critical points to take away from this study on *The Heart of Encouragement* is what happens when we are indifferent to people. We know that if we encourage people, encouragement boosts confidence, which affects performance in a positive way. When we encourage others, they perform better. It's pretty common sense.

Discouragement creates doubt, which kills confidence, which affects performance in a negative way. When we discourage others, there is a negative outcome.

Here is a critical point: When we offer neither encouragement or discouragement, when we are indifferent, it creates doubt, kills confidence, and affects performance in a negative way. So, in giving no feedback, it is the same as giving negative feedback. In some ways, it's actually worse. Sometimes it is better to know that you stand in a negative space with someone than not knowing where you stand at all.

Here is a simple formula to remember: Positive in gets positive out; negative in gets negative out; and nothing in gets negative out.

The verse from Colossians 3:21 reminds us, "Fathers, do not provoke your children, lest they become discouraged." At the same time, don't be indifferent to them either because they will become discouraged.

Going back to the 5:1 ratio we discussed at the beginning of this study, people ideally should receive five positive inputs to every negative input. There are very few people who receive this ratio of encouragement to discouragement. Encouragement can be as simple as a smile, a "thank you," or a "good morning." Anything we can do to put something positive into the mind of our neighbor is a good thing. The thing to remember is that if we ignore our neighbor, it's the same as if we are negative to our neighbor.

Let's think for a second about the person who puts the groceries in our bag at the store. This person receives negative feedback if he or she breaks some eggs or puts too much stuff in a bag. They probably don't receive a lot of positive comments, not because they don't do a good job but because people are too busy looking at or talking on their phones when checking out of a store that they don't notice the people who work there unless they can't find something or unless they do something wrong. A simple "thank you" can go a long way. It means, "I notice you, and I appreciate you." Negative input, of course, will be discouraging in this instance. But no input will leave the person bagging the groceries, thinking that he or she must be doing a bad job because no one is taking notice of them except when they do something wrong.

When someone does something wrong, constructive criticism (notice the use of the word constructive as opposed to destructive, which is tearing someone down and completely shattering their confidence) is warranted. We are all quick to criticize when we don't like something. We can all stand to learn to be better at complimenting when we like something. When someone gets something right, we've all got to do a better job of saying something positive. Just as positive input results in positive output, a positive output by someone should result in a positive feedback, not in indifference.

Many of us have used the phrase, "That's the best twenty dollars I've ever spent." Well, among the best instances of best twenty dollars I've ever spent was when I waited outside while the garbage truck was in my neighborhood and offered the driver twenty dollars to go buy lunch that day. He told me, "I drive this truck alone, and on most days, I speak to no one the entire day. Thank you for making me feel valued today." Money well spent!

We are all quick to point out when something goes wrong. We need to be even more quick when it comes to pointing out when something goes right.

Lord, thank You for the people around me who do the common things that I take for granted, like the clerk at the grocery store who puts my groceries in the bag, the bank teller, or the sanitation engineer who picks up the garbage, who drives alone each day and probably talks to no one. May I have opportunities to encourage and thank these people so that they know they are important. Help me not to take the good things people do for granted but instead to express my gratitude so that others may feel filled with encouragement. Amen.

Encouragement Challenge: Positive in-positive out. Negative in-negative out. Nothing in-negative out. Don't forget to be positive when something goes right.

I Wish the Best for You

May you be blessed by the Lord, Who made heaven and earth!
Psalm 115:15

There is nothing wrong with competition. When we compete against other people, it drives us to be better. For instance, if you are running a race against someone, you are likely to run faster than if you are running by yourself because competition drives us to be better. The same is true when we compete on a team against another team. Competition drives a team to be more cohesive when playing against another team.

Competition is being ruined in four ways in the world today. First, there is so much pressure to win today that it is making people full of anxiety to even get in and compete. People are so afraid to lose or be identified as a loser that they don't even want to get in and try. Second, the pressure to win is so great that people are cheating to get ahead. I have been told by many students that there is so much pressure to get good grades to get into college that many people are cheating to get through school. I've even been told that because virtually everyone is cheating to get a good grade, if one is honest in their studies, they might actually not get the top grade, so people would rather cheat their way through school than be honest because there is that much pressure to get the top grade, whether you've earned it or not. Third, many think that competition is not healthy because when there is a competition, there is, by necessity, winners and losers. So, as to not make the losers feel bad, trophies are given to everyone, which causes there to be no difference between winning and losing when everyone is treated as a winner.

All of these factors make for unhealthy competition. In 2 Timothy 2:5, we read "An athlete is not crowned unless he competes according to the rules." In the ancient Olympics, one was a champion because they prepared to compete and gave the best of themselves. Competing honestly and with integrity was prized as much as winning. People also knew how to lose—they could shake the hand of the one who won and congratulate them on the effort. In the world today, we have forgotten how to lose gracefully and tip our hats to a worthy opponent who bested us.

That brings us to the fourth way that competition has been ruined, and that is, "We've made everything a competition." Because virtually everything has become a competition, when we encourage one another, it seems we run the risk of falling behind or wishing someone well, perhaps to our own demise. This is not how things should work.

Encouragement means, among other things, "I wish the best for you." Encouragement is not about the encourager. It's about the person receiving encouragement. Encouraging others should not take away from our own sense of self-worth. If anything, it should add to it. For instance, if I tell another priest that he gives good sermons, it doesn't devalue my sermons. I want all priests to give good sermons. That's because I see other priests more as brothers and not as competitors.

I'm sure that it is difficult for one student to encourage another student on a test because they are both competing for a grade. If high school senior student A encourages senior student B, and both are applying to the same school, maybe student A fears that student B might get in while student A will not. Hence, student A might discourage or belittle student B, seeing student B as competition.

Competition is good when it inspires people to be the best version of themselves. It becomes a negative thing when competition fosters discouragement and tearing down others rather than encouragement and building others up. Ideally, we need to come to a place where we can encourage others and mean it, where we can say, "I wish the best for you," and really believe that. We should be able to hope for the best for those around us without thinking that their successes will lessen our own successes.

Encouragement really is an art form. It takes a steady hand to make a beautiful painting. And it takes a steady heart to offer encouragement in the midst of a world where everything is so competitive. We all need encouragement. However, if we all see one another as competitors and combatants, it will be difficult to offer encouragement as well as expecting to receive it.

Encouragement means, "I wish the best for you," and we can all work a little harder at saying that and meaning it. We've all got to come to a place where we can sincerely encourage others and understand that their success doesn't necessarily preclude our success or make us more likely to fail. And sometimes when we encourage others, and they do "better" than us, we've got to go back to ancient times and tip our hats to them and congratulate them.

Lord, help me to see the good in others. Help me to truly wish for the best for others, to see others in a positive way and not in a competitive way. Help me to understand that the success of another will not result in failure for me so that I can encourage others without reservation. Help me to know that I am in competition with no one but myself. May I honor you by honoring others. Amen.

It's hard to encourage people if we are sizing everyone up as competition. Encouragement means, "I wish the best for you," and we can all work a little harder at saying that and meaning it.

THE ENCOURAGEMENT WALK EXPERIMENT—
THE GIFT IS YOU

> *So when they were sent off, they went down to Antioch, and having gathered the congregation together, they delivered the letter. And when they had read it, they rejoiced because of its encouragement. And Judas and Silas, who were themselves prophets, encouraged and strengthened the brothers with many words.*
> Acts 15:30–32

A few years ago at summer camp, we tried an experiment. A cabin of teenagers was going to walk from their cabin down to the ropes course, which was a fifteen-minute walk. We blindfolded their three counselors and told the campers (out of earshot of the counselors) that while we were walking down to the ropes course, they were to take turns walking with each counselor, holding their hand, identifying themselves to the counselors, and saying something nice or encouraging to the counselor. A typical comment went something like this: "Hi Jasmin, this is Artemis, and I just wanted to tell you that you are doing a great job as our counselor. I love your smile, and the other day when you told us about some of your college experiences and got really personal with us, it really struck a chord with me. Thanks for being so real with us." As the counselors were walking, not knowing where they were going, different campers would take hold of their hands, offer encouragement, let go, and another set of campers would come in and just pile encouragement on them.

Fifteen minutes later, we arrived at our destination. We took the blindfolds off the counselors, who were all crying. We asked the counselors why they were crying, and they said that they felt so good. They didn't realize they were making such a difference in the lives of their campers. We asked the counselors how they felt, and they said they felt so good receiving such a great infusion of encouragement. Some of the campers were crying. When we asked why the campers were crying, they said that it felt so good to make the counselors feel good. When we asked what it cost us to do this activity, the answer was "nothing." It would take fifteen minutes to walk to our destination anyway. It cost us exactly nothing to do this activity, and yet EVERYONE felt good. Those who were encouraged, and those who had been encouraging—everyone felt good. We call this activity "The Encouragement Walk." And this has become one of the favorite activities at summer camp. People enjoy being encouraged as much as they enjoy encouraging others.

On one occasion when we were doing this, the guys and girls asked if we could do this co-ed, guys encouraging girls, and girls encouraging guys. I asked the guys before they encouraged the girls, "What do you think all those girls want to hear?" They answered, "That they are pretty." It was amazing to watch the care the guys took in speaking to the girls. If only it could be like this all the time.

On another occasion, we did an encouragement walk for the person who had organized our Camp Olympics the previous evening. After the Olympics, everyone was wet and cold and quickly retreated to their cabins to shower and clean up. This person hadn't really received any feedback from the campers, though a few of the senior staff had complimented her. During her encouragement walk, many of the campers told her that the Camp Olympics had been the best ever, how much fun they had, what a good leader she is, and more. When we were done, she told the campers how she had gone to bed the previous evening feeling like she had failed because she had only gotten positive feedback from a few of the senior staff, not from the campers. Everyone had a good time, but if they hadn't told her, she would have actually felt like a failure. Remember "nothing in, negative out?" Here was a classic example of that!

The lesson here is that when you like something that someone is doing, TELL THEM! Parents, tell your kids that you love them and are proud of them because this is what they are literally DYING to hear. Many of them are doing stupid things and dying sometimes because they are seeking approval and not finding it from parents, so they go to other places to find it, and oftentimes these "places" are unhealthy, even dangerous. They want to hear from parents and also from peers. Young women want to hear that they are pretty from their peers, not only from their parents. Young men want to hear that people believe in them and trust them. Everyone wants to hear that they have some value.

This activity has shown us several things. First, it takes next to no time to offer encouragement. This activity is a great example of low cost and high return. Second, it is interesting to hear what people have to say about you, when they really put some thoughts together. Having been on the receiving end of an encouragement walk, it is really an amazing experience to have a ton of encouragement rained down on you, but it is also interesting the things people say. Little things that I don't even remember saying or doing are things that meant a lot to them.

Craig Groeschel, the well-known founder and pastor of LifeChurch in Oklahoma City, did an experiment similar to the encouragement walk at his church on Christmas.[62] They surprised some members of their congregation with gift boxes filled with letters from family members, co-workers, and friends who wrote about all the things they loved about them. Imagine receiving a box of letters offering you affirmation and encouragement. They called this experiment "The Gift is You." Imagine what it would feel like to open a gift box, to find letter about you, and how much you mean to people. What could be a better gift?!

These two examples of a flood of encouragement benefit both parties, the one being encouraged and the one offering the encouragement. The one receiving encouragement will feel affirmed and valued. Also, the helpful feedback will inspire them to continue the work they are doing. When people tell me they really like something I'm doing, it lets me know that I should do that particularly thing more. That's helpful feedback. The one offering encouragement will have to dig deeply to specify what it is that they like about the person they are encouraging. They will feel joy seeing the person they are encouraging feeling joy. And undoubtedly, their relationship will grow closer. Cabins that have done the encouragement walk at summer camp amongst themselves and campers encouraging campers have reported that after doing this activity, the cabin got closer, cliques were busted up, and the cabin became more like a family.

At camp, we hang bags on the wall, and the staff write notes of encouragement to other staff members throughout the week—I've kept my bag each year and reread the notes on a bad day. Whether you do an encouragement walk for someone, an encouragement box or bag, or even just taking the time to write a single letter to someone, telling someone what they mean to you is something that has low cost and high benefit. We all like receiving gifts. But there is a difference in buying something for someone or telling someone "the gift is you" and raining encouragement down on them. This is one of the best gifts you can offer someone, and it is one of the best gifts that someone can receive. And I say this from personal experience. It is a euphoric feeling to have a flood of encouragement poured on you. And it is almost as euphoric to help pour a flood of encouragement on someone else.

Lord, give me the eyes to see people around me who can use some encouragement. Sometimes it takes courage to offer encouragement. Give me the courage to offer the compliment or write the letter of encouragement to someone who needs it. Help me to find joy in offering encouragement to others. Lord, I also need encouragement, affirmation, and feedback. Help others to see this need in me, and for me to see it in them. Thank You, Lord, for the many things You have done for me. There are not enough words to offer to You to thank You for everything that You are to me. Amen.

Encouragement Challenge: When you like something that someone is doing, tell them. That's the only way they will know. And if you really feel bold, organize an encouragement walk or encouragement box for someone. Encouragement is one of the lowest cost, highest benefit things we can offer.

Swimming against the Current

On the way to Jerusalem, He was passing along between Samaria and Galilee. And as He entered a village, He was met by ten lepers, who stood at a distance and lifted up their voices and said, "Jesus, Master, have mercy on us." When He saw them, He said to them, "God and show yourselves to the priests." And as they went they were cleansed. Then one of them, when he saw that he was healed, turned back, praising God with a loud voice; and he fell on his face at Jesus' feet, giving Him thanks. Now he was a Samaritan. Then said Jesus, "Were not ten cleansed? Where are the nine? Was no one found to return and give praise to God except this foreigner?" And He said to him, "Rise and go your way; your faith has made you well."
Luke 17:11–19

Soccer was my sport in high school. Our season ran from November through March. We were not allowed to do drills with a soccer ball in the off-season until November 1. So our coaches had us spend September and October doing conditioning drills. And one of his favorite drills was to have us run laps around a large pool. The depth of the pool was four feet, and so all twenty of us would "run" around the perimeter of the pool. Once we got the current going in one direction, our running was almost effortless. However, just at the moment, the coach would blow a whistle, and we'd all have to stop and start running in the other direction, against the current. This is really hard. Eventually, however, we'd turn the tide and get the current going in the other direction, and then he'd blow the whistle, and we'd reverse again. Here's the thing—we had to work as a team to reverse the tide. If one person stopped and tried to reverse the current of the other nineteen, he would most certainly fail. But when all twenty of us stopped, while we struggle to reverse the current, eventually, with some effort, it could be done.

At the time Jesus walked the earth, there were many currents He encouraged people to reverse. In the verses above, He encountered ten lepers. Lepers lived in isolation, completely cut off from society. And Jesus interacted with them. Jews didn't talk to Samaritans. And yet Jesus talked with them, and in this case, healed one of them. And Samaritans didn't talk to Jews, and in this case, it was the healed Samaritan, and not the other nine lepers, who came back to offer thanks to Jesus. The leper had every reason to feel bitter about his state in life, just like many people do in society today. He realized that His healing had come from Jesus, not of his own doing. He also realized it was a gift. And thus, he expressed thanks rather than entitlement. How many people in today's world in the same situation would have come back to say thank you at all, let alone to an "enemy." Jesus was all about changing the currents of society.

The current of society today is more about competition and cooperation. There are WAY more voices of discouragement than encouragement. People are more fake than genuine. Relationships are inauthentic rather than authentic. People are quick to criticize and often forget to praise. And in an age of technology, people feel more isolated than connected. These, and other currents, need to be reversed.

There is no way to reverse the current of the entire society. But what about changing the course of our small group—our family, our friends, and those we associate closest to. It starts when a small group of people decide to stand against the tide of being competitive, discouraging, fake, inauthentic, and critical. One person stands little chance against the tide. But two or three or five or ten can start a new current.

Lord, help me always to know that You are real. Help me to build an authentic relationship with You. May I be inspired to bring to You my good things and my failings. Please help me to encourage authenticity in my relationships with others. Please bring others to me who will encourage me to be authentic. Give me the courage to stand against the tide of competition, discouragement, and inauthenticity. Bring people into my life who will stand with me. Amen.

Encouragement Challenge: Don't be afraid to stand against the current of inauthenticity. Get a friend to stand with you. And if you see a friend try to reverse the current, run to stand with them.

Practical Ways We Can All Make a Difference

As Jesus went ashore He saw a great throng; and He had compassion on them, and healed their sick. When it was evening, the disciples came to Him and said, "This is a lonely place, and the day is now over; send the crowds away to go into the villages and buy food for themselves." Jesus said, "They need not go away; you give them something to eat." They said to Him, "We have only five loaves here and two fish." And He said, "Bring them here to Me." Then He ordered the crowds to sit down on the grass; and taking the five loaves and the two fish He looked up to heaven, and blessed, and broke and gave the loaves to the disciples, and the disciples gave them to the crowds. And they all ate and were satisfied. And they took up twelve baskets full of the broken pieces left over. And those who ate were about five thousand men, besides women and children. Then He made the disciples get into the boat and go before him to the other side, while He dismissed the crowds.
Matthew 14:14–22

One of the most well-known miracles Jesus did was when He multiplied five loaves and two fish and fed a crowd of five thousand men, plus women and children. Let's conservatively say that each family has three people in it (some have more, some have less); that could mean that as many as 15,000 people ate from five loaves and two fish. That would mean that 3,000 people shared a loaf of bread, and 7,500 people split up a fish. That is ridiculous! How could that happen? To top it off, there were twelve baskets left over—that's a lot of leftover food.

Now imagine being one of the disciples when Jesus suggested feeding the large crowd. Imagine what it would have been like to canvas that crowd, asking for some food. Imagine what it must have been like in the crowd if you had one of those precious loaves set aside for yourself or your family, and now you were being asked to give some food for the masses. Give up what you have and risk going hungry. One miracle was that anyone chanced sharing their meager food with a large crowd. That was a miracle in itself!

One of the many lessons of this story is that when we offer something to God, even something small, He can multiply it and make it go far. Imagine if no one had provided any bread of fish.

This miracle would not have taken place. To multiply something, something has to be offered. Zero times anything is still zero.

Several years ago, I gave a sermon on this miracle of the five loaves and two fish in church. I talked about how offering something small can be multiplied by God into something big. And then I took out a piece of paper and a pen, and I asked the congregation to come up with small things we could all do to reduce anger and infuse encouragement into the world around us. Within a few minutes, they came up with thirty suggestions that I will list here, small and practice ways that we can all make a difference.

1. Give someone a compliment
2. Offer Christian forgiveness
3. Smile to people you encounter
4. Pray
5. Give love
6. Be kind to people
7. Help someone in need
8. Share a meal with someone
9. Call/text someone at random to see how they are doing
10. Thank people
11. Lead by example
12. Don't annoy people
13. Be mindful of how you are feeling
14. Be mindful of how others are feeling
15. No road rage
16. Send short texts of encouragement to people
17. Adjust your own attitude
18. Be there for people when they need it
19. Share
20. Volunteer
21. Give someone a compliment
22. Abstain from social media
23. Have compassion
24. Put others first
25. Seek out someone who needs help
26. Ask how someone is doing and actually listen to the answer
27. Recognize that everyone is battling something
28. Be patient

29. Be encouraging
30. Give positive feedback when you like something

Pick one suggestion a day or even one a week and focus on that. Choose a different one tomorrow next week. If everyone does even one of these to one person a day, you'll be amazed at what could happen. Most of them will cost little time and no money. They are just about all easy things that we can do with a little bit of intentionality. So go make a difference. What is stopping you?

If everyone reading this message (a) did one of the things listed below every day, (b) passed this message on to others, and (c) did these things under the umbrella of God and prayer, we actually could change the world. Just like five loaves fed 15,000, a few hundred people who committed to doing what is listed below could change a few hundred thousand people. It's actually possible.

Lord, sometimes I feel like I'm sitting in that crowd of 5,000 hungry people. It seems that there won't be enough food to eat. In the times when I am hungry for affirmation or encouragement, send people around me who will encourage and build me up. Sometimes I feel like I have one of the loaves of bread, and I am afraid to offer it for fear that I might go hungry. Give me the strength and courage to offer whatever little I have to You and for Your glory. Multiply what I have and what I offer so that whatever little positive thing I offer can affect many others in a positive way. As You continually multiply Your blessings on me, allow me to multiply those blessings I have received from You to those around me. Help me to see the many small ways that a little encouragement can go a long way each day in the situations in which I find myself. Amen.

Encouragement Challenge: Think you can't make a difference? Think again. We all can! Do one of the things on this list today. We can all make a difference!

Who Is Going to Take the First Step?

Behold, now is the acceptable time; behold now is the day of salvation. We put no obstacle in anyone's way, so that no fault may be found with our ministry, but as servants of God we commend ourselves in every way: through great endurance, in afflictions, hardships, calamities, beatings, imprisonments, tumults, labors, watching, hunger; by purity, knowledge, forbearance, kindness, the Holy Spirit, genuine love, truthful speech and the power of God.
2 Corinthians 6:2–7

The choice to be an encourager is just that, a choice. We know that encouragement can lead to more safety, vulnerability, and authenticity in relationships. These things make us better people, better friends, and ultimately, better Christians.

We need more encouraging, more vulnerability, and more authenticity in our society. No, we're not going to have a deep and vulnerable relationship with every person we meet. But sadly, many people do not have even ONE authentic relationship, and that needs to change.

We all know the saying, "It takes two to tango." Well, it takes two to be vulnerable. In our relationship with Christ, He's already made the first move—He died for us—what is more vulnerable than that? Are we ready to make the second move?

In our relationships, it always takes one person going first when it comes to showing vulnerability. It is easier to take that step when another person commits to go second. So, are you willing to take the first step? Are you willing to commit to taking the second step if someone else goes first?

One of my favorite songs is *"If Everyone Cared"* by the group Nickelback. Allow me to share some of the lyrics:

And as we lie, beneath the stars,
We realize how small we are,
If they could love, like you and me,
Imagine what the world could be?

If everyone cared and nobody cried,
If everyone loved and nobody lied,
If everyone shared and swallowed their pride,
Then we'd see the day when nobody died.[63]

In relation to God, we are indeed pretty small. If the Almighty God was vulnerable for us, why can't we be vulnerable to Him? If He took the first step, why can't we take the second? Imagine what the world would be like if everyone had an authentic relationship with Christ? And if everyone had at least one or two authentic relationships with someone else (not ten or twenty, just one or two), so that everyone was caring and everyone was cared for, so that everyone was sharing and swallowing their pride, well, no one would die sad and alone or without Christ. The "day when nobody died" is a vision of heaven. And as Christians, the path to heaven is love, caring, vulnerability, and authenticity with Christ and each other. And encouragement plays a large role in that journey.

There are plenty of people who feel "dead" in this life. If we are honest, all of us have days like this. A little bit of encouragement can lift us up when we feel "dead" and make us feel "alive" again. Encouragement brings vitality into relationships and puts a spring in our steps. Encouragement precedes vulnerability or trust in any relationship. So, take a chance and encourage first. If someone makes the first step and encourages you, make the second step and encourage them as well.

Lord, thank You for the gift of my life. Thank You for my joys and thank You even for my struggles. Thank You that I have another day of life to learn, grow, love, and hope. Help me build an authentic relationship with You. Help me build authentic relationships with others. Help me to be an authentic person. Fill me with joy, hope, and the desire to bring joy and hope to others. Bring me to the day when nobody will die, to salvation in Your heavenly kingdom. Amen.

Encouragement Challenge: Be bold in taking the first step to encourage others. Don't be afraid to take the second step, and encourage someone in return if someone has taken the first one to encourage you first.

WE CAN ALL SOLVE THIS PROBLEM

Your boasting is not good. Do you not know that a little leaven leavens the whole lump? Cleanse out the old leaven that you may be a new lump, as you really are unleavened. For Christ, our Paschal lamb, has been sacrificed. Let us, therefore, celebrate the festival, not with the old leaven, the leaven of malice and evil, but with the unleavened bread of sincerity and truth.
1 Corinthians 5:6–8

One year at summer camp, I was talking with a group of campers who were about to be seniors in high school. This was their last year of camp. All were somewhat nervous as well as excited about finishing high school and heading off to college. Many of them were serious about their Christian faith, which was a good thing. And several expressed concern that when they went off to college, if they weren't interested in the party scene, how might they occupy themselves on a Friday night? Who could they talk to? I answered, somewhat casually, "Why not talk to the people here? You're all nervous about confronting the same problem. Can you see how you can solve this problem?"

It is always interesting when a group of people all agree on a problem and all see the solution. The issue here was people expressing the identical concern with having someone to talk to on a Friday night. And the answer was found in that same circle of people—how about each other? (It kind of reminds me of a time I gathered with a bunch of Christian young adults who were complaining, "Where will we ever find nice Christian people to date?" And the answer was, "Just look around the room.")

If we all agree that something is a problem, and we all agree that we have a solution, why can't we do it?

I think most people would agree that they like being encouraged and lifted up. Most people would probably like to have more encouragement in their lives. Everyone is capable of offering encouragement. So the answer is, if this is something everyone wants and something everyone can do, then why aren't we doing more of it?

On the same note, if everyone is looking for places where it is safe to be honest, if this is a concern for most people, then why aren't more people making sure there are safe spaces to talk?

The Scripture verses from 1 Corinthians talk about leaven. Leaven is a substance that makes dough rise. Centuries ago, people made bread by creating yeast, making dough, and then taking some of the leaven off of the dough and saving it for another day so it could be used as the yeast for more bread. Leaven could last for years, shared from loaf to loaf. If the leaven were ever exhausted, more would have to be made. Only a little leaven is needed to make a loaf of bread. That's why a little leaven can be removed from the dough of a loaf of bread and be introduced into other dough.

We need some new leaven in our society, and that leaven is encouragement. It needs to be taken from relationship to relationship, from high school to college, to adulthood, to different friendship groups, to different cities, and to different life circumstances. It needs to be kneaded into marriages and passed on to children. It needs to be found in workplaces, churches, sports teams, and organizations. Perhaps it might even make its way into politics and other places of hostility.

If we all (or at least most of us) think the world needs more encouragement, then we each hold part of the solution in our minds, mouths, and mannerisms. Look around the room, the house, or the office—we all need more encouragement. We can all give more encouragement. We are the solution to the problem we all face.

As St. Paul writes in 1 Corinthians 6:8, let us not move forward "with the old leaven, the leaven of malice and evil, but with the unleavened bread of sincerity and truth." And let us lead the way there with encouragement, to build up one another rather than tear one another down. No one likes to be torn down. Everyone likes to be built up. So let's stop the destroying and start the building up. Let's destroy the destructive habit of discouragement and build up one another with encouragement, encouragement that is purposeful, sincere, and consistent. We need to change the leaven of our society from anger and rage to encouragement, which will increase overall confidence and joy.

Lord, help me to be an encourager. Kindle in me the desire to encourage others and to provide a safe space for others to talk. Surround me with people who will build me up, especially at times when I feel down. Help me to develop a good group of friends who share a love of You, who can help me love You even more. Help me to always see people who need encouragement and be generous in giving encouragement to others. Amen.

Encouragement Challenge: We all have the same problem. We can all share in the same solution. Everyone needs more encouragement. Everyone can be more encouraging. Let's not stand around bemoaning a problem we can all fix. Let's go fix it.

**Dedicated to Artemis Xenick, Mia Lenardos and Kristina Hixson.

Are You All In?

As for me, I would seek God, and to God would I commit my cause, Who does great things and unsearchable, marvelous things without number.
Job 5:8-9

Several years ago, the Tampa Bay Lightning hockey team had a marketing campaign entitled "All In." All around the Tampa Bay area, there were billboards that read, "Tampa Bay Lightning: We're All In!" The purpose of the campaign was to get fans to go to the games and tune in to the broadcasts. The ownership of the team was going "all in" by signing big-name players to exorbitant contracts and upgrading the stadium where the team was playing, and they wanted the fans to know this and reciprocate in supporting the team. It worked. Games started selling out, and people all over town could be seen wearing Lighting apparel, and the team won the Stanley Cup in 2020 and 2021.

Can you imagine what would have happened if the billboards had read, "Tampa Bay Lighting: We're Half-In!" People would have laughed at that and thought, "This organization is a joke." How will I go all-in on a team whose ownership and players are half-in? It just wouldn't work.

It's hard to think of anything worthwhile in life that we don't go all in on. If we decided to go half-in on a relationship, it probably won't work. If we are half-in at a job, we probably won't be able to keep it. If we go to class half the time, we won't pass the class. If we are truthful only half the time, we'd probably be considered a liar. And so on.

The study has been on encouragement, and as we come to the end of it, we are encouraged to go all-in when it comes to encouraging others. This means that we are consistent and lead with encouragement. It means that we learn to see the best in people. It means that we help people be the best version of themselves.

We have not only talked about how we can best encourage other people. We've encouraged you to the best version of who God created you to be. In the Orthodox church, which I have been privileged to serve as a priest for many years, in our services, there is a petition that invites us to "commit ourselves and one another and our whole life to Christ our God"[64] doesn't invite us to commit half our lives to Christ but our whole lives. Anything worth doing is worth doing fully. And this applies to the encouragement to follow Christ, encouraging others to do so, and also being an encourager of others in all the positive aspects of their lives.

I remember my mom used to tell us, "If you lie 1 percent of the time, you are a liar." I suppose the same could be said that "if you discourage 1 percent of the time, you are a discourager." When it comes to being truthful, we've got to be truthful all the time to be considered a truth teller. And when it comes to encouragement, we've got to be encouraging all the time to be considered an encourager.

"I'm half-in on encouragement" does not make one an encourager. We need to go all-in when it comes to encouragement. As with just about everything else in life, we can all improve when it comes to being a friend, student, spouse, parent, at our jobs, and as Christians. The desire for improvement and going all-in go hand in hand. We can all stand to improve as encouragers. And our desire to improve and going all-in on encouragement go hand in hand.

Lord, thank You for the energy You give me each day, to get out of bed and go and do the things I do in my life. Give me the energy and consistency to be a good encourager and the desire to make encouragement part of my daily life. Help me to go all in on encouragement and on so many other things—love, forgiveness, patience, service, generosity—and the many other things that will bring me closer to You and closer to others. Amen.

Are you all in on encouragement?

Proclaim Encouragement from the Rooftops

Jesus said, "A man once gave a great banquet and invited many; and at the time for the banquet he sent his servant to say to those who had been invited, 'Come, for all is now ready.' But they all alike began to make excuses. The first said to him, 'I have bought a field, and I must go out and see it; I pray you, have me excused.' And another said, 'I have bought five yoke of oxen, and I go to examine them; I pray you have me excused.' And another said, 'I have married a wife, and therefore I cannot come.' So the servant came and reported this to his master. Then the householder in anger said to his servant, 'Go out quickly to the streets and lanes of the city, and bring in the poor and maimed and blind and lame.' And the servant said, 'Sir, what you have commanded has been done, and still there is room.' And the master said to the servant, 'Go out to the highways and hedges and compel people to come in, that my house may be filled.' For I tell you, none of those men who were invited shall taste my banquet."
Luke 14:16–24

In Luke 14:16–24, Jesus tells the parable of the great banquet. The context of this parable is at a dinner where Jesus was eating with the Pharisees, the Jewish temple leaders. The parable of the Great Banquet is about them. The people who were initially invited to the banquet, the ones who made excuses for not going, represent either the Pharisees or the Jews in general, those who rejected Christ. In the parable, the servants tell their master that those who were invited have declined to attend. The master tells the servants to go out to the streets and lanes of the city to invite people to come to his banquet. When the servants tell the master this has already been done and there is still room, the master implores the servants to "go out to the highways and hedges and compel people to come in, that my house may be filled" (Luke 14:32) because the master wants to share his food, his home, and his joy with as many people as possible.

When it comes to encouragement, I feel the joy and urgency of the master in this parable. I want to implore anyone who wants to be an encourager to go proclaim encouragement from the rooftops, go everywhere you can, and spread encouragement to as many people as you can. Help build the confidence of as many people as you can. No one should be hungry when it comes to encouragement. There is plenty of encouragement to go around so that no one feels hungry. Encouragement can almost be described as an inexhaustible resource. I only have so much money I can give away because my income and bills are fixed. There are only so many hours in a day because time is limited. However, when it comes to encouragement, I have more than enough to give away to other people. And the need for encouragement is unending as well. It's something we always have a need for. Virtually no one will say, "I've been over encouraged; I don't think I can have any more." We can oversleep, we can over eat, and we might even get overpaid (it does happen), but no one is ever over encouraged.

Like the servants in the parable, we should go to the highways and hedges and encourage as many people as we can find so that all can feel the fullness of encouragement rather than the emptiness of negativity or indifference. Worse, we don't want to have people who feel isolated and alone. Encouragement reduces both significantly.

Encouragement is not a religion. It is not something we believe in. Rather, it should be a way of life, and it should be something we do with regularity. Being a good encourager will not replace the need for a relationship with Christ. Remember, life is about being godly, not just being good. But goodness is a step toward godliness, and encouragement is a large step toward goodness. Thus, encouragement will help us grow in our faith and bring us closer to Christ.

There are things we think about every day—getting enough sleep, getting enough to eat, making sure we check in with family, doing our jobs, and so on. Encouragement should be something we think about intentionally every day as well. Encouragement will not solve all the problems of society or the world, but it certainly can go a long way to improving our little corner of it.

The master in the parable told his servants to compel everyone they found to come in and eat—he wanted the house full and wanted everyone to feel full, even people he didn't know. In the same way, we want to encourage everyone so that no one feels empty, even the people we don't know. When you think about it, there is something encouraging we can say to just about everyone. Let's see ourselves like servants in this parable, going out to the highways and hedges, going to every corner of our world, and encouraging others so that everyone can feel full, and so that no one feels empty.

Lord, thank You for inviting us to be with You. Thank You for the invitation to share in Your kingdom, both in this life and for eternal life. Help me to be attentive to the invitation. Help me to see encouragement also as a banquet to which to invite others. Give me the desire to go to the "highways and hedges" and compel all to feel encouraged. Bring those who feel empty to me so that I can encourage them. Amen.

Encouragement Challenge: Proclaim encouragement from the rooftops! Encourage everyone!

Go Do It

And there appeared to Him an angel from heaven, strengthening Him.
Luke 22:43

The night before His passion, Jesus prayed in the garden of Gethsemane. He asked His disciples to "watch" with Him. He didn't ask them to do anything, just to be with Him so He wouldn't be alone. Unfortunately, this proved difficult for them, and they fell asleep. Jesus was scared. And even more than scared, He was lonely. He had told His disciples, *"my soul is very sorrowful, even to death, remain here and watch"* (Matt. 26:38). He knew the burden He would carry, and He knew He would carry it alone. His prayer was so sorrowful that the Bible says that He was in *"agony"* and that *"His sweat became like great drops of blood falling down upon the ground"* (Luke 23:44). In the midst of all this sorrow, the Bible also says that an angel from heaven appeared to Him, and it gave Him great strength. I've seen depictions of this scene in paintings and icons. Some depictions show the angel sitting and speaking with Jesus. Other depictions show the angel embracing Jesus like a mother embraces her child. In all the depictions, we can see how Jesus is strengthened by the encouragement He is receiving.

I believe that God brings "angels" into our lives. Some of these angels are the bodiless powers that surround each person, the angels we read about in the Bible. We also know that God works through people. When we look after other people, when we encourage them, we take on an almost angelic role for them. When we allow God to work through us to strengthen others, we take on the role of the angels for one another.

I am thankful to God, and I will always be thankful to Him for people He has put into my life who are sources of encouragement. There are times in my life when I feel down and discouraged, when I doubt my own abilities to do basic things that I am good at doing, even things I enjoy doing can become stressful. There have been times when I have felt paralyzed with fear of failure and an encouraging word from someone has, many times, been THE factor in lifting my spirits and restoring my confidence.

By God's grace, I had the joy of directing our Metropolis summer camp for many years. It is a ministry I truly enjoy. One year, I went up to camp, and on the day the staff arrived for training, when all the preparation was over and the moment of truth had arrived, I found myself paralyzed with fear. I had done as much preparation as I could do, and I was prepared as well as I could be prepared. Yet when the time came to execute not only what I was planning to do but what I was looking forward to doing, I was literally sick to my stomach with nerves. I couldn't eat or couldn't think straight. My mind felt like a convoluted mess, and my mouth felt like it was full of cotton, like I couldn't even get my words out.

As we were about to begin our staff training, I received a three-word text from a friend back home who knew that I was starting staff training but who actually had no idea that I was so stressed out. The text said, "Go do it." That's it. Three words.

However, those words said a lot more to me. They said to me:

- "You've got this."
- "You are going to do great."
- "I believe in you."
- "I trust you."
- "I've got your back."
- "God is not going to let you down."
- "Go do it with God's help."

I felt almost like a shot of energy coarse through my body. I felt like God took over my mind and body. The fog in my mind lifted. My words came out clear. And I had a great day. God did that for me, but it was the encouragement of a friend who reminded me that God was going to walk with me. It was encouragement that reminded me I was not alone. It was encouragement that quieted the voices of doubt and distraction and replaced them with voices of confidence. A three-word text caused one of the most powerful "God-moments" of my life. That is the power of encouragement.

The good news is that we can all be the person who sends the text and says the words that create powerful and empowering moments for others who need them. We can all be an angel to someone who is in need, whose soul is sorrowful, and who needs to be lifted up and encouraged. The challenge is to recognize the importance of encouragement and the crucial role we play in offering it to others.

We all become discouraged when we look at the landscape of our society. We sometimes feel hopeless and wonder, what can I possibly do to make a difference? Well, encouragement is a need we all have. When you build up others through encouragement, you become part of the solution, not part of the problem. If a day comes when everyone is a voice of encouragement, then there will be no more problems. God doesn't expect us to solve all of the problems of the world, just to do our part in our corner. And something we can all do is offer encouragement.

I want to thank you for your prayers and encouragement. Both are vital to the success of the Prayer Team. Your encouragement provides much of the inspiration behind my thoughts and writings. This final prayer is my prayer for you, the priestly benediction of Numbers 6:24–26:

The Lord bless you and keep you. The Lord make His face to shine upon you and be gracious to you. The Lord lift up His countenance upon you, and give you peace!

Encouragement Challenge: Whatever challenge you face today, GO DO IT! GO DO IT WITH GOD!

To Him be the glory to the ages of ages. Amen.

About the Author

Father Stavros N. Akrotirianakis is a Greek Orthodox Priest who serves St. John the Baptist Greek Orthodox Church in Tampa, Florida. He has also authored the books Let All Creation Rejoice: Reflections on Advent, the Nativity and Epiphany; The Road Back to Christ: Reflections on Lent, Holy Week and Pascha; Blessed Is the Kingdom, Now and Forever: Reflections on the Divine Liturgy; The Heart of Encouragement: Reflections on the Sunday and Feastday Scripture Readings of the Orthodox Church; Engaged: Called to Be Disciples, Reflections on What It Means to Be a Christian and Commissioned to Be Apostles: Love, Worship, Community, Learning, Service. He writes a daily reflection called "The Prayer Team," which can be found at www.prayerteam365.com.

Endnotes

Introduction

1. Salem Web Network, n.d. "Salem Media Group." https://www.biblestudytools.com/lexicons/greek/nas/parakaleo.html (accessed Aug. 27, 2022).

2. DeMars Sean, n.d. "Don't Flatter, Encourage." The Gospel Coalition. https://www.thegospelcoalition.org/article/dont-flatter-encourage/ (accessed Aug. 27, 2022).

3. *The Divine Liturgy of St. John Chrysostom,* Translation by the Holy Cross Seminary Press, Boston, MA: Holy Cross Seminary Press, 1985, p. 19-20.

Part Two–Esteem Others Highly

4. Wikipedia, n.d. "Titanic" Film by James Cameron. https://en.wikipedia.org/wiki/Titanic_(1997_film) (accessed Aug. 27, 2022).

5. AOL.Com, Editors "Dr. Martin Luther King's 'I Have a Dream' speech: Full text" January 16, 2017 11:00 a.m. https://www.aol.com/article/news/2017/01/16/dr-martin-luther-kings-i-have-a-dream-speech-full-text/21655947/ (accessed Aug. 27, 2022).

6. Kelly, Mathew, "Become the Best Version of Yourself (Motivational Video) Feb. 7, 2021. https://www.youtube.com/watch?v=mAd3vm9kM6w (accessed Aug. 27, 2022).

Part Three–Be at Peace

7. Wikipedia, n.d. "Let There Be Peace on Earth" Song written by Jill Jackson-Miller and Sy Miller 1955. https://en.wikipedia.org/wiki/Let_There_Be_Peace_on_Earth_(song) (accessed Aug. 27, 2022).

8. THEWhOoT.com, n.d. "66 Positive Things to Say to Kids." (newsletter) https://thewhoot.com/life/66-positive-things-say-child (accessed Aug. 26, 2022).

9. Richards, Fr. Larry, 2018 "F.A.M.I.L.Y." *Sacred Heart Narratives* (blog). Oct. 18, 2018 https://sacredheartnarratives.com/2019/10/21/f-a-m-i-l-y-coverage-of-jp2-benefit-dinner-with-fr-larry-richards-speaking/

10. Keith, Toby, "My List," (song) *Pull My Chain, LyricFind* 2011.
11. Dictionary.com LLC., "Authentic" https://www.dictionary.com/browse/authentic. (accessed Aug. 27, 2022).

Part Four–Help and Be Patient

12. Chapman, Gary, 1992. *The Five Love Languages: How to Express Heartfelt Commitment to Your Mate.* Chicago, IL, Northfield Publishing, 1992.
13. Dictionary.com, LLC. "Admonish." https://www.dictionary.com/browse/admonish. (accessed Aug. 27, 2022).

Part Five–Seek to do good

14. Evens, Timothy Dr., *The Art of Encouragement: Human Relations Training, 1989.* The University of Georgia, Georgia Center for Continuing Education, Athens Ga., pp. 73-74.
15. "Seventh Prayer of the Orthodox Sacrament of Holy Unction," Translated by Fr. George Papadeas, *Holy Week Easter* Daytona Beach, FL. Patmos Press, 2016 p. 157. https://patmospress.com/shop/holy-week-easter/
16. Deselm, Dave, June 28, 2019 "Making Music with the Master," Dave DeSelm Ministries, Inc. 2019 https://www.davedeselmministries.org/devotionals/making-music-with-the-master (accessed Aug. 27, 2022).
17. Warren, Rick, "Conflict Resolution" (Podcast) June 25, 2018. https://pastorrick.com/listen/archive/

Part Six–Rejoice Always

18. Gordon Jon, The Energy Bus, Forward by Ken Blanchard. Hoboken, New Jersey. John Wiley & Sons, Inc., Jan. 22 2007
19. Bible Hub, "3842.Pantote." https://biblehub.com/greek/3842.htm (accessed Aug. 27, 2022).
20. Bible Hub, "5463 Chairete," https://biblehub.com/greek/chairete_5463.htm (accessed Aug. 27, 2022).

21. Bible Hub, "5479 Chara." https://biblehub.com/greek/5479.htm (Accessed Aug. 27, 2022).

22. Bible Hub, "5485. Charis," https://biblehub.com/greek/5485.htm (accessed Aug. 27, 2022).

Part Seven–-Pray Constantly

23. American Carpatho-Russian Orthodox Diocese of the USA., Ecumenical Patriarchate of Constantinople., n.d. "A prayer for acceptance of God's will," https://www.acrod.org/prayercorner/prayer/variousneeds (accessed Aug. 27, 2022).

Part Eight–Give Thanks

24. Wikipedia, "Theosis," (Eastern Christian theology) https://en.wikipedia.org/wiki/Theosis_(Eastern_Christian_theology) (accessed Aug. 27, 2022).

Part Nine–Let the Spirit Lead

25. Greek Orthodox Archdiocese of America, n.d. "The Holy Sacrament of Ordination to the Diaconate," https://www.goarch.org/-/the-holy-sacrament-of-ordination-to-the-diaconate?inheritRedirect=true (accessed Aug. 27, 2022).

26. Greek Orthodox Archdiocese of America, n.d. "Digital Chant Stand of the GOA," https://www.goarch.org/chapel/dcs?inheritRedirect=true

27. Idleman, Kyle, *Not a Fan*. Grand Rapids, Mich. Zondervan, 2011

Part Ten–Hold Fast

28. Wikipedia, "Serenity Prayer," by Reinhold Niebuhr. https://en.wikipedia.org/wiki/Serenity_Prayer (accessed Aug. 27, 2022).

29. Greek Orthodox Archdiocese of America, n.d "1970 Yearbook of the Greek Orthodox Archdiocese of North and South America." New York: NY, 1970.

30. Serota, K. B., Levine, T. R., & Docan-Morgan, T. (2021). "Unpacking variation in lie prevalence: Prolific liars, bad lie days, or both?" *Communication Monographs*, DOI: 10.1080/03637751.2021.1985153 (link)

31. Lucado, Max, "It's Not About Me: Rescue from the Life We Thought Would Make Us Happy," Nashville, TN: Thomas Nelson, 2011.

32. Lucado, "It's Not About Me, p. 109-110.

33. Quinn, Daniel, "The Boiling Frog," *The Story of B*. http://faculty.washington.edu/rturner1/Sustainability/Bibliography/docs/The_Boiling_Frog.pdf (accessed Aug. 27, 2022).

34. Vocabulary.com Inc., "Mantra," https://www.vocabulary.com/dictionary/mantra. (accessed Aug. 27, 2022).

Part Eleven–Abstain from Evil

35. Cherry, Kendra, "What is Passive-Aggressive Behavior? How to Recognize and Respond to Passive-Aggressiveness," Verywellmind,com. June 17, 2022 https://www.verywellmind.com/what-is-passive-aggressive-behavior-2795481. (accessed Aug. 27, 2022).

36. Mallin, Meaghan, head of lower school. "The Starfish Story: Making a Difference," New Canaan Country School. April 11, 2019 https://www.countryschool.net/news-detail?pk=1250796. (accessed Aug. 27, 2022).

37. Glasser, C., Glasser W., *Getting Together and Staying Together: Solving the Mystery of Marriage*. New York, NY: Harper Perennial, 2000.

Part Twelve – Keep Sound

38. Bible Hub, "40 Hagios," https://biblehub.com/greek/5479.htm (accessed Aug. 28, 2022).

39. Greek Orthodox Archdiocese of America, "Christ the True Light," *My Orthodox Prayer Book*. GOA, Department of Religious Education, Brookline, MA, 1985, p. 70-71.

40. Eldredge, John, *Get Your Life Back: Everyday Practices for a World Gone Mad*," (Nashville, TN: Nelson Books, 2020).

41. Eldridge, *Get Your Life Back*. p.xv

42. NASA Science, n.d. "SpacePlace Explore Earth and Space," https://spaceplace.nasa.gov/moon (accessed Aug. 27, 2022).

43. Wikipedia, n.d. "Apollo 11" https://en.wikipedia.org/wiki/Apollo_11 (accessed Aug. 27, 2022).

44. Howell, Elizabeth, "Apollo 11 Flight Log, July 17, 1969: Course Correction to Reach the Moon." July 17, 2019. Space.com https://www.space.com/26565-apollo-11-moon-mission-day-2.html (accessed Aug. 27, 2022).

Part Thirteen – God Is Faithful

45. Greek Orthodox Archdiocese of America, "The Divine Liturgy," p.20.
46. Bible.org. "The Cross Room," https://bible.org/illustration/cross-room (accessed Aug. 27, 2022).
47. Ankiel, Rick, *The Phenomenon: Pressure, the Yips, and the Pitch that Changed my Life.* New York: Public Affairs April 18, 2017.
48. Ankiel, *The Phenomenon. p.* 4.

Part Fourteen – Prayer For Us

49. Bible Hub, "40 Hagios," https://biblehub.com/greek/5479.htm (accessed Aug. 27, 2022).

Part Fifteen – Greet One Another

50. Metrakos, Aris. Fr., "Is Your Parish a Cruise Ship or a Battleship?" Saint Barbara Greek Orthodox Church., 2006. https://saintbarbara.net/articles-is-your-parish-a-cruise-ship-or-battleship/ (accessed Aug. 27, 2022).

Part Sixteen – Read with All

51. Greek Orthodox Archdiocese of America, "The Divine Liturgy" p. 17.
52. Greek Orthodox Archdiocese of America, "The Divine Liturgy" p. 19.
53. Greek Orthodox Archdiocese of America, "The Divine Liturgy" p. 19
54. Greek Orthodox Archdiocese of America, "The Divine Liturgy" p. 24.
55. Greek Orthodox Archdiocese of America, "The Divine Liturgy" p. 25.
56. Greek Orthodox Archdiocese of America, "The Divine Liturgy" p. 26.

57. Merriam-Webster, "Encourage," https://www.merriam-webster.com/dictionary/encourage (accessed Aug. 27, 2022).

Part Seventeen – The Grace of Our Lord

58. Dictionary.com, "Authentic," https://www.dictionary.com/browse/authentic (accessed Aug. 28, 2022).

Conclusion

59. Wikipedia, "The Riddle (Five for Fighting Son," https://en.wikipedia.org/wiki/The_Riddle_(Five_for_Fighting_song) (accessed Aug. 27, 2022).
60. Yeo, Alyssa LPC, CYT., Feb. 24, 2016. "The Story of Two Wolves," Urban Balance. https://www.urbanbalance.com/the-story-of-two-wolves/ (accessed Aug. 28, 2022).
61. Greek Names, n.d. "Stavros, " https://www.greek-names.info/Stavros/
62. Facebook, n.d. "The Gift is You," https://www.facebook.com/watch/?v=2878943925491599 (accessed Aug. 27, 2022).
63. Genius.com, "If Everyone Cared" (Song) *All the Right Reasons,* Track 9 Nickleback., https://genius.com/Nickelback-if-everyone-cared-lyrics
64. Greek Orthodox Archdiocese of America, "The Divine Liturgy." p.3.

BIBLIOGRAPHY-SUGGESTED READING

Ankiel, Rick. *The Phenomenon: Pressure, the Yips, and the Pitch that Changed my Life*. New York: Public Affairs April 18, 2017.

Chapman, Gary 1992. *The Five Love Languages: How to Express Heartfelt Commitment to Your Mate*. Chicago, IL, Northfield Publishing, 1992.

DeMars Sean, n.d. "Don't Flatter, Encourage," The Gospel Coalition. https://www.thegospelcoalition.org/article/dont-flatter-encourage/ (accessed Aug. 27, 2022).

Eldredge, John. *Get Your Life Back: Everyday Practices for a World Gone Mad*," (Nashville, TN: Nelson Books, 2020).

Evans, Dr. Timothy. "The Art of Encouragement: Human Relations Training," Athens, GA: University of Georgia, Georgia Center for Continuing Education, 1989, p. 73-74.

Greek Orthodox Archdiocese of America. "Christ the True Light," *My Orthodox Prayer Book*. GOA, Department of Religious Education, Brookline, MA, 1985, p. 70-71.

Greek Orthodox Archdiocese of America. n.d. "1970 Yearbook of the Greek Orthodox Archdiocese of North and South America." New York: NY, 1970.

Glasser, C., Glasser W., *Getting Together and Staying Together: Solving the Mystery of Marriage*. New York: Harper Perennial, 2000.

Gordon Jon. The Energy Bus, Forward by Ken Blanchard. Hoboken, New Jersey. John Wiley & Sons, Inc., Jan. 22 2007

Idleman, Kyle. *Not a Fan*. Grand Rapids, Mich. Zondervan, 2011

Keith, Toby. "My List," (song) *Pull My Chain*. LyricFind 2011.

Lucado, Max. "It's Not About Me: Rescue from the Life We Thought Would Make Us Happy," Nashville, TN: Tomas Nelson, 2011.

Metrakos, Aris. Fr. "Is Your Parish a Cruise Ship or a Battleship?" Saint Barbara Greek Orthodox Church., 2006. https://saintbarbara.net/articles-is-your-parish-a-cruise-ship-or-battleship/ (accessed Aug. 27, 2022).

Quinn, Daniel. "The Boiling Frog," *The Story of B*. http://faculty.washington.edu/rturner1/Sustainability/Bibliography/docs/The_Boiling_Frog.pdf (accessed *Aug. 27, 20220*).

Richards, Fr. Larry 2018 "F.A.M.I.L.Y." *Sacred Heart Narratives.* (blog). Oct. 18, 2018 https://sacredheartnarratives.com/2019/10/21/f-a-m-i-l-y-coverage-of-jp2-benefit-dinner-with-fr-larry-richards-speaking/

Serota, K. B., Levine, T. R., & Docan-Morgan, T. (2021). "Unpacking variation in lie prevalence: Prolific liars, bad lie days, or both?" *Communication Monographs*, DOI: 10.1080/03637751.2021.1985153 (link)

Seventh Prayer of the Orthodox Sacrament of Holy Unction," Translated by Fr. George Papadeas, *Holy Week Easter.* Daytona Beach, FL. Patmos Press, 2016 p. 157. https://patmospress.com/shop/holy-week-easter/

The Divine Liturgy of St. John Chrysostom, Translation by the Holy Cross Seminary Press, Boston, MA: Holy Cross Seminary Press, 1985, p. 19-20.

Wikipedia. n.d. "Let There Be Peace on Earth," (song) written by Jill Jackson-Miller and Sy Miller 1955. (accessed Aug. 27, 2022).

Wikipedia. "The Riddle (Five for Fighting Song)," https://en.wikipedia.org/wiki/The_Riddle_(Five_for_Fighting_song) (accessed Aug. 27, 2022)

Wikipedia. "Serenity Prayer," by Reinhold Niebuh. https://en.wikipedia.org/wiki/Serenity_Prayer (accessed Aug. 27, 2022).

CPSIA information can be obtained
at www.ICGtesting.com
Printed in the USA
LVHW050806291122
733859LV00005B/367